HUMAN RIGHTS AND THE WORLD'S MAJOR RELIGIONS

Human Rights and the World's Major Religions

William H. Brackney, Series Editor

HUMAN RIGHTS AND THE WORLD'S MAJOR RELIGIONS

VOLUME 5: THE BUDDHIST TRADITION

Robert E. Florida

William H. Brackney, Series Editor

PRAEGER PERSPECTIVES

Westport, Connecticut
London

Library of Congress Cataloging-in-Publication Data

Human rights and the world's major religions.
    p.   cm.
    Includes bibliographical references and indexes.
    Contents: v. 1. The Jewish tradition / Peter J. Haas—v. 2. The Christian tradition /
William H. Brackney—v. 3. The Islamic tradition / Muddathir Abd al-Rahim—
v. 4. The Hindu tradition / Harold Coward—v. 5. The Buddhist tradition /
Robert E. Florida.
    ISBN 0–275–98425–7 (set: alk. paper)—ISBN 0–275–98047–2 (v. 1: alk. paper)—
ISBN 0–313–30134–4 (v. 2: alk. paper)—ISBN 0–275–98045–6 (v. 3: alk. paper)—
ISBN 0–275–98381–1 (v. 4: alk. paper)—ISBN 0–313–31318–0 (v. 5: alk. paper)
    1. Human rights—Religious aspects.   I. Haas, Peter J. (Peter Jerome)
BL65.H78H8595   2005
201'.723—dc22   2003068987

British Library Cataloguing in Publication Data is available.

Library of Congress Catalog Card Number: 2003068987
ISBN: 0–275–98425–7 (set code)
        0–313–31318–0 (The Buddhist Tradition)
        0–275–98381–1 (The Hindu Tradition)
        0–275–98047–2 (The Jewish Tradition)
        0–313–30134–4 (The Christian Tradition)
        0–275–98045–6 (The Islamic Tradition)

First published in 2005

Praeger Publishers, 88 Post Road West, Westport, CT 06881
An imprint of Greenwood Publishing Group, Inc.
www.praeger.com

Printed in the United States of America

The paper used in this book complies with the
Permanent Paper Standard issued by the National
Information Standards Organization (Z39.48–1984).

10 9 8 7 6 5 4 3 2 1

Copyright Acknowledgments

The author and publisher are grateful for permission to reprint material from the following:

Portions of chapters 4, 5, 6, 10, and 11 appeared in different form in Robert E. Florida, "Buddhism and Violence in Modernity," in David J. Hawkin, ed., *The Twenty-First Century Confronts Its Gods: Globalization, Technology, and War* (Albany: State University of New York Press, 2004).

Every reasonable effort has been made to trace the owners of copyrighted materials in this book, but in some instances this has proven impossible. The author and publisher will be glad to receive information leading to more complete acknowledgments in subsequent printings of the book, and in the meantime extend their apologies for any omissions.

CONTENTS

INTRODUCTION TO HUMAN RIGHTS AND THE WORLD'S MAJOR RELIGIONS

THIS BOOK IS THE FIFTH OF A SERIES produced by Praeger Publishers titled Human Rights and the World's Major Religions. The purpose of the series is to define the meaning of human rights in the specific religious tradition and survey its breadth and development across time and cultures. Each author has crafted analytical chapters and selected appropriate primary source materials that illustrate their analyses. Additionally, these books are reference works that include biographical sections, extensive annotated bibliographies, a chronology, and an index. The religious traditions included in the series are Christianity, Buddhism, Judaism, Islam, and Hinduism.

In this volume, Professor Florida begins with an introduction to Buddhism, tracing the origins of Theravada, Mahayana, and Vajrayana divisions and how they are distributed in various countries. Following Robert Thurman's work, Florida uses a pluralistic approach to understanding the Buddhist tradition while recognizing common strands. In discussing the aspect of human rights, the basis of the volumes in this series is the United Nations Universal Declaration of Human Rights, adopted in 1948.

The author is representative in his coverage, first examining how Buddhism historically addresses the notion of "rights" and human dignity, both for individuals and states. Contemporary Buddhist thinkers are examined as well. The Theravada experience is seen through Thai and Burmese lenses, and slavery in Thailand and Tibet is analyzed, as are the circumstances of women in India. Other historical foci look at war and human rights in Japan and Tibet and break new ground.

Robert Florida was selected from a list of distinguished scholars to guide us through Buddhism. He holds first degrees in mechanical engineering and theology from the University of Cincinnati and Tufts University respectively, and his graduate work in religion was completed at McMaster University, where he earned his master's and doctoral degrees. He has taught at the Universities of Pittsburg, Swaziland, and Mahidol, in Thailand, while spending the majority of his career at Brandon University in Manitoba, Canada, where he also served as department chair and dean of arts. Currently Dr. Florida is a fellow in the Centre for Studies in Religion and Society at the University of Victoria in British Columbia where he has been since 2000. He is widely published in Buddhist ethics and Eastern religions, as well as interreligious dialogue. His long-term investigation of Buddhism is evident in the scholarship he displays in this book.

I am pleased to present this worthy addition to the series, as it provides a masterful survey of complex cultures within a tradition of infinite importance to contemporary religious studies. Acknowledging a vast array of literature in the field, Florida's work will challenge several assumptions and provide useful details to the beginning student of Buddhism while it treats topics of high interest to advocates and specialists in human rights.

William H. Brackney
Series Editor

ACKNOWLEDGMENTS

THE CENTRE FOR STUDIES IN Religion and Society at the University of Victoria, British Columbia, provided me hospitality, encouragement, and material aid during the writing of this book, and I would like the fellows and staff to know how much it was appreciated. In particular, thanks to Moira Hill, who helped prepare the documents in chapter 13 for publication, and to Andrew Wender and Benjamin Berger, who gave me the benefit of their comments and suggestions on several of the chapters. Above all, more thanks than can be expressed go to my wife, Janice Florida, for all the help and support she has given me throughout a lifetime in the academy.

NOTE ON TRANSLITERATION

Works on Buddhism provide a challenge in that Buddhist material comes in such a wide variety of languages and has such a rich and varied technical vocabulary. To accommodate the general reader, technical terms have been translated as much as possible, and diacritical markings have not been used. In most cases the Sanskrit form of Buddhist terms has been used; but in the readings when key terms were in other languages, they have been retained. At the first use of each foreign term, it is translated or explained. Foreign words from languages other than Sanskrit are given in their most common transliteration without diacriticals. When Pali terms occur in quotations, they are retained if they are similar to the Sanskrit. For example, *dhamma*, Pali for Sanskrit *dharma* (doctrine), may be found.

Many of the sources used in this study were published in places where English is not the first language, so typographical oddities and unusual punctuations have been standardized without comment.

CHRONOLOGY

c. 566–486 B.C.E.	Life of Gautama the Buddha
	Buddha ordains women and outcastes, will not ordain slaves
c. 500 B.C.E.–0	Early Buddhism develops (India)
c. 410 B.C.E.	The First Buddhist Council
326 B.C.E.	Alexander the Great crosses the Indus
c. 325 B.C.E.	Buddhists divide into two major groups in India
c. 321–184 B.C.E.	Mauryan dynasty (India)
c. 268–239 B.C.E.	Reign of Asoka Maurya, Ideal Buddhist King
c. 250 B.C.E.	Sectarian divisions appear in the Elder tradition
	Asoka's missions to Greek kingdoms and to Sri Lanka
c. 200 B.C.E.	Buddhism into Central Asia following Silk Road
c. 80 B.C.E.	Pali canon written down in Sri Lanka
c. 0–C.E. 500	Development of Mahayana Buddhism in India
c. C.E. 100	Buddhism in Cambodia
c. C.E. 100–200	Buddhism arrives in China
c. C.E. 150	Buddhism in Vietnam
	Nagarjuna, Mahayana thinker, active in India
c. C.E. 200	Lotus Sutra produced, major scripture of Eastern Buddhists

c. C.E. 400	Buddhism arrives in Burma (may have come earlier)
	Buddhism arrives in Korea
C.E. 400–500	Life of Buddhaghosa, Theravada's leading thinker (Sri Lanka)
	Pali Commentaries in written form
C.E. 500–1000	Development of Vajrayana Buddhism in India
c. C.E. 552–600	Mahayana Buddhism enters Japan and becomes state religion
C.E. 600–700	Vajrayana Buddhism enters Tibet
C.E. 618–917	Tang dynasty (China)
c. C.E. 800	Buddhism established in Thailand
C.E. 900–1200	North India conquered by Turkish Moslem tribes; Buddhism becomes extinct in India
c. C.E. 1100–1200	Zen arrives in Japan from China and Korea
C.E. 1173–1262	Life of Shinran, founder of Shin school of Pure Land Buddhism (Japan)
C.E. 1185–1333	Kamakura period (Japan)
C.E. 1222–1282	Life of Nichiren, founder of Nichirin sect in Japan
C.E. 1357–1410	Life of Tsongkhapa, founder of Gelugpa school of Tibetan Buddhism
1603–1868	Tokugawa Shogunate in Japan
1614–1873	Buddhists aid in persecution of Christians in Japan
1617–1682	Life of Fifth Dalai Lama, who took political control of Tibet
1782	Founding of Chakri dynasty (Siam), which successfully maintained a Theravada Buddhist kingdom
1820s–1880s	British and French colonialism destroys Buddhist kingdoms in Sri Lanka, Burma, and Indochina
1868–1945	Buddhists help develop and support Japanese imperialist-militarist ideology
1932	Absolute monarchy ends in Siam
1947	Burma regains independence
1950	Chinese Communists win in China
	Invasion of Tibet by Chinese

1958	Buddhist nationalist policies ignite ongoing civil war in Sri Lanka
1959	Dalai Lama flees Tibet after failed uprising
1966–1976	Buddhism suppressed in China and Tibet
	Cultural Revolution (China)
1989	Dalai Lama wins Nobel Peace Prize
1991	Aung San Suu Kyi of Burma wins Nobel Peace Prize

Part I
Historical Development
and Analysis

1

A Brief Overview

Introduction

BUDDHIST HISTORY SPANS MORE THAN 2,500 years and is
very diverse, with the faith having evolved over the years
and having adapted to local cultures throughout most of Asia. The adap-
tations were reciprocal, with the Buddhist faith changing its host countries in deep and fundamental ways. Buddhism has evolved into three
major strains, called the *Theravada*, *Mahayana*, and *Vajrayana*, each of
them having many subsects, as there is no central authority in either doctrine or discipline. In every Buddhist country there are several different
denominations, sometimes representing different major divisions, most
generally not in vigorous competition with one another, although there
has been serious conflict, sometimes armed, amongst Buddhist sects. Buddhists are rarely exclusivists in religion, so that it is common for a person
to participate in a variety of religious activities and to draw beliefs from
more than one tradition. For example in China, most people practiced aspects of Buddhist, Taoist, Confucian, and local traditions, depending on
context. The picture is made more complex when one takes into account
historical changes. For example, all three major schools developed in India, but all eventually died out there by around C.E. 1300, only to be rein-
troduced by missionaries and exiles in the nineteenth and twentieth
centuries. Thailand, which is now a strongly Theravada nation, at one

time had a thriving Mahayana community as did Indonesia, now predominantly Moslem.

The three major divisions grew in an organic way with each one emerging from the previous ones and coexisting relatively harmoniously. The period for the original development of the Theravada is very roughly from 500 B.C.E. to 0, for the Mahayana from 0–C.E. 500, and for the Vajrayana, from C.E. 500–1000. Theravada means the way of the elders and is the oldest of the three major extant divisions of Buddhism. It derives from the early schools that developed in India in the centuries immediately following the death of Lord Buddha, the founder, who lived in India from around 566 to 486 B.C.E. Nearly all dates in early Indian history are debated, and scholars do not all agree upon the dates of the Buddha. An early form of Buddhism was introduced into Sri Lanka around 250 B.C.E. by missionaries from India, and now Theravada is the dominant form of Buddhism in that country as well as in Thailand, Laos, Cambodia, and Burma. It also exists as a minority faith in other South and Southeast Asian countries. Theravada Buddhists consider themselves to be the most conservative Buddhists and generally think that their way is the closest to what the Buddha taught. Their devotion focuses on the historical Buddha. The governments of Theravada countries, which before the impact of Western colonialism were all absolute monarchies, have been and still are closely intertwined with the Buddhist monastic establishment, each supporting the other in reciprocal ways.

Mahayana (which means the "large vehicle") Buddhism developed in India around the turn of the Common Era, diverging over several issues of discipline and doctrine from the then dominant schools. The Mahayana moved its focus to celestial Buddhas and Bodhisattvas without forgetting the historical Buddha and introduced new doctrines and scriptures. It, alongside the Theravada schools, spread via the trade routes to reach China (C.E. 100), Korea (400), and Japan (500–600). After long periods of assimilation, the Mahayana became the dominant form of Buddhism in these East Asian countries, sharing the stage with various other belief systems and having greater or lesser influence and success often in reaction to government support or oppression. The Mahayana also travelled to South and Southeast Asia, but lost out to the Theravada or to Islam in those areas, for the most part. At the same time, the Theravada died out or became very minor players in East Asia. Mahayana literally means the "large vehicle" and is the name they gave themselves in distinction to what they called the Hinayana or "lesser vehicle," one sect of which developed into the Theravada, which survives today. The larger vehicle saw itself as more inclusive, more generous than the lesser vehicle. The Theravada never calls itself the lesser vehicle and harbors a certain degree of suspicion toward what they see as innovations by the Mahayana.

The Vajrayana, or "Way of the Thunderbolt," also had its origins in India, growing out of the Mahayana roughly from 500–1000 C.E. It retained most features of the Mahayana, including its scriptures and philosophical systems, but also added direct ways of attaining enlightenment through new forms of worship and meditation, adopted various shamanistic practices, and developed new texts, theories, and imagery. Vajrayana also made its way along the various trade routes throughout Asia, penetrating as far as Java and Sumatra, where it faded away centuries ago, and to North Asia, where it persists today in China and Japan as minor schools. In South Asia, it gave way in time to the Theravada. The great success of the Vajrayana was in Tibet and the other Himalayan countries. Tibet saw its first Buddhists around C.E. 600, and eventually became the primary home of Vajrayana, with its own distinctive subsects, literature, and practices. One of the most striking features of Tibetan Buddhism was the way its religious leaders became the political leaders as well. Mongolia, who adopted it from Tibet, is the other major Vajrayana culture. The Vajrayana divides Buddhist practice into three vehicles, interpreted as evolutionary stages for their practitioners to pass through on the way to deliverance. The Hinayana is the preliminary, primarily ethical stage focused on the cultivation of self, leading to the Mahayana stage of focusing on the benefit for all creatures, and culminating in the Vajrayana devotional drive to complete enlightenment. Needless to say, the other schools do not understand themselves as relatively lowly steps on the Vajrayana ladder.

While the Buddhist tradition, for convenience, is often discussed under the three major divisions of Theravada, Mahayana, and Vajrayana, it would be wrong to think of them as completely separate and discontinuous phenomena. They overlap in time and place and practice again and again. In India, for example, for hundreds of years, monks and scholars from all three branches would live and study together in the same institutions, following the same Buddhist rules of morality. Laypeople would donate to mendicants from whatever persuasion, provided they lived purely according to the precepts. Even in rather strict Theravada countries like Thailand today, nearly every temple will have an altar where worshippers make offerings to a Mahayana image of the Bodhisattva Avalokitesvara in the Chinese form of Kwan Yin, another altar for images of the Kings of Thailand/Siam, especially Mahachulalongkorn,* and all will have altars featuring beautifully modelled images of Lord Buddha in the various postures revered in the country.

In light of the tremendous scope, the constant flux, and the amazing variety of forms, languages, scriptures, and other literature that Buddhism has today and has had for the past millennia, it is no wonder that it is questioned "whether one can accurately speak of something called 'Buddhism' or the 'Buddhist Tradition,' or whether those terms are better rendered in the plural."[1] Robert A. F. Thurman, one of the best-known Buddhist scholars in the United States, in his valuable essay, "Human Rights and Human Responsibilities: Buddhist Views on Individualism and Altruism," opts for the plural.[2] The present study strongly favors the plurality of Buddhisms approach and tries to avoid magisterial pronouncements in the name of Buddhism. It is based on the conviction that there is no one normative form, sect, set of scriptures, and so on. Buddhism, or better Buddhisms, like everything else in the phenomenal world, lack eternal essences, are constantly in flux, and are conditioned by the myriad of causes and factors that have led to their arising and will lead to their passing away. Nonetheless, there are certain common threads in thought and "often surprising parallels among the practices of Buddhist cultures widely separated by both history and topography, parallels to be accounted for in large part by a constant retrospection to the figure of the Buddha."[3]

One of the constant themes wherever Buddhists have lived and taught is a focus on and reverence to the three jewels that are invoked in most Buddhist ceremonies. In fact, converting to Buddhism is often referred to as taking refuge in the three jewels, by repeating a prayer or chant that is found in worship services across the Buddhist spectrum: "To the Buddha to refuge I go; to the Dharma for refuge I go; to the Sangha for refuge I go." These terms, here cited in their Sanskrit form, are so standard to Buddhism that they will be used without translation throughout the present study. Briefly, "buddha" is originally an adjective, which means "woken up" or "enlightened." As a noun it refers to the historical Buddha who walked and worked in India some 2,500 years ago, to previous Buddhas, and Buddhas to come into this world in the feature in the lineage of enlightened teachers, to myriads of cosmic Buddhas that feature in the Mahayana and Vajrayana, and to a timeless principle of perfect enlightenment.

Dharma is another term that has many meanings in Buddhism, some of them very hard to penetrate. In the simplest context it means the teaching of the Buddha, believed to reflect his comprehension of the nature of reality, attained as the fruit of meditative concentration. That is, dharma is ultimate truth to a Buddhist. Sangha is the community of those who hear and accept the dharma and try to help each other live according to it, modelling their lives on the career of the Buddha. So to take refuge in the three jewels is to take refuge in the teacher, the teachings, and the community that embodies the teachings of Lord Buddha. In the book that follows, Buddha, dharma, and sangha will be taken up in specific contexts that relate to questions concerning human rights.

SCOPE AND FOCUS OF THE PRESENT STUDY

HUMAN RIGHTS AS defined in the present study are universal moral rights. In the words of the first sentence of the preamble to the United Nations Universal Declaration of Human Rights, "recognition of the inherent dignity and of the equal and inalienable rights of all members of the human family is the foundation of freedom, justice and peace in the world."[4] Chapters 2 and 3 will ask whether Buddhist thought supports this Western-generated notion of rights or whether there are alternative Buddhist visions for societies where human dignity is respected and all members are protected from harmful acts. As the preface makes clear, the Universal Declaration is directed in large part to national governments: "Member States have pledged themselves to achieve, in cooperation with the United Nations, the promotion of universal respect for and observance of human rights and fundamental freedoms." It is indeed the state that can insure that human dignity is recognized and protected; therefore, a major focus of the current study is to examine Buddhist concepts of the ideal state and how Buddhist states have actually functioned in history.

Chapter 4 examines the earliest Buddhist theories and practices in regard to government and its relationship to subjects in ancient India, the home of the first Buddhist polities. Chapters 5 and 6 treat the history of Thailand and Burma over the past two centuries to see how Buddhism, politics, and human rights have worked together in Theravada countries. Chapters 7 and 8 trace Buddhist attitudes and practices in regard to slavery and caste from the earliest period to the present, revealing the surprising history of monasteries owning slaves and of Buddhist support for caste systems in several countries. Chapter 9 looks at how the status of women was affected in ancient India and in later periods by the impact of Buddhist teachings. Chapters 10 and 11 deal with Buddhism, militarism, and human rights in Japan and Tibet, while Chapter 12 offers some concluding reflections.

Chapter 13 consists of a selection of source material drawn from Buddhist writings from the earliest period down to the present. The readings come from a number of traditions and illustrate how major Buddhist thinkers and rulers have dealt with issues raised in the earlier chapters. Chapter 14 has short biographies of more than thirty Buddhists who have been involved in practical ways in struggles to realize Buddhist principles in politics and social issues. An asterisk (*) has been affixed to the first mention in the text of each person who has a biographical sketch in chapter 14. The largest section of this study, a topical annotated bibliography, should be very useful to those who wish to find out more about Buddhists and human rights issues. A chronology of events in Buddhist traditions that relate to the topic is found at the end of the frontmatter.

Examples from all three major divisions of Buddhism and material from earlier stages of Buddhist history and the contemporary period are included. Rather than trying to provide a survey of all Buddhist lands and times, representative topics, places, and periods are presented in some detail. This reflects the author's belief that such an approach is more interesting and more likely to reflect the tradition accurately than a global approach. However, the defect is that, due to considerations of manageable length, some important issues, areas, and individuals were not included in the book chapters, although the reader will find some direction toward them in the biographical and bibliographical sections at the end of this study. For example, China is not well covered; Korea and Vietnam are not covered at all; and the issues around the role of Buddhism in the continuing long-running civil war in Sri Lanka are not taken up.[5] More could have been said about women's issues, as indeed about all of the topics raised, but what follows is offered as a contribution to the scholarly literature on Buddhist ethics.

2

ARE THERE HUMAN RIGHTS IN BUDDHISM?

INTRODUCTION

THE WHOLE QUESTION OF HUMAN rights and justice seems to be a modern introduction to the Buddhist tradition. Buddhists focused much more on perfecting the individual through the cultivation of morality, meditation, and insight rather than on reforming society. Buddhist literature and learning in the areas of philosophy, meditation, and individual moral development are remarkably well developed. These vast and deep endeavors in learning and wisdom constitute one of the great treasures of civilization. On the other hand, Buddhists have never developed any comprehensive social philosophy or theory. Damien Keown, of Goldsmith College, London, a leading authority on Buddhist ethics, noted "For such an intellectually dynamic tradition Buddhism is a lightweight in moral and political philosophy."[1] Keown's own ground-breaking books on Buddhist ethics from 1992 and 1995 hardly venture into social ethics and seem not to mention human rights at all.[2]

The 1991 *Buddhist Ethics and Modern Society*, a compendium of papers from major Buddhist scholars, illustrates the relative weakness of political theory in the tradition. Justice is only mentioned in one passage in the contribution of Sulak Sivaraksa,* the noted Siamese Buddhist reformer. In his paper Sulak argues that there is indirect support in Buddhist thought for a "minimum distributive justice"[3] from general Buddhist principles of the middle way. Sulak notes that there is nothing in the scriptures or in Theravada tradition that directly advocates radical social transformation.

Lily de Silva, a professor of Pali and Buddhist Studies at the University of Perideniya, Sri Lanka, devotes two paragraphs to human rights, the only substantive mention of human rights in the book. She maintains that rights in the sense of a claim or privilege are foreign to Buddhist discourse, although the fundamental rules of Buddhist morality can provide an indirect method to protect fundamental human rights. She stresses that "Buddhism does not speak of rights, but instead emphasizes duties and obligations. . . . According to Buddhism, an emphasis on rights tends to divide society in contending segments, each asserting its own rights, whereas an emphasis on duty is conducive to social cooperation, cohesion, and unity."[4] De Silva, like Sulak, takes the guarded position that Buddhist principles indirectly can work toward the same ends as Western values.

In 1995 the online *Journal of Buddhist Ethics* ran a Web-based conference which resulted in the 1998 book *Buddhism and Human Rights*. Peter Junger, an American Buddhist, who is a professor of Common Law at Case Western University in Cleveland, observed:

> As has been often noted, the concept of "human rights" tends to be based on modern Western European assumptions that, to a large extent, can be traced to earlier Judeo-Christian and Greco-Roman concepts; assumptions that are alien to many, if not all, of the innumerable Buddhist traditions.[5]

In fact, traditional Buddhist discourse even lacks terms that correspond to our Western ideas of "justice" and "human rights." In Maseo Abe's words, "Strictly speaking, the exact equivalent of the phrase 'human rights' in the Western sense cannot be found anywhere in Buddhist literature."[6] For example, until the end of the nineteenth century, the Japanese language lacked any way to express the notion of a "right."[7] A contemporary Thai scholar noted that: "the Thai word for human rights . . . still rings an unfamiliar sound . . . [and] conjures up someone who disregards the traditional pattern of compromise and harmonization of social relations."[8] Peter Harvey, Buddhist Studies scholar at the University of Sunderland, in his recent survey of Buddhist ethics includes a few pages on human rights,[9] noting that Buddhists traditionally have not used rights terminology, focusing rather on duties and responsibilities.

The idea of a human right, as it developed in the West, generally is taken "to mean a kind of universal moral right that belongs equally to all human beings simply by virtue of the fact that they *are* human beings."[10] It emphasizes the individual and has a sense of an absolute entitlement. J. M. Finnis, Fellow at University College in Oxford, expresses it this way in his excellent law monograph:

> [T]he modern vocabulary and grammar of rights is a many-faceted instrument for reporting and asserting the requirements or other implications of a relationship of justice *from the point of view of the person(s) who benefit(s)* from that relationship. It provides a way of talking about "what is just" from a special angle: the viewpoint of [one] to whom something . . . is owed or due and who would be wronged if denied that something.[11]

Since Buddhists teach that the ultimate religious goal for each individual is the elimination of the idea of an independent self through the elimination of craving for benefit, it is no wonder that human rights language sometimes feels very strange to traditional Buddhists. David Chappell, a well-known Buddhist scholar from the University of Hawaii and Buddhist activist, noted, "Scholars have argued that Buddhism has no doctrine of human rights and, technically, they are right."[12] More broadly, it has been argued that not only Buddhists, but all East Asians lack human rights traditions.[13]

It is significant that human rights, both in practice and in theory, evolved in the West in a particular historical and theological context with Jewish, Christian, and classical roots that located rights as part of a God-given order of justice applicable to all human beings, who were understood to be individual souls with eternal essences. In Buddhism, there is neither an exterior theological guarantor for rights nor is there any permanent person for them to adhere to. Wapola Rahula is one of the most highly respected and influential scholar monks from Sri Lanka. In his standard exposition of Theravada Buddhism, he makes it very clear that his nontheistic understanding of moral order is not compatible with Western ideas of justice.

> The idea of moral justice, or reward and punishment, arises out of the conception of a supreme being, a God, who sits in judgment, who is a lawgiver and who decides what is right and wrong. The term "justice" is

ambiguous and dangerous, and in its name more harm than good is done to humanity.[14]

There is nothing comparable in Buddhist texts to the ringing calls for justice, inspired by a vision of a God who acts in history, like those found in Amos and other prophetic sections of Abrahamic scriptures. Such exhortations seem somehow to go against the Buddhist grain.

If it is true that Buddhist thought does not share the theological background of the Western doctrine of natural rights, it is also true that the histories of the two cultures are very different. Buddhist countries never experienced the social, philosophical, and political changes that transfigured the West, leading to a human rights culture. Keown notes that there is no reason for Buddhists to apologize for their failure to come up with a full-blown human rights system, as the Western development was the result of its own peculiar historical situation, and could hardly be expected anywhere else.[15]

GROUNDING RIGHTS IN BUDDHISM, SOURCES

IN THE JOURNAL of Buddhist Ethics[16] there are six papers from the 1995 American Academy of Religion panel, "Revisioning Buddhist Ethics," which reflect some of the current excitement and flux in the field. One of their common themes is that Buddhist traditions and Buddhist scholarship lack common approaches to ethical issues, both theoretically and practically. The papers published in Buddhism and Human Rights (1998) confirm that diversity on the issue of the proper relation of Buddhist thought to human rights. Some of the contributors argue strenuously that Buddhist thought directly supports a modern human rights framework, while two in particular find quite the opposite.[17] Nonetheless, the editors conclude, "[I]t does appear that there is a consensus that Buddhist teachings are compatible with the aims of contemporary human rights movements." Disagreements arise over "how the Western concept of human rights, and human rights language, is to be expressed in an authentically Buddhist form" and how properly to ground human rights in Buddhist teachings.[18] Damien Keown's paper is perhaps the strongest attempt in the conference material to find a firm foundation for human rights in the Buddhist tradition. Keown is undoubtedly one of the most important contemporary writers on Buddhist ethics, and consistently seeks to ground his positions in the early texts of Buddhism. In an earlier work he described his stance as "Buddhist fundamentalism," which does not mean "emotional, anti-intellectual fanaticism, but the requirement that views and opinions be grounded in textual sources."[19] That is, he thinks that perennial moral truths can be found in Buddhist scriptures by means of a critical, historical examination of the texts. Immediately, in Buddhism, the question of which texts to look at then arises.

Keown relies on the Pali canon, the Pali language scriptures which are the standard of the Theravada Buddhists in South and Southeast Asia, as the "core teachings of classical Buddhism as a whole,"[20] arguing that to take one's grounding from Mahayana texts would exclude the earlier Theravada schools. Although the Pali texts, written down in the first century B.C.E., are the oldest extant Buddhist scriptures, they considerably postdate the historical Buddha and can scarcely be taken literally as his own words. Nonetheless, in one sense, Keown is correct as the Mahayana recognizes the Theravada as prior and accepts the Pali texts as canonical. However, in practice, Mahayana believers focus on their own canon, which they believe surpasses the earlier teachings in profundity if not in authority. Thus a framework built solely on a Pali text foundation would be of little value to Mahayana adherents. This would be true in an even more complicated way for Vajrayana Buddhists, as they have their own scriptures that supersede without replacing the sacred texts of both the earlier two schools.

Keown's goal is to consider human rights in the context of an ideal "classical Buddhism," an abstraction which "is neither the same as nor different from Buddhism in any historical or cultural context" in order to come up with a universal Buddhist formulation of human rights.[21] However, Buddhists have never restricted themselves to the study of texts to establish their moral principles and practices. These aspects of their faith issued from a complex of doctrines, behaviors, attitudes, and feelings drawn from meditation experience, rituals, local customs and history, and scripture alike. To insist that any valid foundation must come from Pali (or other) texts alone seems to fit better with the curatorial interests of some scholars than it does with what Buddhists in Buddhist milieus do on the ground. While scriptural sources remain very important, they should be supplemented by other aspects of the tradition and need to be tested against the historical record.

THE BIRTHRIGHT OF KARMA AND GROUNDING HUMAN RIGHTS

BUDDHIST DOCTRINE (*BUDDHADHARMA*) purports to describe the world as it really is as seen through the enlightened eyes of Lord Buddha. His teachings are the dharma, understood to be the truth about the nature of existence, which is seen as a continuous cycle of painful becoming (*samsara*). Dharma also includes a religious path of liberation for all sentient beings from the cycle of *samsara*. All creatures are trapped by selfish impulses of passion, aggression, and ignorance, which cause rebirth again and again. And everyone who is reborn inevitably will suffer, decay, and die again and again, for death is not permanent. It always leads to reincarnation in a precise position that is merited by one's deeds (*karma*) in previous lives. Buddha taught a way of life involving morality, contemplation, and ultimately wisdom—wisdom so deep that it resulted in liberation from the cycle of rebirth and suffering. Such wisdom involves understanding that all beings are contingent and interdependent (*pratityasamutpada*) and leads directly to compassion because the wise know that the suffering of self and others is driven by selfish and deluded grasping, which can be overcome.

Practically, wisdom leads to selfless action for the sake of others. Thus *prajna* (wisdom) and *karuna* (compassion) are the two major Buddhist ideals, the first relating to the ultimate realm and the second to the world of day-to-day existence. Without ultimate wisdom one will be defective in *upaya* or skillful means for helping others. Moral behavior in Buddhist systems then, is not an absolute in itself; it is a means toward a religious end, the transcendence of those selfish cravings that bind all beings to an ongoing round of suffering. Accordingly all moral acts are understood either to be *kusala karma*, skillful deeds which are beneficial to self and others, or *akusala karma*, unskillful deeds which harm self and others. In popular Buddhism *kusala karma* is "making merit" which can be achieved through ethical behavior, generosity (especially to the sangha, or body of monks), and rituals.

The moral quality of the totality of one's deeds or karma determines a person's destiny. Basically the moral consequences of an act are determined by the will or motivation (*cetana*) of the actor. If the will behind an act is driven by greed, hatred, or delusion, which Buddhists understand as the three poisonous roots of selfish craving, then the act is *akusala* or unskillful. Every act involves body, speech, and mind working in conjunction.

Mind starts a train of activity, and if greed, hatred, or delusion motivates mind, then the speech and bodily activity, which follow, are doomed to be unskillful. Unskillful acts always have negative consequences for the actor and generally for the recipient of the act, and on the contrary, skillful acts are beneficial, both in one's current existence and in determining rebirths.

In common with most Indian religious traditions, most Buddhists understand that individual living beings come into a particular existence, in one of six different realms of rebirth, as a result of the moral consequences of their actions (karma) in their previous lives. Each sentient being's particular destination is determined by the karmic consequences of its own prior acts. The six classes of beings are, arranged from the most to the least pleasant state: heavenly beings, humans, *asuras* (titans), *pretas* (hungry ghosts), animals, and hellish beings. A few Asian Buddhists and rather more contemporary Western Buddhists deemphasize or reject "reincarnation," focusing rather on karmic effects in the present life only. This law of karma is not particularly a fatalistic teaching since the Buddhist path consists of practical ways to replace unskillful with skillful acts and thus to improve one's situation here and now and to achieve a better rebirth in the future. And, of course, the ultimate goal is to transcend the cycle altogether, by attaining enlightenment.

Nonetheless, the law of karma may undercut human rights as a theoretical construct. "If one takes traditional ideas of karma at face value, the question of justice [or rights] would not occur."[22] In the case of rebirth as a human being, one's particular gender, class, nationality and so forth are precisely and justly determined by prior karma. Although one's precise fate in the future usually can not be known in detail, one may well have a good idea of the general direction that one's karma is leading. This means that "rights" can hardly be grounds for objecting to harsh conditions or treatment here and now. To put it most bluntly, if you are born into a powerless position in a rigid society with harsh rulers, you deserve it. Your task is to purify yourself from the poisons of hatred, greed, and ignorance and thus to live compassionately in relation to others. Early Buddhist texts reflect the social situation of India some 2,500 years ago and proper, compassionate behavior is understood in the context of the time. The political structures that existed (preeminently absolute monarchy), the social institutions of caste and slavery, and patriarchy as the norm for family structure were more or less taken as given. They were not, however, uncritically embraced and certainly were not taken as eternal god-given structures.

Indeed there is neither a creator deity nor creation in Buddhist teachings; the events of the universe unfold according to the interrelation of causes and conditions within a beginningless cycle. "The theory of karma is the theory of cause and effect, of action and reaction; it is a natural law, which has nothing to do with the idea of justice or reward and punishment."[23] There is no transcendent being in charge who keeps score. Gods exist, but they too are part of the cycle of rebirth, subject to dharma, and destined to suffer and die eventually. Accordingly, Buddhist thought can be characterized as nontheistic. Similarly, the Buddhist doctrine of no-self which states that each individual being has no permanent, essential self-nature but exists by virtue of its interactions with all the other beings in the cycle of life, precludes attributing rights as an essence, or any other essential quality for that matter, to human beings.

Buddhist precepts are the practical moral rules designed to provide guidelines for skillful activity for human beings in their social existence. When they are followed, negative karmic consequences are avoided and good results accrue. From the Buddhist vantage point of the middle way, there are two basic errors one could fall into regarding the nature of moral order and the necessity to follow right principles of conduct. If one denies the reality of karmic consequences, one has adopted the nihilistic extreme view, which tends toward antinomianism and the abandonment of the precepts. The eternalist extreme view takes moral rules as absolute, resulting in inflexible dogmatic positions. There is a tendency in contemporary human rights thinking to take rights as absolute and fundamental, as an inalienable aspect of humanity, which is so clearly expressed in the 1948 Universal Declaration of Human Rights. This sits uneasily with the Buddhist tendency to avoid absolute formulations.

Finally, the precepts of morality laid down by the Buddha are not absolute commandments.[24] They are clearly understood as "rules of training," which the individual undertakes in order to advance along the religious path. Peter Harvey explains it in this way:

> A key aspect of Western ethical systems is that moral prescriptions should be universally applicable to all people who can understand them. Buddhism, though, is generally gradualist in approach, so while it has ethical norms which all should follow from a sense of sympathy with fellow beings (such as not killing living beings), others only apply to those who are ready for them, as their commitment to moral and spiritual training deepens.[25]

In fact, so little are they absolute commandments, that the precepts have been used since the earliest days of the Buddhist community as temporary vows, freely assumed by individuals for specified lengths of time. A lay meditator, for example, might undertake to follow the rule of training to abstain from the misuse of sensual pleasures for the period of a retreat. The relativity of the precepts is further demonstrated by the fact that there are traditionally five for the ordinary person, eight for the advanced laity, and more than two hundred for monks and nuns.

Dr. Hema Goonatilake, a Theravadin Buddhist from Sri Lanka, makes this point very well: "It is . . . to be understood that precepts are rules of training and not commandments from God, the Buddha or anyone else. It is only an undertaking by one, to oneself, if one is convinced that it is a good practice to observe."[26] Note that this refusal to take rules for human behavior as absolute makes it difficult to affirm rights as essential to humanity. Again, this contrasts with current Western mainstream thought. It should be emphasized that the relativity of the precepts does not imply antinomianism. Although they are relative, it is understood that there will be inevitable unpleasant consequences for any who break them. "The law of karma is seen as a natural law inherent in the nature of things, like a law of physics,"[27] thus negative effects must flow from *akusala karma.*

All of these factors together make it difficult to find a solid footing for human rights. If one is morally responsible for one's own karma, which determines one's place in life, then it is not clear that one has a right to any better treatment than which he or she receives. There are no ultimate authorities to which to appeal. Buddhism is a religion that operates without a deity who created the moral order or who judges those within it. There is no appeal to the moral precepts, if this interpretation of their relativity is correct, as an absolute anchor for a theory of human rights.

THAILAND: PHRA PRAYUDH PAYUTTO ON HUMAN RIGHTS

PHRA PRAYUDH PAYUTTO is Thailand's most respected contemporary scholarly monk, whose thoughts on ethics and human rights are directly relevant to the questions under consideration. His writings on contemporary social issues stress the nontheistic nature of Buddhist thought:

[U]nlike the theistic religions, Buddhism does not propose an agent or arbitrating force that rewards or punishes good and evil actions. . . . Ethical laws follow the natural law of cause and effect: virtuous actions naturally lead to benefit and evils actions naturally lead to harm, because all of these are factors in the stream of causes and conditions.

He also is very clear on the relativity of Buddhist ethics: "Given its dynamic view of the world, Buddhism does not put forth absolute rules for ethical behavior."[28]

One of his clearest pronouncements on human rights comes in the preface to his 1996 book, A Constitution for Living, where Phra Payutto again stresses the nontheistic and flexible nature of Buddhist ethics. The book consists primarily of a compendium of lists of moral principles drawn from the Theravada scriptures, with little detailed application to contemporary conditions. In the preface, however, Payutto offers his impressions of the modern condition, and he is far from enthusiastic about human rights as a guiding principle:

Many people today look on life in all sectors as a struggle between conflicting interests—the "bosses" against the "workers," the "government" against the "people," the "rich" against the "poor," and even the "women" against the "men," or the "children" against the "parents." When the aim of life is seen as material wealth or power, society becomes a struggle between conflicting personal interests, and we are in need of an ethic to protect those interests. It is a "negative ethic": society is based on selfish interests—"the right of each and every person to pursue happiness"—and an ethic, such as "human rights," is needed to keep everybody from cutting each other's throats in the process.[29]

In another publication Payutto argues that human rights systems have three fundamental flaws. The first is the one just mentioned: Phra Payutto thinks that they arise from and reflect cutthroat conditions. Second, human rights are merely a human convention; there is nothing permanent about them; they are not part of the order of natural law (dharma). Third, human rights pertain only to the social realm while the truly critical factor in ethical matters pertains to the level of individual human motivation. When the motivation of the actors in society is not pure, then the results will always lead to more conflict and contention.[30]

In contrast he offers a "positive ethic," a Buddhist ethic drawn from the scriptures, which stress "compassion, goodwill, harmony, cooperation and wisdom."[31] The teachings of Buddhism rather "offer guidelines for behavior based on timeless truths—the positive weal created by compassionate, wise relationships—and aimed at the ultimate goal of spiritual freedom: living in the world and yet above it."[32] His Buddhist economics illustrates how a Buddhist "positive ethic" proceeds and why he does not favor human rights approaches. In the first case, he argues that economics is properly understood as integral to the Buddhist path to enlightenment.[33] The eight-fold path, indeed, includes right livelihood as one of the factors.

In Buddhist understanding, human acts done out of ignorance and motivated by craving are unskillful, and thus forge the vicious circle of *samsara*. However, there is also the quality of basic goodness in people. We all have some spark of primordial wisdom, which leads us toward skillful acts. In Phra Prayudh Payutto's words,

> Buddhism states that human beings are naturally endowed with a special aptitude for development. While . . . it is natural for people to have cravings for things, [there is also] the human desire for quality of life or well-being, the desire for self improvement and goodness.[34]

Buddhist economics, then, would be a matter of cultivating the desire for the good; it would be unselfish skillful behavior in line with the eight-fold path. This would mean turning away from ignorant grasping that leads away from enlightenment.

With proper motivation and understanding, "we no longer see life as a conflict of interests with those of society and nature." Buddhists understand that harmony rather than conflict is the right way to organize the economy and other aspects of society. "[A] truly beneficial life is only possible when the individual, society, and the environment serve each other."[35] As would be expected there are different economic expectations for lay Buddhists and for world renouncers. In the *vinaya*, the scriptural rules for ordained world renouncers, Lord Buddha limited monks and nuns to a very few possessions—their robes, a bowl, medicines if necessary, and little else. They were not allowed to handle money, own real estate, and originally could not even store food overnight—what is begged in the morning must be consumed before noon. The point is to be content with what one receives and to live happily with very little as part of the discipline that leads away from bondage to the world.

Lay Buddhists, on the other hand, are encouraged to be prosperous in order to be generous, especially to the religious orders. The middle way extends to the realm of economics; nowhere does Buddha praise poverty. In fact, wealth is celebrated as a good, but selfishness, miserliness, dishonest methods of making money, and attachment to wealth are all condemned as unskillful. Phra Payutto contrasts this Buddhist approach to what he sees as the western fundamental economic principle, "the pursuit of happiness" as it is put in the United States Declaration of Independence. On the whole, he thinks this western "good-hearted aspiration" is conceptually confused and becomes a habitual pursuit of ever-renewed desires. The result is our modern civilization with its "cities filled with limitless distractions and pleasure centers," which "often leads to restlessness and exhaustion in the individual, strife in society and unsustainable consumption of the environment."[36]

Leaving aside the question of whether or not Phra Payutto's assessment of the qualities of the modern West is altogether fair and accurate, he is convinced that its influence in Thailand has been destructive. Thai people, he says, have to a large degree taken up the belief in progress through ever increasing material advance. "Adopting this way of thinking, their whole way of life is affected, leading to a rejection of religion and a decline in morals."[37] His writings, whether on theoretical or applied topics, present traditional Theravada dharma in new ways in an attempt to counteract the decline in faith and morality that he perceives in Thailand today. His negative evaluation of human rights principles follows from his rejection of the presuppositions of the way of life that brought them forth. While human rights structures might be a good thing, perhaps even necessary, to offset the negative effects of the heedless pursuit of happiness, far better are the positive principles of dharma that underlie traditional Buddhist polities, and those traditional Buddhist principles are what he tirelessly presents.

THE FOUR HOLY TRUTHS: INTRODUCTION

KEOWN USES THE Four Holy Truths, or Four Noble Truths,[38] as a lens to evaluate how several contemporary scholars of Buddhism have tried to ground their human rights concerns in the dharma and also as a tool to develop his own position.[39] All schools accept the Four Holy Truths, from the first sermon Buddha preached after his enlightenment, as an essential formulation of basic doctrine. Therefore, Keown's method is quite useful and will be followed here, with rather different conclusions. Very briefly, the first holy truth states that all experience in all the realms of becoming is ultimately unsatisfactory, and the second says that this unsatisfactory state of affairs comes about due to the selfish grasping of the beings caught in the wheel of existence. Things in the world are inherently instable, insubstantial, and painful; and as long as we attempt to hold on to them through selfish, passionate, angry, and ignorant cravings, we will continue to be trapped in a cycle of sorrow. This is quite a gloomy view of the nature of things, and it is unlikely that Buddhism would have had any missionary success at all if the teachings stopped there. But the third holy truth is as hopeful as the first two are dreary. It says that it is possible for people to overcome selfish craving and thereby to become truly free. The noble eight-fold path, the fourth holy truth, is a practical way to attain emancipation by transforming oneself. It consists of moral guidelines, meditation practices, and aspects of wisdom.

The first holy truth, that all is *duhkha* (i.e., all is ultimately unsatisfactory or conducive to suffering), is explained again and again throughout the scriptures and permeates Buddhist thought. One of the classical schemes used to explain the first truth notes that three types of *duhkha* mark every single existing thing in every manifestation of becoming. First there is ordinary *duhkha*, the suffering that comes in everyone's experience of birth, death, old age, sickness, frustration from not getting what is desired, being in contact with the unpleasant, and being separated from the pleasant—all of the things generally recognized by everyone as unsatisfactory. Second is the sorrow that must come because every thing changes. No matter how much we love something, and no matter how much happiness that brings, that state of happiness will fade, as all mental states must, and that fading will bring pain. And, of course, both beloved and lover alike will inevitably decay and pass away, again causing pain. Third is the mark of insubstantiality, *anatman* (no-self or no-soul). This fundamental teaching resolutely maintains that "there is no permanent, unchanging spirit which can be considered 'Self', or 'Soul', or 'Ego', as opposed to matter."[40] Further, consciousness also is not a persisting substance outside the flux of the phenomenal world. Buddhists do recognize that the notion of an "I" or "self," acting in the world with an apparent continuous reality, is necessary for ordinary discourse. The concept partakes of relative truth, but the error comes when the relative self is taken as an absolute unchanging essential being rather than as it really is—conditioned, ever changing, and perishable. In fact, the Buddha was so resolutely opposed to the idea of *atman*, a permanent soul or self, that he stressed that it was to be found neither in the phenomenal world of becoming nor in the realm of *nirvana*, the release from all bonds of the world of becoming.

The second holy truth is that *duhkha* arises in the world from causes and conditions. As thirst or craving, the cause of *duhkha* is a link in a complicated process of interdependent origination (*pratityasamutpada*). Craving, like all phenomena in the cycle of becoming, is part of the world of becoming, not an absolute in itself. Mahayana Buddhist theory in particular stresses the marvelous way that every aspect of the ever-changing cosmos is mutually related in a seamless web. The selfish craving for permanency, for substantiality in the world of flux, is the link that welds one to the pain of unending birth, death, and rebirth. Above all it is the craving for one's own permanence or *atman* that is the problem.

CAN THE FOUR HOLY TRUTHS GROUND HUMAN RIGHTS? KEOWN, IHARA AND JUNGER

KEOWN CONCLUDES THAT human rights cannot be grounded in the first two holy truths as their structure is strictly factual and analytical and thus lacks an ethical component.[41] Following a theme of L.P.N. Perera, a Buddhist scholar from Sri Lanka, Keown looks to the third and fourth holy truths. Perera provides a straightforward article-by-article analysis of the 1948 United Nations Universal Declaration in his valuable 1991 study, which remains the only monograph on Buddhism and human rights. He provides texts from the Pali canon to support the thesis that there is Buddhist support for human rights in general and for each of the specific articles of the Universal Declaration, some of which will be considered in later chapters.

Keown builds upon Perera's commentary on Article One of the declaration, which begins with the statement, "All human beings are born free and equal in dignity and rights." Perera presents several ways that Buddhist thought supports this statement. First is the nontheistic teaching that men and women are part of a natural causal order and have the freedom to determine themselves as there is no deity who is creator, judge, and redeemer to rely upon. Self-reliance extends to the highest possible point: "Buddhahood itself is within the reach of all human beings."[42] This is another way to express the teaching of the third holy truth that it is possible to overcome the factors which bind one to the cycle of suffering. Second, Perera argues that Buddhist texts clearly teach that human beings are of one fundamental nature; they are essentially equal although their specific circumstances differ greatly. This leads, he maintains, to a Buddhist defence of human rights:

> The sense of equality is further reinforced by the Buddhist view that (a) all human beings, in the final analysis, face the same basic phenomena of birth, decay and dissolution, spelt out in the First Noble Truth, and (b) that at the same time human beings are capable of overcoming these problems by attaining the very highest moral and spiritual level by a development of the human potential through and extensions of human capacity. Human life is so placed in the cosmic scheme of things, that human beings alone enjoy the best opportunity of transcending the unsatisfactoriness of existence into the state of Nirvana . . . in this very life. . . . It is from the point of view of its goal that Buddhism evaluates all action. Hence Buddhist thought is in accord with this and other Articles in the Universal Declaration of Human Rights to the extent to which they facilitate the advancement of human beings towards the Buddhist goal.[43]

Perera's point (b), of course, is related to the teachings of the third and fourth holy truths, the extinction of the causes of suffering and the path leading to that extinction.

Building on the second point in Perera's quotation immediately above, Keown attempts to structure a Buddhist doctrine of human rights on the third holy truth, that Buddhahood is within the grasp of all—that *nirvana* can be attained here and now—and the fourth holy truth which lays out the practical steps to realizing one's Buddhahood. "This is because the source of human dignity in Buddhism lies nowhere else than in the literally infinite capacity of human nature for participation in goodness,"[44] or, as it is more often put, "all beings are potential Buddhas or possess the 'Buddha-nature.'"[45] The Buddhist way is not merely theoretical; it involves a day-to-day way of living. Keown's subtle argument boils down to this: In those societies which lack those human rights enumerated in the Universal Declaration, Buddhists and other serious religious seekers are unable to put their faith into practice and thus cannot realize their highest human potential.[46] He argues that without freedom of religion, liberty of the person, freedom from torture and slavery, rights before the law, and so on, it would not be possible here and now to realize the goals that are expressed in the third and fourth holy truths. On the face of it, this seems utterly obvious—who wants to defend the institutions of torture or slavery? But on reflection, it must be admitted that Buddhist spirituality and Buddhist culture reached some of their highest peaks in places and times where slavery and torture were integral to society and where legal rights as per the declaration were inconceivably remote. Even in the modern world where the freedoms and liberties to which Keown refers do seem necessary for serious religious practice to take place, it is not clear that these freedoms and liberties must be understood as "rights."

As Keown ably outlines, Buddhist scripture and Buddhist history fail to develop an explicit human rights doctrine or even the terminology to express the idea of "right" or "rights" in the sense used in current discourse. Keown then is faced with the problem of reconciling an absence of explicit rights in some 2,500 years of Buddhist tradition to his claim that they are necessary for the successful practice of the faith. First, he makes the reasonable point that it is possible for a concept, especially for such a complex idea as rights, to be present in a culture even when it is not expressly developed. "In sum it might be said that in classical Buddhism the notion of rights is present in embryonic form although it is not yet born in history."[47] To continue the metaphor perhaps too far, the obstetrical tool that Keown seizes upon to draw rights into the Buddhist light of day is the moral teaching of the fourth holy truth. In particular, he focuses on the first four of the five precepts, which Buddhists see as fundamental aspects of dharma (the basic truth of the world as it really is) and which are thought to apply to all people.

The first four precepts involve the abstention from taking life (nonhuman as well as human), from taking what is not given, from sexual misconduct, and from false speech. Keown claims plausibly that these things to be abstained from, in common with most secular and religious moral codes, are forbidden because they are evils which destroy the social fabric and which are "antithetical to the human flourishing-in-community"— the whole point of the third and fourth holy truths. The basic precepts, he argues, are paralleled in the various modern human rights declarations, which can be seen "as a translation of religious precepts into the language of rights." But is such a translation justified? Keown thinks it is, but notes that there are obvious difficulties in that "the precepts look and sound very different from contemporary declarations on human rights." Lacking any mention of rights, they are duties under dharma undertaken by the practitioner.

Keown, probably following Finnis as cited above, resolves the problem by positing that duties entail rights. "A direct translation of the first four precepts yields a right to life, a right not to have one's property stolen, a right to fidelity in marriage, and a right not to be lied to."[48] Earlier he looked at the ideal reciprocal relations between husband and wife, ruler and subject, and so forth, as laid out in early Buddhist texts and followed down to modern times, concluding that the duties prescribed mean that something is due to the other party as a right. It is not at all self-evident that these rights, or rights in general, necessarily flow from duties, and in fact, there are good arguments to the contrary.

Craig K. Ihara and Peter D. Junger both offered strong opposition to Keown in *Buddhism and Human Rights*. Ihara, a professor of philosophy at California State University, Fullerton, who has written extensively on Buddhist topics, offers several examples to show that Keown and Finnis are incorrect in positing a necessary progression from duty to right. He discusses the situation of soccer players, who participate together in a co-operative role-based activity that is governed by a set of rules that establish duties of the players in a way that parallels duties laid out in *buddhadharma*.[49] In the context of soccer, all players except the goalies are bound by a rule that forbids them to play the ball with their hands. Players have a duty to follow such rules, and will be penalized for violations. If a player flouts the rules it would spoil the game for the rest of the players and spectators. It would be appropriate for the others to complain that he was incompetent or irresponsible, but as Ihara argues, it would be very strange for them to claim that their rights had been violated. Rights language simply does not apply in such cases although duty language surely does. To take another example, when a speaker undertakes to deliver a public talk, he or she has a duty to present a good one. However, no matter how badly disappointed the audience is, it does not follow that that their rights have been violated.

As mentioned in the previous section, Keown states that the reciprocal duties laid out in the sermons of the Buddha to govern the relationships between husband and wife, ruler and subject, and so on imply corresponding duties. Ihara comments:

The central flaw in the arguments given by Keown and Finnis is to assume that every kind of "ought" or "duty" entails a corresponding right. For Finnis this error takes the form of holding "ought" equivalent not only to what is "due to do" but also what is "due to one." For Keown the mistake is thinking that reciprocal duties always "correspond" to reciprocal rights.[50]

Finnis's error, which in fact Keown shares,[51] from a Buddhist point of view, is the more serious as it tends toward the notion of *atman* by feeding the sense of individual entitlement and undermining mutuality and interdependence.

The specific relationships in the Pali canon that Keown used to bolster his contention that a duty entails a right better support Ihara's position than Keown's. Take, for example, the reciprocal duties of pupils and teachers:

There are five ways in which pupils should minister to their teachers . . . by rising to greet them, by waiting on them, by being attentive, by serving them, by mastering the skills which they teach. And there are five ways in which their teachers, thus ministered to by their students . . . will reciprocate: they will give thorough instruction, make sure they have grasped what they should have duly grasped, give them a thorough grounding in all skills, recommend them to their friends and colleagues, and provide them with security in all directions.[52]

As broad rules for a cooperative role-based school, these principles made good sense in the context of ancient India and, in fact, seem rather sound today. Some of the points could perhaps be translated into rights language, but others seem very resistant to such manipulation. A teacher's dream would be to have students who are always attentive and masterful, but it would hardly be sensible for a teacher to complain that his or her rights were violated if students became inattentive or failed to learn all that was presented. Or, from the students' angle, the teacher may have failed in his or her duty to "make sure they have grasped what they should have duly grasped," but it is difficult to see what the corresponding right of students could be.

As Ihara argues, if the parties involved in such cooperative enterprises chose to focus on individual rights rather than on their reciprocal duties under dharma, something very significant has been changed.

The change to a modern concept of rights is one from conceptualising duties and obligations as the role-responsibilities of persons in a cooperative
scheme to seeing them as constraints on individuals in their interactions
with other individuals all of whom are otherwise free to pursue their own
objectives.[53]

Any sort of a traditional teacher-student relationship would be undermined if either party should apply to a human rights tribunal for redress
when optimum learning failed to occur. Better to attend to one's duties as
an instructor or learner when there are difficulties than to complain that
one's rights are violated, if learning is to flourish.

To return to Keown's line of reasoning, "Human rights can be extrapo-
lated from Buddhist moral teachings in the manner described above using
the logic of moral relationships to illumine what is due under Dharma."[54]
That is, some Buddhist moral duties entail specific rights as found in the
United Nations Universal Declaration. An example would be the right to
life as derived from the first precept, the undertaking to abstain from taking life. Other declaration rights, he maintains, can be deduced from
other Buddhist moral principles. Since human rights in modern formulations and declarations are absolute rights, Keown works backward to argue that the precepts from which he derives such rights are also absolute.

If there are universal and exceptionless rights, as human rights charters affirm, there must be universal and exceptionless duties. . . . The First Precept in Buddhism, therefore, should be understood as an exceptionless duty
or moral absolute.[55]

There are several objections that can be made to Keown's argument and
conclusion.

In the first case, there are passages in both Theravada and Mahayana
scriptures and commentaries, which allow the precept against taking life
to be violated under certain circumstances.[56] Furthermore, using exceptionless rights in modern rights charters to maintain the absolute, exceptionless nature of the first Buddhist precept is suspiciously circular.
And it even goes in the wrong direction on the circle. Surely, arguments
about the fundamental nature of Buddhist principles should come from
Buddhist sources, not from United Nations statements, which in fact de-
clare rather than demonstrate universal and absolute rights.

Finally, his absolutist understanding of the precepts presents an extreme view, erring on the side of eternalism. All doctrines, Buddhist and non-Buddhist alike, including even the precepts, are essentially provisional and not to be clung to, according to both Theravada and Mahayana teachings. However, it should be stressed that there is no consensus on how exactly the precepts should be taken, whether relatively as suggested here, or absolutely as does Keown. All in all, Keown's attempt to establish a certain base for human rights in the third and fourth precepts does not succeed. On the other hand, he is certainly successful in showing that traditional Buddhist teachings about duty are compatible with many of the specific goals and principles of modern human rights declarations.

Peter Junger, professor of law at Case Western Reserve University and active member of the Cleveland Buddhist Temple, also writing in opposition to Keown, develops three broad arguments against introducing rights language into Buddhist ethics. First, as a historian of law, Junger does a thorough job demonstrating that the "concept of human rights is a recent product of the history of Western Europe and of the civil law and common law traditions."[57] Like Ihara, he contrasts modern rights-based thinking, with its focus on autonomous individuals, to the Buddhist way of duty and virtue-based ethics, centred on cooperative traditional communities. His major point is that human rights theory and practice are contingent products of a specific historical development and thus have no legitimate lineage in Buddhist thought and practice. Second, he argues that rights thinking is radically opposed to the first holy truth, which states that all of existence is unsatisfactory, transitory, and insubstantial. Rights language as found in the United Nations Universal Declaration not only reifies the individual person as an autonomous centre of inalienable rights, it also implies that security is actually due by nature to everyone in this world (Article 25). This is, of course, a direct contradiction to what the Buddha taught, namely, that security is the last thing we can expect from the nature of things. What we get from the impermanent world of flux is old age, sickness, and death: *duhkha*, in short.

Finally, Junger thinks that the attempt to find an absolute anchor for human rights, or anything else for that matter, in Buddhism is misguided.

> In the arising and cessation of all things that comprise this ocean of birth
> and death, there is no ground upon which rights could be founded, there is

no ground at all. . . . [T]he concept of human rights is the product of a particular time and place, without any claim to universal validity.[58]

Since rights, as a product of interdependent arising like everything in the phenomenal world, are empty of any absolute reality, Junger reasons, it would be an error for a Buddhist to turn them into absolutes. This does not mean that Buddhist ethical thought justifies acts that lead to child hunger, political terror, religious persecution, and other such things condemned as human rights violations. Buddhists have the duty to follow virtuous rules of conduct based on wisdom and compassion, not because they are based on absolute human rights but "because that practice leads to the cessation of suffering."[59]

To take rights as absolute is to miss the fundamental point of Buddhist analysis: There are no absolutes in the historical process. Indeed it is the seeking for and clinging to apparent absolutes that binds suffering beings to the circle of *samsara*. Peter Harvey also cautions that rights and *buddhadharma* may conflict since *anatman* is antithetical to any idea that there can be one who owns inalienable rights and further notes that "demanding rights" may well lead to the unwholesome mental states of anger and greed.[60] Derek S. Jeffries, professor of religion and philosophy at the University of Wisconsin, sums this issue up very well: "I have argued that, *prima facie*, a human rights *ethic* is incompatible with the no-self doctrine. Although skillfully presented Damien Keown's argument for human rights requires an enduring self."[61] No wonder that so many Buddhist traditionalists are unable to affirm human rights as Buddhist.

BUDDHA AND HUMAN RIGHTS: ROBERT A. F. THURMAN

IN QUITE AN original paper, Robert A. F. Thurman, who holds the Jey Tsong Kahpa Chair of Indo-Tibetan Buddhist Studies at Columbia University, asserts that Lord Buddha's life demonstrated his affirmation of fundamental human rights in several important spheres. For example, he says that Lord Buddha, "in walking out on his father and on his duty as a husband, father, and king, . . . announced in radical terms his right to liberty as a human individual." And for another example, Thurman argues that instituting an order of monks, who lived by silently begging from the laity, whom they never thank, was "a clear expression of a human being's right to have that necessary to sustain life, just because he or she is a human being, without being expected to fulfil any obligation or to make any compensation."[62]

Such incidents do show how strongly Buddha emphasized the importance of individual self-fulfillment over against contemporary standards in India, which insisted that every person conform to meticulously defined and detailed duties within a holistic socioreligious structure. However, when Thurman concludes that Lord Buddha's "life exemplified all the basic human rights," even including a "right to enlightenment,"[63] he is using "human rights" in a very particular and idiosyncratic way. As Thurman agrees, the articulated political-anthropological complex of "human rights" was the product of Western civilization in its move into modernity. Thurman, in fact, thinks of human rights as a Band-Aid applied to mask the gaping wound that the "metaphysical materialism, psychological reductionism, and nihilistic ethical relativism" of modern Western thought has torn from the heart of human dignity, and that human rights offers a very weak buffer against oppressive forces.[64] The fragility of human rights as a bulwark to protect human dignity, he thinks, is shown at its clearest when powerful, industrialized societies encounter any weaker people, especially nonwhite people, who stand in the way of their desires. How quickly the so-called universal and inalienable rights of the poor disappear.

At the same time, he maintains human rights cannot be grounded in theism, as the limitless power of God means his human creatures are absolutely dependent and contingent beings. When everything depends on the will of God, individual human rights evaporate. Thurman maintains that the Buddhist concept of the person, each of whom is responsible for determining his or her own destiny through the workings of karma, provides a metaphysical framework for a way of life based on human rights and freedom. The Buddhist doctrine of nonsubstantial impermanent self, with its potential for liberation, thus occupies the middle ground between the extremes of nihilism and theist absolutism and supports human rights and freedom, as exemplified in the life of Lord Buddha.

While Thurman's characterization of the Buddhist doctrine of the self is sound, there are two major objections to his saying that this concept of a relative self entails human rights. In the first case, "a human right," as a phrase in ordinary educated discourse, refers to a benefit that is owed to every human being; as something inherent to humanity. It is absolute and universal and should never be taken away from an individual. This, as argued above, is never explicit in the tradition, is incompatible with the basic Buddhist avoidance of absolute formulations, is not part of the ethical teachings (which are relative and predicate behavior on virtue and duty rather than rights), and needs an absolute self (a non-Buddhist concept if ever there were one) to work. Thus Thurman's linking of human rights to the teaching of no absolute self, while it has a certain logic of its own, is bound to cause confusion and lead to misunderstanding if adopted.

Furthermore, the episodes that Thurman cites to show that Buddha demonstrated human rights in his actions could be better explained without reference to rights. For example, in taking up the wandering life of a begging renunciant, Gautama, in fact, entered into a well-established tradition of world renouncers in the India of his era. The records of the early Buddhist order show very clearly indeed that Lord Buddha was well aware of what the Jains and other ascetic orders were doing and that he often took the social expectations of the people toward the monks into account in making his rulings. By begging, monks were not asserting their right to be fed just because they were humans. Begging monks had a socially recognized obligation to their donors, the obligation to live up to their rules of poverty, chastity, nonharm, and proper deportment. Those who did not, were not given food by the laity, and were disciplined or expelled from the Buddhist order. Thurman explains such regulations as the result of regrettable compromises that Lord Buddha had to make, because his vision of basic human rights was too radical to be implemented in the social world of his time and place. The people simply would not accept it.[65] While it is true that Buddha and the early order did compromise with public opinion on several points, it was not done regretfully in the spirit of giving up rights, rather it reflected the acceptance of duties and the attempt to live according to virtue.

Although Thurman's adoption of rights language may be somewhat intemperate, his concluding three-point summary of what Buddhist thought has to contribute to human rights discourse and practice is a gem. First, he notes that any compelling human rights position must be firmly based in "underlying metaphysical issues." It will not work if it is "purely dogmatic or purely prudential, absolutist, or spiritually nihilistically relativist." Second, human rights need to be grounded in some "rationally plausible" idea of the irreducible spiritual nature of the individual persons and at the same time there must be a healthy suspicion of any "spiritual rationalizations of injustice." Third, "human rights thought should always be conducted in interconnection with a balancing consideration of human responsibilities."[66] The Buddhist middle way between absolutism and nihilism offers a great deal to the defense of human dignity and the building of decent societies where the humans may truly flourish in community.

FEELINGS, MEDITATION, AND RIGHTS

KENNETH INADA's "A Buddhist Response to the Nature of Human Rights," was reprinted as the first paper in *Buddhism and Human Rights*.[67] Here he attempts to find a basis for human rights in the way Buddhists understand human feelings. He notes that Buddhist ideas about how people should properly relate to one another involve "soft" relationships, based on the interconnectedness of all beings, holism, and the doctrine of emptiness, in contrast to the western emphasis on "hard" relationships. "The Western view on human rights is generally based on a hard relationship. Persons are treated as separate and independent entities or even bodies, each having its own assumed identity or self-identity."[68]

Although Inada does not mention it, traditional Buddhist meditation practice also encourages "softness," both in feelings and in thought process. Meditation in all schools of Buddhism leads, or is intended to lead, to the person experiencing the dissolution of a solid sense of an "I" or "ego" as distinct from other beings. The practice of the cultivation of loving kindness (*mettabhavana*) is another universal technique, which again leads away from selfish considerations to soft feelings of love and compassion for all other sentient beings, expressly including those who appear as personal enemies. Mahayana meditators often undertake to exchange their self-interest for the good of other beings in various ways. Of course, actually coming to know through one's own experience that all phenomena are subject to constant change and empty of any substantial reality is a major goal in meditation. Thus meditation and doctrine work closely together to help Buddhists stay on the path of "softness."

This complex of feelings and ideas surrounding soft relationships, Inada thinks, forms a basis for a Buddhist approach to human rights. However, his position does not precisely support a human rights doctrine in the full sense. He concludes that soft relationships properly manifest as compassion (*karuna*), the basic Buddhist ethical concept. When one cultivates ontological openness and holistic interrelations with other beings, life becomes governed by compassionate feelings and Buddhist virtues like "tolerance, kindness, and non-injury."

It can now be seen that the Buddhist view on human rights is dedicated to the understanding of persons in a parameter-free ambience, so to speak, where feelings that are extremely soft and tender, but nevertheless present and translated into human traits or virtues that we uphold, make up the

very fibre of human relationships. These relations, though their contents
are largely intangible, precede any legal rights.[69]

Inada does not attempt to show in any detail how rights emerge from traditional Buddhist virtues and soft relationships, and nothing could be farther from the tone and subject matter of Buddhist meditation manuals
than human rights.

In fact, Inada's position is very close to that of Ihara and Junger. He
does not provide justification for a full human rights doctrine. An open
ontology centered on emptiness and coconditioned causality cannot generate the kind of fixed framework necessary for a rights-based morality.
His "soft relationships" characterize the sort of traditionalist role-based
behavior that Ihara takes as the norm for Buddhist interaction. In fact,
there is not a hint of rights language or ethos in Inada's description of
"soft relations." Unlike Junger and Ihara, Inada does not find rights language to be a threat to right Buddhist views and actions, although he is
not altogether comfortable with its introduction. He notes that, "Admit-
tedly, the concept of human rights is relatively new to Asians. From the
very beginning, it did not sit well with their basic cosmological
outlook."[70] Inada's paper, while it neither provides a Buddhist grounding
for human rights language nor uses human rights thinking to illustrate
right Buddhist action, may perhaps be seen as an attempt to ally Buddhists with human rights advocates for practical reasons. In any case, Inada has done an important job in laying out some of the underlying
background in feelings and intangible aspects of human relations that do
figure deeply in Buddhist ethical thought. Another useful feature of his
paper is to highlight the bodhisattva figure as the ideal embodiment of
the Buddhist way of life.

SUMMARY

THIS CHAPTER DREW mainly from the teachings of the Theravada Buddhist schools, the schools that represent the oldest historical strain and
which now dominate in South and Southeast Asia. The next chapter of
this study will take up some of the major themes found in the Mahayana
schools, which are strong in East Asia. In particular the bodhisattva ideal
and the Mahayana teachings on the doctrine of "skillful means" will be
examined for their implications in regard to human rights theory and

practice. The remaining chapters will look at Buddhist theory and actual historical practice to see if Buddhist concepts and ways of organizing society helped work toward that admirable goal, which Keown called "human flourishing-in-community." Issues like slavery, imperialism, the status of women, and the relationship of the individual to the power of the state, will be considered in various Buddhist times and places. Are contemporary human rights concepts applicable in Buddhist history? Do they help Buddhists today in their struggles against cruelty and oppression? Or are there, as suggested in the work of Inada, Ihara, and Junger, unambiguously Buddhist values on which to build societies that respect human dignity?

3

HUMAN RIGHTS AS
SKILLFUL MEANS

BODHISATTVA PATH AND HUMAN RIGHTS

IN THE THERAVADA TRADITION, bodhisattva is a term primarily used to refer to prior incarnations of Gautama, the Buddha
for our age. The stories of Buddha in the making, collected in the canon
as the Jataka tales, illustrate the eight-fold path and are widely used to teach
morality. They are very popular in all schools of Buddhism today, and
some of them have been well known for at least 2,300 years. This study
will consider several of the Jataka tales in some detail because they are so
important in the everyday practice of Buddhism. In contrast to the doctrinal and ritual portions of scripture, which were locked in languages understood by few monks and practically no laypersons, these popular texts
were and are generally known to laity and monks alike in all Buddhist milieus. The Jataka stories are particularly useful to illustrate Buddhist principles, as they are well known in both Theravada and Mahayana
communities. However, they have been little used in discussions of Buddhist approaches to issues of justice and human rights.

In Mahayana Buddhism, the term bodhisattva refers both to Gautama
in his previous incarnations and, in general, to any Buddhist practitioner,
who vows to stay in the world helping others until all sentient creatures
have been freed from the sorrows of *samsara*. Bodhisattvas as those who
give up attaining enlightenment for themselves to save other beings epit-
omizes the ideal human type, and indeed the Mahayana path is often

referred to as the bodhisattva path. In addition to the bodhisattva in training, so to speak, in Mahayana thought there are also great bodhisattvas like Avalokitesvara and Manjusri, who have developed their powers to an enormous degree and function somewhat like protective or saviour deities. This study will concentrate on the bodhisattva-in-process. The close look at some of the basic concepts, texts, and stories about bodhisattva-in-process which follows will illuminate Buddhist attitudes toward human rights.

To begin, everything that a bodhisattva does is done from the motivation of compassion (*karuna*); all merit is dedicated to the benefit of other beings: "Through my merit may all those in any of the directions suffering distress in body or mind find oceans of happiness and delight."[1] He vows to stay in the world to take on the sufferings of others as long as it takes to save all suffering beings.[2] In the most common Mahayana formulation of the path there are six perfections or virtues (*paramitas*) that a bodhisattva cultivates on the road to realizing his Buddha nature. They are giving (*dana*), morality (*sila*), forbearance (*ksanti*), vigor (*virya*), meditation (*dhyana*), and wisdom (*prajnaparamita*).

Wisdom, the profound realization that everything and every concept in *samsara* are empty and without grounding, may be considered the culmination of the perfections and pervades the entire path.[3] It might be said that the full attainment of the *prajnaparamita* is nothing short of enlightenment itself. Meditation is the discipline taught by the Buddha of calming the mind and analyzing mental processes, which leads to inner peace and wisdom. Many basic meditation practices are common to the Theravada and Mahayana schools. Vigor means never to give up in laboring for the sake of others. It involves constant vigilance and effort to eliminate one's own flaws and tirelessness in doing good works to lessen the suffering of all sentient beings.

THE JATAKA OF HARITA AND THE PERFECTION OF MORALITY

MORALITY FOR BUDDHISTS generally means to follow the precepts, the basic rules of skillful behavior as taught by the Buddha, but the Jataka stories show a rather surprising flexibility about *sila*, a *paramita* for bodhisattvas. In fact, odd as it may seem, bodhisattvas may indulge in breaking all of the precepts, with the exception of telling a falsehood, as illustrated in the Harita Jataka.[4] Born of a wealthy Brahmin family, the Bodhisattva Harita gave up his wealth and position to become an ascetic of great spiritual attainment. He eventually came to live in the court of great king, who was very pleased to support such a worthy "field of merit." One day when the king was away at war, Harita caught a glimpse of the perfect body of the queen and instantly commenced an ardent affair. When confronted by the king, Harita confessed, thinking, "They who forsake the truth, though they sit in the sacred enclosure of the Bo tree, cannot attain to Buddhahood." The text continues with this commentary: "In certain cases a [bodhisattva] may destroy life, may take what is not given him, commit adultery, drink strong drink, but he may not tell a lie, attended by deception that violates the reality of things."[5] After Harita confessed to the king, the two men discussed the nature of temptations in a high-minded dialogue, and the king urged his guest to conquer the passion of lust. Inspired, Harita returned to his meditation practices, regained all his former powers, and departed for the forest after teaching true doctrine to the court. This story reverses the more usual pattern where the bodhisattva provided the moral example for secular persons. Here the king reminded the ascetic bodhisattva of his duty, showed no anger, and did not even mention punishing the miscreant saint or his queen.

The teaching that even the precept against taking life may be broken is surprising and contrary to what one might expect Buddhists to maintain. The British expert John Garrett Jones reviewed ten Jatakas in which the bodhisattva was implicated in killing, including three where the issue was that he had eaten meat.[6] In all cases, the victim was an animal, not a human. Jataka 128, in which the bodhisattva was born as the king of the rats, is the only one where he directly took life. He ripped the throat out of a deceitful jackal to protect himself and his subjects. There does not seem to be any Theravada canonical justification for the killing of a human being.[7]

While bodhisattvas do sometimes engage in wickedness in the Jataka accounts, in the vast majority of the stories they are exemplary in their morality. The point of the Harita story was that although practitioners may succumb to the temptations of sexual attraction, it is possible to overcome them after confronting the truth and confessing one's mistakes. In the cases of other miscreant bodhisattvas, their unsavory behavior was the result of their unfortunate horoscopes, which John Garrett Jones notes as an apparent contradiction to the law of karma.[8] Astrology generally is taken very seriously in Buddhist cultures, and perhaps the law of karma and astrology could be reconciled by arguing that one's karma in previous lives determines the particular time of rebirth. In the Jatakas, it is clear that errant bodhisattvas are charged with the duty to correct faults in subsequent rebirths.

The moral impact of certain acts is in large part determined by the context of the situation, including the specific social role of the actors. In the case of the Bodhisattva Harita, his sexual affair with the queen was wrong on several counts: it was adultery with a married woman, it violated the hospitality of his host the king, and was a breach of his vows of celibacy as an ascetic. Sexual activity, for lay Buddhists including bodhisattvas, if it is acceptable within the rules of the land and does not violate a vow, is not forbidden. For example, the bodhisattvas born as kings in the Jataka enjoyed their many wives and concubines as befitted their status, as did Gautama when he lived as a prince.

THE JATAKA OF KSANTIVADIN AND THE PERFECTIONS OF FORBEARANCE

THE JATAKA STORIES that illustrate the perfections of forbearance (*ksanti*) and giving (*dana*) bear most directly on human rights issues. The story of the Bodhisattva Ksantivadin is one of the best loved of the Jatakas. It provides a supernal example of forbearance in the face of cruelty and injustice. A king, inflamed with strong drink, found his dancing girls listening to a sermon given by Ksantivadin, an accomplished ascetic. The bodhisattva told the king that he was preaching on patience, "the not being angry when men abuse and strike you and revile you." To see if the ascetic practiced what he preached, the king summoned the royal executioner and ordered two thousand lashes with a scourge of thorns. Questioned again about his doctrine, Ksantivadin replied that his patience was not skin deep. Whereupon the king ordered the sage's hands and feet cut off, and after questioning again, his nose and ears, but the answer remained that "my patience is deep seated within my heart." Kicking and reviling him, the king left the preacher lying in his own blood. The king's general bound the wounds of the bodhisattva and begged him to restrict his anger to the king alone. Ksantivadin replied:

> Long live the king, whose cruel hand my body thus has marred,
> Pure souls like mine such deeds as these with anger ne'er regard.[9]

The earth herself could stand no more, split open, and drew the evil king into the worst of the hell realms. Ksantivadin's attitude throughout this narrative does not reflect human rights concerns. There is no sense of entitlement to fair treatment, no complaint against injustice, not even a hint of any defense offered, and no righteous anger. His selflessness, the essence of the bodhisattva path, provides no support for rights language and rights reasoning. Moral order turns according to the laws of karma, which work with neither heavenly judge nor intrinsic human rights of the persons involved. The king's fate is due to his neglect of his royal duties, his cruelty, and lack of compassion, not because he offended against the rights of Ksantivadin.

The Jataka of Vessantara and the Perfection of Giving

The Vessantara Jataka is very long and intricately constructed with touching details and rather fully drawn characters. It is "the last and best loved of the birth stories."[10] Vessantara's life exemplifies the perfection of giving and often closely parallel's the life of Gautama. It was predicted while Vessantara was in the womb that he was to be a paragon of giving, and at the moment of his birth, he declared, "Mother, I wish to make some gift; is there anything?" She provided a purse with one thousand coins, saying, "Yes, my son, give as you will."[11] He gave away hundreds of thousands as a young child. At the age of eight he reflected that everything that he gave was not from himself and resolved to give away his own heart or eyes or flesh if requested. At this example of extraordinary generosity, the gods rejoiced and earth and heavens gave forth signs, as happened every time extraordinary giving occurred. When sixteen, Vessantara took a wife and sixteen thousand consorts and ascended the throne. The royal pair produced a fine son and a wonderful daughter, while Vessantara continued his lavish giving.

When the prince donated the kingdom's protective white elephant along with all its precious jewels and attendants to help a neighboring country, the people were very distressed and forced the king to banish the prince, who asked for one last chance to be generous. Vessantara then gave the gift of seven hundreds: seven hundred each of elephants, horses, chariots, high-born maidens, cows, men and women slaves along with fine food and strong drink for everyone. In regards to human rights, note that slavery, not to mention giving women in marriage, is simply taken for granted. Indeed giving slaves and giving girls are meritorious acts. After the great ceremony, Vessantara and his wife left the palace in a chariot, accompanied with the two carts full of treasures that the king sent with them so that the prince could continue his largesse. Before they were out of sight of the palace, he had given away all the treasures including the ornaments he wore, the horses, and the chariot. Carrying their children, and protected by the gods, they walked away into the Himalayas to assume their lives in exile as forest dwelling ascetics, living in a hut on the fruits and grains they could gather.

After they lived there simply for seven months, a corrupt and greedy old Brahmin was urged by his young avaricious wife (both stock figures in Indian popular literature) to seek the family out to ask for the gift of their two children to serve as household slaves. Vessantara, who foresaw the request, waited eagerly, "like a drunkard, thirsting for a draught,"[12] overjoyed that he would soon have the opportunity to practice his generosity again. Vessantara readily agreed to give his children as slaves, saying, "Dearer than my son a hundredfold, a thousandfold, a hundred thousandfold is omniscience."[13] When the little boy and girl ran away, terrified by the obviously cruel Brahmin, their father found them hiding and brought them back to be dragged away, bound and beaten, by their heartless new master.

Before giving them away he set the price that would have to be paid for their redemption, a thousand pieces of gold for the boy and much more for the girl as befitting her status as a future bride worthy only for a king. Her redemption price included one hundred each of male and female slaves, elephants, horses, bulls, and gold pieces. As usual, slavery is an unquestioned part of life. Although the sight of his bloodied children being led away moved the father to grief and anger, he could not rescind a gift once given. John Garrett Jones comments that the extravagant giving in this and similar Jatakas goes far beyond human considerations and, further, that Vessantara's gift was self-serving in that he did so confident of spiritual recompense, omniscience in this case.[14] At this point the king of the gods intervened to make sure that Vessantara did not give his wife away, although he was certainly willing, even eager, to do so. This last manifestation of generosity led the king of the gods to let Vessantara choose eight boons. Issues of the rights for the wife and children never arise; their master, the bodhisattva, was even rewarded for his willingness to deliver them into slavery.

With the help of the gods, the two children and their slave master ended up at their grandfather's court, where he paid their redemption price and reunited them with their parents. The story ends happily, with Vessantara returned to the throne, where he resumed old ways of unreserved generosity. Appropriately enough, the greedy Brahmin died from overeating at the feast prepared for the returning prince. When Vessantara returned to his kingdom, he emptied all the prisons and "set free all creatures, down to the very cats."[15] Although not mentioned explicitly, this emancipation presumably included all of the city's slaves, but the motivation behind the act seemed not to be based on any consideration of rights of prisoners, slaves, and other creatures; rather it was a way for Vessantara's to manifest his limitless giving.

THE JATAKA OF KING SIVI AND HUMAN RIGHTS

THE POPULAR, ALBEIT short, Jataka of King Sivi reinforces the selfless nature of the bodhisattva's activities and again shows how foreign human rights to the concerns of a bodhisattva. The action turns on a vow similar to that made by Vessantara. In Sivi's words,

> I vow that if any one . . . name what is part of myself,—if he should mention my very heart, I will cut open my breast with a spear, and as though I were drawing up a water-lily, stalk and all, from a calm lake, I will pull forth my heart dripping with blood-clots and give it him . . . if one say, I can't get my household work done, come and do me a slave's part at home, then I will leave my royal dress and stand without, proclaiming myself a slave, and slave's work I will do: should any men demand my eyes, I will tear out my eyes and give them.[16]

The gruesome climax came when the king of the gods took the form of an old blind Brahmin to test Sivis's resolve. When asked for his eyes, the bodhisattva was overjoyed for the chance to give what had never been given before and summoned the royal surgeon. In an operation that is nearly unbearable to read about, the lurid deed was done, and Sivi handed over the first eye, saying: "The eye of omniscience is dearer than this eye a hundred fold, aye a thousand fold: there you have my reason for this action."[17] And indeed Sivi's gift, like Vessantara's in the previously told tale, was rewarded by the king of the gods, who replaced the eyes plucked out with eyes of omniscience.

THE NATURE OF THE BODHISATTVA

THESE REPRESENTATIVE JATAKA stories illustrate the supremely selfless nature of the bodhisattva. There is surprisingly little difference between the tone of these Theravada narratives and the Mahayana bodhisattva ideal. Both stress that an ideal practitioner will give up everything for the sake of other beings. The noble bodhisattvas of the Jataka could easily have said the following two verses from a twelfth-century Tibetan text, as cited by the Dalai Lama*:

> When others out of jealousy treat me badly
> With abuse, slander, and so on,
> I will learn to take all loss
> And offer the victory to them.
> In short, I will learn to offer to everyone without exception
> All help and happiness directly and indirectly
> And respectfully take upon myself
> All harm and suffering of my mothers.[18]

These supremely selfless ideals, emerging from a metaphysics that dissolves any sense of fixed personhood, reverse the ordinary habitual patterns of looking out for one's own interests first. Once again, the motivation is duty and responsibility that comes from compassion and understanding. The bodhisattva has a duty to exchange his or her self-interest for others, but there is no sense that others have a right to the bodhisattva's ministrations.

HUMAN RIGHTS AS SKILLFUL MEANS

ONE OF THE key concepts in Buddhism, especially Mahayana Buddhism, is *upaya* (skillful or expedient means).[19] It refers to the skills that a Buddha or Buddhist practitioner brings to bear in presenting dharma to people of varying levels of intelligence and accomplishment to help them along the path that leads to the cessation of suffering. Both compassion and wisdom are necessary for the exercise of skillful means. Compassion for the suffering of others provides the motivation, and the wisdom and insight of the teacher enables him or her to find ways to present the dharma that are appropriate to the temperament, needs, and social situation of the hearers. If one fails to engage one's audience, there is no chance to help them, and sometimes rather surprising methods can be used.

A memorable illustration of *upaya* is found in the prologue to Jataka 182, which tells how Nanda, Buddha's younger brother, was helped when he was distracted from his life as a monk by his love for a beautiful woman. By miraculous means, Buddha took Nanda to the Himalayas where they saw a severely disfigured female monkey before proceeding to the heavenly court of the king of the gods. At the court, Buddha and Nanda met five hundred heavenly nymphs, whom Nanda immediately desired. On being pressed Nanda confessed that his earthly beloved was like "that wretched ape" in comparison to the heavenly beauties and then asked Buddha, "How is it possible, Sir, to win these nymphs?" Buddha answered, "By living as an ascetic, Sir." Nanda got Buddha to pledge that such a course of action would ensure him the enjoyment of the nymphs.

By this promise Nanda was inspired to the ascetic life and they returned to the order of monks. When the head of the order found out what motivated Nanda to such ardent asceticism, he shamed him by saying, "If you live chaste just for the sake of women, what is the difference between you and a labourer who works for hire?" Nanda then applied himself to the discipline of a monk for more appropriate motives and quickly attained sainthood. At that point he released Buddha from the promise to grant him the five hundred celestial maidens. This story is a fine example of how dharma was presented skillfully to a rather poorly prepared student. Lord Buddha skillfully offered the lesser prize of the celestial attendants, in order to entice Nanda to return to the order, where the good advice of his fellow practitioners led him to reach the main goal after all. The major point of the Jataka proper was the efficacy of good counsel.

Perhaps the best-known example of skillful means in Mahayana scriptures is from the third chapter of the Lotus Sutra, a preeminent text in Chinese and Japanese Buddhism. The parable of the carts is about a very rich merchant who lived with his three young sons in a vast and dilapidated mansion. One day, when in the courtyard, the father noted with horror that the house was well on fire and that he had no chance of physically rescuing the boys who were playing happily within. So he called to them explaining the danger clearly and carefully, but they could not understand,

and continued heedlessly in their games. The father then thought, to save them from the inferno, "I must now invent some expedient means that will make it possible for the children to escape harm." Remembering what each of them had as a favorite toy, he called out to them:

> The kind of playthings you like are rare and hard to find. If you do not take them when you can, you will surely regret it later. For example, things like these goat-carts, deer-carts, and ox-carts. They are outside the gate now where you can play with them. So you must come out of this burning house at once. Then whatever ones you want, I will give them all to you![20]

The boys, of course, quickly ran from the building and demanded their presents.

There were no toys, but the boys were not disappointed. Each of them got a magnificent, jewel-adorned full-scale ox-cart, taken from the limitless possessions of the father. In the text, Buddha asked the question of whether or not the father was guilty of false speech, which as has been discussed, is the one precept that the bodhisattva is never permitted to violate. The disciple answered,

> No, World-Honored One. This rich man simply made it possible for his sons to escape the peril of fire and preserve their lives. He did not commit a falsehood. Why do I say this? Because if they were able to preserve their lives, then they had already obtained a plaything of sorts. . . . World-Honored One, even if the rich man had not given them the tiniest carriage, he would still not be guilty of falsehood. Why? Because this rich man had earlier made up his mind that he would employ an expedient means to cause his sons to escape. Using a device of this kind was no act of falsehood.[21]

The seriousness of the situation justified the wise and rich father's promise to his sons, which he knew he could not fulfill. Without the ruse of the carts, the fires of the collapsing mansion simply would have consumed the boys. Both this and Jataka tale about Nanda commend the teacher for enticing the learner with a lower prize in order to achieve a higher goal.

So it would seem that wisdom and compassion might lead one to bend or break all the precepts and to stretch the teachings in cases where great harm might ensue otherwise. Mahayana Buddhists go much farther than the Theravada in this respect, explicitly teaching that a bodhisattva may violate all of the precepts if the motives are compassionate and if others are benefited. The Dalai Lama tells of the previous birth of Lord Buddha as a sea captain. One of his crew of five hundred intended to kill all 499 of his shipmates in order to make off with their goods. The bodhisattva was unable to convince the potential mass murderer not to do the deed, and figured that "it would be better to take upon himself the karmic burden of killing one person in order to spare that person the karma of killing 499, [so] he killed the would-be murderer."[22] Since the motive was compassionate, the Dalai Lama concluded that the act of killing actually was very meritorious and in fact fulfilled of one of the minor precepts of a bodhisattva, "to answer appropriately and halt someone who is engaged in a wrong activity."[23]

Peter Harvey identifies the same story as coming from a Mahayana sutra, well known in China and Tibet, and discusses it under the heading "compassionate killing." He notes that a factor in making an act of killing into a meritorious one for the bodhisattva is his willingness to accept any bad karmic consequences. This is, of course, quite a dangerous principle except in the hands of truly advanced bodhisattvas. It is all too easy to think one is practicing skillful means, when one is actually merely self-indulgently breaking the precepts or foolishly getting the doctrines wrong. Mahayana commentators were very aware of the dangers involved, and some even suggested that this teaching should be kept concealed from everyone except advanced practitioners.[24] Keown suggests that there are effectively two levels of upaya.[25] The first applies to beginners on the bodhisattva path, and only allows flexibility in the minor rules of morality. The second level of upaya, which allows the breaking of the major precepts even up to the one against killing human beings, applies only to Buddhas and the highest level of bodhisattvas, those who have reached the penultimate stage of perfection. While there is no Mahayana consensus on this issue, most of the sutras, parables, and commentators stress the importance of following the precepts and do not encourage breaking them as upaya, especially for ordinary practitioners.

The relevant question now is: Can human rights concerns, terminology, and arguments be introduced into Buddhist discourse as a form of upaya? Craig Ihara, as was seen in chapter 2, has very strong reservations against introducing rights language into Buddhist moral discourse, but he

recognizes that there might be practical reasons to do so. In our fragmented modern world, he notes, we have no common history to draw
upon. Customary role-based institutions, as found in traditional Buddhist
polities, are local by their very nature and can hardly be called upon to
provide a model for international standards to protect individuals from
oppressive governments. Furthermore such customary institutions are dis-
integrating everywhere, under the tremendous corrosive impact of the
homogenizing forces of modern transnational institutions and ideologies.

In Ihara's words, it may be "that rights-talk is the best way of coping
with a world without common customs and traditions." Rights language
and rights declarations have the advantages of making universal claims
and of being accepted, at least in theory, by much of the world community. Although he thinks it would be a dangerous innovation, Ihara asks if
introducing rights into Buddhist moral discourse might "serve as *upaya*
(skillful means) toward the overall elimination of suffering."[26] Working
against suffering is, of course, the major purpose of the Buddhist path,
and one mark of a skillful practitioner is the ability to find methods appropriate to the circumstances of the audience so that dharma can do its
good work. In the context of the early twenty-first century, where human
rights language is dominant in the discourse of the most powerful nations
and international organizations, it could perhaps be skillful for Buddhists
to adopt it.

David Chappell, professor at the University of Hawaii and one of the
strongest scholarly voices in contemporary engaged Buddhism, also argues for the practicality of adopting rights language in spite of the fact
that, technically speaking, there is no Buddhist doctrine of human rights.
He makes the point that the Buddhist metaphysics that undercuts any
doctrine of a permanent self [and thus undercuts any support for a notion
of individual rights] also allows the Buddhist to make use of human rights
language without the danger of reifying rights into absolutes. As he puts
it, "the Buddha warned not to take doctrines too seriously." As long as it
is kept in mind that human rights are man-made constructs, they can
safely be used to advance common Buddhist values.

Human rights may not be inherent in people in a metaphysical sense,
but they are strongly supported by Buddhist leaders as a negotiated social
contract based on fairness and respect since everyone wants freedom from
arbitrary arrest and imprisonment, health, food, self-esteem, and education.[27]

Chappell explicitly makes this point in light of what is going on in the contempory world, where human rights have been sorely violated in Burma, Tibet, Vietnam, and other Buddhist societies. Although he does not use the terminology, Chappell is actually making a very clever Buddhist argument for human rights as a skillful device, or *upaya*. He acknowledges that human rights approaches are not found in traditional Buddhist thought and practices, but takes them up in order to alleviate the real suffering caused by oppression.

SOME POSITIVE BUDDHIST ALTERNATIVES TO HUMAN RIGHTS

CRAIG IHARA, PRIMARILY for reasons of political expediency, rather reluctantly agreed that Buddhists could invoke human rights as *upaya* or skillful devices. The reluctance of this concession is clear from a footnote that followed it very closely. In this note, Ihara, in effect took back his provisional endorsement of using human rights language in Buddhism. He gave three reasons: "While Buddhism has a holistic view, the rights perspective is essentially atomistic" and strengthens "the illusion of self." That is, the metaphysics of the two are incompatible. Second, traditional Buddhist social thought is about doing one's duty in cooperative communities, and does not fit well with a morality based on the concern for individual rights. Finally, he notes that there is very little consensus about the number and nature of rights, let alone about how best to put them into practice; thus it might well be much more effective in international affairs to focus on the alleviation of suffering rather than on rights.[28] This last is a refreshing thought—rather than focusing on the ideal of rights, why not do something to address the actual suffering of actual human beings?

The second and third points offer Buddhist alternative principles that could serve well to ground attempts to alleviate the very real problems of oppression and injustice that people all over the world currently face. They point to a social ethic of duty and responsibility tied in with a compassionately motivated drive to diminish the suffering of others, all perfectly in tune with the basic teachings of dharma, and compatible with traditional Buddhist ways of doing things. Donald K. Swearer, an authority on Theravada Buddhism who teaches in the department of religion at Swarthmore College, also discusses whether or not Buddhist thought supports rights language and offers another, similar Buddhist alternative formulation to deal with the pressing concrete problems of modernity. He notes that many commentators have argued that the Buddhist doctrines of no-soul and emptiness make it impossible to sustain the notion of any inherent rights since there is no intrinsic person or self to bear them. Further, the doctrinal thrust of Buddhism centers on wisdom and truth and thus does not lead to "an ethics of rights and principles." "Others," he notes, "contend that the Buddhist critique of inherent self-nature coupled with an emphasis on compassion (*karuna*) provides a unique basis for an ethic of responsibility based on a distinctive sense on intrinsic mutual worth."[29]

Swearer noted that when Gautama attained enlightenment or Buddhahood, his experience went through three stages in the course of a night. First, he recalled all of his previous karmic history in complete clarity and detail. Second, he saw in his mind's eye the painful birth, death, and rebirth of all the beings that whirl about in *samsara*. That is, he saw the reality of the first holy truth, that all of existence is ultimately unsatisfactory. Finally, he came to understand the causal interdependence of all the phenomena in the world (*pratityasamutpada*), the second holy truth. Tying all these factors together, Swearer developed four important points concerning how Buddhist thought and rights thought may come together. The specific issue he considered was whether or not nature, both animate and inanimate, has rights in the context of a response to the Earth Charter, but his reasoning applies equally well to the question of human rights.

First, he maintained that the universality of the Buddhist doctrine of interdependent causality fits nicely with the universalistic claims of modern rights advocates. Second, without concrete actions to bring them into practice, rights claims and proclamations are meaningless. Third, and particularly interesting, he wrote,

> The debate over whether Buddhism's apparent deconstruction of intrinsic nature undermines the language of the rights of nature is a question that "tends not to edification," especially in the light of the urgent call to concrete action that should be the imperative of the Earth Charter.[30]

Questions that tend not to edification are the kind of theoretical questions that can be discussed practically forever without settling them. The phrase comes from the popular parable of Malunkyaputta,[31] where Buddha refused to entertain such questions as they get in the way of the primary business of the Buddhist path, the elimination of suffering in the world. In claiming that the question of the philosophical compatibility of fundamental Buddhist doctrines and of human rights presuppositions is one that does not tend to edification, Swearer also is indirectly invoking *upaya* to admitting rights into Buddhist discourse. Swearer's fourth formulation is that the problems involved in improving the situation are ultimately spiritual, and any solution must involve individual and group transformation.[32]

In conclusion, it cannot be claimed that traditional Buddhist scripture and ethical thought directly support human rights concepts; and, in both theory and practice, the assertive individualism of much of human rights advocacy, goes against the spirit and teachings of buddhadharma. But to hold too tightly to doctrinal formulations—such as the rejection of rights language—may also go against the spirit and teachings of *buddhadharma*. As long as it is kept clearly in mind that rights are transient human constructs and, like all the products of *samsara*, should not be reified into absolutes, it would be safe enough for Buddhists to invoke them. In the light of the terrible treatment meted out to people by governments all over the world and in light of the efficacy of human rights claims, it could even be an example of Buddhist skillful means to defend the oppressed by using the rhetoric of human rights.

However, having conceded that Buddhists many find human rights claims very useful in certain circumstances, the strongest contribution that Buddhists can bring to the effort to overcome oppression and its ensuing misery would be drawn directly from Buddhist scriptures, doctrines, and traditional practices. Therefore, it would not rely very much (if at all) on rights claims. The fundamental teachings of no-self, emptiness, the interdependence of all beings, wisdom, and compassion lead to an ethics of duty and responsibility rather than one based on individual rights as is the case in Sri Lanka today, where those Buddhists who are trying to find ways to stop the war with the Tamil minority do so from "the spirit of compassion." They are not motivated by the idea of minority "rights (a curiously western term with little genuine applicability to non western traditional societies) which the recipient might legitimately expect to receive."[33]

4

STATE, SOCIETY, AND THE
BUDDHIST ORDER

INTRODUCTION

THERE ARE TWO IDEAL FORMS OF POLITY in Buddha's teachings: the way for the order of world-renouncing monks and nuns to live, and the ideal state under a wheel-turning king for the rest of humanity, for the world at large. While the same ultimate laws of dharma apply to both realms—the four holy truths are true for laypeople and monastics alike, on the relative level, different rules and expectations applied for the two realms. As mentioned in chapter one, there are five basic precepts that govern the moral life of all Buddhists. Laypeople are expected to take them on as vows and to follow them to the best of their abilities. They are to undertake to abstain from taking life, from taking what is not given, from sexual misconduct, from false speech, and from taking intoxicants. The use of intoxicants that cloud the mind interfere with keeping the first four precepts, with meditation practices, and with the ability to attain clarity of insight.

The five precepts have stricter interpretations for monks and nuns than they do for humanity at large. Sexual misconduct for people living in the world means sexual behaviors that are not culturally sanctioned, and in Buddhist practice these vary considerably according to the mores of the nation in question. For monks and nuns sexual misconduct involves any sexual activity at all with any gender of any species of being, whether or not physical contact occurs. Flirting or sexual joking are minor offenses for monks and nuns under the *vinaya*, while any sexual intercourse willingly undertaken is a defeat, which calls for the immediate expulsion from the order with no possibility for reinstatement in the present lifetime. Similarly, the restriction on taking life is much harder to follow for the monks and nuns, who may not dig in the earth as that could injure worms and other small creatures, and who may not pour water on the ground if it has mosquito larvae or other small animals in it.

Not only are the basic precepts more strictly applied to monks and nuns, they are also bound by a much greater number of rules. Especially keen laypeople, for limited periods, may undertake to follow the monastic vow of sexual abstention and to assume three additional vows, which also apply to novices in the orders. The three extra rules are to abstain from taking solid food after midday, from adornments and shows, and from sleeping in fancy beds. Fully fledged monks and nuns are bound by more than 225 different rules, including the eight precepts detailed above, and the monks and nuns are examined every fortnight as to their standard of adherence to them. This duality of ethical structure sets up a clear structural demarcation between laity and clergy. Their interrelations are carefully regulated in the *vinaya*, with the monks and nuns becoming exemplars of moral purity and teachers of dharma to the laypeople. The primary duty of the lay Buddhist is to provide food and the necessities of life to the monks and nuns, as long as the individual clerics are seen to live up to their vows.

From the time of the Buddha, the role of the ruler was to protect the worthy monastics in the kingdom. In turn, the realm would benefit from the virtues generated by the moral and meditation practices of the holy men and women living under strict vows. Kings were to seek out and follow the advice of religious adepts and to support them generously. In recognizing two separate though interdependent realms, the Buddha was not concerned with trying to reform the structures of society and government to conform to the highest principles of his teaching. On these matters, Richard Gombrich, the British authority on early Buddhism, has some very wise words:

> [M]y interpretation puts me at odds with those who see the Buddha as a social reformer. . . . [H]is concern was to reform individuals and help them to leave society forever, not to reform the world. Life in the world he regarded as suffering, and the problem to which he offered a solution was the otherwise inevitable rebirth into the world. . . . To present him as a sort of socialist is a serious anachronism.[1]

The remainder of this chapter will attempt to show how Buddhism, the state, and society interacted in South and Southeast Asia and to point out some implications of this on issues of human rights.

KING, SOCIETY, AND RELIGIOUS ORDERS IN BUDDHIST SCRIPTURES

THE *DIGHA NIKAYA*, or *Long Discourses of the Buddha*, is one of the most important collections of scripture of the Theravada school of Buddhism, which dominates in South and Southeast Asia and which is generally considered to be the oldest extant Buddhist tradition. This text contains a number of fundamental teachings that are foundational to Buddhist social thought. The *Digha Nikaya* lays out the essential features of both realms, and will be one of the primary sources for this chapter.

The sixteenth book of the *Digha Nikaya*, the *Mahaparinibbanasutta*, is an account of the last days of Lord Buddha. The sermons in this sutra are thus remembered in the tradition as the last ones that the Buddha chose to deliver, and may well be taken to be especially important. Several of them have political implications. A certain king decided to attack his neighbours, the Vaijjians, and sent his minister to ask the advice of the Buddha. Good kings, in Indian and Buddhist tradition, always seek the counsel of religious advisors before taking important actions. The Buddha replied indirectly, noting seven things about the way that the Vaijjians governed themselves: (1) they hold "regular and frequent assemblies"; (2) they "meet in harmony, break up in harmony, and carry on their business in harmony"; (3) they follow their ancient traditions, neither bringing in new rules nor abolishing old ones; (4) "they honour, respect, revere and salute the elders among them, and consider them worth listening to"; (5) they do not abduct the wives and daughters of their neighbors; (6) "they honour, respect, revere and salute" their religious shrines both home and abroad; and (7) they protect the safety of Buddhist Arahants, those who have followed the Buddhist path to the point of enlightenment.[2]

As long as they follow these seven principles, Buddha said, "they may be expected to prosper and not to decline." The minister took the point, said that the Vaijjians were invulnerable to force of arms, and advised against the invasion. One might expect the moral of this story to be that the Vaijjian semidemocratic model of governance, which had served them so well, should be followed by all nations. But in fact, by the time that this sutra was collected, the Vaijjian republic had already been undermined from within, thereby losing its unity and strength, and had fallen to the Maghadan Empire. Instead the Buddha modified the seven principles of the Vaijjians to be the basic rule to govern his monks. The last three rules for the monastic order or sangha were changed to fit the needs of world-renouncers rather than laity. The monks were enjoined (5) not to fall prey to desires that arise in them, (6) to be devoted to forest dwellings, and (7) to preserve mindfulness. The monastic system of governance was therefore essentially democratic.

He concluded, "as long as the monks hold on to these seven things and are seen to do so, they may be expected to prosper and not decline." At the time when this sermon was fresh, the monks who heard it would have been well aware of the fate of the Vaijjians, which would been quite an encouragement for them to keep to the rules as laid out by their founder. More than 2,500 years later, communities of Buddhist monks and nuns still follow these seven basic laws, making them perhaps the oldest continuously existing social organizations in today's world.

The *Digha Nikaya* collection of scriptures also has some very interesting things to say about civil government as opposed to monastic. The twenty-seventh book, the Sermon on the Knowledge of Beginnings (*Agganna Sutta*), is something like a Buddhist Genesis. It is not really a creation story, because Buddhists explicitly reject the idea of a creator on both logical and moral grounds. Rather they see the world as one great system with no known beginning, which is constantly evolving and dissolving according to the law of interdependence or coconditioned causality. The story in the sutra gives a more or less naturalistic account of how civilization and the four Hindu classes evolved. Originally the beings of the world were ethereal and pure, but through selfish cravings gradually became more and more corporeal, greedy, lustful, and violent.

After aeons of moral decline, laziness and greed led to the institution of private property and theft, lying, and corporal punishment quickly followed. The people met together and lamented how they had fallen so low and decided that they had to act, saying:

> Suppose we were to appoint a certain being who would show anger where anger was due, censure those who deserved it, and banish those who deserved banishment! And, in return, we would grant him a share of the rice.[3]

They approached the most handsome, capable, and pleasant among them and offered him the job as king, which he accepted. This is the origin of the state, of kingship, and of taxes—all brought about by the selfish cravings of the beings of the world.

Note that the class of rulers came first, contrary to the Hindu insistence that the priests have primacy. Note also that there is no divine sanction or mythical cachet given to the social order; it arose naturally, so to speak, as a free human choice to solve the problems caused by earlier, poor moral decisions made by the beings of the world. The foundation of the state seems to be purely pragmatic, with no notion of intrinsic human rights to be protected. While this story justifies the Buddhist practice of admitting people from all castes into the order as equals, there is no attempt to change the social structure of the world outside the sangha.

This has been the major pattern throughout the history of Buddhism. Inside the order of world-renouncers, everyone in terms of spiritual potential is equal, and the distinctions that applied in the secular world no longer matter. However, the sangha is also hierarchical, with senior monks and nuns having precedence over juniors, and with those who are spiritually and morally adept accruing more honour than those of lesser attainment. Another part of the pattern is that there is no attempt to impose the standards of the sangha on society as a whole. In India, Buddha did not try to eliminate the caste system; in China Buddhist missionaries did not attempt to replace the Confucian system of government; in Canada, Buddhists do not denounce the parliamentary system. What they do is withdraw partially from society to set up their own parallel system and hope that the state allows them to run their own religious communities.

Just as individuals had unequal but reciprocal duties toward each other, so too the community of monastics and the secular world had different roles to play and different rules to follow. Civil society was to be ruled by a monarch who should try to live up to the standards of a wheel-turning king. Such a king, by moral example, will create a prosperous and harmonious society, one that will generously support monastic communities. Monks and nuns shall gain respect and support by living as exemplars of the dharma, and will repay their lay benefactors by keeping the traditions pure and strong and by teaching and demonstrating dharma to all, especially to the king. While the world-renouncers governed themselves by frequent consensual assemblies, ordinary people were subject to royal masters. What bound all estates together was adherence to the

basic precepts (not to kill, etc.), dedication to the elimination of the unwholesome impulses of greed, hatred, and ignorance, and ultimately the
common goal of religious enlightenment following the example of the
Buddha.

Details about the wheel-turning king are found in the twenty-sixth
book of the *Digha Nikaya*, the *Cakkavatti-Sihanada Sutta*, or the "Lion's
Roar on the Turning of the Wheel." Again the context is a cosmic one:
Wheel-turning kings like Buddhas occur at certain times during the great
cycles of evolution and decay. Just as worlds and the cosmos as a whole are
subject to the process of evolution and dissolution, so too individual sentient beings are caught up in the wheel of birth, death, and rebirth.
Wheel-turning kings and Buddhas are very similar in that they both are
products of countless lives of virtue, culminating in very auspicious identical rebirths. Each time such a boy appears he will become either a Buddha, if he opts to renounce the world, or a wheel-turning king, if he stays
in. He is called the wheel-turning king because one of his seven sacred
treasures is an actual wheel. Wherever he rolls this wheel, the people are
conquered by righteousness alone and happily join the empire of the
dharma king. Buddhas also are said to set the wheel of righteousness in
motion when they preach the truth that they have uncovered.

In the words of the Turning of the Wheel chapter, the duties of such a
king are suffused with dharma. He is enjoined as follows:

> Yourself depending on the Dhamma, honouring it, revering it, cherishing
> it, doing homage to it and venerating it, having the Dhamma as your
> badge and banner, acknowledging the Dhamma as your master, you should
> establish guard, ward and protection according to Dhamma for your own
> household, your troops, your nobles, and vassals, for Brahmins and house-
> holders, town and country folk, ascetics and Brahmins, for beasts and
> birds. Let no crime prevail in your kingdom, and to those who are in need,
> give property.[4]

Several sociological observations can be made from this passage. Dharma,
or Buddhist law, includes animals as well as humans within its ambit. The
king has a duty to protect all of his human subjects, regardless of social
class or religious affiliation—ascetics, whether Buddhist or otherwise, and
Hindu priests are singled out for concern. On the other hand, there is no
attempt to eliminate social distinctions: The king is greater than his nobles, who are greater than the vassals. The king rules absolutely, and there

is no hint of democratic procedures or egalitarianism. Activities counter to dharma, crime for example, cannot be tolerated, and the king has a responsibility to take care of those who are in need.

"Lion's Roar on the Turning of the Wheel" has a story which emphasizes the duty of the ruler to govern well and to punish those who go against the precepts. The king's first error was to neglect his duty to see that all of the people were provided with adequate livelihoods. He then neglected his duty to maintain order when he failed to punish the first thieves. It is interesting that while his eventual decision to execute those who stole led to general disorder, capital punishment was not condemned. In fact, Buddhist polities have nearly always maintained capital punishment. In this passage, wrongful acts like stealing and killing are not wrong because they involve violations of rights to others' life or property. Rather they are wrong because they represent failures to behave properly according to dharma.

The duties of a king were standardized in a list of ten items, which appears often in the Jataka tales, often mentioned only as the ten royal virtues. In the Jataka (Book 5, story 378), the ideal king described his righteous reign and named the ten virtues:

> My kingdom is in happy case, from all oppression free,
> Held by no arbitrary sway, but ruled with equity. . . .
> And, standing fast in virtues ten, the next world never dread.
> Almsgiving, justice, penitence, meek spirit, temper mild,
> Peace, mercy, patience, charity, with morals undefiled—
> These graces firmly planted in my soul are clear to see,
> When springs rich harvest of great joy and happiness for me.[5]

These ten virtues continue to be republished today in South and Southeast Asia in Buddhist treatises on social ethics. The Venerable P. A. Payutto, Thailand's most authoritative Buddhist thinker today, called them the "ten regal qualities" in his recent book, A Constitution for Living: Buddhist Principles for a Fruitful and Harmonious Life, saying, "The highest person in the land, whether he be an emperor, a king, or a head of state, should possess [these ten] qualities."

In Phra Payutto's translation of the ten royal virtues "sharing with the populace," a bodhisattva perfection, is the first virtue and means that the ruler should serve the needs of the people rather than his own. Next is "maintaining good conduct," also one of the bodhisattva virtues, which entails the king impeccably following the Buddhist code of morals to set the standard for his people. "Self-sacrifice," even of life itself for the sake of the people or the country, is next. "Integrity," "gentleness," "self-control," and "non-anger," are the next three. All of them are explained as mental qualities, and are typically cultivated by Buddhists through meditation practice. "Non-violence" or kindness is the eighth virtue, and "patient endurance," which is also of the qualities of a bodhisattva, is the ninth. Finally "non-deviation from righteousness" involves the king adhering to dharma and promoting it in all his acts. Phra Payutto, in the same section recommends the five duties of a wheel-turning king as found in the "Lion's Roar on the Turning of the Wheel," a sutra discussed above. The five are adherence to the dharma, protection of all the righteous inhabitants of his territories including beasts and birds, opposing and punishing unskillful acts while encouraging and rewarding skillful ones, assuring right livelihood for all and taking care of the poor, and finally seeking out and taking advice from wise and righteous advisors.[6] Both of these classical formulations, in Phra Payutto's rendition, present the duties of the king solely as virtues that he should cultivate, not as obligations that flow from rights of his subjects.

In Asvaghosa's life of the Buddha, written around the turn of the Common Era, there is a series of verses that describe how Gautama's father was an ideal king, who first mastered his own passions, then "conquered his kinsmen and subjects by his virtues."[7] It was said that he was impartial when making decisions in law and that he conquered his opponents by dharma rather than arms. Rather than executing the guilty, toward whom he felt no anger, "he inflicted mild punishments on them, since their release too was looked on as bad policy." His taxation was fair, and he did not covet the goods of others. His tranquil decent mind and actions influenced all his subjects to be the same. Practicing all the virtues and honouring the ceremonies of his Hindu faith, he lived by dharma, and his kingdom followed suit. In short, he ruled in the fashion of a wheel-turning king.

Another text from the Pali sutras that is often used in discussions of social ethics and human rights is *Anguttara Nikaya* (Book V, sutra 177). It concerns the question of what sorts of livelihoods are inappropriate for Buddhist laity, an important issue "right livelihood" is one link of the eight-fold path, the way to salvation that Lord Buddha laid down in his first sermon. The five trades that Buddha recommended not to engage in were: "Business in weapons, business in living beings, business in meat, business in intoxicants, and business in poison."[8] The first precept, which involves abstaining from the killing of any living being, obviously was the reason to avoid dealing in weapons, living beings (to be slaughtered for food), meat, and poisons. The moral precept against taking mind-dulling substances was why the Buddhist layman should not sell intoxicants. Later in this study the applicability of this scriptural passage to specific human rights will be discussed.

BUDDHA AND THE MILITARY

ANOTHER MAJOR ISSUE concerning the relationship of their faith and the state that the early Buddhists had to face was the question of war and the trades of war. The boy named Gautama, who was to become the Buddha, was born into the ruling family of his small state, and therefore gained some personal experience with military matters. In school he excelled in statecraft, archery, horsemanship, and all the other military skills necessary for a king in ancient India. However, as is so well known, he turned away from the throne to found a religion that renounced ill will and violence. Buddhists are recognized amongst the primary architects of the great Indian religious principle of *ahimsa*, or nonharm. In picturing exemplars of the faith today, one thinks of a Theravada monk in his flowing saffron robes, walking calmly and carefully with downcast eyes, so dedicated to the welfare of all beings that he takes care in order not to harm crawling insects. However, in actuality, this image, while true enough for individual monks, does not reflect the complete picture, which is complicated and not nearly so pure as one might expect.

While Buddha called on monks and nuns to follow his personal example and separate from the secular world, renouncing all violence, he never denied that it was legitimate for the ruler to use force both internally and externally, and did not call for radical reforms of the structures and institutions of the world. Accordingly it is not surprising that Theravada scriptures record only a very few incidents where Buddha dealt directly with soldiering and warfare. The *Vinaya* has two accounts of soldiers converting to Buddhism. In the case of the General Siha,[9] who became a lay disciple, Lord Buddha enjoined him to follow Buddhist moral precepts, to purify himself from all evil inclinations of the heart, and to be generous in almsgiving. Although the first precept is to take no life (especially human life), the question of General Siha's line of work was never raised, either by him or by his teacher. For Buddhist laymen it is not necessary to give up being a soldier. In fact, Lord Buddha recommended a military career as a good way to amass wealth,[10] and wealth itself is good for lay Buddhists. Soldiering does not appear as one of the five forbidden forms of commerce, but trading in weapons does.[11] It seems somewhat strange that selling weapons is condemned while using them is not.

However, there is evidence from the earliest times that some Buddhist soldiers found the conflict between the teachings against violence and the nature of their job to be hard to bear. The second *Vinaya* story about soldiers converting was set in the context of a border conflict in the powerful Magadha nation ruled by King Bimbisara, who was one of Lord Buddha's most powerful patrons. At that time, some of the finest soldiers thought: "We, who go (to war) and find our delight in fighting, do evil and produce great demerit. Now what shall we do that we may desist from evil doing and may do good?"[12] They resolved to become ordained as Buddhist monks, whose strict vows of nonharm were respected and protected by the king, thus they would be freed from their soldierly duties to fight and kill. When the officers found that a number of their crack troops had defected to the Buddhist monastic life, they complained to the king, who asked his judicial officers what should be done. Their answer was that the monk who led the ordination service deserved to be beheaded, the monk who recited the verses should have his tongue torn out, and all the others present should have half their ribs broken.

The king quickly had a word with Lord Buddha, reminding him that his order was under royal protection and that an unfriendly king could make life very unpleasant for the monks. He concluded with the request that no more persons in royal service be ordained, and so the Buddha introduced such a rule, which continues to the present time. This story shows a certain moral queasiness in Buddhism about the legitimacy of war, but also that a mutual relationship between the secular powers and the order of monks had to be maintained. A clear indication that early Buddhists wanted monastics to keep a very healthy distance from the military is a series of three minor offenses detailed in the section of the *vinaya*, which monks and nuns recited twice monthly to test their adherence to the discipline. It was an improper for a world-renouncer to go to see an army fight. If a monk had essential business that took him to visit an encampment, he was to limit his stay to no more than two or three nights, and it was an offense to seek out military displays or fighting during such a reluctant military stay.[13]

Along the same lines, Buddha warned that holy men and world-renouncers should avoid all talk about unedifying topics, which included "kings, robbers, ministers, armies, dangers and wars" at the top of the list.[14] He also warned laymen against a standard list of disasters that included kings and thieves, which could be warded off with the proper use of honestly earned wealth.[15] Clearly, while Buddha did not call for a religiously inspired transformation of the state, he was very suspicious of its powers to corrupt those persons engaged in the religious life. The state was a necessary evil, or more accurately, a lesser good, which had to be accommodated to sustain the orders of Buddhist mendicants. Without the power of the state, which in the Indian traditional view necessarily involves the use of force, the material conditions necessary for the existence of the religious life cannot exist. Therefore, certain rules to exclude soldiers, thieves, slaves, debtors, and others from ordination were enacted in order to maintain the existing social order. Those soldiers wanting ordination in order to practice the principle of nonharm and to improve their karma would first have to get a discharge from the military.

One of the fundamental notions in Buddhism is compassion, the deep intuitive reaction to the suffering of one's fellow human beings, and indeed of all sentient beings. This is both one of the fruits of attaining great insight through meditation practices and a quality to be cultivated by all persons who are on the path of enlightenment. In the biographical accounts of Lord Buddha, and of other Buddhist saints and sinners, incidents motivated by compassion play a major role. There is one scriptural example where Lord Buddha himself intervened for compassionate reasons to prevent a war.

It involved a quarrel between his countrymen, the Sakhyas, and their neighbors, the Koliyas, over water rights in a time of drought.[16] The situation quickly escalated to blows and serious name-calling among the laborers, and when the kings heard of what had been said, they called out their armies and prepared to fight. Using his supernormal powers, Lord Buddha saw what was happening and said, "If I refrain from going to them, these men will destroy each other. It is clearly my duty to go to them." He flew through the air and floated midway between the two armies. On questioning, the king of Sakhya had to admit that he did not know what they were fighting about, so Buddha asked the commander in chief, who also did not know. He went down the chain of command until the slave-laborers told him, "The quarrel is about water, Reverend Sir." Lord Buddha then asked the king, "How much is water worth . . . ?" "Very little, Reverend Sir." "How much are [warriors] worth, great king?" "[They] are beyond price, Reverend Sir." Lord Buddha ended the conflict with these words: "It is not fitting that because of a little water you should destroy [warriors] who are beyond price . . . Great Kings, why do you act in this manner? Were I not present today, you would set flowing a river of blood. You have acted in a most unbecoming manner." The story ends with three verses from the *Dhammapada*, which extol living in freedom from hatred, sickness, and desires even in a world that is afire with all three. In this case, all three of the fundamental poisons were the driving forces of war. The first problem was a selfish refusal to share a scarce resource. This rapidly led to hatred and escalating violence, and it was all steeped in delusion—none of the officers had the slightest idea what had started the war. When Lord Buddha, acting from wisdom and compassion, made all this clear to the combatants, the quarrel naturally evaporated.

The passages discussed above present a Theravada scriptural approach to war and the military. First, the orders of monks and nuns, who are set apart from the world to perfect themselves, are to have nothing to do with the business of shedding blood. War intrinsically leads to breaking the precept against killing, and war feeds on the three fundamental moral poisons of hatred, selfish grasping, and delusion. However, because the ordinary world is such as it is, a strong state and an even an army are necessary evils; therefore, it is permissible for a lay Buddhist to serve as a ruler or a soldier. In order not to disrupt the political order and in return for legal recognition of their vows, monastics undertake not to ordain soldiers.

Buddhist kings in Theravada countries were nevertheless generally very warlike, and Buddhist symbols were important in their military activities. For example, the "Emerald Buddha," which sits in the Royal Chapel in Bangkok serves as the protective talisman for the entire Thai nation. It was the property of several royal families of neighbouring kingdoms until it was taken as war booty by King Rama I,* the first monarch of the current Thai dynasty, and brought home to the new capital around 1800. Following the custom of Buddhist kings from the past, each Thai king, except for Rama VIII* who died before his enthronement, set up a Buddha image called the "Lord of Victory." These images are carried with the king on his military campaigns and are meant to ensure his victory and the safety of the nation.[17]

THE WHEEL-TURNING KING AND EMPEROR ASOKA

THE KING WHO is remembered by Theravada Buddhists as coming the closest to being a wheel-turning king, the ideal Buddhist monarch as described earlier in this chapter, was the Emperor Asoka. He ruled the Mauryan Empire in India some two hundred years after the time that Buddha taught. In fact, as Gombrich noted, Asoka's career was so like that of the ideal kings described in the texts discussed above that some scholars have argued that the scriptural stories are late and based on the historical Asoka. Gombrich, for good textual and historical reasons, thought that the influence was the other way around—that is, Asoka modelled himself on the Buddhist descriptions of ideal king.[18] In any case, he ruled from around 269 to 232 B.C.E., with the precise dates (as always in ancient India) subject to debate. He expanded the boundaries of the nation founded by his grandfather and expanded by his father to include the entire subcontinent, save the southernmost tip, which made the Mauryan Empire the first really large political entity in India. It was one of the most successful states ever in India. Unfortunately, the Mauryan experiment did not last long after Asoka's death with the empire breaking up into a number of warring states, the most usual pattern in Indian history.

Asoka had a number of inscriptions engraved on pillars and natural stone faces in various strategic places, leaving the most detailed historical record of any ancient Indian monarch. These inscriptions, some forty-five pages long in translation, laid out his general political principles, proclaimed some of his legislation, detailed some historical details of his reign, and put all of this in the context of his understanding of the Buddhist dharma. They were intended to educate the Mauryan subjects to follow the vision of their king. The inscriptions themselves were relatively soon lost and forgotten, to be recovered only in the nineteenth century. However, Buddhists in the Theravada tradition kept the stories of Asoka in amplified and somewhat legendary forms in noncanonical, but very influential chronicles. They remembered and revered Asoka as an ideal monarch, one who approached the status of a wheel-turning king, and he was a model for many later monarchs.[19] In the present study, the primary sources for Asoka are the Edicts.

At first Asoka continued the bellicose project of his ancestors to extend the boundaries of the nation through conquest. His last great campaign was against the Kalinga nation, and the inscription that recorded that war described the destruction of the Kalinga army is included in chapter 13. Shortly after this victory, Asoka became "intensely devoted to Dharma" and thereafter resolved to war no more. While he expresses remorse for those he killed in battle and promises clemency to practically all, he reminded the recalcitrant hill tribes in his territories that he continued to exercise "the power to punish, despite his repentance, in order to induce them to desist from their crimes and escape execution."

After the Kalinga campaign, having given up conventional warfare, except in self-defense, he established the policy of "conquest through righteousness" (dharma), sending missionaries to his neighbours and as far away as Europe. Although the record is not altogether clear, he claimed that many kingdoms joined the empire because they saw the advantage of living under the rule of dharma. His words on conquest through dharma, as found in the inscription that regretted the harm done the Kalingans, were the words of a wheel-turning king: "King Priyadarsi considers moral conquest [that is, conquest by Dharma . . .] the most important conquest. . . . Wherever conquest is achieved by Dharma, it produces satisfaction." Although conquest through dharma was the ideal and the most efficacious way to expand sovereignty, his chilling warning to the hill tribes quoted above showed that he did not renounce violence altogether and that he was willing to use the standing army he maintained.

Asoka's practical focus was on human relationships, the distribution of wealth, and kinship. Two inscriptions said that dharma consisted of the proper treatment of slaves and servants, obedience to mother and father, reverence to teachers, liberality to friends, acquaintances, relatives, priests, and ascetics, and limiting violence to all living creatures.[20] With the addition of the nonkilling of animals, these Edicts had precisely the same message as the *Sigalaka Sutta* (chapter 13, document 7), including admonitions against "meaningless" ceremonies. Gombrich noted that the Buddha portrayed the ideal king as the ideal Buddhist layman "writ large," which in turn applied perfectly to Asoka.[21]

Although Asoka probably did not abandon the death penalty, he did very much temper the violence of traditional rule and tried to set higher standards for the administration of justice. "This edict has been inscribed here to remind the judicial officers in this city to try at all times to avoid unjust imprisonment or unjust torture."[22] He initiated public health projects for human beings and for animals, built public works,[23] and generally looked after his subjects as though they were his own children.[24] For example, his dharma officers had the practical duties of looking after the all the people of the realm, with particular help to be given to the poor, the elderly, and the children of prisoners. He also commissioned his officers to pardon those prisoners who had reformed, who were led into crime by others, and those who were very old.[25]

He was a patron of Buddhist and other religious sects and undertook to regulate the activities of all the religious orders in the empire.[26] The idea of separation of organized religion and state did not fit in at all with the way of politics in ancient India. Asoka established a class of government officials to make sure that dharma was implemented throughout the land and to administer the charitable gifts of the royal retinue. While they were all supposed to concern themselves with the general principles of dharma, some were assigned to oversee various specific ascetic orders. He mentioned major sects—the Buddhists, the Jains, the Brahmins (Hindus), and Ajivakas—by name, and said that other unnamed sects were also under the control of the dharma officers. But the good king did not leave all of this important job to his officials, he transformed the pleasure tours and the hunting trips that Indian kings loved to take into dharma-tours, where, "He visits priests and ascetics and makes gifts to them; he visits the aged and gives them money; he visits the people of rural areas, instructing them in Dharma and discussing it with them."[27]

Again, Asoka's actions in supporting religious leaders and organizations of various sorts were consistent with the duties laid down in the Theravada canon for righteous monarchs. Dharma was not understood in a narrow sectarian way, but was taken in its broadest sense of universal law or proper order of the world, the common meaning in all the sects of India, not only in Buddhism. Accordingly, he encouraged "members of all faiths to live everywhere in his kingdom,"[28] honoured "men of all faiths, members of religious orders and laymen alike, with gifts and various marks of esteem," and strongly encouraged mutual respect amongst the various faiths.[29] One wonders that laywomen and female world-renouncers were not mentioned in the passage quoted immediately above, as they were very active in the Buddhist and Jain traditions at the time of Asoka. This probably was merely a matter of grammar, where the male gender was used to stand for both men and women, since other inscriptions do recognize Buddhist nuns and laywomen.[30]

While Asoka was generous with his purse and his praise for all religious orders, he had a special, personal attachment to the three jewels of Buddhism, and took an active interest in the affairs of the monastic orders. He went so far as to recommend a list of texts to be studied and meditated upon by monks and nuns, laymen and laywomen alike.

You know, Reverend Sirs, the extent of my reverence for and faith in the Buddha, The Dharma, and Samgha. Whatever the Lord Buddha has said, Reverend Sirs, is of course well said. But it is proper for me to enumerate the texts which express true Dharma and which may make it everlasting.[31]

Two other edicts recorded an especially important feature of Asoka's patronage of the Buddhist orders.[32] He undertook to enforce the rulings of the democratic assemblies of monks and nuns, and ruled that those individuals who disrupted the unity of the orders must disrobe and leave. Without the power of the state to enforce their decisions, the orders were more or less helpless to maintain the standards of behavior called for in the *Vinaya* and the purity of the teachings passed down from Lord Buddha. Later Theravada chronicles reinforced this point with accounts of the great Council (the third) of Buddhist clerics, which met only after Asoka intervened to evict false monks and which established the Theravada canon.[33] Although the Third Council was not mentioned in the inscribed Edicts, the Edicts do show that the emperor was concerned both unity and the textual purity in the Buddhist orders.

This relationship between Asoka and the Buddhist orders became the norm for Buddhist countries. The monks and nuns proved their worthiness by the purity of their lives and the careful preservation of the dharma. They exemplified dharma by example and provided teaching and advice to the monarch. In return, the monarch protected and provided for the monastics, taking on the responsibility to see to it that the texts were preserved and passed on properly and to cleanse the monks and nuns of unworthy members. In fact, this system never managed to maintain absolute unity in the Buddhist world or in any Buddhist country. But the principle that the state, generally in the person of the monarch, had a duty to intervene to purify the order and to settle disputes and the corollary principle that the Buddhist order had a responsibility to support the worldly order were well established.

Robert Thurman has some very interesting insights on Asoka and his style of rule and how it has worked in Buddhist Asia. Asoka's autocratic form of "monarchical socialism," Thurman claims, is very hard for Westerners steeped in their traditions of democracy and individual freedom to understand.

However, it is clear that in the Indian case, as often in the Chinese, it was the emperor who was the guarantor of the rights of the individual, forcing the pace of social change and protecting the individual from the oppressions of various intermediate elites.[34]

While describing how the king modelled on the Buddhist wheel-turning ideal worked for the benefit of his subjects in both secular and religious spheres in terms of "rights" is somewhat misleading, Thurman's description of the benefits that the Asokan monarch could bring to his people is accurate. Unfortunately, he is also right in pointing out that the Buddhist pattern of kingship in Asia, which involved the acceptance of a "righteous king as the chief layperson, supporter of the order, and defender of the faith," more often than not resulted in "a pattern of despotic behavior vis-à-vis lay subjects, coupled with generosity and tolerance vis-à-vis the monastic order."[35] The following chapters will offer examples of both righteous Buddhist monarchs and dharma-rajas gone awry.

5

Buddhism and Human Rights in Thailand

Thailand: Modern Monks and Politics, Background

THAILAND, WHERE MORE THAN 90 percent of the people are Theravada Buddhists, is where the traditional pattern of Buddhist rule is most intact today even though the revolution of 1932 ended absolute royal powers. All of the other Theravada states that used to follow the ancient model like Laos, Cambodia, Burma, and Sri Lanka have been changed fundamentally by years of western colonial rule, and in the case of Laos and Cambodia, by communist regimes as well. Somboon Suksamran, a leading Thai political scientist at Chulalongkorn University in Bangkok, summed up the way that the vast majority of Thais understand their nation:

> In Thai thinking the foundation of Thai society is based on three related pillars. They are the nation . . ., religion . . ., and the monarchy. . . . The religion—Buddhism—serves as the moral tone and social force of the society, while the monarchy is the morale and bond of unity of the Thai nation. It is further held that these three entities form a threefold moral bond and cohesion; that they are the pillars of freedom; and that Buddhism is the most important symbol of, and primary base for, a feeling of national and cultural identification. Thus, the prosperity of the nation is thought to be related to the prosperity of Buddhism and vice versa; and that the stability of the nation and religion cannot be separated.[1]

This three-pillar ideology was formulated by the last successful absolute monarch of Thailand, King Vajiravudh, or Rama VI* (r. 1910–1925).

In traditional Siam the monks most often minded their religious business and stayed out of direct involvement with politics. Subsequent to the 1932 democracy revolution in Thailand, from the 1940s up until the early 1990s, Thailand was under direct rule by the army or by their right wing civilian surrogates with a few relatively short intervals of more democratic regimes.[2] Rightist regimes relied heavily on the people, religion, and monarchy ideology for legitimacy. Their particular slant identified the army as representing the people and pictured the military as the protectors of the king and of the religion. Religion, that is Thai Buddhism, was understood primarily as the order of monks and the clerical hierarchy. When there were democratically elected more liberal regimes, the same three-fold ideology was used, but it was argued that the message of the Buddha implied social justice, democratic values, and human rights. After 1932, with no ruling monarch at the center, there was always a rather severe dislocation in the system. The kings had very limited powers, from 1934 to 1946 they languished in exile in Europe except for very brief visits, and were generally neglected until the regime of General Sarit in 1958.[3] Neither the military leaders nor the democratic politicians were very convincing pretenders to the role of wheel-turning monarch.

In 1950, a rightist government became worried that some monks seemed susceptible to communist subversion and enlisted the religious establishment in a propaganda campaign against the red danger. They issued posters which represented communism in the form of a demon shown razing temples and torturing monks with the slogan, "If communism comes, Buddhism, [temple], and monks will be destroyed."[4] Such posters were widely used for the next two or three decades. Thai anticommunist activities from this time on were encouraged, funded, and assisted by American government.[5] Sarit Thanarat came to power in a two-stage military coup in 1957–1958, his council justifying their usurpation of power with the following reasons. First: "The growing menace of communism was undermining the basic foundations of the state by attempting to uproot the monarchy, destroy Buddhism, and overthrow institutions of all types which the Thai nation cherished."[6] Second, they argued that democracy had been perverted selfishly with the results that economic development had been retarded and that the nation had been divided into opposing camps. The third major reason offered was that Thailand needed strong leadership to counter the threat from communist advances in Indochina.

Sarit and his successors held power from 1957 to 1968 and 1971 to 1973 and had a particularly bad record of disregarding human rights. Trade unions were banned, newspapers censored and shut down, political opponents punished by courts martial, others killed extrajudicially, and mob violence encouraged against dissenters. On the more positive side, there were great efforts to make use of the national symbols of the monarchy and religion to help out with the government's programs of national integration and development. The Thai Buddhist hierarchy, which Sarit made sure was led by monks sympathetic to his aims, helped by providing moral support for the monarchy and army and by supplying monks to work in missions to the non-Buddhist, non-Thai hill tribes and in development work with the peasants as part of government plans to integrate and strengthen the nation. Poor peasants and hill people were the most fertile recruiting fields for the communists and other leftists, which partly explains the government's interest in helping at this particular time.

Using monks in such work was a rather radical departure from the traditional role of the monk in Thailand, who had been expected to serve the faith through fastidious observance of the monastic rules of morality and deportment, by providing religious services and sermons, and by meditation and scholarship in the scriptures and doctrines. Except for teaching basic literacy and dharma, monks were not traditionally expected to take an active role in the affairs of the world—on the contrary, in fact. The sangha leadership justified their new directions in a series of linked arguments, which can be summarized in three major points.[7] First, monks are dependent on the laypeople, government, and king for their livelihood and thus owe a debt of gratitude, which needs to be repaid by taking practical steps to help the nation and monarchy proper. Second, Thai Buddhism and the Thai way of life are endangered from the pressures of communist ideology and from the erosion of traditions under the onslaught of modernization. Since these external and internal forces will not disappear on their own, the sangha must take positive steps to counteract them, to develop the country in ways that are in concord with the values of Buddhism and inspired by the monarchy. Finally, acts that help others develop and prosper are in accord with the teachings of dharma, particularly the virtue of generous giving, and are thus consistent with the time-honored practices of making religious merit.

Somboon concluded that the first years of these government-sangha cooperative ventures, from the 1960s through the early 1970s, were not terribly effective in achieving their specific local objectives to enhance community development and national integration.[8] A substantial number of monks in the field saw the new demands as being contradictory to the spirit of the *vinaya* and resented being steered by the government in a way they felt led away from the dharma. Many laypeople also disliked the new direction because they had always respected those monks who kept themselves pure and separate from worldly concerns. Workers and peasants did not trust any initiatives coming from a government hostile to their concerns.

Still, since the government controlled the finances and promotions system of organised Buddhism, and since many of the leadership and ordinary monks were convinced that participation was consistent with Buddhist values, a considerable number of monks volunteered to work in community development, education, and national unity programs. Such monks, who work with local parishioners on practical improvements, are known as development monks as distinguished from political monks, who get involved in attempts to effect changes in government policies or even in direct political action. Development monks, on the whole, have gained the respect of the Thai people, while political monks remain very controversial.

Somboon's later assessment was that, on balance, development monks have been a success and represent a positive force for the continuing strength of Thai Buddhism. He noted several good effects of monks' involvement in development work.[9] In the first case, these efforts, which are built entirely on voluntary participation by the villagers, build individual and community self-confidence with growth in community spirit, cooperation, and political know how. The goals of these programs are down-to-earth and practical and constitute a middle ground between the unbridled acquisitiveness of raw Western capitalism and traditional Thai values, which are stressed at all times by the monk practitioners. By showing concern for the suffering and poverty of their parishioners, and by helping provide practical remedies, the prestige of monks and the sangha itself grows in the eyes of the affected laymen. Buddhism is seen to be useful in the day-to-day economic and other practical concerns of the people as well as providing religious training and solace.

It must be remembered that much of the motivation official sponsorship of the participation of monks in development came from the fear of communism that pervaded governments and the religious establishment from the 1950s onward. The fear was grounded in reality, as communist regimes in China and North Vietnam were not at all friendly toward Buddhist believers and institutions. By enlisting the sangha to work for national unity and prosperity, the establishment was able to draw on the most respected and potent symbols and organizations in the country. Nonetheless, some men and women in Thailand, inspired by communist insurgents' successes in China, Indochina, and Malaya and deeply disturbed by the actions of Thai dictators, took to the hills and jungles in the South and North in a guerrilla action that lasted from the late 1950s into the 1980s. An additional very important factor was the involvement of Thailand in the Vietnamese War in the 1960s and 1970s. American troops were stationed in Thailand, and the Thai military establishment and their governments generally supported American aims, allowing the United States Air Force to operate from Thai bases and participating in some joint combat operations. Left-wing Thais and some traditionalists were not pleased with the effects of cooperation with the Americans.

In 1973 students and workers spearheaded a popular movement against the military government with huge demonstrations in Bangkok in which a few young, radical monks participated. After a bloody response by the military and the intervention of the king, the military regime fell in October 1973, ushering in a three-year period of relative political freedom and openness, although behind the surface conservative military and bureaucratic forces kept most of their real power. It was in these complicated and difficult circumstances in the years immediately after 1973 that political monks, that is, monks who took an active and organized role in political events, came in force onto the Thai scene. The remainder of this chapter will focus on that three-year period, which ended with another military coup, because its events well illuminate human rights issues in contemporary Thai Buddhism.

THAILAND: POLITICAL MONKS ON THE LEFT (1973–1976)

MOST OF THE left in Thailand was quite moderate, consisting of those who wanted the basic freedoms and values found in Western democratic states to apply at home. They were loyal supporters of the institutions of the monarchy and Buddhism, but were looking for "freedom of the press, speech and assembly; . . . minimal equality before the law; sympathy with the oppressed and the exploited; opposition to imperialism and any kind of foreign domination." A smaller radical segment supported a rather Marxist analysis that understood the problem to be a struggle between the people and a class of "feudalist-capitalists, imperialist-backed militarists, and dictatorial rulers"[10] that held on to power for their own ends. On the far extreme were those very few communist insurgents and their supporters who were calling for the overthrow of the royal family and the privileged place of Buddhism in Thai culture, rarely going so far as to kill monks and to extort donations or protection money from temples as part of the armed struggle.[11]

Left-wing monks[12] obviously were located on the moderate end of the spectrum. They were concerned that the political and economic systems were unfair to the ordinary Thai people and resented the authoritarian nature of the sangha governance as well as the support that the sangha hierarchy gave to the military and to the economic elite. A few of them worked in elections for socialist candidates, but most restricted their efforts to reform within the order of monks. On the whole, left-wing political monks were neither numerous nor well organized. The most radical group, which supported a socialist overhaul of the entire structure of society, for example, barely had a score of members. Perhaps the most impressive action of the left-wing political monks took place in November of 1974 when a number of them marched in demonstrations in Bangkok, where some 40 to 60 thousand poor farmers supported by trade unionists, student, and other progressive citizens rallied for ten days to present their grievances to the government. The size and nature of the demonstration and the involvement of monks were unprecedented in Thai history. The crowds were well organized and took great pains to demonstrate their peaceful support for the monarchy and Buddhism.

Subsequent to the march, a success as the government went along with most of the farmers' demands, Jud Kongsook, the monk who led the monastic side of the protest, circulated a leaflet justifying why they had demonstrated. He wrote:

We take pity on the farmers who are the backbone of the country and who toil and shed their sweat to feed the world. They are poor and neglected by the privileged classes. But they are contributing to the prosperity of Buddhism no less than the rich. Now they are miserable and suffering social injustice. We (the monks) must help them because, firstly, they feed us and are our benefactors; helping them in time of difficulty is thus an expression of gratitude; secondly, monks and farmers are related as kin by religion and by social ties.[13]

Although the pamphlet denied that the monks' actions were in any way political or that they violated the *vinaya* and disgraced religion, high government figures and the sangha hierarchy were deeply shocked, some feeling that the very existence of Buddhism in Thailand was under attack.

According to contemporary accounts and informal surveys done by the press at the time, public opinion about the monks who demonstrated broke into three camps. First, many agreed with the cabinet, arguing that any overt political action on the part of an ordained man was against the precepts of the *vinaya* and thus brought shame on organized religion. Monks should restrict themselves to traditional rituals and practices. The second group agreed with the leftist monk Jud, thinking that the activists were following their duty under dharma by sacrificing their own interests to help an oppressed class of society. Although the data were not systematically gathered, Somboon thinks that most Thais fell into a third group of opinion, which lay between the extremes. They thought that monks could legitimately take an active role in trying to help solve social problems, but "that the action of the monks in the farmers' demonstration had gone too far, because it undermined the prestige of the Sangha."[14] Finally, many right-wing people feared that the farmers and their supporters were tools of communist agitation and believed that those monks who were actively involved posed a real danger to the faith.

On the day after they marched, Jud and three other monk leaders were expelled from their monasteries. His supporters organized rallies and produced pamphlets in his support, and armed rightists converged on the temple, while others organized counterdemonstrations and publications condemning those monks who had marched, arguing that they brought Buddhism into disgrace by their actions. Senior members of the governing council of the sangha, including the supreme patriarch, added their voices of condemnation to the left-wing political monks, asking the government to act and calling for the public not to support such monks.

In reply, the leftist Buddhists pointed out that monks of all ranks were constantly involved in political acts in support of right-wing and capitalist causes, such as performing blessings for armament factories and for the opening of massage parlors, nightclubs, breweries, and other dubious enterprises. High sangha officials also officiated at the founding of political parties and blessed government soldiers and mercenaries going to war against communists. Such observations were true enough and have often been repeated by reform-minded Thai Buddhists from the 1950s into the twenty-first century. The sangha hierarchy was quick to condemn political activity by the left-wing monks, but never seemed to mind when monks gave their public support to the institutions that represented the status quo. In any case, it should be noted that performing blessings and rituals for commercial, government, and military units fell squarely within the traditional role of monks and can be seen as evidence of just how thoroughly Buddhism permeates every aspect of Thai life.

As to the situation of the monk Jud, the secular authorities simply waited the situation out until the demonstrations withered away. Jud found a place as an unofficial guest with friends in another Bangkok monastery. Jud's supporters asked the highest sangha governing body to reinstate him to his home monastery, which led to a very clear ruling delivered on December 2, 1970: "It was not appropriate for monks to join in the demonstration by the peasants and that the abbots have the duty to determine punishment."[15] These reaffirmations of the traditional interpretation that monastic rules did not allow monks to participate in political demonstrations and of the disciplinary power of the abbot, were confirmed several times by the ecclesiastical council in that period. However, although the abbot was upheld, the offense was seen as rather minor, and Jud regained his place in due time.

THAILAND: POLITICAL MONKS ON THE RIGHT (1973–1976)

A VERY IMPORTANT ultraright nongovernmental organization dates to 1974. Founded by senior military men, high bureaucrats, and very wealthy businessmen, it was called NAWAPOL.[16] To join, the initiate took an oath before the triple gem of Buddhism and other symbols sacred to Thais, swearing to dedicate his or her life to the defense of nation, religion, and monarch on pain of unimaginable catastrophes should the oath be broken. While the ideology stressed the Buddhist ideal of a middle way and claimed to avoid such extremes as right and left, in fact, the organization worked tirelessly to oppose all leftist initiatives, tarring them with the brush of communist subversion and as their proponents as enemies of king and religion. One of the most effective tools they had was radio and television broadcasts as all stations were under military or government control. Songs branding student activists, organized workers and farmers, and writers who criticized the government as a "burden of the earth" and "scum of the earth" were played frequently; and, in 1975, the deputy prime minister broadcast with the slogan "Right Kill Left." Perhaps it is not surprising that in this period murders of farmer organizers, student activists, and socialist politicians increased rapidly. Such murders were never solved—there were never even any arrests.

Donations for NAWAPOL came from anticommunist businessmen, from members of the officer elite, from the Buddhist organizations of Bhikku Kitthiwuttho*,[17] and from membership fees. Without a doubt, the activities of Kitthiwuttho in this period made him into the most striking example of a right-wing political monk. Although lacking a formal Buddhist education, honors or position in the sangha hierarchy, Kitthiwuttho came into prominence by the force of his charismatic personality, dynamic preaching, and organizational skills, building one of Thailand's largest Buddhist educational foundations. In the 1960s the message of Bhikku Kitthiwuttho was not overtly political. For example, rather than supporting rightist or leftist causes, he stressed that all Thais had the duty of "gratitude, affection, and loyalty to the nation, religion, the king, and the government"[18] and that monks had a duty to help the people prosper through right livelihood: that is, making a living in accord with Buddhist ethical principles.

Kitthiwuttho was very upset with the results of the democratic revolution of October 1973, which he believed was a communist-inspired assault on the three pillars of Thai civilization. He was even more disturbed by how the Cambodian and Laotian communist regimes attacked Buddhism and abolished their monarchies. By 1975 Kitthiwuttho was actively supporting NAWAPOL by speaking on their behalf in public meetings and on the state-controlled electronic outlets. He let them use his institutional facilities, donated funds, and provided a considerable amount of intellectual support. In line with the NAWAPOL message, he identified student activists, labor organizers, the liberal press that criticized him, left-wing political monks, and democratic politicians all as enemies of the nation, monarch, and religion—all agents, witting or not, of a communist scheme to overthrow the traditional order, which had borne fruit in China and Indochina and was growing dangerously in the Thai communist insurgent movements.

In January 1976, working with NAWAPOL, he mobilized a large demonstration of village and regional headmen who marched on government offices in Bangkok. They demanded that the government step up efforts to wipe out the communists, called for parliament to expel some socialist and liberal members, and even suggested that the government resign in favor of a military-led "National Reform Council." Kitthiwuttho participated in these events and even took credit on national television for advising the headmen, although he denied leading the demonstration.

As Somboon noted, "Kitthiwuttho's participation in the demonstration appears to be in no way different from Jud's case two year's previously—it was undoubtedly political."[19] When exactly this point was made in the press, the supreme patriarch, who had been a patron of Kitthiwuttho for at least ten years, said that the appropriate judicial body of the sangha would look into this affair. In a newspaper interview, the supreme patriarch said it seemed to him that Kitthiwuttho had committed a minor offense, and if so found by the council, he ought to get off with a reprimand as it would be his first conviction. He also commented, "If the facts be that Kitthiwuttho acted to protect the country, that is a good purpose; but I do not see that what he did was of any utility and also as monks it is not necessary to act like this."[20] If the ecclesiastical council did in fact take up his involvement in the May 1975 agitations, nothing ever came of it, and Kitthiwuttho continued as before.

The most notorious event involving right-wing political monks began in June 1976 when an interview with Kitthiwuttho was published in a secular liberal magazine. After noting that more than ten thousand Thai soldiers had been killed fighting leftist guerrillas, Kitthiwuttho considered whether or not killing communists was a demeritorious act. This was a critical question for a Thai Buddhist, as the popular faith in large part was about the accumulation of merit, by doing those things in accord with the precepts, and the avoidance of demerit, by avoiding those actions contrary to Buddhist ethical teachings. Every Thai would know that abstaining from taking life, especially human life, was the first and one of the weightiest of the Buddhist precepts. Therefore, Kitthiwuttho's answer was a real blockbuster.

> I think we must do this [killing], even though we are Buddhists. But such killing is not the killing of persons. Because whoever destroys the nation, religion and the monarchy is not a complete person, but Mara [a being that leads people into evil]. Our intention must be not to kill people but to kill [Mara]. It is the duty of all Thai.[21]

He continued that the demerit of killing a subhuman being was much less than the merit accrued by defending king, country, and Buddhism. "It is just like when we kill a fish to make a stew to place in the alms bowl for a monk."[22] The demerit of killing a fish is far outweighed by the merit of the giving to the sangha.

There was widespread public opposition throughout the country to what he said, with progressive scholars and journalists denouncing his ideas as a dangerous misinterpretation of the dharma, and with some public demonstrations against him.[23] Sulak Sivaraksa's NGO, the Coordination Group for Religion and Society, was particularly active and outspoken in this crisis, and Sulak had to accept exile for his own safety.[24] Not only was Kitthiwuttho's message in opposed to Buddhist teachings, it was also highly inflammatory in such a time of conflict. Just a few months before in March 1976, the supreme patriarch had condemned the growing tide of political murders, particularly of left-wing politicians. In an address to the nation on his birthday, he had said:

> Murders and killings should never take place in Thailand because the majority of the people are Buddhists. Lord Buddha's teachings specifically state that killing is forbidden. It is therefore tantamount to a sinful, shameful act for Buddhists especially in a Buddhist country like Thailand— we are behaving unreasonably, killing each other as if we are worse than animals.[25]

Kitthiwuttho seemed energized by the controversy and continued to spread the same violent message.

On the second of July 1976, he delivered "Killing Communists Is Not Demeritorious" to a gathering of some 3,200 monks who were attending a course at his Chittapawan College. This speech, which elaborated on the points made in the earlier interview, was published as a pamphlet and was widely circulated. Urged on by moderate and left-leaning Buddhists, the ecclesiastical authorities decided to investigate Kitthiwuttho on the charge that his behavior had been unsuitable for a monk. He continued to defend his position vigorously in speeches and newspaper interviews, and attacked anyone who supported the democratic revolution of 1973, especially the organized left-wing monks, as enemies of religion and the king, and amplified his line that violence against communists was not demeritorious. For example, on July 8, 1976, in a speech to army officers, he argued that killing some 5,000 enemies to save all 42 million citizens was a sacrifice toward the greater good, and that "whosoever thinks of doing this will not go to hell, but will acquire merit."[26] Not only do these teachings violate fundamental Buddhist principles of skillful action, they are in flat contradiction to the supreme patriarch's condemnation of political murders. In both Buddhist and in human rights terms, Kitthiwuttho was particularly dangerous as he stripped his opponents of their human status, explicitly stating they were not persons.

The highest ecclesiastical court made its ruling on August 11, 1976, and essentially dismissed the charges against Kitthiwuttho on technical grounds. They did not seem to consider the content of his "Killing Communists Is Not Demeritorious" speech and pamphlet, nor did they comment on his participation in the January 1975 demonstration where the marchers called for a military-dominated government. Especially when one compares this ruling with the condemnation of the left-wing monk Jud a few months earlier, it seems the sangha hierarchy willfully turned a blind eye to Kitthiwuttho's words and actions, which were certainly political, inflammatory, and contrary to fundamental Buddhist teachings as recently reaffirmed by the supreme patriarch and hierarchy. All the parties involved in these disputes framed their positions and arguments in traditional Thai Buddhist terms. They all saw themselves as having a duty to uphold the institutions and truth of Buddhism, as loyal defenders of the monarchy and faithful sons of the nation. The left-wing protagonists stressed their dedication to the Buddhist virtue of compassion and argued that their religious faith required them to take on the suffering of others. The right maintained that every Thai had a sacred duty to defend the nation, the king, and Buddhism from current and potential threats. Neither right nor left framed their positions in terms of rights.

THE END OF THE ERA OF POLITICAL MONKS IN THAILAND, OCTOBER 1976

KITTHIWUTTHO'S OPPONENTS WERE not satisfied with the results of the investigation into his behavior, but political events moved too fast for there to be any continuation of legal process. At the end of August, Thanom, one of the former military dictators who had been overthrown and exiled in 1973, was said to be intending to return to Thailand to become a monk, which he did in mid-September, receiving full ordination in one of Bangkok's most prestigious royal monasteries.[27] It could be argued that, by allowing this ordination, the sangha hierarchy had tacitly aligned itself with the right. There was immediate turmoil in the streets that culminated in large demonstrations in early October led by the students of Thammasat University in Bangkok, an eerie parallel with events of October 1973, that brought down a dictatorial regime. This time, police with the help of right-wing mobs attacked the demonstrators. "Hundreds of students were killed, lynched, or badly wounded and thousands were arrested."[28] On the sixth of October, the army overthrew the government and set up a National Reform Council, which "abrogated the constitution, abolished parliament, and brought to an end the three year experiment with democracy in Thailand."[29]

At first glance it seemed that the monk Kitthiwuttho's message had been listened to and implemented with a vengeance. Many of those labelled as communist enemies of the monarchy, nation and Buddhism were dutifully killed. The coup reversed the reforms of 1973, and the new authorities soon moved against all those segments of society that Kitthiwuttho had condemned. They closed down the very publications that had criticized Kitthiwuttho. Left-wing student and monk organizations were banned or rendered ineffective as were those labour and farming organizations that called for serious reforms. Many activists on the left, those who had been lucky enough to escape death or arrest, fled to join the communist fighters in the forests. The monk Jud, the most prominent left-wing leader, left the order and joined the communist rebels.

However, as Charles Keyes, professor of Anthropology at the University of Washington, pointed out in a prescient piece of analytical writing, Kitthiwuttho and NAWAPOL did not carry the day completely. Although his call to a "Buddhist holy war" was influential in energizing the forces that led to the coup, both the content of his message and the mere fact that a monk was delivering a political message were seen as going beyond what was proper according to the traditional role of the sangha: "Militant Buddhism as it has been formulated by [Kitthiwuttho] and institutionalized in the [NAWAPOL] movement, is markedly discordant with . . . the civic religion of Thailand, both traditional and modern."[30] Men associated closely with NAWAPOL were not appointed to the new government, which reflected the general distrust and unease Thais felt with the furor caused by political Buddhism from 1973 to 1976. Since then, members of the sangha have mostly kept away from overt political activity. Given the structural relationship of the sangha and its hierarchy to government, it is not surprising that the indirect political action of the Buddhist establish-ment has continued to support the status quo. Kitthiwuttho and his or-ganizations have continued to flourish and to be controversial, but have stepped back from direct political action.[31]

The violent events of October 1976 were very traumatizing in Thai-land, and still deeply affect those who were involved or who witnessed them. Nonetheless, since 1976, the political climate of Thailand has slowly moved more securely in the direction of democracy, with the com-munist insurgency finally ended after a slow and brutal conflict, and after several painful changes from military dictatorships to elected civilian governments and back. The latest military government was overthrown in 1992 after a bloody confrontation between yet another people's move-ment and the army. It ended with King Bhumipol,* Rama IX, intervening to restore peace and good order, no doubt inspired by the model of the ideal Buddhist monarch.

SULAK SIVARAKSA, BUDDHISM, AND HUMAN RIGHTS

SULAK SIVARAKSA IS justly known as Siam's most outspoken defender of democracy and justice against a whole series of authoritarian regimes over the past forty years. Sulak uses the older term Siam rather than Thailand, which was finally adopted for the country only in 1949, because it repre-sents to him the loss of traditional Buddhist values under dictators and because it is disrespectful to non-Siamese minorities in his country.[32] From a middle-class Bangkok family, Sulak obtained his undergraduate and legal education in Great Britain. On his return to Siam in 1961, he married and settled into one of the few old-style neighborhoods surviving in Bangkok and immersed himself in attempts to influence and reform his society in line with Buddhist principles. Two of his major activities have been writing, publishing, and distributing critical literature, and founding and maintaining an important bookstore. His output in the Thai lan-guage is very great indeed, and many of his works have been translated into English. In the 1960s he was a founding editor for the influential scholarly journal, *Social Science Review*, the voice for critical analysis and reform of Thai society and culture, which helped fire the progressive movement of the 1960s. Sulak has edited and published many of his own works, journals of his organization, and works of others interested in the religious transformation of society.[33]

In 1971, Sulak founded the Komol Keemthong Foundation, one of Thailand's first NGOs, which undertook to do community development work outside the control of the government sponsored projects. This foundation was named after an idealist Siamese scholar who took a job as a schoolteacher in the south of Thailand, where communist insurgents were strong. Komol tried to inspire his students with his vision of a "new sense of Siamese identity, one defined neither by the policies of a development-minded national government nor the radical politics" of the communists. For this the communists murdered him, and some very important Thai civic leaders asked Sulak to organize the Komol Foundation to keep his ideals alive. In Sulak's description of the foundation's goals is a clear expression of his intent to make the principles of Buddhism the practices of the world:

> This was probably the very first social action project to take place . . . outside of government to do something for the people. Our main objective was to promote idealism among the young so that they would dedicate themselves to work for the people. We tried to revive Buddhist values. . . . We felt that the monkhood could play a role again through education and public health.[34]

He has founded or participated in literally hundreds of local and international organizations, committees, seminars, and workshops on issues of nonviolence, sustainable development, Buddhist economics, environmental protection, and women's issues.

His writings on human rights are very interesting in the way they balance traditional Buddhist thought with the concerns of modernity and practical action. Consider the definition of politics he uses in his important essay "Buddhism and Thai Politics." "It is a framework where justice, peace, mercy, decency, friendliness and basic human rights can be conducted."[35] His most extended piece on the issue of human rights is his "Buddhism and Human Rights in Siam," which starts with a discussion of how human rights are affirmed as universal rights both by international bodies and on the level of the people. He then goes on to note that from the point of view of dharma, since all entities including nation-states, individual persons, and the idea of rights, are the product of coconditioned causality and lack any permanent reality, "Buddhist discourse [about human rights] therefore deals with the empirical, relative self and *upaya* or skilful means." He also notes that Buddhist traditional texts do not make any mention at all of rights at any level; rather they focus on "duties and responsibilities." Nonetheless, Sulak affirms that since the destruction of traditional social structures has "undermined the ethical bases of most societies and produced the need for the *upaya* of systematic standards and promises of protection provided by human rights." Thus he uses human rights discourse as skillful means while denying that human rights is ultimate truth or dharma.

Sulak, like his teachers Phra Payutto and Phra Buddhadasa, emphasizes that the Buddhist path necessarily involves the transformation of society as well as the individual practitioner. Buddhists need to work courageously to "enlighten politics" in order to realize their duty to alleviate the suffering of other sentient beings. To combat such evils successfully, Sulak argues, Buddhists must eradicate the root causes of all suffering, "greed, hatred, and delusion, not only in the individual person but in their social and structural dimensions." The way to accomplish this is very traditional. All Buddhists should apply themselves to the practice of mindfulness meditation in order first to diminish the root causes of suffering within themselves, which then enables them to work tirelessly for the elimination of the causes of suffering in the larger social realms. Sulak cites Thich Nhat Hanh,* the Dalai Lama, and Aung San Suu Kyi* as examples to emulate in this regard and insists that the task is a possible one, when undertaken with the assistance of spiritual friends, the community of committed Buddhists. If the task is difficult enough in Buddhist societies with leaders like the Dalai Lama to inspire the masses on the way, how much more difficult is the task in the non-Buddhist consumer societies of the West.

This ambitious program to "reconstitute our societies to be free from oppression and exploitation" obviously "goes beyond the human rights conventions." What he is calling for is nothing less than "the eradication of evil . . . to provide a groundwork for the development of a more full spiritual life, for a reintegration, in Taoist terms, into the higher levels lost before the discussion of justice was ever necessary."[36] Thus it is very clear why Sulak places human rights and justice in the realm of *upaya*, the realm of relative truth. They are useful concepts to secure minimum standards in societies corrupted by the negative values of consumerism and nationalism. In cultures permeated by dharma, where everyone carefully follows the eight-fold path—as Sulak characterizes Siam before the people heedlessly abandoned their traditions—human rights are redundant as the conditions that demand them do not arise.[37]

While social and ethical problems in Siam have generally gotten worse as a result of partially adopting economic and cultural values from the west, Sulak goes too far in idealizing traditional Siam and other premodern Buddhist states. All of them had their own forms of oppression and structural violence, such as slavery in Siam and caste practices in Tibet and Sri Lanka. It also seems that Sulak's goal of the complete eradication of evil through Buddhist transformation of society goes beyond what is possible in Buddhist theory. Society and the individuals that constitute it are the products of coconditioned causality; that is, they are part of *samsara*, summed up in the first holy truth as fundamentally unsatisfactory. As long as there are beings in society, there will necessarily be at least a residue of greed, anger, and delusion, the root causes of oppression and exploitation. Thus the complete eradication of evil is virtually self-contradictory. Still, there is no doubt that individual Buddhists are called upon in all streams of the tradition to eliminate selfish cravings in themselves, to work compassionately for the sake of others, to live according to the precepts of morality, and to follow the Buddhist regulations for interpersonal relations, all of which lessen suffering in the world.

Sulak's ambivalence toward human rights as a tool for social reform is very clear in what he wrote about his own dangerous situation in Thailand in the 1990s.[38] Early in 1991 military men yet again seized the government of Thailand, and Sulak responded with a speech at Thammasat University in August of the same year. General Suchinda Kraprayoon had him charged with lèse-majesté and defamation, and the case continued even after a popular democratic mass movement in 1992 overthrew Suchinda and his National Peace Keeping Council. Sulak went into exile until democratic rule was restored, and after he returned his trial lingered before the courts from March 8, 1993, through April 26, 1995.

His defense was spirited and uncompromising. He maintained it was his duty as an intellectual, a democrat, and a Buddhist to oppose the "corruption of the military dictators" who regularly used the Thai courts to silence opposing voices. Furthermore he pointed out that he never impugned the crown in his speech, and in fact had an extensive public record of recognition for service to the monarchy. The court ruled very strongly in his favor, dismissing the charges and condemning the military coup leaders both for violating the basic principles of democracy and for using the monarchy to further their own political aims. They noted that Sulak's speech, for which he was indicted, encouraged his student audience to live according to Buddhist values and to support the ideals of

justice and democracy. They also found that nothing in the speech undermined the office of the monarchy; rather it explicitly supported it.
The judges said this about the defamation charge:

> As for whether the defendant defamed Suchinda Kraprayoon or not . . .
> normally those who are involved in politics and public affairs need to listen
> to both praise and blame. Suchinda was the deputy leader of the NPKC
> and was criticized and resisted because of the coup. This kind of criticism
> is for the protection and benefit of the country and the people.[39]

In short, Sulak was vindicated fully. As he said, his case was framed and
decided according to "Western civil and political human rights language
and practice" and was one of many around the world that used such
methods "in the struggle for genuine democracy and civil liberties."

Sulak expressed his gratitude for all the international support that he
received from human rights advocacy community saying, "At this personal level I am the last person to criticize what is valuable in Western
human rights theory and practice." However, he immediately pointed out
that his objectives as a Siamese and as a Buddhist were not in complete
accord with those of his Western friends. In the first place he did not
claim an "absolute right to free speech,"[40] affirming the legitimacy of the
law against undermining the monarchy. His defense and legal vindication
rested on his innocence: His speech in no way defamed the crown. He
reaffirmed his responsibility as a Siamese citizen to respect the legitimate
authority of his king and the legitimacy of the law against lèse-majesté.
Secondly, he stressed that his criticisms of his society and the remedies
proposed both came from a Buddhist point of view. He condemned the
forces of greed, hatred, and delusion undermining the good things in
Siamese life and proposed to counter them with the time-honored Buddhist antidotes of morality, meditation, and insight—the eight-fold path.
As he noted, people of other traditions would have different diagnoses of
the problems of their cultures and would offer different remedies according to their own lights.

It is clear from Sulak's analysis of his own case why his support for human rights rhetoric and action is both limited and guarded. First, the
means of human rights come from Western theory and practice and do
not sit well with traditional Buddhist and Siamese ideas and customs.
Second, the ends of the Buddhist endeavor are transcendental, the complete transformation and enlightenment of men and women, ends which

far exceed those of human rights advocacy, ends which may even work against each other. Nonetheless, as a practical man of action, Sulak recommends that Buddhists should align themselves on the side of human rights activists, arguing that the precept against false speech supports such action. "Out of the networking of the global peace, justice and human rights movements arises a radical discourse, a pluralistic, insurgent understanding, a dynamic truth which threatens the power of the forces of violence, greed and ignorance."[41] It seems that "human rights" enter into his rhetoric as skillful means, as a tool for reaching his transcendent goal. This would explain his tireless work on international bodies for just economic development, for peace, and for justice, and why he encourages all Buddhists to do the same.

6

BUDDHISM, DEMOCRACY, AND HUMAN RIGHTS: THE BURMESE CASE STUDY

INTRODUCTION

THE CASE OF BURMA AS IT ADAPTED to modernity provides some interesting insights into how Buddhism, politics, and human rights issues interact. Burma, a Buddhist monarchy of the common South Asian pattern, from at least the time of the Pagan Dynasty (eleventh century C.E.), had times of great military success, becoming a major imperial power in the area, and, at other times, was sorely pressed by neighbours like Siam and China and invaders from afar like Kublai Khan. Melford Spiro, emeritus professor of anthropology from the University of California, characterized the traditional Burmese politico-religious order as a symbiotic relationship: "the state having the responsibility of purifying the Order, and the Order having the responsibility of assuring that the state keep steadfast to Buddhist principles." Furthermore, "Buddhist ideology [was] the reservoir from which the monarch derives charismatic authority,"[1] or in the poetic terms of a Burmese metaphor, the great king who shines like a golden sun should be balanced by the "pure and radiant moon of a monkhood living by orthodox teachings of the Buddha."[2] This metaphor of sun and moon captures very well the wariness of the relation between the ruler and the monastics—although revolving around each other in an intimate interrelationship, there is always a respectful distance that separates them. That the realm of the religious practitioner needed to be separate from that of the ruler was expressed in

another Burmese proverb, which "includes rulers among the Five Enemies, together with Fire, Thieves and Pestilence."[3]

BURMA: RESISTANCE TO THE BRITISH

IN THE NINETEENTH century, in a series of wars, Britain made Burma
part of the empire. The Burmese resisted fiercely and never accepted the
new regime. Although King Thibaw (r. 1878–1886), whom the British
deposed, had been weak, unwise, and unpopular, he nevertheless was a
traditional Buddhist monarch, understood to be the central point of the
mandala of sacred and secular life, holding the Burmese world together
and giving it meaning. King Thibaw's last words to his people called for
them "to resist the English barbarians, who had made harsh demands calculated to bring about the destruction of Burma's religion, the violation
of national traditions, and the degradation of the race."[4] Very quickly the
newly conquered territories, which had been declared a province of
British India in February 1886, descended into chaos, with the sources of
traditional authority pushed aside, and with unpaid and unsupervised soldiers and officials left to fend for themselves. Armed bands of villagers,
some of them mere bandits but others traditional self-defense groups,
took matters into their own hands.

In reaction to the brutal attempts of the British to restore order, by
midyear in 1886, the scattered armed actions in the newly annexed areas
had grown to a general rebellion throughout Burma, even in the areas occupied for some generations by the British. This rebellion was very strong
but lacked any national figure around which the whole nation might
unite. Even though the struggle remained a series of local campaigns, it
expressed a general Burmese revulsion for the way their country had been
forced to give up its traditional ways, and the Burmese never became eager to assimilate into a British European mold. The nicely named pacification took some four years, needing some 30,000 soldiers and 30,000
military police to complete, and was ruthlessly pursued.[5]

During this war of resistance against British imperialism, Dr. Vinton,
an American Baptist missionary to the Karens, a non-Burmese tribal people, noted in his correspondence that some monks led anti-British fighters
and "actually fought themselves." As the missionary noted, "this is un-
heard of in history," so much so that his Karen converts took it as a sign
from their new God that Buddhism was about to be destroyed forever.

Encouraged by Dr. Vinton and other missionaries, who supplied arms, the Karens defended themselves effectively against the Burmese and proved very useful to the British. Dr. Vinton, in the midst of the war, judged it to be a good thing as something to "put virility into our Christianity."[6] It should be noted that the armed struggle between the Karens and other non-Burmese peoples on the border and the Burmese has continued to the present time.

These yellow-robed warriors in the 1880s marked "the origin of the political monk"[7] in Burma. From then on, a relative small minority of monks, feeling freed from the restraints of the vinaya rules about political activity after there was no longer state support of the sangha, took an active role in the political struggle to regain independence. They were the major organizational and inspirational force behind the resistance. Although it is not at all easy to know precise numbers, the vast number of monks, especially those in monasteries outside the major cities, continued with their traditional duties of preaching, meditation, performing rituals, and providing primary education, and as world-renouncers left the dirty business of politics to the laity.[8]

Just as it is difficult to determine how many monks were politically active in the resistance to the establishment of British sovereignty over Burma, it is also very difficult to know what their motivation was. The British in the field tended to judge that the politically active monks, particularly those who took up arms, were not sincere in their religious convictions. Sir Charles Crosthwaite, who was in charge of the pacification of Burma after February 1887, agreed:

> In common with others who know Burma better, I doubt if the religious orders as a body had much influence on the course of events, or took an active part in the resistance to us. When a monk became a noted leader, it was a patriot who had been a monk and not a monk who had become a patriot. At the same time some of the most serious and deepest-laid plots were hatched in monasteries or initiated by [monks].[9]

Spiro agreed with Crosthwaite and added that many of the Burmese political monks, from the time of their first appearance down to the current time, were more political than religious, that many were "merely disguised in the yellow robe as a cover for their political activities."[10] Still, since the Buddhist establishment and the stability of the state were understood to be inextricably intertwined, it seems that a Burmese Buddhist who worked for independence would likely have been motivated both by religious and nationalistic factors, which cannot be very neatly separated.

Even in the uprising that enflamed the country in 1887, some monks worked for the return to peace and good order, which does seem to be a better fit with general Buddhist ethical principles and the specific rules for the deportment of monks than the activities of those who participated in the fighting. Crosthwaite, who seemed to have good relations with the supreme patriarch and rather good impressions of Burmese Buddhism, believed that a number of the monks he encountered regretted the upheavals caused by the armed resistance, and "would have been glad to work for peace."[11] The events of the nineteenth century set the pattern for subsequent Burmese history. First, Buddhist clergy and Buddhist ideology were major sources of political thought and action, and the political monk has remained a force. Second, the country has a tendency to descend into turbulence and violence in times of pressure. And finally, issues with non-Burmese minorities have never been resolved, and habitually generate armed conflicts.

Buddhism suffered in two ways, particularly, under British Indian governance. First, the new rulers did not follow the Burmese practice of the head of state appointing the supreme patriarch for the country, even though they were asked to do so by some leading citizens early on. Their refusal was a result of their attempt to remain neutral in matters of religion, while the Burmese depended upon the central authorities to make the critical appointment. In fact since the Burmese Buddhist establishment was highly fragmented with some nine major schools and many minor sects, they would have found it very difficult to agree upon a choice. When the British said they would be happy to confirm whoever the Burmese would choose, there was an impasse, each side being rather bewildered by the position of the other.[12] This meant that the organized religion lost authority and support of the state and made it more difficult for the hierarchy of the sangha to maintain discipline within the ranks, especially after British courts, as early as 1891, overturned rulings of ecclesiastical councils.[13]

Second, before being annexed to British India, Burma had a very high standard of literacy, accomplished through the monastery schools, which functioned in every village. Indeed in the early nineteenth century, there was effectively a system of universal education throughout the country, something far above the contemporary British system. Not only did the children learn to read, they were also taught the fundamentals of Buddhist doctrine, steeped in Buddhist ethics, and learned to honor Burmese Buddhist customs that stressed harmony, respect, and mutual responsibility. British administrators did not choose to build on the indigenous school system, but rather introduced English-style learning, often taught by missionaries under the auspices of Christian church organizations. These schools were concentrated in the major centers and mainly attracted the children of the economic elite, who learned to devalue their Burmese Buddhist heritage, either because it was ignored in the curriculum or because it was presented as inferior to British learning. Furthermore, without government support, the monastery school system weakened, and without royal patronage, the literary and material arts suffered. The net effect was that the level of education and Buddhist culture in Burma declined under British rule.

There was continuous opposition to British rule in Burma with many small rebellions, riots, and reprisals. Political monks, always fewer in number than those who stayed focused on life within the walls of the monastery, were very active and provided much of the leadership to Burmese nationalism in the 1920s and 1930s. Buddhism was the central intellectual and cultural force in country, and since British policy was not to interfere in religious matters, it provided a safe refuge to organize opposition. Some aspects of political Buddhism were quite negative. In particular, Buddhist nationalism fed xenophobia and helped fire violence against minorities in the country. By making Burma part of the Indian empire, the British imposed Indian law and legal systems on the country and opened it up to immigration as well. Most of the army, police, and much of the civil service were Indian, many Indian workers were brought in to fill jobs (menial and otherwise) primarily in the modern sectors of the economy, and Indian entrepreneurs and moneylenders came to control much of the business life. In 1930, Indian dock workers went on strike for better wages, and Burmese strike breakers were hired as replacements. When the strike was settled, all the Burmese were fired, which brought the resentment to a boiling point. They formed mobs, and bolstered by religious tattoos, hunted down and killed hundreds of Indian inhabitants of Rangoon, most of them unconnected with the strike. Similar riots, which also targeted the Chinese minorities, spread to other parts of the country in 1930 and 1931, and no one was ever brought to trial for their acts. These disturbances were the direct source of the *Dohbama* movement, the cry "we Burmese" that rallied the rioters. The *Dohbama* movement later was called the Thakin Party, whose leaders like U Nu* and Aung San, were central in liberating the country from the British and the Japanese. Its chauvinism was all too clear in the party slogan, "Race, language, religion."[14]

While the 1930–1931 xenophobic riots and attendant murders did not apparently have any direct involvement of Buddhist leaders, the disturbances of 1938 were a different matter. The report of the official inquiry set the casualty figures at 192 Indians killed and 878 injured with some 171 Burmese casualties inflicted by the police, and the actual numbers were thought to have been much greater. In Rangoon, the Indian community lost an incalculable amount of wealth to the mobs, which pillaged Indian homes and places of business. To give an idea of the magnitude of the troubles, the 4,306 persons charged by the police for their activities in the riots were admitted by the authorities to be only a token number of the rioters. As to assigning blame for starting the fire and keeping it fanned, the inquiry found that the culprits were the press and certain agitators, who included monks as well as laymen. In the words of the report,

> In our evidence we have a mournful record of these so-called [monks] up and down the country promoting meetings . . . for political or subversive ends, participating in rioting and, arms in their hands, leading or accompanying crowds of hooligans, committing assaults, looting and even murder, and in general breaking the civil laws of the country and laws of their own order.[15]

There were 132 well-authenticated such cases, and there were many other well-documented instances where monasteries were used to shelter rioters and to store loot, taking advantage of the reluctance of the police to enter religious sites. Throughout the report, it was stressed that there was a real difference between the young political monks and the genuinely pious, mainly older, members of the sangha.

BUDDHISM AND HUMAN RIGHTS IN BURMA UNDER JAPANESE OCCUPATION

BURMESE NATIONALISTS FIRST supported the Japanese, whom they saw as liberators from the British. A group of around thirty patriots trained under the Japanese Army outside the country. They recruited and trained several hundred Burmese in Thailand. This core of the Burma Independence Army (the B.I.A.)[16] helped the Japanese army in its invasion of Burma, which began late in December 1941, only a few weeks after Pearl Harbor. The three hundred soldiers of the B.I.A. were neither well equipped nor thoroughly trained. Nonetheless, they fought bravely and were well received by their countrymen, many of whom quickly joined, with the B.I.A. numbering some ten thousand men by the time they entered Rangoon in March 1942.[17] British forces and their Chinese allies were quickly defeated, routed even, and by April 1942 had fled back to India and China.

For a few months, April through June 1942, the B.I.A. was in charge of parts of lower Burma, and things went very badly. This period was called a "reign of terror."[18] The British Indian Army did not allow Burmese to enlist, but Karens and other hill tribes were, and many of them had fought alongside the British, the Indians, and other commonwealth forces in Burma. When the army collapsed, the Karen soldiers returned home with their weapons, which the B.I.A. attempted to confiscate. Very soon fighting broke out, and there was quite a nasty war, with brutality on all sides, but triggered mainly by the B.I.A. There were horrible atrocities—torture, mass execution, slaughter of men, women, and children in villages—against the Karens and the Indians who had fled for safety to Karen territory. Aung San, father of Aung San Su Kyi, was the senior Burmese officer in the B.I.A. and tried to gain control of his troops. Since they had recruited nearly anyone who asked to join, including criminals let out of jail when the British administration disintegrated, and since they were mainly untrained and undisciplined, it was only when the Japanese Army took control after mopping up operations that intercommunal violence came to an end. The B.I.A. was dissolved on July 24, 1942, and replaced by the Burma Defence Army, which had been formed from the better elements of the earlier force. They were again under the command of Aung San, who was closely supervised by the Japanese, and they gradually became an effective, trained fighting force.

At first the Burmese, including many monks, welcomed the Japanese forces, seeing them as liberators from their colonial masters, and expecting that Japanese who were fellow Asians and Buddhists would be both friends and allies. Dr. Ba Maw, who had served as the first prime minister under limited British home rule, was originally very positive about the Japanese takeover of Burma.

Looking at it historically, no nation has done so much to liberate Asia from white domination, yet no nation has been so misunderstood by the very peoples whom it has helped to liberate or to set an example to in many things.

He also said, "in suppressing the new B.I.A. terror the [Japanese] militarists employed their own brand of terror, and the two terrors together let loose hell."[19] Ba Maw attributed the "reign of terror" under the Japanese as being the product of fundamental "racial" misunderstandings between them and the Burmese. In particular, he blamed those Japanese who had served in Korea, Manchuria, and China and had become absolutely convinced of the superiority of Japanese people and culture to all others. Ba Maw believed this explained their arrogant and brutal behavior to the peoples of the Greater East Asia Co-Prosperity Sphere, which Japan used to plunder local resources for the Japanese military machine. In Burma perhaps the harshest example of these policies was the use of Burmese forced labor in the construction of the infamous Burma-Thailand railway. Dr. Ba Maw's government was rather successful in looking after the welfare of its people who had been conscripted in contrast to the horrors inflicted on prisoners of war and conscripted Asians on the Thai side of the project.

One thing that all the Burmese recall with great distaste from the Japanese "reign of terror" was their practice of slapping the face of anyone who provoked them. While this was the accepted practice within the Japanese Army, it was enormously offensive to the Burmese, who understand the head of a person as the most important part of the body, never to be treated disrespectfully. In fact, the practice of slapping faces was perhaps even more offensive to the Burmese than the British insistence on wearing boots or shoes in temples—these two things, which mirror each other in a peculiar way, were guaranteed to offend Burmese sensibilities in the worst way. Even though most Japanese are Buddhists, the occupying forces were extremely disrespectful to Burmese Buddhist institutions. Soldiers slapped monks in the face, used monasteries to stable their horses and as slaughter houses, pillaged and destroyed religious images, wrapped their horses' feet in the yellow robes taken from monks, and generally behaved atrociously to all the Burmese civilians. Professor Aung summed it up in these words: "The period of Japanese military rule lasted only three years, but to the Burmese people it was more irksome than some sixty years of British rule."[20]

The Japanese eventually in August 1943 granted nominal independence to Burma, but actually kept the country carefully under the thumb of the military secret police. Burma immediately entered the war on the side of the Japanese. Dr. Ba Maw, the new head of puppet state under the Japanese, quickly took on the trappings of the Burmese monarchy, adopting the official title of *Adipati*, a title used in Theravada countries for a royal prince. He was "Lord of Power, the Great King's Royal Person" and took "Great Prince" into his official title. He pledged to uphold the time-honored traditions and laws of the country, and assumed the role of the protector of Buddhism, planting a tree that symbolized the center of "the traditional ideal of the mission of Burma's rulers to unite the Entire abode of Men," ruling from the center of the cosmic mandala. The soil used to receive the tree came from the homeland of the Buddha of the future, and it was believed that showers of gold and silver would flow from the tree to all the people of the realm. The official newspaper of the Adipati Ba Maw regime promised that when the Axis powers won the war, then Burma would be turned into "the Earthly Nirvana," a perfected prosperous land under the rule of dharma. It is interesting that "Earthly Nirvana," a phrase originally coined by Burmese socialists who attempted to synthesize Buddhist dharma and Marxism, could be used in such an overtly fascist context.[21]

Trevor Ling (1920–1995), late professor of comparative religion at the University of Manchester and a leading authority on Buddhism in Southeast Asia, noted that Ba Maw's personal commitment to Buddhism was very doubtful, since he was born into a Christian family, was educated in England and France, and spoke in very disparaging terms about the qualities of Burmese monks.[22] Whether or not his Buddhism was genuine, the Adipati attempted to gain the support of the organized sangha and to utilize their prestige to reinforce the aims of the ruler, as would be expected in a traditional Buddhist monarchical polity. To this end he established a ministry of religion and propaganda, the very title of which casts some doubt as to the religious purity of his motives.[23] He attempted to unify the major Burmese sects and to mobilize a unified sangha to support the nation through the "Burmese People's Monks' Association." The association called for all monks to

(1) collaborate in the construction of New Burma; (2) purge Burma of all enemies of Nippon and Burma; (3) foster friendly Nippon-Burma relations; and (4) carry out a positive religious programme of benefit to the Burmese people.[24]

The Adipati's efforts to assume the mantle of a traditional Burmese monarch and to mobilize the Buddhist establishment to support the fascist state were not successful. The various sects continued to compete with one another, and even those monks who benefited from the relationship with the new government were not at all interested in undertaking the sort of practical nation-building role expected of them. The traditionalist wing of the sangha continued its opposition to monks undertaking political activities, and the people did not seem to accept Dr. Ba Maw's aspiration to be seen as a wheel-turning king. Above all, the Burmese were deeply offended by the Japanese army's behavior. There was no way to reconcile the rhetoric of the government, which urged the Burmese sangha to support closer ties with Japan and Japanese Buddhism, with the continuing disrespect shown by the Japanese forces of occupation to Burmese Buddhist institutions. Neither did the brutality of the military police, who routinely used torture, and the looting of the economy for the benefit of Japanese interests did not reconcile the Burmese to their allotted place in the Co-Prosperity Sphere. Ling concluded that by the end of the Second World War, monks had become completely "disenchanted with the political realm and alienated from the affairs of the state."[25]

BUDDHISM AND HUMAN RIGHTS IN INDEPENDENT DEMOCRATIC BURMA (1948–1962)

BURMA EFFECTIVELY GAINED its independence by force of arms. General Aung San had long distrusted the Japanese and planned to resist them after they failed to grant real independence and because of their mistreatment of his people. In 1945 he led the Burmese in guerrilla warfare against the Japanese under the banner of the "Anti-Fascist People's Freedom League," providing considerable help in the British reoccupation of the country. However, it was clear to the Burmese that the Fascists they opposed included "Japanese militarists and the English racists,"[26] and after the Japanese were defeated, Aung San's forces kept their arms and refused to accept the administration that the colonialists attempted to impose. Outgunned on the ground and unwilling to go to war, Britain granted Burma independence as a secular state in 1947, with Aung San slated to be the first leader. However, before the transition, on July 19, 1947, Aung San and his cabinet were murdered by political rivals. U Nu, who had served in the cabinet of Dr. Ba Maw's puppet regime, fortunately had not been at the fatal meeting, and was asked to form the new government.

Without the strength of character and personal charisma of Aung San to hold the country together, the first few years of independence went very badly indeed, with various ethnic groups and political groups taking up arms against the newly independent state. "Almost the entire country was overrun by the various factions of Communists, mutineers, Karens and other separatists,"[27] but U Nu with the aid of the commander of the army, General Ne Win,* somehow managed to reestablish the unity of the country without abandoning the principles of democracy. By 1951, the major fighting was over, although armed troubles with Communist insurgents, the Karens, and some other minorities have continued as a major destabilizing factor even to the present day (2003).

The Burmese government was also faced with a devastated economy after decades of British policies that had impoverished the average person, two very destructive wars of conquest and a civil war in less than a decade, and three years of Japanese looting. The answer they chose was a form of democratic socialism, understood as being compatible with Buddhism and, by most, to be opposed to communism.[28] U Nu and other politicians and thinkers sought to justify their socialist policies by citing various Theravada texts. While some teachings in the sutras may support democratic socialist principles, others are quite useful to capitalists, but most support autocratic monarchs. Quickly U Nu took on the traditional role of a Burmese Buddhist monarch in the Asokan model, supporting the sangha and using Buddhism as the basis for his rule. Just as in Thailand at the same time, the army used many of these initiatives effectively in its efforts to combat communist rebels.[29]

U Nu's proudest religious accomplishment was his Sixth Buddhist Synod (1954–1956), convened to celebrate the 2,500th anniversary of the *parinirvana* of Lord Buddha. U Nu proudly connected himself to the lineage of the Emperor Asoka, credited with having convened the Third Synod (c. 241 B.C.E.) and King Mindon, the last great Burmese king, who had convened the Fifth Synod in Mandalay in 1871. He also came to think of himself as a bodhisattva,[30] another traditional attribution to an ideal Buddhist monarch. He had the Pali scriptures translated into Burmese, so for the first time, every literate person could read them.

In the 1960 election, U Nu campaigned on the promise that he would make Buddhism the state religion, but he came into conflict with the political monks who opposed his attempt to follow the Asokan model of supporting all the religions in the realm. Late in 1961, things came to head when fifty monks occupied a partly completed mosque and began a noisy denunciation of the U Nu and other cabinet ministers. The police told them to leave as they were in violation of the law, but the monks refused, and continued their agitation. Rather than attempting to enforce the law and evicting the monks, the government asked their abbots to reason with them. After all, according to the *vinaya*, such political activity was quite out of order, but the young monks would not listen. The government decided to wait them out, and after two weeks, the monks got completely out of hand. They destroyed the structure they had occupied, set fire to another mosque, and led a mob of some 1,500 supporters on a rampage in the Moslem quarter, a smaller version of the intercommunal violence of 1938. Two Moslems were murdered, and the police shot two Burmese lay rioters to death when they fired on the crowd to restore order. Of the 371 men arrested, 92 were wearing the yellow robe.[31] The government treated the rioters with considerable leniency.

BUDDHISM AND HUMAN RIGHTS UNDER THE MILITARY REGIME (1962–   )

BUDDHISM NEVER GOT to function as the state religion in a democratic Burma. The army, under General Ne Win, caretaker premier from 1958 to 1960, opposed the new status of Buddhism, fearing that such a change would even further destabilize the country and was concerned about the increasing economic problems and political instability. The monks who encouraged violence against the Moslems in Rangoon and those who contemptuously agitated against securing minorities' religious freedoms alarmed the non-Buddhist Burmese, sparking the formation of the Kachin Independence Army, and also alarmed secularist officers in the army. The contribution of religious agitation to unrest and U Nu's religious response to the worsening situation of the country—he had 60,000 sand pagodas built all around the country and sponsored spirit-propitiations—did not reassure General Ne Win and like-minded army officers, so they mounted a successful coup on March 2, 1962. One of the first acts of the new regime was to reverse the laws that made Buddhism the state religion.

Burma has been under military control ever since, under a regime widely condemned for its oppressive practices toward its citizens, and for its dismal management of the economy. General Ne Win was inspired by Stalin and tried to synthesize centralized authoritarian socialism with aspects of Buddhist thought to come up with a "Burmese Way to Socialism."[32] The results in practice have not been encouraging. Besides having wiped away such niceties as freedom of the press, freedom of assembly, parliamentary democracy, and the like, the military regime has persistently and widely used or sanctioned torture, rape, forced labor, forced migration, forced relocation within the country, child soldiers, and other abuses, making Burma one of the most sorely oppressed nations in the world today. A devastating mixture of corruption and ideological mismanagement has ruined the economy. Twenty-five years into the military regime, "Only three weeks before the celebration of the fortieth anniversary of Burmese independence [1987], Burma achieved 'Least Developed Nation' status in a United Nations General Assembly vote."[33]

RESISTANCE TO THE MILITARY (1988–PRESENT), DAW AUNG SAN SUU KYI, BUDDHISM AND HUMAN RIGHTS

DAW AUNG SAN Suu Kyi is the daughter of Aung San, the charismatic freedom fighter against both Japanese occupiers and British imperialists in the 1940s. He was murdered in 1947, a few months before independence, when Aung San Suu Kyi was only two years old. Educated first in Rangoon, she did her secondary education in India and studied political science for two years at Delhi University, after her mother was appointed Burmese ambassador there in 1960. No doubt her Indian education contributed to her admiration for Gandhi and her adherence to nonviolent methods.[34] She then did a degree at Oxford (1964–1967), reading the Modern Greats—Politics, Philosophy, and Economics.[35] After working for the United Nations in New York and Bhutan from 1969–1972, she married Dr. Michael Aris, whom she had met at Oxford, and spent from 1972 to 1988 raising her two sons as the wife of a British academic, while pursuing her academic interests as much as possible, producing several substantial pieces of work on Burmese issues.[36] Her life changed in the most spectacular way imaginable in 1988 while visiting Burma to tend her mother who had suffered a stroke.

At that time, Burma had been under a brutal, corrupt, and economically inept military dictatorship since 1962, led by General Ne Win, a wartime colleague in arms of Aung San. During Aung San Suu Kyi's 1988 visit to help her mother, there was a student-led popular uprising against the regime, triggered by Ne Win's decision to resign on August 8, 1988— 8.8.88, a most auspicious number in Chinese-Burmese numerology. This led to popular demonstrations which the army suppressed with great brutality in four days of slaughter, August 8 through 12. At least three thousand people, mostly students, were killed and thousands more fled to the jungle to continue resistance or to seek refuge in Thailand. It was at this point that Aung Sang Suu Kyi entered politics, although her earlier writings show that she had long been inspired by the memory of her father and the struggle of the Burmese people. In her, the people of Burma saw the outstanding leadership qualities of her father, who remained the most revered of the freedom fighters that had led Burma out of colonialism.[37] In return she was energized by them and their struggle and quickly found herself at the center of the democratic movement.

On August 26, Aung San Suu Kyi along with other leaders spoke to a crowd of perhaps 500,000 people in the capital, calling for nonviolent action to return to democracy. In this speech, she tied the current situation to the struggle her father had led a generation ago, saying that "I could not as my father's daughter remain indifferent. . . . This national crisis could in fact be called the second struggle for national independence."[38] The army's response, under the guidance of General Ne Win, came quickly on September 18, in the form of a violent coup, establishing the State Law and Order Restoration Council (SLORC), which has governed ever since.[39] Shaken by the scale of public support for change, SLORC pledged to allow elections, and on September 24 the National League for Democracy (NLD) was formed to participate in the elections scheduled for May 1990. Aung San Suu Kyi was chosen general secretary of the NLD, but she was not allowed to run for office, although she campaigned vigorously throughout the country, giving close to a thousand speeches before she was put under house arrest in July 1989.

Aung San Suu Kyi was often harassed and threatened in the course of the election campaign, as were most of her party's supporters and candidates. Soldiers frequently warned citizens to stay away from NLD meetings, yet the crowds were always impressive. In spite of all the difficulties that the NLD faced, they won the election by a landslide. However, the military refused to implement the results and has resolutely clung to power, increasing the level of oppression and injustice. Since then Aung San Suu Kyi has spent her life under house arrest or close supervision, always witnessing for peace and justice through nonviolent change, while devoting herself to meditation, study, and writing. Her influence and popularity in Burma has remained high, and she has been well honored abroad for her work for human rights and democracy. Her greatest award of many was the Nobel Peace Prize in 1991. In May 2002, she was freed from house arrest, but a year later in another round of violence by the military against her party and supporters, she was once again taken into "protective custody" where she remains at the time of writing (October 2003).

What then does she have to say about Buddhism and human rights? "In Quest of Democracy," written in the difficult period leading up to her first house arrest on July 20, 1989, is her longest work on the topic. This piece, which is excerpted in chapter 13 of the present study, was originally meant to be part of a volume on human rights and democracy dedicated to the memory of Aung Sang, her father. Her major point is that the Burmese people know that democratic representative government and human rights are necessary if they are to have a decent way of life, and further, they are consistent with the basic tenets of Buddhism. Her expansion on the Ten Duties of Kings surely was intended to condemn the military junta whose venality and brutality is in such vivid contrast to the high-minded and noble qualities expected of a Buddhist ruler.

She cites Theravada scriptures about kings to provide a Buddhist charter for democratic representative forms of government, but do they? The general answer, it seems, must be no. The ideal form of Buddhist governance for the world that Lord Buddha taught in the scriptures was the righteous monarch, the wheel-turning king, enjoined to govern according to dharma. Except for the mythical story of the first king in the *Agganna Sutra*, elections of the ruler by the people were never recommended or even mentioned as a possible course of action. Buddhist kings most often attained the throne hereditarily, or in some cases by force of arms. Even less a possibility was democratic governance by the people as a whole or through representative assemblies. He had a duty to govern according to dharma, but no particular responsibility to consult the will of the people, though in many cases that would be a prudent thing to do.

One of the most interesting sections of "In Quest of Democracy" linked the Universal Declaration of Human Rights to Buddhist teachings about the preciousness of human person, "who alone of all beings can achieve the supreme state of Buddhahood."[40] Therefore, the goal of

Buddhist government should be to ensure the conditions that allow individuals to proceed on their religious quest. She concluded that this Buddhist affirmation of the human potential for perfection or recognition of the "inherent dignity" of persons meant that human beings have "equal and inalienable rights."[41] This central doctrinal point was quoted in the Nobel Prize acceptance speech given by her son on her behalf. L.P.N. Perera and Damien Keown posit the same argument to sustain a Buddhist basis for human rights and equality as absolute values, but as argued at length in chapter 2, absolute rights can be seen as contrary to basic Buddhist doctrines. Furthermore, equality of individuals was never part of the tradition, which rather prescribed reciprocal duties within social hierarchies.

Still, her basic point is well taken—it is a perversion of Buddhist thought and values for authoritarian governments like Burma's military regime to denounce human rights as antithetical to indigenous values. While it is very difficult to find a Buddhist doctrinal grounding for absolute human rights as expressed in the Universal Declaration, it is very easy to show that corrupt, brutal, and authoritarian regimes that beggar their nations and oppress their people are antithetical to the Buddhist picture of the righteous ruler. Burma under Ne Win and his successors have steadily moved away from establishing the conditions conducive to the well-being and religious advancement of people in society, the ideal function of the state as taught in Buddhist traditions.

In 1995–1996, Alan Clements, a Western Buddhist and author, who had previously been a monk in Burma for several years, was allowed to visit Daw Aung San Suu Kyi several times and to tape their conversations. This was during a remarkable gap in the generally tight web of censorship that military intelligence had woven around her. These conversations, which were published in 1997, show her to be a resolute defender of nonviolence in the struggle for democracy, and add a few valuable insights into her view of human rights and Buddhism. She noted that she did not consider religion and politics as separate at all and that she believed that Buddhists should be "engaged Buddhists." In particular, she said, "there was nothing in democracy that any Buddhist could object to," thus monks and nuns ought to become active politically in order "to promote what is good and desirable." This would be done "by preaching democratic principles . . . and by trying to persuade the authorities to begin dialogue."[42] To her, engaged Buddhism meant getting involved in the world through active compassion or loving-kindness, because the law of karma does not advocate passivity; rather, it advocates taking responsibility for one's own karmic future.[43]

In one respect she thinks that the military regime shows some progress in morality in comparison with the traditional absolute monarchies of Burma's past. The ancient kings did not hesitate to torture and execute their enemies or those subjects who displeased them, and they did this publicly and without shame. Now, although SLORC does routinely torture and kill its accused enemies, they conceal and deny their deeds. This is because human rights as recognized in the Universal Declaration have become the international standard of civilized behavior, and the military clique that routinely abuses the people is at least ashamed to admit it.[44] Finally, her support for human rights, in common with thoughtful Buddhists everywhere is guarded. "I think that people everywhere [not just in the Western world] do try to take advantage and misuse their rights." She says that when Burma regains her freedom through democratic means she "would like our democracy to be a better, more compassionate and more caring one" than is found in the West. This means that Burma would use her "freedoms more responsibly and with the well-being of others in mind."[45]

All in all, Aung San Suu Kyi's thought is an admirable synthesis of her Burmese Buddhist and political heritage, her immersion in Indian thought and culture, and her first-rate Western education in politics, philosophy, and economics at Oxford. Her political career shows her to be a woman of incredible courage and levelheadedness, who is committed to nonviolence. Her devotion to Buddhism, human rights, and democratic politics have every mark of deep and sincere conviction, and one trusts that they would guide her actions and pervade her policies should her party ever take power. Burma, however, has proven very difficult to unite and to govern well, and the devastation of the last half century would make building a decent new regime very difficult. Furthermore, the involvement of Buddhist monks in politics, which she endorses, has often had bad results in the past. Still, this remarkable woman might well be able to succeed in spite of all the difficulties to overcome.

THE ROLE OF MONKS IN BURMESE POLITICS SINCE 1988

JUST AS IN all Burmese political movements in the last 100 years, the events of 1988 involved politically active monks. In Rangoon, the Young Monks Association, took a leading role. This is the same group that was formed in the 1938 xenophobic riots and violently opposed U Nu's attempts to support the freedom of religious minorities. In part, some of the monks and abbots had been upset by the military's efforts in the 1970s to gain more control over the sangha and to try to eliminate corrupt monks, those who flaunted the rules of the *vinaya*. During the run up to the disturbances, monasteries were used as safe places for the student and other dissidents to meet, and once demonstrations started, monks marched along to protect the others from the army, who they hoped would be unwilling to risk the religious demerit of firing upon the clergy. This probably did have some effect; nonetheless, a number of monks were amongst the thousands of people shot down.

Officially Burma, under the current regime, was to be a secularist state in the tradition of Aung San and the original constitution. However, in practice the military government has assumed the role of a traditional Buddhist ruler by providing material support to the organized sangha and by taking steps to regulate and purify its operation. As usual the rulers' motives were no doubt mixed, in part an expression of their attachment to their Theravada faith, in part a hope to gain legitimacy from support and blessing from the Buddhist establishment, and an attempt to bring the sangha under firmer control by the state. In 1965, 1980, and 1985 Ne Win's government sponsored councils to reform the sangha, and has been more successful than any previous government in bringing the sangha under central government control and imposing discipline on errant monks, using Thai-style bureaucratic methods.[46]

Due to the effective isolation of the country and the efficiency of the secret police, regrettably one of the few functioning government services,[47] it is not at all clear exactly how effective the military has been in bringing the monks under state control. One scholar, who is very positive about the military regime, reported that after 1980, "there were no longer any organized factions of political monks."[48] There has, however, continued to be some organized Buddhist resistance to the army, with the most famous being the "overturning the begging bowl" protest of 1990,[49] where an estimated 20,000 monks across the country refused to accept alms from anyone in military uniform in protest to their continuing armed brutality toward the population as a whole. By refusing to accept gifts from the soldiers, the monks kept them from acts of merit, the most important religious practice for Burmese laymen, and effectively said the military was behaving as non-Buddhists. The public at large showed their agreement by refusing to share public transport with soldiers or to sell to their families in the market.

According to a 1992 Human Rights Watch report, "the Burmese military government actively endorses Theravada Buddhism in practice, as have previous governments—both civilian and military," going so far as to use forced labor and forced donations to build Buddhist structures. Human Rights Watch reports that the army's patronage of Buddhism was not solely to gain legitimacy, but also has a component of genuine devotion.[50] Unfortunately, there is considerable evidence that the government and monks have worked together in the systematic repression of the Moslem minority that has continued since Ne Win took power in 1962.[51] For example, the government in 2001 used monks to distribute anti-Moslem pamphlets,[52] and monks participated in the widespread violence against Moslem communities in Burma throughout 2001. Some of the 2001 riots were triggered by the destruction of the colossal Buddhist statues in Bamiyan, Afghanistan, by the Taliban regime in March, and some were reactions to the al-Qaeda attack on New York City and Washington, D.C. on September 11 of that same year. The underlying causes were deeply rooted in Burmese xenophobia and economic resentment against Moslem merchants and moneylenders, and the violent attacks on innocent minorities are depressingly similar to those of the 1930s.

One scholar concluded, in spite of such outrages in the name of Buddhism, there is no major official Buddhist xenophobia today in Burma.[53] Perhaps not, but popular Buddhist feelings against the Moslems have contributed to the climate of governmental violence and repression in Burma. Furthermore, today's communal violence by Buddhist rioters fits uncomfortably well into the pattern of similar carnage over the last seventy-five years, and nonethnic Burmese are worried that Aung San Suu Kyi and her party are not sympathetic to their concerns.[54]

CONCLUSION: BURMESE POLITICAL BUDDHISM AND HUMAN RIGHTS

IN 1965, DONALD Eugene Smith, now professor emeritus in the South Asia Studies Department of the University of Pennsylvania, after reviewing all of the various ways that Buddhism had been used in Burma to legitimate political movements, concluded that "Buddhism might be used to legitimate any conceivable political system."[55] He was writing before the military regime unofficially came to treat Buddhism as the state religion, while they were still promoting a secular state, so now it could be said that Buddhism in Burma has legitimated traditional despotic monarchies, mystical revolutionary movements, fascism under the Japanese, democratic and tolerant socialism under U Nu, authoritarian militaristic socialism under the generals, and the campaign for democracy and decency led by Daw Aung San Suu Kyi. Smith pointed out that Buddhism does have affinities with democratic values, such as its emphasis on individualism and self-reliance in the religious quest and, ideally at least, tolerance and compromise with different beliefs and practices. However, as he noted, in Burmese history Buddhism flourished for centuries under traditional absolute monarchies.[56] It is also significant that as a traditional Theravada culture, Burma never developed democratic structures of government or the legal structures and cultural values that seem to be necessary steps before democracy can develop. All this argues against Professor Perera's claim that representative democracy based on inherent human rights is the natural form of government that flows from basic Buddhist principles.[57]

In Burma the religious-political mold, constantly returned to, was that of a traditional Buddhist monarch understood as the center of his nation, who legitimated his power by upholding dharma in the world, in short, a wheel-turning king. Such a ruler could also be interpreted as a Bodhisattva or even as Maitreya, the Buddha who will mark the end of this age. None of these ideas relied upon or supported human rights notions or practices in any direct way. Therefore, it is hardly surprising that those Buddhist monks and laymen in Burma who opposed British rule did so without making human rights claims or arguments. In fact, it is sad to report that in many cases, under all sorts of regimes, political monks' actions actually encouraged or abetted the violation of the most basic human rights, those of freedom from violence and intimidation for non-Buddhist minorities in the country.

General Aung San, Burma's greatest hero of the revolutionary struggle, who was slated to be the first prime minister, was assassinated at the age of thirty-two just before the country regained independence in 1948. He, like U Nu, consistently opposed the involvement of monks in politics, from the time of his first speech in college to one given in the year before his death.[58] For him, the best thing for a monk to do in the service of his country would be to proclaim the Buddha's message of universal love and brotherhood, leaving the worldly business of politics to laymen and lay-women. Aung San Suu Kyi, the daughter of Aung San, who has taken on the leadership of the second struggle for independence against military tyranny does not share her father's and U Nu's opposition to political monks. As an "engaged Buddhist" she would welcome more active in-volvement in democratic politics by monks and nuns, saying that they have a duty to preach democracy and human rights, and to encourage the government to enter into dialogue with the opposition.[59] In fact, in De-cember 1990, parliamentarians elected from Aung San Suu Kyi's party, the National League for Democracy, who had managed to escape, along with the All Burma Students Democratic Front, and the All Burma Young Monks Union formed the Democratic Alliance of Burma,[60] a par-allel government that continues to operate in the rebellious areas of Burma and in exile. The fact that the Young Monks Union has often been involved in agitation and violence against non-Burmese minorities gives one pause. However, in all of Aung San Suu Kyi's writings, speeches, press releases, and actions there has been an unwavering support for the Buddhist ideals of nonviolence and loving-kindness in the struggle against the current oppression.

BUDDHISM AND SLAVERY

INTRODUCTION

SLAVERY IS A LIMITING CASE FOR HUMAN rights, the point where rights for individuals approach zero. Therefore, the ways that Buddhists handled the issues of slavery are important windows on fundamental approaches to human rights. First, however, it should be made clear that slavery as practiced in ancient India was not nearly as brutal an institution as occurred in the Greco-Roman world and later in Christendom.[1] Megasthenes, an ambassador to the Mauryan emperor from the Selucid successors to Alexander the Great, noted around 300 B.C.E. that there was no slavery at all in India. In this he was wrong, because it is known that captives taken in war including women and children were often enslaved, and their descendents would remain as property of their owners. Such slaves could be bought and sold. It was also relatively common for people to sell themselves and their families, or their children, into permanent or temporary bondage in times of famine or to settle heavy indebtedness. Slaves could rise to positions of power and authority and could buy their freedom. It was not permitted for a master to kill a slave, and most were domestic servants and treated rather well. These were so much milder than conditions in the Greco-Roman world that Megasthenes did not even recognize that there was slavery in India.

SLAVERY IN THE SCRIPTURES

WHAT DID LORD Buddha have to say on slavery? To turn to the *Digha Nikaya*, the primary scriptural source for this chapter, there are three substantive references to slavery. In the sutra regarding "The Fruits of the Homeless Life" the Buddha engaged in a dialogue with the Magadhan king Ajjatasattu. To answer the king's question about the fruits of the homeless life of a monk, Lord Buddha presented the hypothetical case of a slave owned by a king. The slave, after reflecting on the hardship of his life in comparison to the godlike existence of his owner, decided to join the Buddhist order and did so, shaving his head and donning the saffron robes. After a while, it was reported to the king that his slave had become a monk and had successfully mastered the discipline. Buddha asked the king, "Would you then say: 'That man must come back and be a slave and work for me as before'?" The king replied, "No indeed, Lord. For we should rise and invite him and press him to receive from us robes, food, lodging, medicines for sickness and requisites, and make arrangements for his proper protection."[2]

Later in the same sutra, as part of his exhaustive answer to the king's question of the benefits of entering the life of a world-renouncer, Lord Buddha described five unhappy circumstances that people often fall into in ordinary life: debt, illness, incarceration, slavery, and dangerous travel. Of the slave he said: "a man might be a slave, not his own master, dependent on another, unable to go where he liked," but once freed he would "rejoice and be glad." He concluded that when a monk had successfully followed the path to fruition, "it as if he were freed from debt, from sickness, from bonds, from slavery, and from the perils of the desert."[3] It is clear from this text that the Buddha saw the life of the slave as a very great misfortune and viewed those in bondage with compassion.

There was no permanent or intrinsic stigma attached to the person who was in servitude. Lord Buddha accepted the king's slave as a full and equal member into the monastic life, and then the king himself offered the full respects due to a monk to his former slave. Note, however, that there was no implication in this sutra that slavery per se needed to be eliminated. Perhaps the doctrine of karma can be used to explain the Buddhists' acceptance of slavery: a slave, after all, was a slave as a result of his or her previous unskillful actions, and could expect an improved situation if his or her behavior warranted it in the future, whether in this life or a future one.[4]

The second reference in the *Digha Nikaya* that touches on slavery is found in "The Marks of a Great Man," which discusses the thirty-two physical marks that Buddhas and wheel-turning kings share. Here a great man is one who in former lives worked for the "welfare of the many . . . thinking how they might increase in faith, morality, learning, renunciation, in Dhamma, in wisdom, in wealth and possessions, in bipeds and quadrupeds, in wives and children, in servants, workers and helpers."[5] The message is curiously mixed. Although the sutra identifies a great man as one who works for the material and spiritual benefit of the many, it unself-consciously includes wives, children, servants and workers in a list of wealth and possessions seen to be desirable for everyone. It was also virtuous to make a gift of one's slaves, and in the famous example of the Bodhisattva Vessantara discussed earlier, giving one's children and wife into slavery was supremely meritorious.

The third reference to slavery in the *Digha Nikaya* occurred in the *Sigalaka Sutta* (Advice to Lay People), which closes with the Buddha outlining the six principle relationships in lay life and spelling out the responsibilities on each side of them. The six are child-parent, student-teacher, husband-wife, friend-friend, master-servant, and layperson-clergy.[6] As to masters and servants (which included slaves), there are also five duties on each side. The master should arrange the work according to the strength of the workers, supply them with food and wages, take care of them when ill, share delicacies with them from time to time, and let them off work when it is time. It is also mentioned in the duties of a wife that she should be kind to the servants. In turn the worker should get up before the master, go to bed after him, take only what is given, complete the work well, and praise the boss. Each side has reciprocal duties to the other, proportioned to the station of the individual. The point is not to demand one's rights, but to perform one's duty in such a way as to ensure a harmonious, prosperous community where dharma can flourish.

This was the traditional Buddhist position on slavery, reflected in Theravada and Mahayana scriptures and cultural institutions.[7] In Mahayana scriptures, slaves were included in the standard lists of what a notable man would possess and give away. The Lotus Sutra, a Mahayana work from India which became the preeminent Buddhist text of China and Japan, quoted Lord Buddha saying that, as a bodhisattva perfecting the virtue of giving, he never begrudged bestowing "elephants, horses, or the seven jewels; nor realms or walled cities [including the people therein, of course]; nor wife nor children, slaves and servants, nor head, eyes, marrow, trunk, and flesh, arms and legs; not begrudging bodily life it-self."[8] Slavery was an accepted part of civil society, but all men and women were seen as spiritual equals in that every person had the poten-tial to become enlightened, and there was duty to treat slaves decently ac-cording to dharma.

The story cited above from the *Digha Nikaya* about the king whose slave became a monk suggested that slaves could be easily admitted into the order of monks. However, the *vinaya* section of the canon, which rec-ords the rules and the early case law that bind the monastics, states that the practice was later changed by the Buddha. The case that forbids the ordination of slaves, which is presented in full in the readings section of this volume,[9] comes from a section of the *vinaya* that explains why vari-ous classes of persons may not be ordained. In general, the pattern of these cases is that Lord Buddha ruled against the ordination of criminals, debtors, soldiers, escaped prisoners, minors, and other categories of indi-viduals after there were complaints from the laity that someone had joined the order to avoid his or worldly obligations. King Bimbasara, monarch of the Magadhan Empire, on becoming a patron of the early or-der, ruled that "No one is to do any harm to those who are ordained [into the Buddhist order]; well taught is their doctrine; let them lead a holy life for the sake of the complete extinction of suffering," thereby protecting the monk or nun from the arm of the law. The case in question was one where the owners of a slave, who had become a monk, were stopped from taking him back due to the king's decree. They complained and Lord Buddha adjudicated that, thereafter, no slave could receive ordination. Of course, a redeemed or released slave could join freely, and would be treated as an equal. In general, great care was taken to avoid those things that would undermine the respect and support given to the monastic or-ders by their lay supporters, and especially not to lose royal protection.

Although slavery in ancient India was less terrible than that of Greece or Rome, Buddhist texts show that some owners sorely abused their slaves with overwork, mutilation, sexual attack, and even death.[10] That Bud-dhist masters were under a duty to treat their slaves and servants decently, as taught in the *Sigalaka Sutta* reviewed above, and in other Theravada and Mahayana admonitions, may have provided some protection. How-ever, once again, there was no attempt to make radical social reforms, and canonical texts simply accepted slavery as part of the landscape, so to speak.

SLAVERY IN BUDDHIST INDIA

IT IS CLEAR then that slavery was not an "issue" to Buddha, to the early Buddhists, or indeed throughout the history of Buddhist lands. In fact, very early on in India, the Buddhist order itself came to own slaves as shown by inscriptions found on Buddhist structures and from pilgrims' reports. This may seem to be somewhat strange since Lord Buddha taught that world-renouncers were to keep themselves free from all but the most basic possessions. In the scriptures there are stock lists of things that monks and nuns ought not to own, as possessions are only encumbrances on the way to salvation. For example, the sermon on "The Fruits of the Homeless Life" in the *Digha Nikaya* included the following items which a monk must not accept: silver or gold, uncooked grain, raw meat, women or girls, bondmen or bondwomen, sheep or goats, fowls or swine, elephants, cattle, horses or mares, and cultivated or waste fields.[11] These things were not bad in themselves; they were what successful householders would normally acquire. However, for the monk or nun, they were encumbrances.

In the early years, when monks and nuns moved constantly, these rules could be kept with little problem. However, as time went on, settled communities came to be the rule, and donors, including royal benefactors, gave property, silver and gold, and other goods for the use of the community. So that the monks and nuns would not break the rules, a lay official (*kappiya-karaka*), the "legitimizer"[12] or the "one who makes arrangements,"[13] received the forbidden items on behalf of the monastery. Once monasteries became elaborate institutions, with endowed lands, keeping them up became quite a responsibility. The *vinaya* and other traditions stressed that monks and nuns could not farm or do any productive work appropriate to a householder. Thus land gifts came with bound laborers included, and wealthy donors gave slaves to work for the benefit of the dharma and, of course, to accrue merit for themselves. Like any other slaves, monastery slaves could not be ordained until after they were freed. In large monastic establishments, there could be a number of lay officials to manage the numerous workers and complicated affairs of the institution. These officials were the legal owners of the slaves and other property and probably took most of the responsibility for day-to-day management although the clerics might be involved.

KING ASOKA AND SLAVERY IN BUDDHIST INDIA

ASOKA, THE GREATEST monarch of ancient India, ruled the Mauryan Empire in the third century B.C.E. He became attached to the three jewels of Buddhism and attempted to rule the largest and most successful empire of traditional India using the principles of dharma. The various edicts that he inscribed in prominent places throughout the realm provided a record of his deeds and his political ideals. Three of these inscriptions deal directly with slaves and are similar in content.

> Whatever good deeds I have done the people have imitated, and they have followed them as a model. In doing so, they have progressed and will progress in obedience to parents and teachers, in respect for elders, in courtesy to priests and ascetics, to the poor and distressed, and even to slaves and servants.[14]

"Proper treatment of slaves and servants" was the recommendation to further dharma in the other two direct references to slaves in the inscriptions.[15] The message of these passages was very consistent with what the Buddha taught in his sermon on the proper behavior for laymen.

Indirectly, slavery was touched upon in the famous inscription where Asoka described the misery that attended his conquest of the Kalinga nation.[16] He mentioned that some 150,000 persons were taken captive, which in the context of ancient India meant that they were taken into slavery. In his lamentation and regret about the suffering he caused the people of Kalinga, there was not a hint that Asoka ever considered liberating the slaves taken there. Similarly, in several of his inscriptions he noted that prisoners were pardoned, but he never boasted of freeing slaves. This position was consistent with both the scriptures and general Buddhist practice in India—one had a duty to treat slaves and other relatively powerless people with respect and even courtesy, but reforms like abolition were not considered.

SLAVERY IN SRI LANKA

THERE IS NOT a great deal of detailed information available about the details of day-to-day management of monasteries and monastic workers in ancient India. However, in the case of Sri Lanka, enough records have survived to give a reasonably clear picture of how the monastic economy functioned with slaves in the ninth and tenth centuries of the Common Era. In the largest, best-endowed monasteries, there were elaborate management structures, which included laity and monks alike on the steering committee. Monks were directly involved in the administration, and in fact received remuneration in gold for the their services, which goes against the *vinaya* rules. Another violation of *vinaya* principles became customary in Sri Lanka after a king in the first century B.C.E. gave a monastery as a personal gift to a monk. Down to the present day, some monasteries are the personal property of their abbot, who determines who should receive it on his death.

Some of the monastic estates were so large and powerful that they had their own systems of justice for the villages they controlled. From the second century C.E. on, monasteries behaved like any other large business enterprise, buying and selling, lending and borrowing, with monks taking an active role in the transactions. When a monastery was given land and villages, the labor of the people living there also was bound to a greater or lesser degree to the religious proprietors. Inscriptions and chronicles from the seventh through ninth centuries show that monasteries owned both hereditary and bought slaves. Some were captives of war donated by kings and some were crafts workers and laborers. Poor people sometimes bound themselves to monasteries in order to make a living, and some were forced to sell their children into slavery by debt. Inscriptions show that some slaves bought their freedom, at a considerable price, from their monastic owners. Although many Theravada monks in Sri Lanka entered into various aspects of commerce regularly, it does not seem that they owned slaves directly as personal property. Slaves including those owned by monasteries were not allowed to be ordained until freed. Slavery as practiced by monasteries seemed to have paralleled the system of slavery in society at large where it was accepted without question.

Probably in emulation of the extraordinary generosity of Prince Vessantara of the *Jataka* tales, a Sri Lankan king in the first century C.E. gave himself, his wife, and two sons as slaves to the monks, and then redeemed the gift with a massive money donation.[17] This sort of fictive slavery to the sangha became a popular way to make merit for nobles and wealthy commoners in the medieval period.[18] While giving slaves for the use of monasteries was very beneficial to the donor, freeing slaves was an even more efficacious way to make merit. A fourteenth-century monk wrote "that in order to liberate oneself from evil tendencies one should liberate slaves."[19] There are stories about poor men who sold their children into debt slavery in order to make gifts of food to monks. One even used the money he had saved to redeem his daughter after six months' hard labor in order to buy a meal for a monk who was in danger of going hungry for a day.[20] It seems that fictive slavery was out of the reach of the poor.

SLAVERY IN SIAM (THAILAND)

GENERAL CONSIDERATIONS

Slavery was known in Buddhist Siam at least as early as the Sukhothai dynasty (c. 1240–1378),[21] and was not seen to be in conflict with Buddhist values and teachings. In 1805, King Rama I, the first monarch of the Chakri dynasty, which continues today as the ruling family, codified the ancient laws of the preceding Ayutthyan regime, which showed that the complex conditions of slavery were relatively harsh.[22] Jeremias van Vliet, a trader for the Dutch East India Company, a long-time resident at Ayutthya, recorded in 1640 that a particularly cruel and capricious king who ruled at the turn of the seventeenth century had some 1600 royal boatmen burnt alive because of a docking error.[23]

Under the traditional monarchy all Siamese save the king were less than free. This hierarchical structure was highly codified in the *sakdina* system, which assigned a numerical value to everyone in the country according to his or her position.[24] The Thai term *sakdina* comes from *sakti*, related to the Sanskrit word for power, and *na* (mark) and literally means "power" or "dignity" mark. The *sakdina* number indicated the nominal amount of arable land that every person or position was allowed by the king, and all this was codified as early as 1454 C.E.[25] The king had infinite value, and the highest princes had a value of 100,000. Thirteen lower noble classes ranged from 50,000 down to 800 points. Then there were one mixed noble-commoner class with a range of 1000 down to 200 points, four commoner classes ranging from 800 down to 10 points, and four groups (beggars, mendicants, slaves, and descendents of slaves) all with a value of 5. Monks were also assigned sakdina grades according to their position in the sangha and their individual attainments in dharma with a minimum number of 200 for novices who knew nothing of the doctrine.[26]

The Siamese legal system was fully integrated with *sakdina* principles, with compensation for physical injury being calculated from tables that recognized forty-two levels of damage and twenty-seven different levels of *sakdina*. The amount of court award for a given injury was proportional to the injured person's place on the *sakdina* scale. For example a noble at 10,000 *sakdina*, whose limb had been broken unlawfully would be awarded between 6,280,000 and 8,792,000 cowry shells, while a slave (5 *sakdina* units) could receive from between 50,000 and 70,000 cowries.[27]

The general term for slave in Thai was derived from the Sanskrit word for slave or servant found in the Buddhist scriptures.[28] The 1805 codification of the laws on slavery described seven licit ways that slaves could be acquired: through indebtedness; from the children of slaves living in the household of the master; by gift from their parents; by gift from a third party; by redeeming a condemned criminal from execution or from a fine; by feeding someone in a time of want; and by capture in war.[29] Some crimes were punished by sentences of enslavement for the guilty person and even for the family as well.[30] All slaves were not equal in their degree of servitude. The least bound class was the redeemable debt slaves, also called fiduciary slaves. In the mid-nineteenth century, Bishop Pallegoix, the head of the Roman Catholic Church in Siam, estimated that more than one quarter of the total population of the country was made up of slaves, the vast majority of whom were fiduciary slaves.[31] He commented that slaves made up the bulk of the wealth of the propertied classes. Slaves were used in all aspects of the economy save government administration and mining.[32] Other classes of slaves, like the many monastery and war slaves, were much more deeply bound to servitude than fiduciary slaves.

SLAVERY ASSESSED

Obviously, the Siamese system of slavery was very complex and different in kind from the harsh form of chattel slavery practiced in contemporary European empires and the United States. Slaves were not a separate caste, absolutely segregated from civil society. In Siam, everyone from the highest noble to lowest slave was tied together in a system of mutual relationship, all subject to the king. As noted above, in the *sakdina* classification the human value of a slave, even of most extreme form of absolute slave, was not zero; all slaves had a certain number of legal protections. Although corporal punishment was permitted on an increasing scale according to the degree of bondage, the slave owner could be tried for homicide should he or she kill a slave. Furthermore, the owner had to provide compensation for permanent injuries incurred in a beating. Contracts for debt slaves were recorded and regulated by the state with maximum values set for buying out one's freedom. Marriage for slaves had the same legal status as for free men. If a master should be convicted of committing adultery with the wife of his slave, then the slave husband would be manumitted and his wife as well, if she chose to come along.[33] Slaves were granted automatic freedom on becoming monks; however, to join the order, it was necessary to have permission from their masters, which was consistent with ancient practice and the teaching of Lord Buddha in the canon. Freeing slaves so that they could become ordained monks was a particularly powerful way for the owners to gain religious merit, and such ex-slaves retained their freedom should they decide to leave the order. Once inside, *sakdina* ranking was put aside; monastic seniority and spiritual attainment became the measures of worth.

Western observers in Thailand often noted that slavery was very gentle there in comparison to the kind of slavery they were familiar with at home. In 1854, Monseigneur Pallegoix, Roman Catholic prelate of Siam, wrote that slaves were treated very humanely in the kingdom, comparing their lot to domestic servants in Europe.[34] Sir John Bowering, the British ambassador to the Siamese court and himself a noted abolitionist, in 1856 commented:

> Slavery is the condition of a large part of the population of Siam—not absolute slavery, perhaps, as formerly existed in the West Indies, or now exists in the United States, but such as implies a dependence far less tolerable than that which belongs to domestic servitude. . . . I saw few examples of harshness in the treatment of slaves.[35]

Bowering quoted "a gentleman resident at Bangkok" who believed that Siamese slaves were actually treated better than domestic servants in England and noted that the worst treated slaves in Siam were those owned by the Christian community.

Still, the state of slavery was negative enough. In an oath taken by witnesses in court, we find the following passage, outlining the consequences of giving false testimony:

> [M]ay I after death migrate into the body of a slave, and suffer all the hardship and pains attending the worst state of such a being during a period of years measured by the sands of the four seas: or may I animate the body of an animal or beast during five hundred generations; or be born an

hermaphrodite five hundred times; or endure in the body of a deaf, blind, dumb houseless, every species of loathsome disease during the same number of generations: and then may I be hurried to [a hell].[36]

Clearly the company that slavery keeps in this list shows that it was not a preferred fate. This oath also illustrates that slavery was seen as a punishment for one's own misdeeds, in this case, perjury.

Absolute slaves, indeed, were simply another form of property to be bought and sold like elephants, horses, cattle, gold, silver, boats, tea, or rice, as one of the Siamese laws put it. When slavery was abolished in Burma after the British conquest (1885–1886), runaway slaves from the border areas of Thailand fled for refuge in Burma. The profusion of laws concerning runaway slaves and the many different abuses of slaves that were mentioned in the law codes suggest that the lives of Siamese slaves could be very grim indeed. Before the nineteenth century absolute slaves had very little protection in law from harsh treatment and overwork. Still, it is true that nineteenth-century sources agreed that the lot of the slave in Siam was surprisingly good.[37] While it would be tempting to attribute this state of affairs to the influence of Theravada Buddhist ideals of compassion and the duties taught to treat subjects and slaves well, the relatively harsh treatment of slaves in the adjacent country Burma, which was also a Theravada kingdom, prevents such an easy answer.[38]

THE GRADUAL ABOLITION OF SLAVERY IN SIAM

Throughout the nineteenth and into the twentieth century, under the kings of the Chakri dynasty, there was a continual movement of liberalization in the matters of slavery and corvée labor. Lingat provided the most detailed account of this process, reviewing the law codes and decisions of the early nineteenth century that regulated slavery and the twenty-seven different decrees and statutes promulgated between 1858 and 1923 that step-by-step dismantled the legal support for forced labor, debt bondage, and outright slavery.[39] For the purposes of this chapter, a very brief summary is all that is needed. In the realm of Rama I (r. 1772–1809), the law of slavery from Ayutthyan times was revised, and later the king decreed that the children of the absolute slaves, should become redeemable slaves, who were treated with the most leniency. By the time of Rama III* (r. 1824–1851), redeemable debt slaves far outnumbered the other sorts, and by all accounts fared rather well.

The great king Mongkut, or Rama IV* (r. 1851–1868), was a very able and learned man, who learned English and Latin from missionaries and who was the leading Buddhist scholar of the era. Before becoming king, he served for twenty-seven years as a monk, reforming the clergy and founding the most strict and elite order of monks. Mongkut worked carefully to reform and modernize the economy and government of Siam, moving very carefully not to alienate traditionalist subjects. He successfully minimized the incursions of British and French colonial imperialists on his borders. In the last year of his life, he repealed the ancient law that allowed a husband to sell his wife or other dependents into slavery without their consent, or even without their knowledge.[40] This decree also abolished the right of parents to sell their children without their consent, but did nothing to abolish the institution of slavery itself.[41]

Much earlier in his reign, in the context of a case in favor of a girl forced to marry against her will, King Mongkut showed his distaste for the custom that allowed parents to sell their children into bondage:

> The fact is undeniable that people of lower birth are more interested in acquiring wealth than in furthering the welfare of their children. As a result, children, who should receive nothing but kindness and mercy from their parents, are oft consigned by the latter to miserable slavery in mere exchange for gold and silver. Therefore, the rule of free will must be made applicable so as to prevent havoc being brought upon the persons of women off sold into bondage by their parents.[42]

Mongkut's legal reasoning here reflects the general Buddhist principle that parents had a duty to provide for their children with care, but he raised no particularly Buddhist arguments or reasons against slavery as an institution. The king knew his Buddhist texts very well, and they taught it was permissible, and sometimes commendable, for a husband to deliver his dependents into slavery.

By the time of Mongkut, economic life in Siam was very different from that at the beginning of the nineteenth century. Land was no longer cheap, having been developed into small privately held rice farms, a cash economy had become predominant, and labor was at premium. "Slavery and bondage under such circumstances lost their economical basis and ceased to be an indispensable institution; thus in the course of time they could be abolished without any disturbance being caused in the system of production in the country."[43] It had become clear that the corvée was a very wasteful way to finance public works in a modernizing economy, and under King Mongkut the first steps to replace it with wage labor had been taken.[44]

Mongkut's son Chulalongkorn (Rama V*, r. 1868–1910) is remembered in Thailand as Mahachulalongkorn, or Chulalongkorn the Great.[45] Because his father was aware of the importance of understanding Western powers, Chulalongkorn learned English in the palace school under an American governess and was encouraged to learn as much as he could about Europe and America as well as being given a fine classical Siamese education. When Mongkut died in 1868, his son was too young to govern, so a regent guided Siam for a period of six years. During this time of apprenticeship, Chulalongkorn travelled to the Dutch East Indies and to the British territories of Penang, Rangoon, Singapore, and India to get first hand knowledge of modern administration. On taking power in 1874, Chulalongkorn immediately set out to make major reforms in the Siamese tax system, judiciary, and government administration as well as moving to abolish absolute forms of slavery.[46]

He set out his thinking on slavery in a position paper presented to his advisory council on July 12, 1874:

> I feel that children born to slaves in their creditor's houses, who are slaves as from the time of delivery and are worth something even beyond 100, have not been treated kindly. Children thus born have nothing to do with their parents' wrong doing. The parents have not only sold themselves into slavery but also dragged their innocent children into lifetime slavery and suffering on their behalf. But to emancipate them straight away now would put them into the danger of being neglected and being left to die by themselves, since unkind creditors, seeing no use in letting mothers look after their children, will put these mothers to work.[47]

Accordingly, he proposed a system whereby such children born into slavery would have their value reduced at a yearly rate from the ages of eight to twenty-one, when their value would be zero and they would automatically be emancipated. The king was concerned that liberated slaves would be vulnerable to reenslavement under the existing tax system and proposed reforms to protect them.

On August 21, 1874, Mahachulalongkorn proclaimed an act for the gradual abolition of hereditary slavery in Siam.[48] This law generally followed the reasoning and method laid out in the earlier discussion paper and was retroactive to 1868, the year that he assumed the throne under the regency. Although there did not appear to be much opposition to this law, other reforms, to change government structures, provoked a serious reaction, and there was real danger of a coup. Accordingly, Chula-longkorn reiterated that his reform of slavery was to be slowly imple-mented in order not to upset the country too much.

As it turned out, it took more than thirty years for the legal basis of slavery to be eradicated in central Siam, with the law of 1905 which emancipated the monastery slaves who were excluded from the earlier acts. Even though some of the slaves did not want to be free at the time,[49] Thais count emancipation as one of the greatest accomplishments of Rama V. As Lingat noted, one of his greatest titles to fame is that he rec-ognized both the necessity of eliminating slavery if Siam were to be a modern country and the dangers of moving too quickly.[50]

What motivated Mahachulalongkorn? His primary inspiration was probably his father, King Mongkut, who had stopped the practice of sell-ing one's dependents without their permission and who expressed more discomfort with the practice of selling of one's children than did Chula-longkorn himself. While Chulalongkorn noted the internal opposition to abolition, from both the slave owners and some slaves, he was also aware of the social and political disruptions that the precipitous emancipation of the serfs in Russia and the slaves in the United States had recently caused. One of the fears in Siam was that newly freed slaves would be worse off than before, with no means to support themselves. Accordingly, Chula-longkorn asked wealthy Siamese to help in the emancipation process by donating the required redemption fees for slaves. He set an example in this respect by making a generous gift of money that freed some forty-four slaves on his twenty-fourth birthday and by providing them with land grants and the necessary tools to make a living.[51] In general, the king showed great interest in the welfare of his subjects and took unprece-dented steps to mingle with ordinary people to find out how they lived and what their problems were. No doubt some of his concern for slaves and others came from his having been taught the traditional duties and qualities of an ideal Buddhist king and his desire to practice compassion, the prime Buddhist virtue.

It has been suggested that abolition was done "mainly with a view to Siam's image abroad."[52] Perhaps there is something to this: His Ameri-can teacher may have influenced Chulalongkorn's thinking, and many Thai intellectuals of the era were attracted to western ideas.[53] Indeed,

Chulalongkorn did embark on his reforms shortly after visiting European territories in Asia. Later his first voyage to Europe in 1897 seemed to revivify his enthusiasm for reforms. In July 1898, the king met with one of his Belgian advisors, and the discussion turned to the slow pace of the abolition of slavery following the law of 1874. Chulalongkorn was reported to have said: "I met opposition not only from the slave masters but from the slaves themselves who dreaded being thrown on themselves entirely and having to earn their own living."[54] When the advisor suggested doubling the rate that the value of a slave would decrease in order to speed up the elimination of debt slavery, the king agreed that it was time to do it, and shortly implemented the new rates.

It has already been pointed out that bonded labor in Siam was far from efficient and was seen as a brake on the progress toward a modern economy, which would have provided good reasons for the king to move against it. At the same time, slaves formed a major part of the wealth of the nobility and traditionally were the means for conspicuous consumption and to manifest personal power. Therefore, since one of Mahachulalongkorn's prime objectives was to increase and centralize power in the office of the king, it was beneficial to him to eliminate slavery, a major source of prestige for potential rivals.[55] Furthermore, he—the central government—would benefit from collecting taxes from freed slaves, since slaves paid none. The arguments against the continuation of slavery put forward by Mahachulalongkorn and his advisors were based on general principles of fairness and on the desirability of modernizing the country to secure her independence and to advance economically. There seem to have been no particularly Buddhist discussions that advocated abolition.

CHINESE BUDDHISM AND SLAVERY

BUDDHISM FOUND ITS way into China and then adapted to become an integral part of Chinese culture, in a centuries-long process where the religion grew to fit into its new environment and in turn profoundly changed Chinese thought and life. Non-Chinese Buddhist teachers entered China from Central Asia as an adjunct to the trade carried out along the fabled Silk Road sometime in the later years of the Han Dynasty (206 B.C.E.–C.E. 220). Buddhist ideas and practices were very different from Chinese norms, as different perhaps as the Sanskrit language of the Buddhist scriptures is from Chinese. Needless to say, translation of texts, ideas, institutions, and practices was neither easy nor quickly accomplished.

One aspect of Chinese culture that the Buddhists had no trouble adapting to was slavery. There is considerable evidence that, just as in India and Sri Lanka, slaves and bound labor formed an essential part of the monastic economy. Large clerical establishments with estates attached to them as endowments arose from the generosity of wealthy donors. These establishments followed the normal Chinese practice of using slaves and other nonfree workers as a matter of course.[56] The *vinaya* rules that governed the lives of monks clearly forbade the practice of agriculture. They could not dig in the ground as that caused harm to the creatures living in the soil, they could not cut trees in order not to injure the sprits that made their home in trees, nor could they water plants as that would harm the small creatures that teem in standing water. Monks were expected to follow all these rules by donors, rules that were enforced by the central government after they assumed responsibility for regulating the sangha. Accordingly, the monasteries turned to slaves, tenant farmers, and novices to work their lands and do the other forbidden tasks necessary to maintain their establishments. Those who did this work were called "the pure people" because they spared the monks performing impure acts.

Monks and monasteries in China were receiving slaves as early as the second half of the fourth century C.E. as a donation of three slaves to a monk show. A Chinese version of the *vinaya* that dates to the early fifth century C.E. permitted "human goods" to serve the monks and to tend the property as well as all sorts of "nonhuman" livestock for the benefit of the community.[57] It is not clear whether or not such servants were directly under the control of ordained personnel or lay officials. In a will dated 865 C.E., a nun left a slave to her niece. It was noted that this slave had been born into the nun's family and was her only possession.[58] At the beginning of the sixth century, a Chinese writer estimated that there were some 500 Buddhist monasteries in Nanking, with some 100,000 monks and nuns. They were very wealthy establishments, and it was reported that they had an unspecified number of slaves, obliged to wear green garments like all slaves of the period.[59] A ninth-century C.E. document estimated that there were some 150,000 slaves and another 250,000 serfs and peasants bound to Buddhist establishments in China.[60]

The vast monastic holdings, all tax exempt, had serious repercussions on government revenues, and the number of slaves and bound laborers they controlled affected government corvées and military drafts. Accordingly, from time to time, the state moved to reduce the wealth of the Buddhist establishments. Emperor We-tsung's "Edict on the Suppression of Buddhism" in C.E. 845 complained that the Buddhists had extravagantly wasted the wealth of the nation on building elaborate temples, which threatened "to outshine the imperial palace itself," and undermined the nation by drawing away men and women to a nonproductive life of celibacy in the monasteries. "In destroying law and injuring mankind indeed nothing surpasses this doctrine!" The emperor therefore decided to destroy Buddhism in the country, which he failed to do, but Buddhist organizations and prestige were sorely damaged. This was the worst persecution of the faith in China until the even worse depredations under Chairman Mao in the twentieth century. The emperor's account of what was done gives some idea of how powerful and wealthy the monasteries had become and how many slaves and serfs they owned.

> The temples of the empire which have been demolished number over 4,600; 26,500 monks and nuns have been returned to lay life and enrolled as subject to the Twice-A-Year Tax; over 40,000 privately established temples have been destroyed, releasing thirty or forty million *ch'ing* of fertile, top grade land and 150,000 male and female servants who will become subject to the Twice-A-Year Tax.[61]

Where did the monks and nuns acquire their slaves? According to Gernet, monastic slaves were given by the state from those condemned to death, from ordinary prisoners, and from public slaves. The monasteries purchased other slaves. Another major source of temple slaves was the impoverished mass of peasants who had lost their land to large landholders, including the monasteries, and debtors who were willing to sell themselves into bondage.[62] The provenance of slaves, therefore, was quite the same as it was in South Asia, as was the work they did: the construction and cleaning of monasteries and the labor for the fields and gardens. In the sixth century, most slaves were obtained by breeding them, and many were ordained on reaching the proper age. However, in 517 the government of the northern Wei kingdom banned the ordination of slaves and ruled that anyone who violated this would be laicized and that those ordained would revert to slave status.[63] By the twelfth century, there were a number of secular officials who complained that the monks had far too many slaves, some of whom had been reduced to slavery by unfair taxation.[64]

A seventh century edifying text mentioned the bad karma that accrued to a monk who misappropriated monastic goods for his own use. The moral drawn was that any monk who misused the common goods for his own benefit would as a minimum consequence come back as a domestic animal or a slave, and at worst would burn in a hell. Other similar texts from the same period made similar points.[65] One of them told of two monks who were eventually reborn as domestic slaves in their previous monastery because one of them gave ten pieces of cloth from the common store to the other. The karmic consequences were quite appropriate; the punishment for misusing the property of the monastery was to come back as property of the monastery—a domestic beast or a domestic slave. These Chinese examples provide very good evidence of how unproblematic slavery was in Buddhist thought. After all, to a large extent, according to the laws of karma, a slave was a slave due to his or her previous unskillful acts.

CONCLUSION

HAVING LOOKED AT slavery in several key Buddhist times and places, and finding that Buddhists did not see slavery as an important ethical issue, the next step will be to consider what contemporary writers on Buddhist ethics have had to say on the issue. The short answer is that, with one exception, they have said very little. This may be because slavery is no longer a live issue, having been abolished in all Buddhist lands, or perhaps it is because Buddhists traditionally did not see slavery in itself as an ethical problem.

In Peter Harvey's important recent survey, *An Introduction to Buddhist Ethics* (2000), the only reference to slavery was a single paragraph. He noted that Theravada and Mahayana scriptures advocated treating workers and servants well, that Asoka did not abolish slavery but stressed that slaves should be treated decently, and that slavery in Thailand was not as degrading to those in bondage as was the practice in the West.[66] Harvey did not raise questions of whether or not slavery is consistent with Buddhist principles.

Damien Keown was the only essayist to discuss slavery in *Buddhism and Human Rights*. The two sentences he wrote were:

A right not to be held in slavery, for example is implicit in the canonical prohibition on trade in human beings [*Anguttara Sutta* iii, 208]. These rights are the extrapolation of what is due under Dharma; they have not been "imported" into Buddhism but were implicitly present.[67]

For an extended theoretical discussion that explains why the present study generally opposes Keown's extrapolation of rights from duties in Buddhism, please refer to chapter 2 above. In this specific case, there is an additional problem of interpreting the scripture passage cited. This well-known text lists the five livelihoods that are not permitted to Buddhists because their practice either directly violated the five precepts or encouraged and abetted such violation. Peter Harvey glossed the verse as follows: " 'Wrong livelihood' is trade in: weapons (being an arms salesman), living beings (keeping animals for slaughter), meat (being a slaughterer, meat salesman, hunter or fisherman), alcoholic drink, or poison."

As Harvey noted, this prohibition against trading in living beings has only recently been extended by Buddhists to include such activities as trading in human beings for the purpose of prostitution.[68] In at least one case, a contemporary Asian Buddhist writer has interpreted this admonition as being directed against slavery. The writer was a high-ranking monk in the Thai Buddhist hierarchy, Phra Nyanavarotama, who wrote: "[I]n [the *Anguttara Sutta*, iii, 208] there is mentioned one of the ways of earning a livelihood that lay Buddhist disciples are not allowed to do. This is to trade in human beings (i.e., slaves)."[69] While this does not do violence to the text as "living beings" certainly include "human beings," Buddhists until the twentieth century never took it as a reason to abolish slavery. Slave trading existed, in some form or another, wherever Buddhists owned slaves. On the same note, the inclusion of trading in arms in the list of wrong livelihoods did not lead Buddhists to call for disbanding their countries' armed forces.

Phra Nyanavarotama, in his single page discussion of slavery, presented the novel argument that, although it persisted in the Kingdom of Thailand until 2448 in the Buddhist Era (C.E. 1905), in fact Lord Buddha had abolished slavery in his own lifetime. "It was clear that the Buddha as the initiator of this abolition project had tried to do whatever was possible for him to promote human dignity and abolish slavery."[70] In support of this, he adduced the text against Buddhists trading in living beings just discussed and the *vinaya* rules discussed at the beginning of this chapter, which forbade monks and nuns to own slaves or to accept them for ordination. However, as argued above, these texts did not at all advocate the abolition of slavery in the reading of traditional Buddhists.

The most extended discussion of slavery in the context of Buddhism and human rights was Dr. L.P.N. Perera's discussion of the fourth article of the United Nations Universal Declaration of Human Rights regarding anti-slavery.[71] His major point was that slavery was fundamentally incompatible with key Buddhist concepts like no-soul, universal flux, interdependence, and concern for the good of the whole of society. "With such a philosophical outlook and psychological attuning, there is no justification in Buddhist philosophy for slavery in any form." With this as a starting point, it would be difficult to explain the history of slavery in Buddhist countries, but Perera avoided this claiming, "Slavery, as understood in the West, never existed in the East."

What of Perera's claim that slavery as understood in the West never existed in the East? In the first place, "West" and "East," only mask the complexity of the issues involved. Degrees and structures of bondage, servitude, slavery, and so forth varied immensely from era to era and place to place in both East and West. Undoubtedly slavery in various forms did persist in most Buddhist countries well into modern times. In fact, extralegal forms of debt bondage are still prevalent in South and Southeast Asia, with individuals selling themselves or their dependents into service. Perera acknowledged that Indian Buddhist texts list the various ways that a person can be "reduced to servitude"—capture in war, as the result of legal penalty, voluntary servitude for atonement or for debt, and being born to someone in servitude. He also commented that Asoka enslaved the Kalingans and taught that there was a duty to treat slaves decently. While he stressed that former slaves were welcomed as monks and nuns by the Buddha, he failed to mention that there was a restriction against ordaining slaves until they had been freed by their masters. One wonders why he did not mention the slavery that was common in his own country, Sri Lanka, where monasteries as well as lay Buddhists often were slave masters.

In discussing the *Sigalaka Sutta*, Perara noted that it says slaves and servants should be well treated in a spirit of "mutual love, trust, and service" but also insisted that the overall social teaching of Buddhism was the equality of all humanity. Surely slavery and egalitarianism are self-contradictory. There is no contradiction when, as in the present study, Buddhist traditional social philosophy is understood to be based on hierarchical relationships, governed by mutual duties and responsibilities of socially unequal persons, all under the umbrella of dharma. This is nowhere clearer than in Buddhist legal systems. For example, in Thailand, a Theravada country, there was the *sakdina* schema, where individuals were given numerical values to determine legal rewards and penalties according to their social status. Tibet, a Vajrayana country on the other end of the Buddhist spectrum, had its own forms of bonded labor[72] and followed the *tong* system, whereby people were assigned different values for "blood money," compensation in murder cases, depending on where they stood on the nine-level social pyramid.[73]

Perera's attempt to say Buddhists opposed slavery from a philosophy of social equality can not convince. However, loving-kindness, compassion, and nonviolence, which he also cited, provide a strong Buddhist base against slavery. The situation of a slave in relation to his or her master was intrinsically one of suffering, as Buddha himself noted in his sermon on "The Fruits of the Homeless Life."[74] Wisdom and loving-kindness guiding the Buddhist in his or her duty of compassion and nonharm, point to the abolition of slavery. There is no need to import non-Buddhist notions of rights to achieve this goal.

8

BUDDHISM AND CASTE

INTRODUCTION

LORD BUDDHA RATHER CLEARLY addressed the caste system, one of the defining social structures of the Hindu tradition. While it is not certain exactly what form of the system prevailed in India where Gautama grew up and lived, there are a number of references to issues that arose from it in the Buddhist canon. The basic idea of the Hindu caste system is that all human beings belong to a particular social slot by virtue of birth, and that one's social duties, responsibilities, and benefits are clearly laid out according to one's position in the hierarchy. Every particular rebirth into the social system is understood as being the fruit of one's personal karma in his or her previous existences, which in effect means that whatever one gets one deserves.

In practice, in India the caste system is very complex indeed, with many local variations, but the basic idea is that there are four classes, which were established in primal times by divine activity. Therefore they are immutable, holy, and understood to be a fundamental expression of the law that governs the whole of creation (dharma). To break the laws of caste is not only a human error to be punished here and now, it also violates the divine order. Functionally the four classes from the highest down are priests (*Brahmins*), warriors or rulers (*Ksatriyas*), merchants (*Vaisyas*), and servants (*Sudras*). The Sudras at the base were there to serve all the others.

Lower than the four classes, there were also the "outcastes," groups who were said to have come from those who violated the laws of dharma, by improper intermarriage for example, and were therefore thrust out from society altogether. Outcastes were considered so polluted that to touch them would corrupt a member of a higher class; even to be touched by their shadow could render another person unclean. These so-called untouchables were restricted to the dirtiest work of toilet cleaning, removing dead beasts and tanning their hides, scavenging, and the like. They could not use wells used by others, lived outside of the village proper, could only wear clothing made of cast-off rags, could not enter Hindu temples, and were generally treated as inferiors. Since they were thought to have achieved their lowly condition due to their own previous sins, they were scorned as moral outcastes as well, who deserved their miserable lot. This description of the outcastes is drawn from the situation in modern India, and most likely some of the detail would not be true of the India of Lord Buddha. However, outcastes did exist in his time.[1]

While Lord Buddha was not primarily a social reformer, he rejected some aspects of the caste system. In the *Agganna Sutta*[2] he scorned the Hindu orthodox view that the priestly class was born from the mouth of divinity, the warriors from the arms, the merchants from the thighs, and the servants from the feet, noting that "the wives of Brahmins . . . menstruate and become pregnant, have babies and give suck" just like all women from every class. Later in the same sermon, in his myth of the origin of human society, he taught that the first rulers were elected and above the priestly class. Humanity evolved as part of a karmic process rather than coming to be through divine creation. In the *Esukari Sutta*,[3] he dismissed the fundamental premise of the caste system, that the very nature of the lower orders is to serve the Brahmins, as a self-serving prescription on the part of the priestly class. Lord Buddha taught service should be undertaken not as a matter of birth, but after considering whether or not the service would make one a better person. This was very much attuned to a fundamental principle in Buddhist ethics, that an act is good (skillful) if it helps those involved on the path to enlightenment, or bad (unskillful) if it leads in a wayward direction.

Both these sermons insist that the worth of an individual is to be measured by the quality of his or her deeds. There are good people of very base birth, and very base people from the aristocracy. Whoever follows the precepts of morality is a noble person, regardless of birth. Similarly men and women of all social levels may develop purified minds. In these documents, and throughout the teachings of the Buddha, all considerations of caste were to be put aside within the Buddhist monastic order, with men or women from all four classes as well as outcastes accepted as members. The *Aggañña Sutta*, for example, began with a complaint from a Brahmin who had become a Buddhist monk that members of his birth caste were rebuking him for consorting with fellow monks, who were "dark fellows, born of Brahma's foot." Buddha's answer subverted the purported religious basis for the caste system, and reaffirmed the Buddhist principle that true "brightness" comes by successfully following the way of the world-renouncer to enlightenment.

Merit comes by eliminating the poisons of hatred, greed, and lust so that body, speech, and mind operate together in a harmonious way in the service of dharma. Merit is not a matter of one's parentage, wealth, or beauty. Still, he did not completely deny caste altogether. "Indeed caste is accepted as a fact of life on a par with other forms of status; to be reborn in a low and unimportant family is the result of demerit in this life."[4] The teaching on caste is clear enough: caste is not an eternal god-given structure, but something that has emerged through the processes of natural evolution. Rulers, not the priests, are at the top of the hierarchy and skillful or unskillful behaviour is found in individuals from all classes. Finally, the best way of life is to renounce ordinary society and to live as a Buddhist monk or nun, in a new social order where caste is altogether left behind. Lord Buddha welcomed outcastes into the order as well as men and women from the four castes, and used the metaphor that all persons on entering the order are like streams that enter the sea—they lose their previous identity and become known as the great ocean. "It is quite definite that there was no caste difference whatever in the Sangha at the time of the Buddha."[5] However, in several different times and places, Buddhist practice has diverged considerably from the theory.

CASTE IN BUDDHIST SRI LANKA

SRI LANKA, ONE of the first places outside of India to receive Buddhist missionaries, is predominantly Theravada Buddhist. Like so many South Asian cultures, Sri Lanka has been deeply influenced by India, the dominant cultural power of the region, and in an attenuated form, has become a caste-based society. The castes may have come about as a result of immigration from the Tamil regions of India and from the families of laborers bound to Buddhist temples, who became low caste.[6] Currently in Sri Lanka there are three separate monastic orders for men. In these orders there are strict caste differentiations, something that goes against the sermons of Lord Buddha and the ancient monastic regulations. Caste practices have been traced to the earliest period of Buddhist activities in the country, the first centuries of the Common Era, and have been continuous ever since.

Today, the three "denominations" have identical doctrines, and differ in a few minor monastic customs; their serious differentiation comes from how they treat caste issues. "On entering the order, monks showed no sign of losing their caste identities; on the contrary, they continued to be highly conscious of their caste."[7] The most exclusive Buddhist order will only ordain candidates from the highest caste. The middling group does not ordain from the lowest castes. The reforming order, in theory, maintains that Buddhism should be without caste considerations, but finds it difficult to accept recruits from the lowest orders. In fact, one subdivision of the reforming sect will only ordain the highest caste. Some monks from the highest castes refuse to accept donations from laymen and laywomen of the lower castes. Caste does permeate Sri Lankan Buddhism, so much so that laypeople of high birth often refuse to honor monks from lower castes or to donate to them. Monks who have attempted to reform these ordination customs have suffered at the hands of their hierarchies as well as losing lay supporters.[8] Until recently, people from the very lowest caste were not allowed to enter monasteries or Buddhist temples at all, but now, most monks allow them in, if not always into the most sacred precincts. Professor Gombrich noted that the monks are aware of the contradiction between their practices and the teachings, and most are a bit embarrassed and reluctant to discuss the issue, although some of the usually older, more reactionary monks defend their discriminatory ways. However, all agree that all men and women are equal in their capacity to achieve enlightenment by following the path.

In contemporary popular lay Buddhism there are some relatively new rituals centered on the worship of exemplars of the Bo Tree, the tree under which Lord Buddha attained enlightenment. These ceremonies utilize some doctrine and texts from mainstream Theravada tradition, but they usually focus on attaining practical worldly benefits for the worshipper, something that in the past had been thought to be in the job description of the gods, while the Buddha was understood to transcend mundane desires. One of the hymns used includes the following purposes for the rite: "To be born in an honourable caste, to possess as much wealth as one wishes."[9] Even more shocking is to find out that these BoTree services have been used to seek success for the government's army, nearly completely made up of Buddhists, in the war against the Tamil rebels. However, most Sri Lankans think that this is fundamentally opposed to the nondiscriminatory aspects of the dharma and that it is wrong to use Buddhist rites against a particular ethnic group. In fact, as this satirical verse shows, there are some who reject caste altogether on Buddhist grounds:

> One master taught all these people the path
> Now we find divisions amongst lay and clergy both
> Caste system too has crept in fast
> These quacks are supposed to be showing the spiritual path.[10]

Article 1 of the Universal Declaration of Human Rights states, "All human beings are born free and equal in dignity and rights"; and Article 2 speaks of the entitlement of everyone "to all the rights and freedoms set forth in this Declaration without distinction of any kind, such as race, colour, sex, language, religion, political or other opinion, national or social origin, property, birth or other status." In discussing these two Articles,[11] Professor Perera, the Sri Lankan Buddhist scholar, argues forcefully that Buddhism maintains human equality, and is opposed to any discrimination on the basis of birth or social origin, which logically preclude caste distinctions, especially within the sangha, because such discrimination is explicitly excluded in the regulations as given by Buddha. Sri Lankan caste practices in society at large do not meet these standards, and caste pervades Sri Lanka monastic Buddhism. At the very least, this poses some difficult questions to Sri Lanka, which prides itself on having the oldest and purest Buddhist pedigree, questions which are not raised by Dr. Perera, himself Sri Lankan.

CASTE AND BUDDHISM IN JAPAN

CURRENTLY THERE ARE at least some three million people of the 120 million population of Japan who are members of a "formerly" outcaste group, the *burakumin*. Their name comes from *buraku*, the name of the ghettos to which they were restricted under Tokugawa (1603–1868) regulations. Although theoretically liberated in 1871 during Japan's rush to modernization, there is still widespread discrimination against burakumin, who are concentrated in some six thousand buraku. They are discriminated against in housing and marriage, refused employment in many companies, and even humiliated in funerals by the Buddhist establishment. Over the centuries, names used to distinguish such groups in Japan have changed, but there has been a consistency in that they have been seen as polluted or ritually unclean. Under the Tokugawa, society was divided into four classes, samurai, farmers, craftsmen, and merchants. There were two classes of outcastes regulated by law, the *eta* and the even lower group, the *hinin*. Both *eta*, which means "defilement abundant," and *hinin*, or "nonhuman," are still used today to refer to the burakumin.[12] The *eta* were restricted to occupations thought to be defiling, and the *hinin* were not allowed to work at all; they were restricted to beggary.

Although there are various theories as to the origin of these groups, the most plausible traces them to certain hereditary occupations, especially those that entail contact with dead animals, like butchers, leather workers, executioners, and people who tend the human dead. In Shinto, the indigenous strain of Japanese religion, there was a very strong sense that any contact with a dead human body made one ritually unclean. After Buddhism came into the country in the seventh century of the Common Era, the Shinto taboos surrounding dead people "became linked to Buddhist prohibitions on the taking of any life."[13] Even though Buddhist dietary rules were not rigidly observed in Japan, there were regulations passed prohibiting one who had eaten meat from going into a Buddhist temple. At the end of the Tokugawa era, just before Japan began to modernize, the status of the *eta-hinin* was reinforced by the Confucian ideology of the rulers that systemized society into four classes and the outcaste groups and insisted that every individual be carefully regulated in his or her activities. "The Confucian obsession with completeness and wholeness complemented the Buddhist and *Shinto* ideas that ritual impurity was associated with those who performed pariah tasks on the margin of society."[14] In 1859, there was an infamous magistrate's decision in a murder case, where the judge ruled, "An *eta* is worth 1/7th of an ordinary person. If you would have me punish the guilty party, let him kill six more of your fellows."[15]

Under the Tokugawa, the *eta* were given a monopoly in leather working and had other useful but lowly roles, such as drum makers, bamboo utensil makers, special militia, and road menders, which gave them some economic security and leverage. Owners and middlemen in the larger *eta* enterprises became relatively wealthy. After the formal emancipation, the economic situation of the burakumin worsened with competition in their traditional trades, and great reluctance to hire them in the mainstream society. In rural areas, many became sharecroppers, and in the cities, day laborers. Non-burakumin workers refused to work alongside "outcastes" for fear of pollution through contact, and prejudice against them continues into the present. They continue to be segregated in slums, to be considered impure and unreliable. They have much higher unemployment rates and are considerably poorer than the general population. In the 1970s it was discovered that private detective agencies were preparing detailed lists of all the buraku residents in the country to sell to employers and to families checking out the pedigrees of potential mates for their children to make sure that they would not hire or wed anyone of the polluted group in case they were understandably attempting to conceal their origins.[16]

In the matters of faith, most of *eta-hinin* gravitated to the Jodo Shinshu Pure Land Buddhist sect, which was the most egalitarian of all the Japanese schools.[17] Rennyo (1415–1499), the leader who revived and reorganized the faith, made a special effort to minister to and to recruit members from the "outcaste" groups. However, Jodo Shinshu institutionalized discrimination against the outcastes, setting up temples where no *etas* could attend, special temples (*eta-dera*, or polluted temple) within the buraku for *etas* alone, and temples where both *etas* and non-*etas* attended (*eta-za*). In the mixed temples, segregated seating was provided for the outcastes. Priests who served the *eta* were often *eta* themselves.

In the Tokugawa era, Buddhism was the state religion, and local temples across the country served as part of the government bureaucracy. Every person in Japan was required to register as a member of a local temple, and the temple records were an official governmental register, enabling supervision and control of the population. In the eighteenth century, the government made it manditory for all temples located in buraku to come under Shin jurisdiction and insisted that separate registers for *eta-hinin* be kept in every temple in the country. These registers became a major tool used to track down those outcastes who tried to conceal their origins.[18]

Since the Meiji reforms beginning in 1868, the vast majority of the burakumin continued to be active members of Jodo Shinshu sect. In the years immediately following the abolition of the caste system (1871), the burakumin were energized, building many new temples and seeking proper recognition in their Shin denomination. However, in 1899, during a commemorative ceremony for the 400th anniversary of the death of Saint Rennyo, the priests from the temples in the buraku were denied their proper seats, and the Shin hierarchy ignored their protests. In 1902 a Jodo Shinshu priest defended the practice of having separate temples for the *eta-hinin* "and was heard to say that since even *eta* donate money to the temples, humans should contribute more."[19]

In the first decades of the twentieth century, there were a number of progressive and radical social and political movements that arose in Japan, largely inspired by Western groups and drawn from people who were dissatisfied with the way that Japan was embracing modernity. In 1911 some three hundred buraku priests of the Jodo Shinshu formed a "Harmony Association," and shortly thereafter an "Improvement Group" that included mainstream Jodo Shinshu priests and government officials. These associations, which were neither supported nor opposed by the sect's hierarchy, worked quietly for greater integration of the burakumin.[20] One of these was the *Suiheisha* or Levelers Association founded in 1922, a movement dedicated to the eradication of discrimination against the burakumin and inspired by a peculiar mixture of socialist, Christian, and Buddhist ideas.

Their first conference was attended by between one and three thousand delegates, who adopted three principles as the foundation for their movement: (1) the burakumin will liberate themselves through their own efforts; (2) they demand economic freedom and the ability to choose whatever occupation they please; and (3) they vow to "awaken the fundamental principles of human nature and march toward the perfection of mankind."[21] They also adopted a stirring declaration,[22] vowed to oppose anyone who referred to them as *eta* or in other insulting terms, and promised to approach the Jodo Shinshu headquarters to find out what the leaders had to say about the movement. Perhaps they were hoping to receive support from the Buddhist sect, which had the membership of most of the burakumin, or perhaps they were reacting to continuing discrimination in the temples and hierarchy.

A group of younger priests in the Nishi Honganji responded to the Levelers by forming the Black Robe League, who called for radical reform within the denomination. "In particular, they demanded the removal of the rules which segregated *eta* temples, the abolition of separate seating arrangements at other temples," and the abolition of the different colored robes, which distinguished the ranks of their priests, proposing that all should wear the same black gowns.[23] The Nishi Honganji leadership responded in 1922 by issuing an order "to remove the old mistaken customs and notions and renew the church atmosphere," and "to consider everyone as a fellow-believer bound by Buddha's will, associate with everyone and appreciate the highest joy."[24] In 1924 and 1926 the Nishi Honganji formed groups to support and to implement government plans to improve the living conditions for the former outcastes. The records of these groups are scanty, and it is not clear how much effect they had.

In any case, the Levelers were not appeased by the efforts of the Nishi Honganji, and one segment of them became more and more radical, taking a Bolshevik turn. In the 1920s and 1930s the Levelers Association organized thousands of aggressive, public campaigns to eliminate discrimination in schools, public places, and temples, censuring a number of priests. In the early 1920s, the Black Robe League supported some of these protests, but as a separate organization soon disappeared. By the late 1920s the Levelers were calling for the burakumin to suspend their contributions to the Jodo Shinshu, denouncing the influence of religion as an ideology that reconciled the burakumin to their fate: after all, the bad karma of killing animals and working with their flesh could be used to explain the lowly place of those workers.[25] Further, they argued that it was a waste of effort to try to reform the Buddhist establishment. As Japan moved to become a totalitarian state in the 1930s and then into the Great Pacific War, the Levelers Association was diverted from its original aims into becoming yet another patriotic front.

After the war, the burakumin regrouped to fight the continuing discrimination against them, and since 1955, have gone under the Buraku Liberation League. They have continued their struggle against the Jodo Shinshu, with public demonstrations and calls to reform. Finally in 1969, the Honganji accepted responsibility for discriminating against the burakumin and expressed regret for the suffering that had been caused.[26] Since soon after the Second World War, the Jodo Shinshu has had practical undertakings to combat discrimination against the burakumin, with programs of education stressing their traditions of brotherhood and welfare and development activities in the buraku designed to raise the living standards and educational levels of the people. However, in 1983, it was noted "There is relatively little action taken by either Christian or Buddhist organizations in Japan to alleviate Burakumin oppression."[27] In recent years, this has improved. The largest branch of Rinzai Zen apologized for their treatment of outcastes,[28] a new antidiscrimination law was passed in 1969, which continues to fund integration and development projects, the Buraku Liberation League has redoubled its efforts and has forged international links with outcaste and human rights groups, but the problem has far from vanished.

In Japan, Buddhist priests play a very important role in the rituals around death. Every traditional person will have a Buddhist funeral and will receive a special Buddhist name, which is recorded in the temple register and carved on the tombstone. The Buraku Liberation League discovered that many priests in many different sects in all regions of the country had been assigning derogatory names like "animal-man," "leather woman," and "*candala*," the Sanskrit word for outcaste. While this practice was very common in the past, it has diminished since the Second World War, but still happens today. In 1984, after earlier denying the existence of discrimination in Japan, the Soto sect of Zen Buddhism publicly apologized for the various ways it had harmed the burakumin in the recent past including the use of the Tokugawa registration system for discrimination, using the register of funerary names to discriminate, the assigning of derogatory funerary names, and even prescribing a special discriminatory ritual for as late as 1973 burakumin funerals.[29]

A NOTE ON THE ROLE OF ORGANIZED BUDDHISM IN THE PERSECUTION OF CHRISTIANS IN JAPAN (1614–1873)

As MENTIONED IN the preceding section, the Tokugawa (1603–1868) rulers established Buddhism as the state religion and state registry system. Every person in Japan was compelled to register at the local temple as a Buddhist. This system was initiated with the Edict of 1614 as part of the intensified persecution of Christians, and "it was made clear that its purpose was the elimination of Christianity."[30] Shogun Ieyasu feared that the many Japanese, who had been converted to Christianity in the previous century of turmoil, were a destabilizing force. Portuguese priests had been allowed to operate in the country with considerable success during the times of civil war. The Edict of 1614 expelled all foreign priests and closed all churches; later edicts sought to root out and eliminate lay Christians, starting with members of the samurai class and eventually including everyone. By 1638 it was compulsory for every household to be examined annually at a Buddhist temple to make sure that there were no Christian members with temples certifying their status. Those detected as

Christians would be executed, often with horrible tortures, if they refused to renounce their faith. In Nagasaki, where there had been a concentration of converts, the local officials instituted an annual ceremony around 1630, where everyone was required to trample an image of Christ to prove non-Christian status. For the general population, in time, this became just another part of the New Year's festivities, but it was always a horrible experience for the *kakure kirishitans*, the hidden Christians, who managed to persist for over two hundred and fifty years without priests or contact with the church.

CASTE IN BUDDHIST TIBET

AT THE BOTTOM of Tibet's hierarchical class system were groups of hereditary outcastes called by various names depending on which part of Tibet and which cultural subgroup they came from.[31] They were restricted to the lowest of occupations, were considered unfit to marry people from other classes, and could never rise in status.[32] In the Lhasa region they were called *ragyapa* and specialized in defiling jobs that involved "blood, death, and dirt."[33] They were the general scavengers, butchers and fishermen, removers of dead animals and humans, weapon makers, and also beggars. They were the people who executed the sentences of bodily mutilation and the death penalties that were features of Tibetan justice. In 1934 they bungled removing the eyeballs of a high-ranking prisoner convicted of plotting against the Dalai Lama. "The method involved the placement of a smooth, round yak's knucklebone on each of the temples of the prisoner. These were then tied by leather thongs around the head and tightened by turning the thongs until the eyeballs popped out."[34] It had been so long since that penalty had been used that no one had seen it done, so they did their best from what the elders remembered.

The outcaste stigma was hereditary and usually came from the line of the father, although sometimes from the mother. Outcastes were "regarded as both polluted and polluting," and in many places were not admitted into monastic orders. Tibetan legal codes separated the population into nine different categories, with three subdivisions of three classes, aristocrats, commoners, and outcastes. The outcastes were divided into the highest of the low, blacksmiths; the middle of the low, butchers; and the lowest of the low, executioners. They were forbidden to share food or cups with anyone outside their group and were not allowed to marry or to have sex with outsiders. They did not use the government's legal system and had their own association to settle disputes within the community. Buddhist doctrine explained their status as the result of breaking the precepts, and nothing could be done in this life to move to higher class.[35] It was estimated that in central Tibet the outcastes made up from between five to 10 percent of the population.[36]

There seems to have been no questioning of the theory or practice of the outcaste system by Tibetans from Buddhist principles or from any other angle in traditional times. Under the Chinese regime, members of the former outcaste groups have gained high positions in the Communist Party and administration.[37] Article 8 of the Draft Constitution of the Tibetan Government in Exile,[38] adopted on the initiative of the current Dalai Lama, guarantees equality for all citizens and bans discrimination on the basis of social origin or birth, which of course, would eliminate the basis of the caste system.

BUDDHISM VERSUS CASTE IN CONTEMPORARY INDIA, THE WORK OF DR. AMBEDKAR

AS SKETCHED IN chapter 13, Dr. Bhimrao Ramji Ambedkar (1891–1956)* was a tenacious and accomplished fighter on behalf of his people, the untouchables, the outcastes of the Hindu social system. Ghandi thought that the outcaste problem should be handled by getting the caste Hindus to moderate their position and behavior, and by raising the quality of life of the untouchable people through education and development projects. But Ghandi, as a good, if unconventional Hindu, did not think that the caste system itself was problematic. Dr. Ambedkar decided that the Hindu system itself was the root of the oppression of his fellow outcastes, and announced as early as 1935 that he would not die as Hindu, but would convert to another faith, one which would aid in the liberation of his people. A few months before his death, he chose to convert to Buddhism, and some 500,000 of his untouchable followers joined him. The Trailokya Bauddha Mahasangha Sahayaka Gana (TBMSG),[39] the group he founded, has continued to function and to grow both in numbers and in sophistication. In 1951 the census of India reported 180,823 Buddhists, mostly from hill tribes in border areas, and in 1981, the number was 4,719,028 the vast majority of whom were followers of

Dr. Ambedkar from the former Mahar caste of untouchables in Maharashtra State.[40]

Ambedkar's great speech where he publicly announced his intention to leave the Hindu faith said why he believed it was necessary:

> If you want to gain self-respect, change your religion.
>
> If you want to create a cooperating society, change your religion.
>
> If you want power, change your religion.
>
> If you want equality, change your religion.
>
> If you want independence, change your religion.
>
> If you want to make the world in which you live happy, change your religion.[41]

One is struck by the intensity of this call, which reflects the powerless and oppressed situation of the people to whom it was addressed. The reasons he gave to change are all practical, worldly concerns. The ten thousand untouchables who heard this call unanimously endorsed it, but some twenty years of discussion and debate went by before Dr. Ambedkar led his people into Buddhism.

From 1951 to 1955, Dr. Ambedkar devoted all his efforts to compiling a book summing up the life and the message of the Buddha, published posthumously in 1957 as *Buddha and His Dhamma*, the book that would become the primary scripture for the TBMSG. In the introduction, he says that there are several problems in the Buddhist tradition, which need to be dealt with. For example, the story of the Great Renunciation with its miraculous encounters was neither plausible nor reasonable. In Ambedkar's version of the biography, the Great Renunciation was to solve a political problem in Gautama's kingdom.[42] Second, he sees the Four Holy Truths of Buddhism as presented in the first sermon as a great stumbling block, as something added to the original teachings by the order of monks. Third, he thinks that the doctrines of karma and of no-soul as presented in the tradition are contradictory. Fourth and finally, he rejects the idea of the order of monks having been created to enable the members of monastic sangha to perfect themselves through withdrawal from worldly concerns and self-cultivation. Rather, he says the monk "as a social servant . . . may prove to be the hope of Buddhism,"[43] which is a radical new interpretation of the role of the monk.

Many Buddhists and scholars were shocked at the time of publication of *Buddha and His Dhamma*, and suggested that what Ambedkar was teaching was not really Buddhism, perhaps it should be called "Ambed-karism"[44] or neo-Buddhism. Indeed, his version of the first sermon is startling to one who knows the original. He altogether leaves out the transcendent aspects of the third noble truth, that the goal of the religious path is for the individual practitioner to attain the supernal state of nirvana. In his words, the Buddhist message is focused solely on this-worldly concerns: "The centre of his Dhamma is man and the relation of man to man in his life on earth . . . how to remove . . . suffering from the world is the only purpose of Dhamma."[45] In his version of the eight-fold path, he stresses that its purpose is to "remove all injustice and inhumanity that man does to man,"[46] and does not mention the higher meditative states. Ambedkar's recasting of buddhadharma, although somewhat pale and pedestrian, is nonetheless consistent with the worldly motives he gave for conversion in his famous speech from the 1930s. It also fits in with his three fundamental rules for determining what teachings are truly Buddhist: First, if something is not rational or logical, it can not be from the Buddha; second, everything that Buddha said relates to man's welfare; and third, Buddha's statements can be divided into those where he expressed certainty and those where expressed his view tentatively. His no-nonsense, down-to-earth approach are probably linked to his experiences at Columbia University from 1913 to 1916, where he studied with John Dewey, and would have been exposed to the social gospel that dominated the intellectual milieu at that time.[47]

In practice, the TBMSG has certainly helped many of its members into a better life in face of the continuing oppression and miserable poverty that is the lot of the outcastes in India in spite of the Constitution (drafted under Dr. Ambedkar's leadership) and the laws and regulations that are meant to protect them. In spite of its radical changes and omissions, it can be argued that Ambedkar's interpretation of Buddhism was far better suited to the needs of his people than a traditional form would have been.[48] In fact, as shown in the earlier parts of this chapter, traditional forms of Buddhism in Sri Lanka, Japan, and Tibet, all tolerated or supported social systems with miserably maltreated groups of outcastes. In any case, the Mahar Buddhists deeply appreciate what Dr. Ambedkar did for them, as this song they sing in his honor shows:

> He gave us the conversion at Nagpur
> He threw his light in the darkness
> He never was the slave of anyone

He showed us the way of the Buddha
He gave us salvation.[49]

Even more striking is their version of the refuge vows, chanted in most services. There are no longer three refuges, but four: "To the Buddha for refuge I go; to the Dharma for refuge I go; to the Sangha for refuge I go; to Ambedkar for refuge I go."[50]

THE STATUS OF WOMEN
IN BUDDHISM

THE EARLIEST BUDDHIST WOMEN

AFTER HIS ENLIGHTENMENT, BUDDHA decided to seek out an audience in order to bring others to enlightenment. His first listeners were five male ascetics, who instantly responded to his sermon and became his first disciples. Achieving insight into the true nature of the world, they too became enlightened and undertook to spread the word to others. The first few years of the Buddhist mission were very successful with many men renouncing the world and joining Buddha and his original followers to form a community of monks, a high proportion of whom became enlightened themselves. Buddha's message and example was attractive to women as well as men, but for the first few years no women were admitted to the order. They were welcome to hear the teachings, to adopt the lay precepts, to make donations to the order, but they were not allowed to become full monastic disciples. According to scriptures,[1] Maha-prajapati Gautami, his aunt who had served as Gautama's wet nurse and foster mother (his own mother died shortly after bearing him), along with some five hundred women from his home nation, came to have a strong desire to "renounce their homes and enter the homeless state under the doctrine and discipline proclaimed by the [Buddha]." Three times she begged Lord Buddha to ordain them, and was denied three times without explanation.

Nonetheless, the women cut off their hair, put on saffron robes, and followed their teacher on foot to his next destination, some 150 miles.

"And Maha-prajapati the Gotami, with swollen feet and covered with dust, sad and sorrowful, weeping and in tears, took her stand outside the entrance hall." Ananda, Buddha's young disciple noted for his sweet nature, saw her there and inquired as to why she was in such a state. When he heard that her sorrow came because Lord Buddha refused to ordain women, Ananda immediately approached the master and intervened on their behalf. After being so refused three times, Ananda decided to try a reasoned argument in favor of allowing women into the order.

He asked if women could benefit from renouncing the world and following the discipline. Would they be capable of serious progress on the Buddhist path? Could they become enlightened? The Buddha replied positively, and then Ananda clinched the case by reminding Lord Buddha that "as aunt and nurse she nourished him and gave him milk." Lord Buddha admitted Maha-prajapati as the first Buddhist nun on the condition that she accept eight special rules (to be discussed later). Of course, nuns were also to be bound by all of the rules for monks as well. She readily agreed and became the first Buddhist nun. The Blessed One commented that if women had not been ordained then the dharma, that is the Buddhist religion, would have lasted for one thousand years in its full purity, but now with a female order it would persist only five hundred. He went on to explain that they were now like a house with many women and few men, easy prey for robbers, or like crops stricken with mildew or blight, they were not destined to last long. Nonetheless, he immediately gave Maha-prajapati permission to ordain her five hundred friends under the same conditions as she was admitted, and she did so at once.

This narrative presents some obvious interpretive problems. Why was Gautama so reluctant to admit women? Should one focus on the high estimation he gave to women's ability to achieve the highest level of religious attainment or on his comparison of women to the diseases that destroy healthy fields of plants? The story itself shows that Maha-prajapati and her five hundred companions were far from weak wilting flowers. After all, even after three rebuffs from the master, they undertook to adopt the shaven head and robes of the Buddhist wayfarer and then walked barefoot in the heat of India some one hundred and fifty miles to press their case. Maha-prajapati was called the Gautami in the text, a title that is the feminine form of Lord Buddha's given name. This parallel suggested by her name is carried through in her canonical biography, which models her life on the career of Lord Buddha. It began with her previous existences, detailed her involvement with Gautama as a child, and emphasized her full enlightenment, her mastery of the doctrine, and her ability to perform miracles. In her biography, it is the Buddha himself who asks her to demonstrate supernormal powers for the benefit of "fools who doubt that women too can grasp the truth."[2]

Perhaps the most surprising detail was the final one, the focus on her passing away from this life. Fully enlightened beings like Lord Buddha have broken the chains of death and rebirth and thus do not die in the precise sense of the term when it is time to depart from their last existence. Rather it is said that they pass permanently into the nirvana state, or experience *parinirvana*, which is what Maha-prajapati did. In fact, the text goes so far as to say that her *parinirvana* was even greater than that of the Buddha.

> The Buddha's great nirvana, good,
> but not as good as this one:
> Gotami's great going out
> was positively stellar.[3]

Lord Buddha was present at her *parinirvana* and funeral and praised her in the highest terms,[4] recognizing her wisdom, her supernormal powers, and her complete enlightenment, saying: "All imperfections were destroyed; she'll have no more rebirths."[5]

If Maha-prajapati's attainments were not impressive enough, it should be noted that five hundred of her fellow nuns also achieved the *parinirvana* state at the same time[6] after performing miracles on their own. The five hundred received the same honors. Nonetheless, Buddha did institute a number of special restrictions for all nuns to follow. First, and most startling is, "A [nun], even if of a hundred years standing, shall make salutation to, shall rise up in the presence of, shall bow down before, and shall perform all proper duties toward a [monk], if only just initiated."[7] In the order of monks, strict seniority was observed, the youngest always deferred to his elders, but Lord Buddha insisted that every nun is junior to any monk, no matter what the chronology of ordination was. Maha-prajapati objected to this rule, asking that monks and nuns be put on an even footing. Buddha refused, saying, "This is impossible, . . . and unallowable, that I should so order. Even those others, . . . teachers of ill doctrine, allow not such conduct towards women; how much less, then can the Tathagatha allow it?" He then ruled that any monk who should "perform those duties that are proper (from an inferior to a superior)" toward a nun is guilty of an offence that must be confessed and atoned for.[8]

The other seven primary special rules for women all reinforce the principle that the women's order must be under the supervision of the monks. Women, for example, have to be ordained and disciplined by properly constituted assemblies of both the male and female orders, while nuns may not participate in the ordination of monks. The order of nuns is forbidden to lodge an official admonition against any monk, while monks as a body may chastise nuns.

The Buddha ruled that nuns and monks could not be treated as equals in social relations which would have been shocking to contemporary society. Since competing faiths like the Jains kept their male ascetics at the culturally acceptable higher level of status, it would have been quite imprudent to allow Buddhist nuns to be treated on a par with monks. If they had done so, donations would have dried up, and the order could not have survived.

As a matter of fact, admitting females into holy orders did give rise to a number of problems, which Lord Buddha dealt with. Some had to do with the appearance of impropriety involved when nuns came to monks for the guidance and teaching that was necessary because of their subservient position. "The people murmured, and were indignant, saying: There are their wives, there are their mistresses; now will they take pleasure together."[9] Buddha solved these sorts of problems by increasing the authority of the nuns to discipline and teach themselves so that they would no longer have to approach their male counterpoints. Another series of rulings had to do with the tendency of the nuns to go a little overboard in adorning themselves. Part of the monastic life involves great simplicity in dress and keeping possessions to the very minimum, including a single set of robes, a needle and thread, a begging bowl, and medicines if necessary. Some nuns took to decorating their robes with various sorts of fringes, being scrubbed by others while bathing, wearing perfumes and make up and other such worldly practices, which upset the laity. Because of their monthly cycles, nuns were allowed to add a loincloth and a hip string to their permitted possessions, but some nuns began to wear their hip strings as a fashion accessory. All of these were banned as minor offenses.

As one might have expected, some monks behaved toward nuns in a way that we would call sexual harassment today. The Buddha condemned them and ruled that monks who were guilty of such behavior had committed a minor offense and would no longer be saluted by the order of nuns, a severe public rebuke. When some nuns misbehaved in the same way, it was also ruled to be a minor offense with a different penalty, since monks were already forbidden to salute nuns.

The most prestigious life for a Buddhist monk is the life of the solitary forest monk, who lives most austerely and concentrates on meditative practices. Nuns naturally were attracted to this pattern as well, but it proved too dangerous. Forests were the refuge of thieves and ruffians as well as ascetics, and the forest nuns became prey for rape. Accordingly, the forest path was forbidden for women. Aside from the rules against nuns having authority over monks, this restriction against females being forest solitaries is, I believe, the only one where the Buddha limited what nuns could do in terms of religious practice. After some bad experiences, in order to protect nuns from rape, Buddha made a rule forbidding them to bathe in isolated bathing places. In resolving all these issues, the Buddha showed concern and compassion for women and an understanding of their needs and respected the autonomy of their order.

In summary, the story of Maha-prajapati and the rules adopted for her followers illustrate the basic views on the nature of women that have pervaded Buddhist thought. First, from the point of view of absolute truth, women are the spiritual equals of men. They can and do achieve the highest levels of religious attainment. Maha-prajapati's career can be taken as the model for women's spirituality—nothing was beyond her capacity, and any woman who follows her example may also attain permanent release from the sufferings of the world. Since the Buddha's goal was to establish a world-renouncing community of followers to be supported within the existing social order, he did not try to challenge ancient Indian ideas about the relative status of women in relation to men. Because women had such a weak position in the culture of the time they needed to be under the protection and regulation of males. Therefore, Maha-prajapati and her order of nuns could not be granted social equality with the order of monks. From practical "rice-in-the-bowl" considerations, that would have been fatal to the entire Buddhist enterprise as such an affront to public sensibilities would have dried up the gifts necessary for the monks and nun to eat.

Rita Gross, a feminist and a Buddhist scholar of the very first rank who teaches at the University of Wisconsin-Eau Claire, develops an interesting point from the story of Maha-prajapati's difficulty getting Lord Buddha to agree to her ordination. She notes "this is the only instance on record of the Buddha changing his position due to persuasion and arguments from his disciples."[10]

> He changed his mind despite misgivings, practical difficulties, and negative
> anti-women public opinion. This is, in fact, the most usable model we
> could have. . . . All that is really required is that when women object to
> unreasonable and inhumane discriminations and present a program that
> corrects the problem, men stand not in opposition, trying to maintain their
> gender-based privileges and power.[11]

She only wishes that the men in the Buddhist hierarchies today would
follow the Buddha's example in this regard.

As it turned out, the early generations of Buddhist nuns were highly
successful in gaining members and donations, and many nuns and even a
few laywomen became enlightened.[12] The spiritual accomplishments of
the early nuns were recognized and highly praised by the Buddha himself
as we have seen in the case of Maha-prajapati. Indeed, the wisdom of the
early nuns was so respected by the entire Buddhist community that an entire section of the canon, the *Therigatha*, collects some seventy-three po-
ems attributed to them. Some of Maha-prajapati's words are included.
The name of the book, *Therigatha*, means hymns (*gatha*) of the female
elders, and there is a corresponding book of hymns composed by male
elders. Note that the verses of the nuns are completely equal in all respects to those of the monks. Rita Gross finds the *Therigatha* particularly
valuable as it offers a glimpse into the world of early Buddhist women
undistorted by patriarchal lenses and regrets that the androcentric
worlds of practicing Buddhists and of Buddhist studies have made so little
use of it.[13]

There are, however, also a number of antiwoman passages in early Buddhist scripture, many found in the Jataka tales. One of the longest
Jatakas, number 536,[14] is a collection of rather nasty lessons about the un-
trustworthy nature of women. The framing story, which makes it clear
that the point is to counteract the wiles of the former wives of some dis-
content monks, ends with these words of the Buddha,

> Surely, Brethren, even when I was in an animal form, I knew well the in-
> gratitude and immorality of women-folk, and at that time so far from being
> in their power I kept them under my control.[15]

The general pattern of several of the stories in Jataka 536 is the same. A
lovely young woman is married to a powerful, handsome, wealthy, and
generous man, who adores her for her beauty and charm. In spite of all

she has, she falls in love with an inappropriate man and betrays her husband. One of the stories even has the girl married to five wonderful brothers, each totally devoted to her. In her case, the lover was a humpbacked palace slave. When she is found out, her five husbands had her punished and saw the futility of trusting women, who are judged to be universally deceitful. In another of the stories in this Jataka, the king's advisor saved a flagrantly adulterous queen from execution on the grounds that she was only following her nature. Any woman, he argued, would have done the same if she had the chance.

> Thus does a wife forsake her lord, though lusty he and strong,
> And will with any other man, e'en cripple vile, go wrong.[16]

By far, the majority of the Jataka teachings about women are unflattering to say the least, with some showing real hatred of women.[17]

There are also a number of stories in the Jatakas that praise virtuous women in contradiction to tales that slander them. One of the strongest declared that there is no place in all the worlds, except the Brahma world, where women are excluded and commends them very highly.[18] Another praised a queen for her great devotion in caring for her husband afflicted with leprosy. She followed him into the forest, where he went in despair, and lovingly tended his wounds and foraged for his food. Through her loyalty and an act of truth, she miraculously cured his vile disease. In this case the king subsequently proved to be disloyal, failing to give her proper honor and spending all his time with other women in the harem. He was rebuked by the Buddha-to-be with these words: "An act of treachery to a friend like this is a sin."[19]

A similar theme is found in the story about another queen who accompanied her royal husband into the forest, where he had been unjustly exiled. Her honest and steadfast support were recognized in these verses:

> Known to fame as peerless wife,
> Sharing weal and woe of life,
> Equal she to either fate,
> Fit with even kings to mate.[20]

A very important Jataka[21] concerns a king who had been misled by false teachers. They turned him from the path of virtue by denying the basic principles of morality. His very beautiful daughter, however, knew the truth of the law of karma (that one's acts in this life determine one's fate and place in this and subsequent lives), which she explained to him very clearly. Although she failed to convince her father, it took a miracle to do that, she was praised for her understanding and devout preaching. Many of the Jatakas in fact show specific women to be much better morally than the men in the stories, but there never seems to be any corresponding generalization about the depravity of males.

Early Buddhist texts are very consistent in praising the devout Buddhist laywoman, who was the pillar of support for the Buddhist monastics. In fact, Vishakha, a very wealthy and very generous donor, not Maha-prajapati, is the woman who has the greatest number of pages devoted to her in early Buddhist documents.[22] In an oft-cited sermon, the Buddha outlines the reciprocal duties of wife and husband. It starts with some general principles: that both parties should follow the four basic Buddhist precepts, should avoid the states of mind that lead to evil acts, and should stay away from bad companions and low places of temptation. Then the specific spousal duties are outlined, five for the husband and five for the wife. He should honor her, treat her with courtesy, be faithful, allow her to manage the house, and provide her with ornaments. Her duties are to manage the affairs of the house to the best of her ability, to be hospitable to his family and friends, to be faithful, to safeguard his property, and to be diligent in fulfilling her duties.[23]

While these rules do protect the wife, they presume her secondary place in the scheme of things. It is his property and his friends that she has to look after. Nonetheless, by the standards of ancient India, and even by the standards of many places in today's world, this teaching of mutual respect and reciprocity of duties between husband and wife is commendable. Even so, several of the verses of the *Therigatha* show that some of the nuns, who left marriages to enter the order, felt absolutely liberated when they no longer had to look after their households and their husbands. The mother of Sumangala's poem in the *Therigatha* has these lines:

> Free, I am free.
> How glad am I to be free from my pestle.
> My cooking pot seems worthless to me.
> And I can't even bear to look at his sun-umbrella
> —my husband disgusts me![24]

In this context, it is interesting to note that the Buddha protected the nuns against becoming housekeepers for the monks, making it a minor offense to do their laundry or any other chores.[25]

Lord Buddha was very open to women of all castes, marital statuses, and occupations. Anyone who sincerely wished to follow the way of life of the world-renouncer was welcome to join. For example, women honored in the *Therigatha* include wealthy married women, impoverished Brahmins, washerwomen, courtesans, prostitutes, and never-married virgins. Among the five hundred Sakya women who followed Mahaprajapati as Buddhist nuns, there were twelve who had been in Gautama's palace as his harem girls, before his great renunciation and enlightenment. Seven of his ex-playmates are honored as elders with their verses included in the *Therigatha*.[26] Similarly, pious laywomen of all sorts, including prostitutes and courtesans, were praised for their virtues and support of the Buddhist order. On the whole, Buddhists considerably opened up the possibilities for freedom and respect for women 2,500 years ago in India. In addition to providing them a way to live nearly completely independently from men as nuns, Buddha also made it respectable for a girl to remain at home without marrying, permitted considerable choice in choosing a husband, and very much improved the status of widows, allowing them to remarry, for instance.[27]

In contemporary Theravada or southern Buddhist lands, there is still relative social freedom and opportunity for laywomen. In Thailand, for example, women run many of the most successful businesses, and they have free access to higher education and the professions. Aung San Suu Kyi is the leader of the Burmese opposition to the current repressive military government, and Sirimavo Bandaranaike* (1916–2000) former prime minister of Sri Lanka was the first female prime minister in world history. On the other hand, in all the Theravada countries, the order of nuns has disappeared, or was never established, and currently the male hierarchies of all the denominations oppose its renewal on technical grounds.

IMAGES OF WOMEN

IT IS NOT too surprising that some monks had some difficulty with their vows of celibacy. They were particularly tormented by tempting visions of women that arose during meditation. Most of the monks would have been sexually active before their ordination, and memories of their past lovers, not to mention imagination for those with or without sexual experience, could pose problems. Some of the Jataka tales that slander women were attempts to deal with these temptations. One of the major points of the Buddha's message is that ignorant attachments to anything at all are the root cause of suffering and weld us all to a never ending round of birth, death, and rebirth, and attachment to sexual objects and sexual pleasure is one of the strongest fetters. If one really sees the truth that all tempting things are without permanent substance, constantly changing, destined to dissolution, and ultimately disappointing, then it is possible to break free.

In the biography of the Buddha, his decision to become an ascetic was triggered by his first disturbing encounters with old age, sickness, and death at a very late age, since his father had protected him from all the unpleasant things in life. When the court noticed how upset Gautama was by his encounters with bodily decay, they arranged a great party for him in his harem, trusting that he would be kept in the world by the beauty and pleasures it had to offer him. However, after the party, when all the girls had fallen asleep in less than alluring poses, he reflected that the pleasures of sensuality were fundamentally marred by over-ripeness of the body, which inevitably declines to death and then corruption. At this point, he resolved to become a homeless seeker for religious insight, and said goodbye to his wife and infant son.

One of the meditation techniques that Buddha recommended for his followers was to go to the charnel ground to observe bodies as they progressed in returning to the earth. This as well as reflecting on the various disgusting substances and parasites found in the body and on the secretions that flow from the nine orifices helped one combat pride in and attachment to the flesh. When bothered by lustful images, monks were advised to superimpose a rotting corpse, or to think of the organs, secretions, sinews, bones, and so forth that lie beneath the deceptively attractive external body.[28] While some interpreters have taken these contemplations and Lord Buddha's statements at his great renunciation as attacks on women, they can also be read as commentaries on the weakness of men, who are so easily duped by surface illusions.

For example, "The Tale of King Udayana of Vatsa," a scripture of the later Mahayana school, which originated in Central Asia or China before the eighth century of the Common Era, can be read in several ways. This complicated story begins with an account of a devout and virtuous Buddhist queen, who was a generous donor to the Buddhist orders.[29] The jealous second queen misled the king by flattery and falsely accused the good queen of disloyalty. In a fit of anger the king shot an arrow at the good woman, who stopped it in midair with miraculous powers she received through Buddhist practices. The sutra proper consists of a sermon by the Buddha to the king, who had gone to the Buddha in repentance for his unjust headstrong acts.

He asked about the nature of women's treachery so that he would no longer be misled. The Buddha replied, "Your majesty should first know a man's faults. Then he'll have insight into those of a woman." The first fault of men as he explained it is "they are addicted to desire, insatiably looking at women for their own self-indulgence."[30] The verse puts it memorably:

Fools
Lust for women
Like dogs in heat.
They do not know abstinence.
They are also like flies
Who see vomited food.
Like a herd of hogs,
They greedily seek manure.[31]

The second fault that Buddha detailed is that men, addicted to the love of women, squander their parents' wealth and betray their filial duties. The third fault is that some men are misled by false views. "[M]en who do not know that their bodies are soon extinguished"[32] waste their time seeking sensual pleasures that lead to the worst of fates.

Diana Paul takes this sermon as a "vituperative polemic against women"[33] but its condemnation of foolish men seems at least as strong as its denigration of deceitful women. When the king asked to be taught about the evils of women, Buddha's reply was that men's lust and men's ignorance are men's real problems. This is very consistent with the fundamental Buddhist teaching that every individual is responsible for cleaning up his, precisely "his" in this case, state of mind. This sutra ends with the king converting to the Buddhist path taking his first steps as a layman,[34] while it began with his virtuous queen already far advanced in that same journey. In my view, although there are certainly harsh things said about deceitful women and the destructive power of witless lust, the

sutra can also be read as high praise for the ability of women to lead ignorant and brutish men in the spiritual life.

What then of nuns? Were they not tormented by images of men's bodies, drawing them into the hot confusions of lust? Apparently not.

> Whereas Buddhist monks are frequently haunted by images of women, or
> shaken in their resolve by thoughts of wives or lovers, the nuns do not
> speak of a comparable temptation by former husbands or lovers. The im-
> pression is that, when these women had strong sexual feelings, they didn't
> project them outwards or blame men for them.[35]

It would seem that nuns had considerably less problems with celibacy
than men did.[36]

It is interesting that when nuns were tempted, it was their own bodies
they saw as subject to deterioration and decay, thereby counteracting sensual desires. For example, Khema, who was remembered as a spectacularly
gorgeous woman, gained enlightenment when the Buddha showed her a
fast-forward vision of a goddess, more beautiful than any human could be,
as she rapidly aged and withered.[37] Later the *Therigatha* records the nun
Khema's account of her temptation by a supernatural being, who took the
form of a lusty young man. His line:

> Come on Khema!
> Both of us are young and you are beautiful.
> Let's enjoy each other! It will be like the music of a symphony.

Khema's reply:

> I'm disgusted by this body.
> It's foul and diseased.
> It torments me.
> Your desire for sex means nothing to me.[38]

SEXUAL TRANSFORMATIONS

ONE OF THE recurring themes in the early texts, especially those written
by women, was that one's sex had nothing to do with one's capacities to
prosper in the Buddhist enterprise. As we have noted, Buddha was quick

to acknowledge that women and men are equal in their ability to attain the highest fruits of the religious life. This theme was carried forward in a number of Mahayana scriptures in vivid episodes where spiritually adept females readily changed themselves into males, manifesting the characteristics of Bodhisattvas or even Buddhas, the highest level of attainment possible.[39] These stories are effective counters to the androcentric notions that to be born as female is a misfortune and the resulting doctrine, which actually contradicts the teachings of spiritual gender equality, that one may never attain Buddhahood in female form. One must wait for rebirth as a male. The best known of these transformations is in the Lotus Sutra (composed in India, c. second century C.E.), the preeminent scripture in China and Japan.[40] Here an eight-year-old Naga (semidivine serpent) princess, when her widely renowned wisdom and depth of Buddhist practice were challenged by men, transformed into a male and instantly manifested the marks and powers of a Bodhisattva, then a Buddha. The point is that her essential enlightened nature had nothing whatsoever to do with her bodily form. All external forms are empty and insubstantial, merely masking the Buddha nature within.

The *Vimalakirtinirdesasutra*, a Mahayana text composed in India (c. first century B.C.E.) in which a wealthy and worldly layman, Vimalakirti, is the primary teacher, contains perhaps the funniest passage in Buddhist scripture, and it is remarkable how few jokes there are in sacred texts. It comes in a dialogue between Sariputra, Buddha's most learned disciple and a goddess. Sariputra is a man who knows every doctrine in detail, but who often fails to get the point. After a long discussion with the goddess, who impressed him with her deep wisdom, he said, in effect: If you're so smart, "why don't you change your female sex?" She replied that after twelve years of searching, she had not been able to find any "innate characteristics of the female sex" and noted that all such markers are illusory. Then she changed him into her bodily form and simultaneously assumed his form. Sariputra was bewildered, and had no idea what to say when asked, "Why don't you change your female sex?" Eventually she changed her-him back to his original illusory male form, and he finally got the point, saying, "The female form and innate characteristics neither exist nor do not exist."[41]

From the point of absolute truth, then, sex and gender do not matter. However, in countries where Mahayana Buddhism was a powerful force, sex and gender mattered a great deal on the level of relative truth in day-to-day life. In China and Japan, for example, where Buddhist ideas were very powerful intellectual forces, gender equality in the family and society was very weak, with Confucian patriarchal structures retaining their hold. However, when the order of nuns in China was established, it did offer an alternative way of life for women who wanted to live more independently, and to the present time Chinese nuns have very strong communities, probably stronger than the monks. In Taiwan, the nuns are especially active in humanitarian work and social services. In Japan, a fully fledged order of nuns was never established, but there are a relatively small number of nuns who follow the lesser precepts.[42] There are also a number of women who serve as teachers in the Zen tradition and as priest-nuns in Pure Land Temples.[43]

SOME RECENT DEVELOPMENTS

IN TAIWAN, THE Fo Kuang Shan[44] temple is the largest one on the island. Founded in 1967 by Master Hsing Yun in the south of Taiwan, it has branches all over the country and has also opened several branches abroad including a large one in Los Angeles. In China the continuity of the order of nuns never was broken, and in contemporary Taiwan, more nuns than monks are being ordained. Fo Kuang Shan has been particularly supportive of the educational advancement and social action activities of its nuns, and has also facilitated the reestablishment of the Theravada order of nuns, having sponsored an ordination ceremony in India in 1996, where a number of Sri Lankan women were given full ordination.[45] This ordination and the subsequent ordination of Thai women by the Sri Lankan nuns have not been fully recognized in their home countries due to resistance from the all-male sangha hierarchy and some doctrinal issues. In the Thailand the Buddhist scholar and feminist, Chatsumarn Kabilsingh* was one of the women ordained. While the controlling fathers of the order firmly rejected the validity of the ordination, there is a growing group of strong women determined to be recognized as fully ordained Theravada nuns, and their wishes may come to fruition. Phra Payutto, the most respected Thai Buddhist monk and thinker, has called for the female order to be recognized, but not at the expense of violating *vinaya* regulations, and has stated that the present controversy is a matter of persons holding extreme views on both sides.[46]

One of the issues around the ordination of women today is the status of the special eight rules for nuns, those rules which ritualize female subordination to male in the monastic orders. Since they are clearly part of the *vinaya* and are attributed to Lord Buddha, they are difficult to avoid, just as they are difficult for modern women to accept. The solution of Fo Kuang Shan is perhaps useful as a model.

> The traditional sharply drawn hierarchical relationship between male and female monastics is not observed. . . . The eight rules are there in the *Vinaya* that is transmitted to each [nun] when she is ordained, but though known, they are not acted upon.[47]

In any case, the nuns of Taiwan are flourishing, well respected, and exemplary in their compassionate service to those who need it most.

CONCLUSION

RITA GROSS TACKLES the contradictory teachings about women in Buddhist history head-on and makes some very sensible suggestions to deal with them.[48] As she puts it,

> From the beginning, the Buddhist position is unclear and ambiguous. By quoting only part of the record, one could easily paint a portrait of Buddhism as hopelessly negative to women or as very egalitarian in its treatment of men and women.[49]

One solution might be to argue that the misogynist texts are later interpolations, and there is some scholarly evidence for this, but it really begs the question as the Buddhist tradition has always accepted and transmitted the canon as a whole.[50]

The contradictions in the teachings about women were noted early on in the tradition and obviously perplexed the faithful. *The Questions of King Milinda*, a popular noncanonical Pali text, which dates from early in the Common Era, is in the form of a dialogue between a Greek Bactrian king, who was interested in the Buddhist faith but who had doubts and questions, and a very learned monk. The king noted that the Jatakas taught in one passage that any woman will take the opportunity to go astray sexually if the right man comes along and if she will not be found out,[51] yet another tale praised a wife who remained faithful under great temptation while her husband was away travelling.[52] He set the problem:

Now if the first of these passages be correct, the second must be wrong; and if the second be right, the first must be wrong. This too is a double-edged problem now put to you, and you have to solve it.[53]

The monk's answer was that the ostensibly virtuous woman was not really virtuous. Her restraint was not from lack of desire, but from fear of consequences and lack of an attractive sexual partner. Furthermore, she knew that secrecy was impossible. Finally, since her husband was the paragon of good qualities, no suitor was "right."

This answer really does not resolve the contradiction. The first misogynist Jataka tale tars all women as insatiably unfaithful, incapable of truly virtuous behaviour. The second story praises a virtuous woman, and the monk's answer in effect confirms her exemplary character. In his reinterpretation, she intelligently applies the principles of Buddhist moral reasoning. She affirms the laws of karma and the force of conscience and recognized the virtues of her husband. Rather than resolving the contradiction, the monk's reply seems to deepen it, and one is rather surprised that King Milinda, a very sharp critic, so readily accepted this piece of casuistry. At least the dialogue does not repeat or justify the stories in the Jatakas that denigrated women.

Gross's solution is to acknowledge that both strains are part of the history of the faith and frankly admits that the Buddha failed to transcend the bounds of the society that he lived and worked within. She thinks that the major reason that Buddha resisted the ordination of women and later kept the nuns under the control of the male order was because to do otherwise was too unconventional. His goal was to facilitate personal salvation by establishing "a path of individual self-removal from conventional society" not to reform the "social injustices and inequities" of the world.[54] Thus he allowed patriarchal and androcentric considerations to limit his radical insight that women are equal to men at the most important fundamental level.

While recognizing the patriarchal and androcentric elements in Buddha's words and acts, which Gross admits may count against claims to his omniscience,[55] she stresses the positive side of the record. In spite of the male-dominated milieu of early Indian Buddhism, and even though the scriptures were orally transmitted and authenticated by monks, the canon somehow managed to include considerable material which celebrated the very high accomplishments of nuns and laywomen.[56] To sum up Gross's position, she argues that the Buddha was not misogynist, although he did shape his teaching to the common androcentric views of the time. His essential message about the nature of the world as insubstantial, ever changing, and full of suffering and the noble eight-fold path he prescribed to overcome the pain of ordinary existence do not support a gender hierarchy with males superior to females. Therefore, Buddhists of the past and particularly Buddhists of today are called upon to purify the theory and practice of their religion from male-centred cultural accretions and patriarchal structures.

Japanese Buddhism, Militarism, and Human Rights

Buddhism, Militarism, and the State in Traditional Japan

SOME THOUSAND YEARS AFTER ITS founding in India and after considerable transformations in its journeys through central Asia, China, and Korea, Buddhism entered Japan during a time of tremendous change. Japan was still an unlettered, fragmented nation, coming to be a unified literate nation inspired by the examples of Korea and China. Buddhism was neither quickly nor easily assimilated into Japan. At first it penetrated only into the highest levels of the aristocracy; the texts portray Buddhism as being a gift from a Korean monarch to the emergent royal family of Japan. Many conservative families felt that Buddhism was a dangerous import, which would only offend the indigenous deities, the kami of Shinto faith. Indeed the first two attempts in C.E. 584 to establish Buddhist images, texts, and temples ended in their destruction after outbreaks of illness were attributed to the anger of the kami.

Eventually Buddhism did develop indigenous Japanese forms, well integrated into the culture. The general way that Buddhism and other Chinese influences were absorbed by Japan is laid out as early as the "Constitution of Prince Shotoku," Japan's first, which dates to C.E. 604 and combines Confucian ideals of social harmony, reverence for the three jewels of Buddhist thought and practice, and strict obedience to the edicts of the emperor, seen to be much greater than a mere human being.[1] This synthesis took centuries to mature fully in theory and practice, and there was always a certain undercurrent of resentment against Buddhism as a foreign religion.

Japan never really achieved lasting civil harmony and stability. During times of turbulence and civil war, some Buddhist sects went to war, putting armed monks into the field, even killing, sacking and pillaging at other Buddhist temples over issues of power, doctrine, land, and finance. One of the last examples of a Buddhist group taking up arms occurred around 1500. At that time a branch of the Pure Land or Shin school inspired a village-based, religiously-motivated popular uprising. They controlled considerable territory for some ninety-three years before the forces of the Shogun eventually wiped them out.[2] This revolutionary movement was not supported by the mainstream Shin establishment, which took particular pains to insist that good Buddhists owed their loyalty to the Emperor and his local representatives.[3] To oversimplify, in times of stability the Buddhist organizations tended to integrate into the official bureaucracy, while during political upheaval, old issues resurfaced and things became difficult between civil authorities and the Buddhist schools.

BUDDHIST IDEOLOGY AND JAPANESE MILITARISM, FROM THE MEIJI ERA TO WORLD WAR II

WHEN JAPAN WAS forced by the United States to open its borders to the world in the middle of the nineteenth century, the nation was shaken to its very depths. After a few false starts, Japan vigorously embraced modernization during the Meiji regime (1868–1912). In the first few years of Meiji, Buddhism came under very strong attack, perhaps the greatest persecution since its earliest days in Japan. Government authorities denounced Buddhism as "corrupt, decadent, antisocial, parasitic, and superstitious." They claimed that it was a major impediment to modernization and once again rejected it as a foreign religion fundamentally opposed to native sensibilities. Local organizations lost their financial base when the government abolished the system wherein every family had to register with and support a parish temple. For a while, Buddhist temples were forcibly closed down, endowment lands were confiscated, and some thousands of priests were compelled to return to lay life, with those between the ages of eighteen and forty-five being conscripted into the new Imperial Army.[4]

While Buddhism had become rather too comfortably enmeshed in the state apparatus and was not a particularly robust source for innovation at the time, the Meiji reformers had been wrong to think that individual Buddhists and Buddhist organizations were disloyal toward the Emperor and the state. Popular protests and riots in support of Buddhism showed that the reformers had also not understood just how completely the faith had woven itself into the national consciousness, and the suppression was stopped quickly enough (1873). By the end of the Meiji period (1912), Buddhist leaders had worked out the basics, in theory as well as practice, of a new relationship between Buddhism and the state.

This came about in the course of Japan's amazingly quick modernization, which manifested especially in warfare against much larger and traditionally stronger neighbors. From 1894 to 1895 they fought and beat China in the first Sino-Japanese War, which increased their influence in Korea and resulted in the Japanese colonization of Taiwan that lasted until the end of the Second World War in 1945. Although many Buddhist leaders supported this war vigorously in words, they were rather embarrassed by the Japanese Christians, recent converts since the opening of Japan to the West, who were even more enthusiastic verbally and who provided much medical aid to the wounded and financial aid to soldiers' families. Ten years later Japan decisively won the Russo-Japanese War (1904–1905), which led to the annexation of Korea and saw the establishment of strong Japanese influences in Manchuria.

D. T. Suzuki (1870–1966), well known and highly respected as the foremost interpreter of Zen Buddhism to the West through his books and lectures, was also very influential in formulating the ideology used to justify Japanese imperialism and militarism. This aspect of his work, which has only been discussed extensively in the last few years, has been rather a depressing shock in Buddhist circles. In 1896, just after the first Sino-Japanese War, and just a month before his enlightenment experience, he published a book in Japanese, never translated into English, in which he developed three points. First, since there was an absolute identity between religion and the state, Japanese national interests were nothing less than "the perfection of morality." Second, "if a lawless country comes and obstructs our commerce, or tramples on our rights" Japan was duty bound to take up arms in the name of "justice." Third and finally, he taught that soldiers (whether Buddhist or

Christian) have a religious duty to offer up their lives for Japan, and "should they fall on the battlefield they have no regrets."[5] In short Japan's war against China was "a religious action."[6]

During the Russo-Japanese War, Leo Tolstoy wrote to the Rinzai Zen Master Soen to try to get a joint Christian-Buddhist condemnation of the conflict. Soen replied (1904):

> Even though the Buddha forbade the taking of life, he also taught that until all sentient beings are united together through the exercise of infinite compassion, there will never be peace. Therefore, as a means of bringing into harmony those things which are incompatible, killing and war are necessary.[7]

Even stronger is the message of the Inoue Enryo, a well-known scholar-priest, also writing in 1904:

> Buddhism is a teaching of compassion, a teaching for living human beings. Therefore, fighting on behalf of living human beings is in accord with the spirit of compassion. In the event hostilities break out between Japan and Russia, it is only natural that Buddhists should fight willingly, for what is this if not repaying the debt of gratitude we owe the Buddha?
>
> It goes without saying that this is a war to protect the state and sustain our fellow countrymen. Beyond that, however, it is the conduct of a bodhisattva seeking to save untold millions of living souls throughout China and Korea from the jaws of death. Therefore Russia is not only the enemy of our country, it is also the enemy of the Buddha.[8]

All major Buddhist sects and thinkers came to accept these ideas along with those articulated by D. T. Suzuki earlier. Thus by the end of the Russo-Japanese War, the Buddhist ideological foundation for the absolute support of Japanese military and cultural imperialism was nearly complete.

In summary, the six ideological pillars of Japanese militaristic Buddhism are:

1. In the words of D. T. Suzuki, "every action and movement of the state takes on a religious character, and . . . every word and action of religion takes on a state character."[9] Thus Japan's interests are holy and intrinsically just.

2. Any opposition to Japan's interests by a "lawless nation" is to be met by the use of arms.

3. Japan's soldiers have a religious duty to sacrifice themselves for the nation.

4. War (that is war on behalf of Japan) is an expression of Buddhist compassion.

5. Dying on the battlefield is a way to return one's debt of gratitude to the emperor and to Lord Buddha.

6. Japan's army is, in theory at least, made up of bodhisattvas, all eager to sacrifice themselves for the good of others.[10]

In the next three decades, Buddhists continued to develop this into "Imperial Way Buddhism," "Imperial-State Zen," and "Soldier Zen."[11]

While there was some reluctance, and even some isolated resistance, from a few Buddhists to go along with the complete merging of national interests and religious teachings, the vast majority of the Buddhist clergy, thinkers, and laity sincerely and enthusiastically supported imperial ideology. Daiun Harada Roshi, in the course of the First World War when Japan fought against Germany and its allies, coined the phrase "War Zen." He became one of the strongest voices in favor of Japanese nationalism, writing in 1934:

The Japanese people are a chosen people whose mission is to control the world. The sword which kills is also the sword which gives life. . . . Politics conducted on the basis of the constitution are premature, and therefore fascist politics should be implemented for the next ten years.[12]

In 1938, D. T. Suzuki published his long essay entitled "Zen and Swordsmanship" where he also speaks of the "sword which gives life."[13] It is clear that he reaffirms his position taken up in 1896—fighting for Japan's interests is a sacred duty.

The sword comes to be identified with the annihilation of things that lie in the way of peace, justice, progress, and humanity. It stands for all that is desirable for the spiritual welfare of the world at large. It is now the embodiment of life and not of death.[14]

In his essay "Zen and the Samurai," Suzuki also notes approvingly that Zen can adapt

> itself to almost any philosophy and moral doctrine as long as its intuitive teaching is not interfered with. It may be found wedded to anarchism or fascism, communism or democracy, atheism or idealism or any political or economic dogmatism.[15]

As Arthur Koestler noted in a spirited attack on Suzuki's thought some forty years ago, such moral relativism is very dangerous, unable even to condemn Hitler's gas chambers.[16] This led to a spirited exchange of articles in *Encounter*, drawing in such luminaries as the psychiatrist Karl Jung and the leading English Buddhist, Christmas Humphries. But it does seems odd that none of the partisans mentioned Japan's Second World War crimes against prisoners and subject peoples. Why focus on the affinity of Zen with Nazism when Japanese recent history was so much more to the point?

BUDDHISTS AND THE JAPANESE EFFORT IN WORLD WAR II

BY THE END of the 1930s, all organized opposition to war in the major schools of Buddhism had been crushed. Buddhists provided chaplains to the Armed Forces and teachers to inculcate the national ideology. Zen theory and practice were particularly useful with officers undergoing Zen training to enhance their military skill and discipline. Some Zen practitioners, who were military officers, became national models as patriotic Buddhist heroes and martyrs. Zen writers in the Meiji era were major populizers of Bushido, the "Way of the Warrior," a major support for Japanese totalitarianism and inspiration for the war effort through 1945. In January 1941, the Army issued its *Field Service Code*, which was strongly influenced by Zen Buddhist doctrines and teachers. This code which taught that surrender was a shameful disgrace encouraged the pointless death of hundreds of thousands of soldiers and civilians as the war turned against Japan.[17]

D. T. Suzuki continued his efforts to support militarism. In 1941, just before Pearl Harbor, he contributed a chapter to a book that was designed for Japanese military men. His section summarized his ideas on the compatibility of Buddhism, Bushido, and Japanese imperialism.[18] In 1942, his striking essay "The Japanese People's View of Life and Death" strongly argued for the Zen warrior spirit to dominate in Japan. When life and death were seen as without distinction, then all of Japan's problems can be "swept away as if at the stroke of a sword."[19] However, his support for the war machine was not a total one. During the war he published several articles in Japanese journals that in a guarded way questioned the military establishment,[20] and in 1946 condemned Zen leadership that had called for the Japanese to throw their lives away. As Brian Victoria* noted, this condemnation seems less than impressive from a man whose teachings on the "Zen view of life . . . served as the foundational element of the Japanese military spirit."[21]

Another way that organized Buddhism served the imperial aims of Japan was to provide missionaries in the colonial empire, especially in Taiwan, Korea, and China.[22] The Japanese Buddhist missions are interesting in that they were inspired by the belief in the superiority of Japanese religion and culture to those of their subjects. Burmese Buddhists were treated with great contempt.[23] In Taiwan and Korea there was a concerted effort to replace indigenous Buddhism with Japanese forms, Japanese language was imposed, and the locals were forced to take Japanese names. In Korea, to this day, Buddhist organizations suffer from and resent the changes imposed on them, particularly the Japanese insistence that the Korean clergy drop celibacy to follow the Japanese norm of married priests. Japanese Buddhist missionaries in the conquered territories also cooperated with the secret police to keep them informed of any possible trouble brewing.

JAPANESE BUDDHISM, MILITARISM, AND WAR CRIMES

JAPAN BEGAN LARGE-SCALE warfare with China from its Manchurian toehold in 1931 and expanded the conflict further in 1937. Thus the Second World War lasted some eight years longer for China and Japan than it did for Europe and Canada and some ten years more than for the United States and Russia. Japan was never able to control China completely, but for a while did establish quite an empire, conquering most of the French, Dutch, American, and British Asian colonial territories in Southeast Asia to add to Taiwan, Korea, and the extensive areas of China they already controlled. Ienaga, in his popular history of the Pacific War, as they call it in Japan, details how the "Greater East Asia Co-Prosperity Sphere" was little more than a vehicle for Japanese exploitation of its subject peoples, who were often treated with contempt and brutality. Of the Imperial forces, he says, "atrocities on an unprecedented scale . . . were an infamous hallmark of the Japanese military."[24]

Fukushima Nichi'i, a Nichiren priest, served as an army chaplain in Manchuria from 1937 to the last months of the war when he was drafted as a soldier. He was one of the very few Buddhist chaplains who published a wartime memoir, which shows how brutal the Japanese occupation was.

> At the front we reduced villages to ashes as we searched for spies. There were always prisoners. It made no difference whether they were young or old, we first had them dig their own graves and then forced them to kneel down beside them. Following this, soldiers were selected who were skilled swordsmen.[25]

Nichi'i then coolly described the technique of beheading and the clinical details of death. There was not a hint of reflection on the morality of their actions or any suggestion that their hunting down and slaughter of "spies" might have contradicted Buddhist compassion and loving-kindness. Unfortunately this is very consistent with Japan's overall record, which shows no instance of Buddhists speaking out against similar outrages. There are a few documented incidents where soldiers did refuse to participate in such widespread practices as using live prisoners for bayonet practice. But it is not clear that the teachings and spirit of dharma explicitly motivated their resistance.

The teachings of "Soldier Zen" as manifest, for example, in the *Field Service Code* may have established an atmosphere that encouraged atrocities. By completely identifying political goals with religious ones, by making obedience to Imperial Edicts (identified with military orders) a religious duty, by declaring non-Japanese nations inferior, by equating surrender with dishonor, and by glorifying death and devaluing life, Buddhist thinkers left no theoretical foothold for a Buddhist to resist orders, no matter how repugnant they may have been to conscience.

For example, in October 1937, a Soto Zen scholar published an article justifying the expansion of the war in China, arguing that it was theoretically impossible for Japanese soldiers to behave incorrectly.

Wherever the imperial military advances there is only charity and love. They could never act in the barbarous and cruel way in which the Chinese soldiers act. . . . In other words, brutality itself no longer exists in the officers and men of the imperial military who have been schooled in the spirit of Buddhism.[26]

Two months later, the Japanese army perpetrated the Rape of Nanking, where tens of thousands of unarmed military prisoners as well as male and female civilians, including children, were murdered over a period of some six weeks. Unrestrained looting and rape, with the rape victims (often small girls) then mutilated and murdered, marked this atrocious episode, arguably Japan's worst single crime of the Pacific War.

The case of General Matsui Iwane, who was the commander of the army that perpetrated the outrage at Nanking and who was committed to Buddhism, illustrates some of the theological dilemmas that arose when Buddhism was used to justify militarism. In 1939, General Matsui Iwane sponsored the Koa Kwannon temple in Japan dedicated to the benefit of both the Chinese and Japanese combatants who had fallen in battle. On the grounds of the temple, which was of the Rinzai Zen sect, the general enshrined a large ceramic statue made from bloodstained clay taken from the battlefields of China. He hired a priestess to chant prayers and weep for the Chinese war dead. In the ceremony of dedication Matsui expressed grave regrets for the "killing of neighboring friends. This is greatest tragedy of the last one thousand years." The next sentence, however, shows clearly that he also adhered to the doctrines of Imperial Way Buddhism: "Nevertheless this is a holy war to save the peoples of East Asia. . . . Invoking the power of Avalokiteshvara, I pray for the bright future of East Asia."[27] His apparently sincere expression of compassion for the victims of the war and his regret for the violence are in line with the basic Buddhist teachings of nonharm and nonaggression, which cannot be reconciled with the theory and practice of Japanese militarism.

In his last days, General Matsui's major concern was to see that the temple was properly endowed to ensure continuing services for both the victims and perpetrators of Nanking.[28] Koa Kwannon also interred the ashes of seven war criminals executed by the Allied powers after the war, including those of the temple's sponsor, General Matsui, convicted by the Allied powers in the Tokyo war crime tribunal for his role at Nanking. In fact, General Matsui arrived at Nanking exhausted from a bout of tuberculosis after the slaughter had begun and tried unsuccessfully to stop the crimes, severely rebuking his officers and even expressing his dismay to a *New York Times* correspondent.[29] Rev. Shinsho Hanayama, the Buddhist chaplain to the Japanese war criminals, reported the following statement by Matsui, made while he was awaiting execution:

> The Nanking Incident was a terrible disgrace. Shortly after entering Nanking, when memorial services were being held for the dead, I mentioned that services should be performed for the Chinese dead also; only the others, including my Chief of Staff, said that the Chinese would not understand. . . . At the time of the Russo-Japanese War, treatment of Russian prisoners, to say nothing of the Chinese people, was excellent. Things went along nicely. They did not, this time. . . . I wept tears of anger before [the higher officers at Nanking and] told them all that after all our efforts to enhance the Imperial prestige, everything had been lost through the brutalities of the soldiers. And can you imagine it, even after that, these officers laughed at me. To take an extreme example, one of the Division Commanders even came up and asked, "What's wrong about it?" . . . After things turning out this way, I am really eager to die at any time.[30]

General Matsui certainly bought into the Buddhist ideology that justified the war in China and held it to the very end. On the night he was executed, he wrote to his wife,

> My deepest regret is that I was unable to realize Sino-Japanese Cooperation and a new life for Asia. . . . My spirit shall remain in the Koa-Kwannon in Izuyama for all time, to live on in the Sutra of Kwannon and protect and guard the great undertaking of Asiatic revival.[31]

At the same time, his repentance for what the army did at Nanking also seems sincere. This suggests that doubts, bad conscience, and ambiguities lingered in the minds of Buddhists like General Matsui in spite of being reassured by their religious leaders that they could do no wrong in the holy cause. After all, the fundamental thrust of the dharma is to eliminate suffering by eliminating ill will. How can one reconcile Suzuki's sword of "peace, justice, progress, and humanity" with the reality of the sword as wielded in the Greater East Asia Co-Prosperity Sphere, for example, at Nanking in December 1937? According to Hanayama's evidence, in the time they had before being executed, Matsui and the other high- and low-ranking condemned war criminals deepened their religious faith and turned against the ideology of war.[32]

What can be made of the statement of Rinzai Zen Master Nakajima Genjo (1915–2000), who was serving aboard a ship at Nanking during the atrocities? Genjo's enlightenment preceded his enlisting in the Navy.

> I have heard people claim that a great massacre took place at Nanjing, but I am firmly convinced that there was no such thing. It was wartime, however, so there may have been a little trouble with the women. In any event, after things settle down, it is pretty difficult to kill anyone.[33]

Blindness in the face of one of the best documented massacres of the war is a peculiar manifestation of enlightenment, but as Victoria noted, such denials of wrongdoing and complete lack of concern for the suffering Imperial troops inflicted are very common in Japan. The first public admission by a soldier of what they had done in Nanking was in 1995, nearly sixty years after the events.

General Cho Isamu[34] (1895–1945) was the staff officer at the Rape of Nanking, who claimed responsibility for giving the order to slaughter all prisoners. Later he was stationed in Manchuria, where he was responsible for destroying villages and the summary execution of civilians. There Fukushima Nichi'i, mentioned earlier in this chapter, served as his chaplain. They studied the Lotus Sutra together, and Nichi'i gave his disciple a Buddhist name meaning "Courageous Sun [residing in] the temple of Abundant Compassion." Later Cho was chief of staff at Okinawa, where he led the defense against the American invasion. It was he who ordered the soldiers and the island people alike to die rather than to surrender, and he forbade the army to feed starving civilians, policies which led to tens of thousands of senseless deaths. Cho disembowelled himself in a cave at the end of the battle, and much later Nichi'i dedicated a memorial to Cho at the site. At no time did the Buddhist chaplain question Cho's brutal acts, show any concern (let alone remorse) for the suffering of his victims, or have any second thoughts about calling Cho "Abundant Compassion." An Okinawan poet had a more realistic view of Cho and his fellow militarists' actions: "The irresponsibility, recklessness, terrorism, stupidity, debauchery, amorality, and cruelty of the Imperial Army had no confines."[35] Chaplain Nichi'i by confirming General Cho as his worthy Buddhist disciple, by accepting the Buddhist war ideology, and by his blindness to the immoral acts of his religious protégé, surely shares some of the responsibility for the evils perpetrated. And this relationship is typical of the relationship between Buddhist leaders and Japanese militarism and all its excesses.

BUDDHIST WAR RHETORIC

THROUGHOUT THE WAR no major voices spoke out against it, and Buddhist organizations and thinkers continued in their whole-hearted support of the military machine up to the end.[36] Soldiers and workers were given Zen training to improve efficiency and morale, Buddhist organizations collected money to buy warplanes, and priests went to work in armaments factories. All major denominations performed rituals for the defeat of the enemy, and the flood of propaganda continued unabated. The attack on Pearl Harbor, which occurred on December 8 in Japan thanks to the international date line, brought forward this statement in a Soto Zen journal:

> December 8th is the holy day on which Sakyamuni [Lord Buddha] realized the Way, and [for this reason] it has been a day for commemorating the liberation of humankind. It is exceedingly wonderful that in 1941 we were able to make this day also into a holy day for eternally commemorating the reconstruction of the world. On this day was handed down to us the Great Imperial Edict declaring war aimed at punishing the arrogant United States and England, and the news of the American forward bases in Hawai'i spread quickly throughout the world.[37]

Unfortunately this praise of the Pearl Harbor attack as the realization of Sakyamuni Buddha is not an extreme example; it is typical of what the Buddhists journals published throughout the war.

Daiun Harada Roshi said, "We must push on in applying ourselves to 'combat zazen,' the king of meditation,"[38] in 1943. And as the war situation got more desperate, he wrote in 1944:

> It is necessary for all one hundred million subjects to be prepared to die with honour. . . . If you see the enemy you must kill him; you must destroy the false and establish the true—these are the cardinal points of Zen. It is said that if you kill someone it is fitting that you see his blood. . . . Isn't it

the purpose of the zazen [sitting meditation] we have done in the past to be of assistance in an emergency like this?[39]

In the last days of the war, Masunaga Reiho, a Soto Zen priest and scholar, published a series of articles in the Buddhist press in praise of the "Special Attack Forces," the kamikaze pilots and sailors who crashed their planes and vessels in suicide attacks on Allied shipping. He called their sacrificial acts "the achievement of pure enlightenment."[40]

Some of the most shocking material comes from a book published by Yasutani Roshi (1885–1973), the founder of the Sanbo Kyodan Zen sect, the Zen group that has had the most successful missionary role in the West since the war. Written in 1943, it remained unknown in the West until 1999, when it, along with defenses by four Western students of Yasutani, appeared in *Tricycle*, a widely read popular Buddhist magazine. Yasutani followed the general theoretical line about the superiority of Japan and Japanese Buddhism, which he said justified extreme acts in the ongoing war:

> Of course one should kill, killing as many as possible. One should fight hard, kill everyone in the enemy army. . . . Failing to kill an evil man who ought to be killed, or destroying and enemy army that ought to be destroyed, would be to betray compassion and filial obedience, to break the precept forbidding the taking of life. This is a special characteristic of Mahayana precepts.[41]

Yasutani singled out Jews as the source of the ideology of freedom and equality that Japan was called on to destroy. He describes the Jews as evil, demonic schemers, who preach the love of money, pleasure seeking, and individualism, all antithetical to Japanese Buddhist values. Anti-Semitism without Jews—what a blot on the history of the dharma.

OTHER BUDDHIST VOICES

WHILE THE VAST majority of Buddhists, especially officials of Buddhist organizations, were firmly behind the imperialist ideology and the way that the war was prosecuted, there were a few dissenters. One was Ekai Kawaguchi (1866–1945), the Zen monk, who travelled to Nepal and

Tibet at the turn of the century in order to collect Buddhist scriptures in the belief that the Tibetan texts might preserve more of the original dharma than those texts available in Japan. Kawaguchi was gifted in his ability to learn languages, and after mastering Tibetan was able to penetrate the borders sealed against foreigners to live as a Tibetan monk in one of Lhasa's major monasteries. Kawaguchi came up with a plan to unite East Asian countries under the guidance of their common faith, Mahayana Buddhism and to combat Western imperialism, which he wrote in English in a beautifully handwritten memorial presented to his acquaintance, the ruler of Nepal.[42] The idea was to ensure that economic development was for the benefit of Asians, and Kawaguchi also advocated building up strong modern armies to keep their independence. This was not so different from the theory behind the Greater East Asia Co-Prosperity Sphere, but in Kawaguchi's plan, there was great respect for the other Asian peoples. In fact, during the time of Japan's imperial adventures in Asia, Kawaguchi curtly refused to provide the military with information about Tibet and Nepal.[43]

As we have seen, there was widespread and very strong support for the war and war ideology in all its manifestations in the Zen community, but there is no record of any protest or dissent. Ichikawa Hakugen (1902–1986),[44] a Rinzai Zen priest and professor at Hanazono University, where he studied and worked from 1921 until his retirement in 1973, was strongly influenced by Western socialist writers as a young man. After the Pacific War, he was one of the very few intellectuals to express regret about not speaking out against Buddhist war ideology but devoted his considerable energy and scholarship to rectify his earlier silence. His critique appeared in *Zen and Contemporary Thought* (1971), *Buddhists' Responsibility for the War* (1971), and *Religion under Japanese Fascism* (1975), none of which are available in translation. It seems that his work elicited little response from Buddhist individuals, leaders, or institutions, but it did serve to inspire Brian Victoria in his subsequent work.

Ichikawa's assessment of Japanese Buddhists' responses to militarism was based on strong scholarship and firsthand experience, and it was scathing:

With what has modern Japanese Buddhism harmonized itself? With State Shinto. With state power and authority. With militarism. Accordingly, with war.

To what has modern Japanese Buddhism been nonresistant? To State Shinto. To state power and authority. To militarism. To wars of invasion.

Of what has modern Japanese Buddhism been tolerant? Of those with whom it harmonizes. Of its own responsibility for the war.[45]

In addition to detailing the history and details "Imperial Way Zen," a phrase he coined,[46] he also attempted to explain it theoretically, uncovering some twelve contributing factors.[47] Ichikawa did not spare the Kyoto school of philosophy, an informal group centered on the work of Nishida Kitaro (1870–1945) Japan's foremost Buddhist philosopher of the time, which he censured for its authoritarianism, its emperor worship, and its de-facto support of the wars of aggression.[48]

The only major Japanese intellectual who wrote in a forthright way against the Kyoto school's nationalist philosophy during the war was Nanbara Shigeru (1889–1974), who published his *State and Religion* in 1942, where he bravely linked Tanabe's thought with Nazism, and rejected it. Tanabe was one of the Kyoto-school philosophers. For this extremely courageous stance, given the intense pressures to conform to the militarists at the time, Nanbara has been spoken of in Japan as "our pride for having protected the smoldering wick of conscience in the Japanese academic world."[49] Since he was writing as a Christian, the Buddhists' record of nonresistance to fascist ideology remains unblemished.

The Jodo Shinshu, also called Shin Buddhist or Pure Land Buddhist, schools in Japan, which trace back to Honen (C.E. 1133–1212), had some tendencies in their early history to resist government pressures to conform. They also gave rise to popular egalitarian movements, which formed effective local governments and protected the Shin followers in turbulent times. They have been Japan's largest Buddhist sects for centuries, and although they have had enormous influence on the day-to-day life of the Japanese people, they have not attracted much scholarly or general interest from the West. As the quiet faith of ordinary citizens, perhaps it lacks the exotic attraction of Zen and the New Religions, which certainly have had considerable ink dedicated to their exposition. In 1207, at the age of seventy-four, Honen was banished unjustly from his home. Other cobelievers were banished and some were executed for their religious innovations—all at the urging of the current Buddhist establishment. Honen was allowed to return four years later in broken health, and he soon died.

Shinran (C.E. 1173–1262), who was Honen's greatest disciple and the effective founder of the Pure Land dynasties, expressed his disapproval of the way the government had treated Honen. Shinran also suffered exile. He wrote,

> The emperor and his ministers, opposing the dharma and violating justice, harbored anger and resentment [against the Pure Land teaching]. Because of this Master [Honen], the great promulgator of the true teaching, and his followers were, without consideration of their crimes, arbitrarily condemned to death or deprived of their priesthood, given [secular] names and sentenced to distant banishment. I am one of those. Hence I am neither a monk nor one in worldly life.[50]

Now, Honen and Shinran alike generally stressed that it was best to conform to the secular authorities and to established social norms, and by the twentieth century Shinshu had long become part of the establishment. Therefore, this extraordinary passage, scripture in the Shinshu traditions, was troublesome as it clearly condemned the emperor as arbitrary, unjust, and an opponent to dharma. In the militaristic imperial atmosphere of the time, which Shin thinkers had helped to create,[51] Shinshu authorities in 1940 took the extraordinary step of censuring their religious texts, removing these critical words of Shinran and excising other passages from Mahayana sutras and Shinran's hymns that might be interpreted as lowering the prestige of the emperor. They were not replaced until the 1977 edition of the service materials.[52]

While some Shin priests protested as late as 1942 against changing even a single character of their scriptures, the overwhelming voice of the sect was in favour of the militaristic ideology of the state and the war it supported. For example, in 1942, a Shinshu scholar, Shigaraki, published an untranslated book entitled *A Theory of the Oneness of Benevolence: The Essence of Imperial Way Buddhism*, where he maintained "the oneness of the emperor's and Amida's benevolence," Amida being the Buddha that was the central point of Shinshu devotion. The author went so far as to say Shin Buddhists, "are to take imperial law as fundamental and submit absolutely to the [emperor's] command; this is basic to Amida's intent. Those who oppose [this] are, consequently, excluded from Amida's salvation."[53] While some of the Buddhist New Religions did not accept Imperial Way Buddhism,[54] their voices and those of other isolated dissenters, like those few Nicherin followers who resisted the official ideology,[55] were small and quickly silenced, leaving the stage clear for the official Buddhist spokesmen to beat the drums of war.

Postwar Reactions

Yasutani Roshi received dharma transmission from his teacher in 1943, the year of his anti-Jewish pro-war writing. It is more than a little unsettling to find anti-Semitism in the writings of an enlightened Zen master, and even more unsettling to find that he never renounced such teachings. There has been quite a controversy in the columns and letters of *Tricycle*, with his American successors trying to make the best of the situation. Very recently, as a result of the controversy, Kubota Roshi, the dharma successor to Yasutani, issued an apology for what his master said and did in support of the war.[56] Kubota apologized for Japan starting the war and for the horrible experiences of their victims, noting that the Japanese people also suffered terribly from the war. He also apologized to any Zen student who might be offended or shaken by what Yasutani had said.

The basic problem of this chapter, which Kubota and the other leaders of his sect confront, is how to reconcile the attested spiritual attainments of a teacher (or Japanese Buddhism in general) with the obviously poisonous nature of their nationalistic doctrines, which led to many horrible acts. In Yasutani's case, his students claimed that in his postwar Zen practice, he said nothing of politics, and that his students benefited from his spiritual instruction. Yasutani was persuaded to hand over the leadership of the sect in 1967 to a politically more moderate Zen master. Some supporters try to justify the words and acts in support of Japanese imperialism of men like D. T. Suzuki and Yasutani Roshi on the grounds that they were caught up in a totalitarian state, which "subjected [them] to nearly total thought control and indoctrination."[57] This really will not wash because, as we have seen, these and other Buddhist intellectuals were major contributors to building the totalitarian ideology and then were wholehearted supporters of it. Victoria has replied to the defenders of Yasutani, documenting that he continued his right-wing antidemocratic pronouncements long after the war, even after stepping down as head of the sect. Furthermore, Victoria asked some pointed questions about why Yasutani's American dharma successors turned such a blind Zen eye toward their lineage's complicity in Japan's rush to war and war excesses.[58]

On the whole, very few individuals have apologized for or recanted their pro-war Buddhist triumphalism. In contrast to individuals, a number of Buddhist organizations have expressed deep regret for what they said and did to aid Japanese imperialism. However, they were rather tardy in their apologies. The intellectuals of the Soto Zen sect produced a great deal of the ideology of Imperial State Buddhism, and they had one of the largest and most vigorous missionary programs in the subject nations. They published *The History of the Soto Sect's Overseas Evangelization and Missionary Work* in 1980. This book praised Japanese militarism, denigrated the people they missionized, and reaffirmed the Imperial policy of assimilation. Due to reactions to this publication, they reexamined their past, withdrew the book and issued a strong and sweeping apology in 1993. It says, in part:

> We, the Soto sect, have since the Meiji period and through to the end of the Pacific War, utilised the good name of overseas evangelisation to violate the human rights of the peoples of Asia, especially those in East Asia. . . . [W]e despised the peoples of Asia and their cultures, forcing Japanese culture on them and taking actions which caused them to lose their national pride and dignity. This was all done out of a belief in the superiority of Japanese Buddhism and our national polity. Not only that, but is was done in the name of Buddha Shakyamuni and the successive patriarchs. . . . There is nothing to be said about these actions other than they were truly shameful.[59]

They explicitly acknowledged that this apology was too late in coming and very much regretted publishing such an insensitive history of their actions some thirty-five years after the war.

Much weaker was the Rinzai apology issued in response to the events of September 11, 2001. On September 27, 2001, the General Assembly of the Myoshinji Branch of Rinzai Zen, which is the largest branch of the sect, proclaimed,

> Even though it was national policy at the time, it is truly regrettable that our sect, in the midst of wartime passions, was unable to maintain a resolute anti-war stance and ended up cooperating with the war effort. In light of this, we wish, first of all, to confess our past transgressions and critically reflect on our transgressions.[60]

This disingenuous statement was hardly an apology at all, but on October 19, 2001, the Administrative Head of the Myoshinji Branch, recognized their complicity in actively promoting militarism both ideologically and by contributing war goods, and noted that the earlier statement was only a first step. Furthermore, he credited the publication of Brian Victoria's *Zen at War* as the reason for their recent concern and reflected that they seemed unable to reflect on their own mistakes until prompted by outsiders.[61]

The much stronger Soto statement is a good place to end. It is a good summary of the shameful facts and does not attempt to explain them away. "There is nothing to be said about these actions other than they were truly shameful." Perhaps there is no way to explain how enlightened Buddhist teachers could go so far astray.

TIBETAN BUDDHISM, SOCIAL STRUCTURE, AND VIOLENCE

INTRODUCTION

BUDDHISM HAS THE IMAGE OF A FAITH dedicated to peace and peacemaking, even as a way of pacifism, but as shown in the preceding chapters, there is another and darker side to the picture. However, in the case of Tibet, one instantly thinks of the current incarnation of the Dalai Lama, head of the Gelugpa sect and figurehead of the Tibetan Government in Exile, who has tirelessly worked to try to resolve the confrontation between the Tibetans and the Chinese by peaceful means. A well-deserved Nobel Prize in 1989 recognized these efforts, which will be reviewed at the end of this chapter. However, the earlier history of Tibet shows that the Buddhist establishment was steeped in violence and supported surprisingly rigid class and caste systems.

BUDDHISM, SOCIETY, AND WAR IN TRADITIONAL TIBET

VERY LITTLE IS known of Tibet's earliest history, but by the early seventh century of the Common Era, Tibet was the most powerful state of Inner Asia. The texts that record the events of this era were composed long after the events and reflect a strong Buddhist bias, so critical historians question many of the details. Nonetheless these chronicles reflect Tibetan Buddhists' self-understanding. King Songtsen Gampo (r. c. C.E.

614–650), revered as Tibet's greatest king, united the country and defeated armies from China, Nepal, and India, and the Turkish and Arab armies. Although at that time some neighboring countries had had strong Buddhist communities for some time, it would seem that the faith had not become well known in Tibet. As was common practice, the kings of Nepal and China each sealed their treaty with Tibet by sending a daughter to marry King Songtsen Gampo. The queens were both Buddhists and brought sacred Buddha images with them to Lhasa. It is taught that these foreign wives convinced the king to accept dharma and that he then became a lavish benefactor of the faith. Besides building numerous temples, he is credited with sending scholars to India to collect Buddhist texts and to develop a written language for Tibet in order to produce translations of the scriptures. As with Buddhists everywhere, the Tibetans did not abandon their earlier religious traditions, rather they integrated local deities, rituals, and other practices to come up with their unique variety of tantric Buddhism.

Buddhism in Tibet flourished under royal patronage for some two centuries after its introduction, and Tibet continued as the major political power of the region.[1] The kings were believed to be divine and there was an elaborate politico-theological system, which had some features like animal sacrifice that did not fit well with Buddhist thought and practice. Monasteries were built, many Indian Buddhist texts were translated, and Chinese Buddhist schools and influence weakened. This first introduction of Buddhism ended with the reign of King Langdarma (c. 836–842), who is remembered as a thoroughly evil enemy of dharma, although modern scholarship suggests that perhaps his crime was no more than the withdrawal of patronage from Buddhist institutions.[2] The chronicles report that his reign ended with his assassination at the hands of a Buddhist monk and that two centuries of political and religious chaos followed.

In the centuries of chaos that followed, there was a second gradual diffusion of Buddhism from India into Tibet. In the vacuum of power and chaos of the times, the monasteries came to be major powers. They built fortifications, engaged in commerce, controlled much of the land and laborers, and by the thirteenth century became the rulers of the country. This came about when in 1244 the very powerful Mongol ruler of China gave sovereignty over Tibet to the head of the Sakyapa Buddhist sect. For a long period, power shifted between the Kagyupa Buddhist lineage and secular kings until 1642, when the Mongols threw their weight behind the Gelugpa sect, appointing the fifth Dalai Lama to rule the country.

The transition of leadership was not achieved easily, and armies of monks led by their lamas fought several bloody campaigns in the fifteenth century, levelling each other's monasteries,[3] with the Gelugpas eventually coming out on top.

Although never completely without conflict, Tibet's peculiar political system, with the head of state also being the head of the Gelugpa sect, lasted from 1642 until 1959 when the current Dalai Lama, the fourteenth, fled into India to escape the Chinese communists, who had occupied the country in 1950. With political and economic power concentrated in celibate monks, there was an obvious problem of succession, which Tibetans solved in a singular way, with their *tulku* system. Standard Buddhist doctrine teaches reincarnation, that all sentient beings are bound to be reborn again and again as the result of their moral actions or karma until they follow the Buddhist path to its end of complete liberation. In Tibet, important religious teachers are called "lama," from the Sanskrit "*guru*," which Tibetan glosses explain as "highest" or as "exalted mother."[4] Certain very advanced lamas, who are ready to enter the enlightened state, choose rather to be reborn again in order to help all beings. These special lamas, the *tulkus*, leave clues as to when and where they will incarnate and thus the power, wealth, and religious lineage are all passed on from generation to generation. This system has been in force in Tibet since the fourteenth century for all the sects with their being some three thousand different *tulkus* in all.

Tibet was never a homogeneous country with a uniform social system for all of the areas within the Tibetan cultural sphere. The best documented system was that of the agricultural area surrounding Tibet, where there was a well-ordered strict hierarchy of social classes.[5] In simplified form, there were four hereditary classes with hereditary lamas occupying the most prestigious positions. Next were the lay aristocrats. Both of the top two groups were quite small in numbers but had authority over quite large estates. The lamas (through their *labrangs*), the aristocrats, the monasteries, and the central government controlled all the productive land. Chinese authorities recently estimated that religious estates comprised some 37 percent of this total, aristocratic estates 25 percent, and governmental land 38 percent.[6]

The next class, the *mi-ser*, constituted some 90 percent of the population and were divided into households of varying categories and prestige. These included full taxpaying members of the community (relatively few), tenant farmers and itinerant laborers (the majority), traders, hereditary servants, crafts workers, and lay religious practitioners. All *mi-ser* had heavy tax, corvée, and other duties to their hereditary superiors. Through hard work and skill, *mi-ser* often prospered, and some through strategic marriages moved up to the aristocratic level.[7] The lowest social group in traditional Tibet, perhaps 5 to 10 percent of the population, were the outcastes—beggars and others. While the above description of social divisions applied best to central Tibet's agriculturists, other segments of traditional Tibet had similar class structures with pastoral peoples distant from Lhasa being the most egalitarian.[8]

The controversy centers on how to characterize the *mi-ser* grouping and how to describe the system as a whole. Samuel puts the issue nicely:

A major area of disagreement in the literature is over Goldstein's insistence that the situation of the Tibetan peasants can appropriately be referred to as "serfdom." The dispute refers more to nomenclature than to substance (see Michael 1986;[9] Goldstein 1986,[10] 1988;[11] Miller 1987[12]) but it has obvious political overtones, in view of Chinese attempts to display the Lhasa government as an oppressive and exploitative feudal system and so to legitimate their overthrow.[13]

According to Goldstein, in his important paper published in 1970, the situation was very clear in Tibetan society: "With the exception of a handful of aristocrats, all laymen in Tibet were serfs hereditarily linked by ascription to estates and lords."[14]

Were the Tibetan peasants serfs, and was Tibet a feudal society? The Chinese communists believe so and justify their occupation of Tibet and the radical changes they made on that basis. "The essence of the system of 'combined political-clerical rule' in old Tibet was the dictatorship of the serf-owners over the serfs. Brutal suppression upheld cruel economic exploitation."[15] Similarly, another Chinese publication maintains that all "serfs" were doomed to the most appalling poverty and were treated like beasts with unrelenting cruelty.[16] Epstein's *Tibet Transformed*, in chapters 2 and 3, presents a similar, though less lurid, picture of darkness, but his ninth chapter, "The Accusers," is unrelenting in its focus on the worst excesses only.[17] Such Chinese literature exaggerates the cruelties and iniquities that afflicted some of the *mi-ser*, ignoring that many of the common men and women led decent, prosperous, and relatively independent lives. Indeed, a very good case has been made that the policies of the People's Republic of China, especially during the Cultural Revolution (1966–1978), were more brutal and surely more deadly than the policies of the ancient regime.[18]

Goldstein defended his position forcefully, maintaining that the *mi-ser* system had nothing to do with Chinese justifications at the time for their occupation of Tibet, and in fact they maintained the old forms of bound labor for the first years of their governance, from 1951 to 1959.[19] All of the writers mentioned above substantially agreed with Goldstein's description of how the Tibetan estate system worked, with the vast majority of peasants being hereditarily bound to particular estates and having their lives controlled to a considerable extent by the masters of the estates. And all agreed that the lands of the central government, aristocrats, monasteries, and hereditary lamas constituted nearly all the useful land in Tibet. While the status of the *mi-ser* was considerably better than slavery, there was at least one outlying Tibetan community, the Nyinba of Nepal, that had a system of chattel slavery.[20]

DALAI LAMAS

THE MOST FAMOUS *tulku* of course is the Dalai Lama (or "Ocean" Lama), whose third incarnation was given the title by the Mongol Khan in 1578.[21] He is understood to be an incarnation of the Bodhisattva Avalokitesvara, one of the most spiritually advanced and powerful beings in the Mahayana hierarchy. The Dalai Lama's political power came in large part from his status as an incarnation of the highest order, which tied in neatly with the ancient Tibetan system of divine kingship. However, in practice, the incarnation's managers handled most of the day-to-day secular governance.[22] Because of the considerable time lag between the recognition of the new incarnation as a young child and his taking power around the age of twenty-one, during most of the Gelugpa hegemony, regents ruled the country. Also, many of the Dalai Lamas died very young, perhaps under "encouragement," which meant that power remained with regents and officials. From the death of the Great Fifth Dalai Lama in 1682 to the Great Thirteenth Dalai Lama*, who reigned from 1895 to 1933, none actually governed for more than a few years.

While the Dalai Lama was said to be the head of both the religion and the state in Tibet, the situation was really much more complex. Tibet was never a fully unified state. The so-called central government really was in tight control of only the region around Lhasa. In the outlying areas, individual monasteries and estates held by hereditary nobles had more political power than the central government. Furthermore, the Dalai Lama was head only of the fractious Gelugpa school, with practically no direct influence over the other Buddhist sects. There were four major Tibetan Buddhist schools, several minor ones, as well as the non-Buddhist Bon tradition, all with distinctive practices and doctrines, all led by incarnate lamas, and all in competition for political, economic, and spiritual power. As an additional complication, there was a dual bureaucracy, with most of the important posts in the central government being held by two persons: a monk chosen from the higher ranks and a layman from the hereditary nobility.

MONASTIC GOVERNANCE

THE TIBETAN SYSTEM of governance, with direct rule by Buddhist monastics, was unique in the Buddhist world, and some of the ways that their monasteries functioned were found only in Tibet. A very high proportion of the population of Tibet lived as monks.[23] In 1951 there were around 2,500 monasteries in Tibet, with some 115,000 monks, or between 10 to 15 percent of the male population. The custom in Tibet was for families to place their sons as novices at the age of seven or eight, and the boys were expected to stay until they died. In contrast, most Thai monks enter the order for only a few months or years as young men, and there is no disgrace if one chooses to return to the secular world. The proportion of men who are monks in Thailand has been put in the range of 1 to 2 percent.

Some Tibetan monasteries had thousands of residents, supported by endowments of money, land, and bound labor, and were managed to generate enough profit to support the religious activities of the monks and their supporters. Others were very modest indeed. Monasteries had considerable autonomy and the central government rarely intervened in internal issues, with the larger monasteries having the authority to discipline their members for all crimes save treason and murder. The three largest Gelugpa monasteries, known as the Three Seats, all near Lhasa, were enormously powerful. These mass institutions were by no means quiet retreats for scholars and meditators, although they did produce and maintain a certain relatively small number of excellent scholars and practitioners. Most of the monks were engaged in practical pursuits to support themselves and their monasteries. Many worked on building and maintenance projects; some poor monks were servants to the higher monks; some served as administrators of the vast monastic holdings. Non-scholar monks, in addition to the moneymaking work they did, also participated in rituals as musicians, dancers, chanters, and the like. Goldstein reports that the Three Seats had around ten thousand, seven thousand, and five thousand monks respectively in 1951.[24] Those engaged in higher studies constituted some 30 percent of the total, with most of those never advancing far in their learning.[25]

One of the most striking things about Tibetan monastic life was the class of warrior monks, or *dobdos*,[26] who made up from 10 to 15 percent of the population of the Three Seats. They arose during the centuries of struggle after the collapse of the early powerful monarchies and served to defend their monasteries against internal and external enemies. They also provided a role for that proportion of the mass of monks who were really not well suited for the contemplative or scholarly life. *Dobdo* was a nickname, which means something like swank, and refers to the special way they dressed and adorned themselves. They wore special doubled-over pleated skirts, and their upper garment was worn like a shawl rather than as a sash, the normal method. Instead of having completely shaven heads, they allowed a lock of hair to grow behind each ear, which was shaped and draped over the ears. They used eye shadow and always carried at least one weapon, often an oversized metal door key or a crescent knife, which were sharpened and tied to a string. These were thrown and retrieved something like a yo-yo and were useful against a man armed with a sword, because of their long range. The *dobdo* often carried a long knife on his back, concealed by his robes.

They trained in six militaristic sports events, including jumping off a platform, placing a knife in a target, and various sorts of stone throwing, and had periodic tournaments between monasteries. However, the real interest of the *dobdos* was in fighting, as individual and group prestige depended on success in battle. There were official challenge battles between institutions, arranged fights between fellows of the same monasteries, and spontaneous brawls. If they came across a fight between laymen, they usually waded in on the side of the losing party. Another function of the *dobdos* was to keep order during two annual festivals in Lhasa, during which the secular authorities withdrew.

A rare eyewitness account of the details of monastic life in the Three Seats comes from a Japanese Buddhist priest and scholar, Ekai

Kawaguchi[27] (1866–1945), who spent some three years in Tibet at the turn of the twentieth century. Tibet was closed to foreign travelers, but Kawaguchi was able to pass as a Tibetan, due to his mastery of the language and his appearance. He enrolled as a student in the Sera Monastery, one of the Three Seats and the one with a reputation for having the fiercest *dobdos*. He noted that, although they were very poor, the *dobdos* were able to get by as they worked as guards or laborers.[28]

Kawaguchi had some medical knowledge and became friends with the *dobdo* whose wounds he treated after duels. He noted that, "They scarcely ever fight over a pecuniary matter, but the beauty of young boys presents an exciting cause, and the theft of a boy will often lead to a duel."[29] Although homosexuality was strongly condemned for Tibetan laymen, it was tolerated for monks (so long as there was no penetration) and was widespread in Tibetan monasteries, especially in the ranks of the *dobdo*.[30] In their duels, they fought with swords and other weapons, generally until one or both were wounded, and then retired to the inns of Lhasa to reconcile over drinks. In the case of death, they tried to conceal the evidence from the monastic and secular authorities to avoid punishment. While the Japanese priest was put off by their rude manners and uncouth appearance, on the whole, Kawaguchi admired the fighting monks for their good-natured honesty and valour.[31]

MONASTIC OPPOSITION TO REFORM IN TIBET (1900–1950)

FROM 1913 TO 1933, the thirteenth Dalai Lama attempted several modernizations in Tibet, in large part because he had become convinced in his period of exile that the future independence of the country could only be maintained through building a modern army and improving other state facilities. He fled to Mongolia and China after the British military excursion into Tibet in 1903 and 1904, then to India when the Chinese occupied Lhasa in 1909. All in all he was gone from 1904 to 1912, returning when China was in turmoil from the Republican revolution. The young army officers, who had fought the British and the Chinese and who knew first hand that their traditional fighters, no matter how courageous, could not withstand modern armies, were the strongest supporters of modernization. While religion provided the most powerful uniting force for the Tibetans and the various competing factions genuinely acted with the intention of benefiting their faith, the "essential flaw in the Tibetan politico-religious system was . . . that while religious priority was universally accepted, the definition of what benefited religion was often contested."[32]

The group that most strongly opposed change was the Three Seats, supported by their squadrons of *dobdos*, which in fact outnumbered the government's army. According to Goldstein, supporting the great mass of monks and paying for the annual cycle of religious festivals was extremely costly, which led the monasteries to resist any attempts to tax or limit their land holdings or other revenues.

> It also made them advocates of the serf-estate system and, thus, extremely conservative. As Tibet attempted to adapt to the rapid changes of the twentieth century, religion and the monasteries played a major role in thwarting progress.[33]

This judgment is echoed by the contemporary Tibetan historian, Tsering Shakya, who concluded, "High lamas and the monasteries used their enormous influence to obstruct reforms that were desperately needed to transform Tibetan society."[34]

At first the thirteenth Dalai Lama was inclined to follow the advice of the soldier faction and proceeded slowly to build up a strong, modern army to protect the borders and sovereignty of the country and to provide a countervailing force to monastic troops. In 1921 he used the small but effective army against the Loseling College of the Drepung Monastery, one of the Three Seats. In the 1911 to 1912 war with Chinese forces, Loseling supported the Chinese side, refusing to send warrior monks to help rid Lhasa of Chinese forces and then protecting the Chinese political officer when he fled. In the context of a conflict over property, the central government punished two high college officials who had helped the Chinese, and then a crowd of monks from Loseling besieged the Dalai Lama, who was in retreat in the Norbulinga, his summer palace.

> While the senior monks shouted and prostrated, the younger monks urinated and defecated all over the Dalai Lama's gardens, pulled up and trampled the Dalai Lama's flowers, broke the statues, and sang as loudly as possible in order to disturb him.[35]

At that moment, there were not enough troops to control the situation, but within a few days, some three thousand soldiers were brought together to confront the college, which backed down without a single shot being fired. About sixty ringleader monks were seized and punished by light flogging, shackling and placement in cangues, and then were put under house arrest under the care of various nobles. There was no general punishment and no confiscation of property. This incident changed forever the relationship between the forces of the central government and the forces of the Three Seats and showed the value of an effective army to the Dalai Lama. It also reinforced the conservative forces in their opposition to a modern army and other progressive changes.[36] Another reason that Tibet failed to modernize its armed forces was that Buddhist values against killing made soldiering an unattractive option, especially for the hereditary aristocrats who saw a military career as a degrading option.[37]

Buddhist institutions in traditional Tibet loaned out their enormous endowments at 20 to 30 percent rates of interest to support their annual cycle of rituals and other activities. In 1944, a group of monks mostly from Sera Che college were sent to Lhundrup Dzong, a district north of Lhasa, to collect the interest on such a loan. This ordinary act precipitated an incident, which had dangerously destabilizing effects on the country. It illustrated the political power of the ecclesiastical institutions, showed how tenaciously they defended their economic interests, and also showed how ordinary citizens were protected to some degree by the central government from the demands of their overlords.[38] It began when the debtor peasants complained to the district commissioner that they could not afford to pay what they owed. The central government had a new policy to relieve some of the financial burdens of the peasantry, and the commissioner instructed the monks not to force payment until the government had investigated the situation, much to the anger of the loan collector monks. The abbot of the college instructed them to do whatever they had to do to get the money owed to them.

Around November in 1944, the party of collectors presented themselves to the district commissioner, bringing with them traditional gifts, including a dried leg of mutton. Each side stubbornly held its position. "In the series of increasingly insulting exchanges that followed, one monk, in a frenzy, started hitting the district commissioner on the head with the dried meat."[39] The others joined in, stabbing and pummelling the hapless official with tea utensils and whatever else came to hand. He was very severely injured and died a few days later after the number and nature of his wounds were carefully cataloged. The central government appointed a very high-level committee of inquiry into this violent act and ordered that the college hand over the monks who were involved for questioning. The college refused, saying that the monks were not acting for themselves and never meant to show disrespect to the government. They offered instead to pay a fine on behalf of the institution. Neither side would compromise. The government quietly waited while reinforcing its troops around Lhasa, and acted in June 1945 to remove the abbots of Sera Che and the other college that supported them. At first the abbot wanted to offer armed resistance—they had some two thousand rifles and the usual cadre of fighting monks—but the largest subunit of the college would not agree. The abbot fled to the Chinese controlled section of Tibet, with his bodyguards fighting the pursuing troops. He later returned to Lhasa with the Chinese People's Army.

With the abbot out of the way, the government seized all of the monks that were directly involved in the Lhundrup Dzong killing. Two of them, the most defiant, were whipped severely in the course of the hearings, and fourteen were convicted and punished. Two years later, things came to a head again when the monks of Sera Che revolted against the central government.[40] It began on April 16, 1947, when the unpopular new government-appointed abbot publicly supported the regent in a move against his rival. Spontaneously a group of his monks armed themselves with swords, knives, and an axe. They pursued the abbot across the roof of Sera Che, eventually cornered him, and then stabbed and hacked him to death. The rebellion lasted with sporadic fighting until the twenty-ninth of April when it was put down in a decisive battle by the government forces. One of the most violent episodes occurred on the twenty-third and twenty-fourth, when a force of armed monks surrounded and slaughtered a small group of soldiers who were guarding a confiscated property.

In the days of fighting, it was estimated that perhaps two hundred or three hundred monks were killed, with only some fifteen soldiers having died. Twenty-two monks who led the rebellion were flogged severely, with one hundred to two hundred lashes, and then placed in irons and in cangues. Five received life in prison, and the others were kept under house arrest in various aristocratic estates. While the rebellious monks were completely crushed, the country was left "hopelessly fragmented . . . [with no] chance that Tibet would be able to present a unified front to the inevitable Chinese threat to its de facto autonomy."[41] At the time of all this turmoil, it should be remembered that the fourteenth Dalai Lama, who remains the incumbent today, was only thirteen years old and that officers of his regency made all of the political decisions. It was reported that he was most distressed by the harsh treatment of the leading rebels.[42]

TIBET, THE FOURTEENTH DALAI LAMA

IN 1950, AFTER the Chinese invasion of Tibet, the young Dalai Lama, only fifteen years old, was raised to his full power to govern in order to deal with the crisis facing the country. Besides trying to deal with the representatives of the People's Republic of China to guard Tibet's interests as much as he could, he also felt it necessary to make internal reforms to modernize the government and society to make matters fairer to all. In his memoir published in 1962, he described the Tibetan system in these words:

> Outside the monasteries, our social system was feudal. There was inequality of wealth between the landed aristocracy at one extreme and the poorest peasants at the other. It was difficult to move up into the class of aristocracy. . . . But on the other hand, promotion to higher ranks in the monasteries and among the monk officials was democratic.[43]

As he said, boys of any social class could enter the monastic life and could advance through the ranks by skill and application, and the hereditary lamas often chose rebirths in humble families like his own.

He came to see, "Our inequality in the distribution of wealth was certainly not in accordance with Buddhist teaching," so he instituted reforms in tax collection, land tenure, bound labor, debt relief, and most importantly, the reform of the feudal system that prevailed on the estates of the hereditary aristocracy. These improvements were all undertaken in the early 1950s and met with considerable resistance from those whose time-honored powers and privileges were reduced. There was not enough time to see if they would have been effective and popular, because the Communist Party soon overruled them with their own policies. Still it is obvious that the fourteenth Dalai Lama, from a very early age, was dissatisfied with the status quo of old Tibet, though he did note that the Buddhist doctrine of karma had the double effect of making one accept one's lot in life, while simultaneously striving to do better, to improve one's karmic situation through good works and charity. This meant that Tibetans, although generally acquainted with poverty, on the whole were relatively happy and content and did not question their social system. Finally he noted, "And feudal though the system was, it was different from any other feudal system, because at the apex of it all was an incarnation of [the Buddha of Mercy]," that is, himself, whom the people revered and trusted completely.[44]

In 1962, he explained his vision for the future of Tibet, rejecting the feudalism and isolation of the past, and pledging to continue in his mission of reform. At the time, he was "drafting a new liberal and democratic constitution for Tibet, based on the principles of the doctrine of Lord Buddha and the Universal Declaration of Human Rights."[45] Promulgated on March 10, 1963, the fourth anniversary of the uprising in Lhasa against the Chinese that led to the Dalai Lama's exile, the Draft Constitution drew heavily on the United Nations Universal Declaration of Human Rights. Although implemented as much as possible by the Tibetan Government in Exile, they have been meticulous in referring to it as a draft until such time as it is hoped all the Tibetan people will be free to ratify it democratically. The preamble is very interesting indeed:

> WHEREAS it has become increasingly evident that the system of govern which has hitherto prevailed in Tibet has not proved sufficiently responsive to the present needs and future development of the people
>
> AND WHEREAS it is deemed desirable and necessary that the principle of justice, equality and democracy laid down by the Lord Buddha should be reinforced and strengthened in the government of Tibet.
>
> AND WHEREAS it is deemed essential that the people of Tibet should have more effective voice in shaping their destiny
>
> NOW, THEREFORE, His Holiness the Dalai Lama has been pleased to ordain, and it [the Constitution] is hereby ordained . . .[46]

Perhaps the most striking thing about this was that, in the interests of democracy, the Dalai Lama, befitting his status as a divine head of state, imposed a new liberal order on his people, who really did not want it and were rather bewildered altogether.[47] Tibetans particularly objected to Article 36e,[48] which allowed the National Assembly by a two-thirds vote to strip the Dalai Lama of his executive powers should the interests of the country require it. In 1990, the Dalai Lama said of this controversy, "I had to explain that democracy is very much in keeping with Buddhist principles and, somewhat autocratically perhaps, insisted that the clause be left in."[49] In fact, while having many democratic features and protecting human rights, the Constitution and the Government in Exile does retain a fair degree of autocratic power for the head of state, the Dalai Lama. In 1996 he was accused by one group of Tibetan Buddhists for attempting to restrict their religious freedom by his opposition to the worship of a Tibetan deity, Dorje Shugden, which he and his close advisors denounce as a dangerous and harmful "cult."[50]

It is striking that, in the preamble to the Constitution and in his 1962 autobiographical statement, the Dalai Lama said that the principles taught by Lord Buddha and the United Nations Declaration on Human Rights were compatible, if not identical. Furthermore, chapter II of the Draft Tibetan Constitution, "Fundamental Rights and Duties," enshrined many of the specific rights found in the United Nations Universal Declaration.[51] The defense of human rights from very basic Buddhist principles has been a constantly recurring theme in the speeches and writings of the Dalai Lama for some forty years. José Ignacio Cabezón, an authority on Tibetan Buddhism who teaches the philosophy of religion at Iliff School of Theology, has reviewed and analyzed these teachings by the Dalai Lama in a very fine essay. He notes first that the Dalai Lama's efforts are grounded in the current political and historical suffering of the Tibetan people, who have been oppressed, at varying degrees of intensity under Chinese communist rule since 1950.[52] As the hereditary spiritual and political leader of the country, the Dalai Lama has tried to inspire his people to defend themselves using nonviolent Buddhist principles, and he has consistently preached and practiced compassion, loving-kindness, and nondiscrimination toward the Chinese.[53] He has also attempted to negotiate just and peaceful political settlements, but with no real progress. In fact, the Chinese seem to be gradually succeeding in their plans to integrate Tibet into their system through a combination of repression, development, education, and population transfer. Nonetheless, the international community has generally responded very favorably to the message and activities of the Dalai Lama, as his Nobel Peace Prize in 1989 demonstrates.

Cabezón shows that the philosophical basis for the Dalai Lama's affirmation of human rights lies in the basic Buddhist teaching of the interdependence of all beings and in the idea that all human beings, by virtue of their fundamental Buddha nature or "potential for perfection," are equal.[54] In the Bodhisattva practice, which is the core of the Mahayana, this equality of self and other is worked out in the selfless service and sacrifice of the practitioner for the sake of other sentient beings, to bring them all to enlightenment. According to the Dalai Lama, such compassion for others is based on the fact that all of us "want happiness and do not want suffering,"[55] and this directly leads to a doctrine of rights. In his disarmingly simple words,

> If you ask, "Do humans have rights?", yes, there are human rights. How is it that humans have rights? It is on the basis of the valid innate appearance of an I to our consciousness that we naturally want happiness and do not want suffering, and that wanting of happiness and not wanting of suffering itself, with this appearance as its basis, is the very reason for there being human rights.[56]

This reasoning bases human rights on the universal human experience of wishing to avoid suffering and to have happiness. Although it is very consistent with the basic teachings of the Four Holy Truths and other basic Buddhist doctrine, it does not rely on any particular Buddhist text or teaching to make its point, and thus should appeal to all humanity.

It seems obvious, however, that he is not maintaining that human rights are absolute. Since they derive from "the appearance of an I to our consciousness," human rights are in the realm of relative truth. The idea of a permanent, absolute self or "I" is one of the fundamental errors that the Buddha dispelled and which, of course, the Dalai Lama constantly guards against. Since there is no absolute ground for human rights, they are in the realm of *upaya* or skillful means. This also ties in very well with the concrete situation out of which the Dalai Lama's teachings about rights and the inclusion of them in the Draft Tibetan Constitution arise. All those rights found in Chapter II of the Constitution would serve very well to protect the happiness of Tibetans and to save them from suffering. Furthermore, as the Dalai Lama argued so eloquently in his 1993 statement to the United Nations World Conference on Human Rights and Universal Responsibility, such rights are universal in their application:

> Recently some Asian governments have contended that the standards of human rights laid down in the Universal Declaration of Human Rights are those advocated by the West and cannot be applied to Asia and others parts of the Third World because of differences in culture and differences in social and economic development. I do not share this view and I am convinced that the majority of Asian people do not support this view either, for it is the inherent nature of all human beings to yearn for freedom, equality and dignity.[57]

This 1993 statement by the Dalai Lama is perhaps the best single document to observe how he based universal human rights on the universal human capacity for love and compassion and the universal human desire for happiness and against suffering. It would seem that his view of human rights affirms their universality but does not claim they are absolute.

CONCLUSION

WHILE INDIVIDUAL BUDDHISTS are encouraged to cleanse their own hearts from violent impulses and to avoid violent acts, Buddhists generally have not advocated pacifism as a policy for the state to follow. Buddha's social and political thought had rather a hard-nosed realism to it, recognizing that men and women in society were caught up in webs of delusion and desire, which inevitably led to injustice and violence. A strong ruler, who combined a concern for the practical welfare and spiritual progress of his people, was the solution offered. Such a ruler, by the very nature of social reality, would have to use force to restrain and punish the most greedy, violent, and lustful of his subjects when they oppressed their weaker neighbors. The ruler also had the positive duty to take steps to see that the nation prospered and then to see that the wealth was used to support spiritual groups, particularly, the Buddhist orders.

Individual monks and nuns, who renounced the world to live in the Buddhist orders, were expected to live according to much higher moral standards than the laity. Their lives were regulated by strict rules conducive to nonviolence, chastity, and nonacquisitiveness. In large part, the monastics were supported or not depending on how well kept their many precepts. This, of course, was not easy to do in traditional times and even less in modernity. In Thailand, this interrelation between the worldly and the world-renouncers has been maintained as an ideal, but has been put under considerable strain by the threats to the country from both western imperialism and by communist expansionism.

Tibet's Buddhism evolved very differently, with the governance of the state overlapping considerably with the monastic establishments. Monks held key political offices, participated fully in the economy, and even served in military positions. This was a unique Tibetan solution to the traditional tension found in Buddhist countries between the religious establishment, as embodied in the purified monastic sangha, and the political realm, as embodied in a sacral king. In the figure of the Dalai Lama the religious pole of authority and the secular pole were unified in a single figure a monk, who was the incarnation of the Bodhisattva Avalokitesvara and wheel-turning king all in one.[58] While this system provided relative stability and reasonably good government for some centuries, in the modern era it would seem that the political and economic interests of clerical forces fatally undermined the independent survival of the country as a whole. As Tsering Shakya put it, the failure of the Tibetan elite to come to terms with the challenges that faced them in the first half of the twentieth century meant that, "By 1949 . . . Tibet was not equipped to oppose China either militarily or socially."[59] This sort of outcome vindicates the Buddha's teaching that monks should keep themselves at arm's length from political, economic, and military power. Of course in the case of Tibet, where the monasteries were mass rather than elite institutions, effectively autonomous as economic, political, and even military structures, it was not possible to follow the rules that separated monks from worldly spheres of activity.

Kawaguchi, one hundred years ago, noted approvingly the words of his Tibetan teacher:

> I do not know whether to rejoice at or to regret the presence of so many priests in Tibet. Some seem to take this as a sign of the flourishing condition of the national religion and on that ground seem to be satisfied with it. I cannot quite agree with this argument; on the contrary I rather hold that it is better to have even two or three precious diamonds than a heap of stones and broken tiles.[60]

In exile today, the Dalai Lama and his followers have renounced most direct political power and have reformed many of the economic and other practices of the monasteries. In Tibet, the monasteries, which have begun to rebuild after the worst excesses of Chinese repression were relaxed, are limited in size and restricted from political and economic activities and are monitored to see that they support the current regime.[61]

12

CONCLUDING REFLECTIONS

ARE THERE HUMAN RIGHTS IN Buddhism? It is clear that in traditional Buddhist sources there is nothing like a fully developed theory of human rights. In fact, "rights" as a concept does not exist in any explicit form. However, some Buddhist scholars argue that rights are implicit within the core of dharma and that it is possible, desirable, and perhaps even necessary, to derive a Buddhist doctrine of human rights. On the other hand, as maintained throughout the present study, there are strong counterarguments that suggest that human rights theory, which ineluctably carries with it a huge baggage of Western concepts, attitudes, and history, simply is not a good fit with Buddhist thought and practice. The Western-based notion of a human right as an absolute and universal good, owned by and owed to autonomous individuals, may well be fundamentally inconsistent with the Buddhist avoidance of absolute formulations, teachings of interdependence, and doctrine of no-self.

On the other hand, there are a number of indisputable, unambiguously Buddhist ideals, which if implemented, lead in the direction of wholesome, flourishing societies where human dignity and individual persons are respected and cherished, the point of human rights systems. On the level of personal virtues, Buddhists are encouraged to live with compassion, to practice nonharm, to be generous givers of self and goods, to work for the cessation of suffering, and to strive for the happiness of all beings. On the social level, there are the values of cooperation, interdependence, peace, forbearance, and relations built on the basis of mutual duties, responsibilities, and respect. A nation of people that lived up to these great ideals would have no need for a human rights doctrine, as the dignity and welfare of all would be the at the heart of all. Such an ideal Buddhist society would not need to compromise or undermine the fundamental principles of dharma by trying to squeeze them into the framework of a human rights system, yet it would have much in common with an ideal Western society where human rights were sincerely respected by individual citizens and carefully guarded by the state. Unfortunately, as the historical record reviewed above suggests, Buddhist states have rarely been successful in ordering themselves according to the highest ideals of dharma—not to imply that Western ones have very often, if ever, been exemplary in living up to their finest principles.

Minor and Ann Rogers commented that the Mahayana Buddhist tradition

> has the intellectual resources . . . to offer a critique of prevailing social norms: it has the sociological resources, through the community of monks, to offer an alternative to and a refuge from society for the individual.

However, in Japan the Buddhist community failed "to seek and find conceptual and institutional expression for a tradition of transcendence that would provide an alternative to and a basis for critique of the existing social order."[1] Rather the Buddhists in Japan nearly always sought to support the political order, with its tradition of state-centered religion, by seeking to ally themselves intellectually, ritually, and personally with the emperor as the embodiment of worldly law and order.

While the Rogers's comments concern Japan, they fit rather well with what happened in other traditional Buddhist polities. The radical insights of the dharma, calling for a life of freedom both aiming for and grounded in transcendence, was actualized in the monastic sangha for the relatively few who chose to renounce the world. For the rest, it was best not to disturb things over much. The world of flux always ends in disorder, death, and rebirth, according to the laws of karma and the first holy truth, which states that all phenomena entail suffering (*duhkha*). Furthermore, the monastic orders depend upon the stability and generosity of the ordinary world, from which they receive all their needs. Political order, as part of the realm of relative truth, never was a major concern to Buddhist thinkers, yet the tradition did lay down general principles, lists of virtues, and traditional models for rulers to follow (none of which included human rights), and in so far as they were implemented, life was relatively sweet in the realm.

Although there were these general guidelines for governance, there were never any detailed blueprints laid down for all Buddhist nations and rulers to follow. Therefore, there have been numerous forms of government in the various times and places that Buddhists controlled nations and empires. When Buddhists came to a new place, it took many generations to grow into it, and to modify it in return. For example, in China, there was no tradition of supporting begging monks, and celibacy was taken as a threat against the cultural imperative to carry on one's family name and responsibilities from generation to generation by producing an heir. Thus in China, it was not easy to establish the monastic sangha, which was one of the three fundamental jewels of Buddhism. In the past, the Buddhist state was always centered on a king or emperor, who in one sense or another was more than an ordinary man, who connected the human social realm with the cosmic order. In Japan, there was a divine emperor, in China an emperor who ruled with the mandate of heaven, and Tibet came to be ruled by Buddhist clerics who were understood to be incarnate Buddhas.

In modernity, from the beginning, say, of the nineteenth century of the Common Era, new forms and ideas have entered into Buddhist thought and political practice in Asia. Various parties in the Theravada country of Burma, for example, have interpreted their religious tradition to support a surprisingly diverse number of different types of state in the last 150 years, from traditional Southeast Asian monarchy drawing on the Asokan ideal, through democratic state socialism (U Nu), to military dictatorship (SLORC), and the hope of parliamentary democracy based on universal human rights under the party of Aung San Suu Kyi. In Tibet, the current Dalai Lama, the incarnate Buddha who heads the Tibetan Government in Exile has also espoused human rights and has given them a central place in the Draft Constitution.

If it is true, as maintained throughout this study, that Buddhist thinkers never developed human rights principles, that Buddhist societies were not governed by them, and that the rhetoric and content of human rights discourse may actually go counter to the spirit of traditional dharma, how can it be explained that the two Buddhist Nobel Peace Prize laureates both champion human rights?[2] The writings of the Dalai Lama offer the beginning of an answer:

> Although compassion is explained mainly in the Bodhisattva scriptures—
> the Great Vehicle (*Mahayana*)—all Buddhist ideas are based on compas-
> sion. All of Buddha's teachings can be expressed in two sentences. The first
> is, "You must help others." This includes all the Great Vehicle teachings.
> "If not, you should not harm others." This is the whole teaching of the
> Low Vehicle [Theravada]. . . . It expresses the basis of all ethics, which is
> to cease harming others. Both teachings are based on the thought of love,
> compassion. A Buddhist should, if possible, help others. If this is not possi-
> ble, at least do not harm others.[3]

This passage is very like a verse found in the *Dhammapada* that summa-
rizes and simplifies all of the complexities of Buddhist thought and practice into one simple sentence: "Not to do any evil, to cultivate good, to
purify one's mind, this is the Teaching of the Buddhas."[4] Note that, according to the Dalai Lama, not harming others is at a lower level than
helping them. Human rights laws prohibit acts that harm others. If motivated by compassion, human rights as relative values are compatible with
basic dharma. The potential danger is that, if human rights are taken as
absolutes inherent to persons understood as substantial selves, they will
lead in the direction of selfish motivations. When human rights lead an
individual to grasp for a good that he or she believes is due as one's right-
ful possession, then they counter buddhadharma and will lead to unskillful acts.

On the mundane level of politics, it seems clear that such human rights
protections as are offered in the Draft Constitution of Tibet under "Safeguards in Judicial Proceedings" and "Prohibition of Inhuman Treatment"
would, if implemented, protect the Tibetan people from many of the
abuses they have suffered under the Chinese. At the same time, the new
Constitution would provide a framework to reform the abuses of the prior
Tibetan regime. The current Dalai Lama believes such reforms must take
place in order to make the system viable in the modern world and, more
critically, to bring it into accord with the Buddhist ideals of good governance, which he notes had been violated in the past. Here one is reminded of what Phra Payutto, the influential Thai Buddhist scholar and
monk, wrote about human rights. At best they might prove useful in the
dog-eat-dog world of modernity:

> It is a "negative ethic": society is based on selfish interests—"the right of
> each and every person to pursue happiness"—and an ethic, such as "human

rights," is needed to keep everybody from cutting each other's throats in the process.[5]

In short, human rights in this Buddhist understanding are relative and not absolute goods. They are a matter of *upaya*, or skillful means. In the Dalai Lama's overall message, using human rights to prohibit harmful acts is not nearly so central as his constant call to live according to the Buddhist virtues founded on compassion, to do good, and to help others selflessly.

Aung San Suu Kyi, like the Dalai Lama, is faced with the pressing political reality that the people she leads are suffering greatly under their current political leaders. The umbrella of human rights as detailed in the Universal Declaration of 1948, if implemented in Burma, would greatly diminish the evils done and the suffering felt in her country. This would be (Buddhist) justification enough for her advocacy of human rights, which she sees as consistent with Buddhist teachings, although she does not demonstrate such a consistency. Furthermore, the positive political principles she puts forward are traditional Buddhist virtues and rules for the ideal monarch, so it would seem that human rights are only the first step necessary to restrain the doing of evil, and by no means an absolute value. That Aung San Suu Kyi studied Western politics, philosophy, and economics at Oxford and lived in the United States and Great Britain for a number of years may also help explain the seemingly effortless way she has assimilated democratic and human rights values and espouses them for Burma and other non-Western cultures.

This leads into the final question of this study, the place of human rights in Western Buddhism. Buddhism entered the West over the last 150 years, through the influx of Asian Buddhist migrants and the conversion of Westerners to the dharma. Both of these streams have increased significantly in the last fifty years. In reality, the job of Buddhism evolving its Western forms has hardly begun, and it is not a certainty that the seedling will hold and flower. However, it does seem clear that Western Buddhism, especially the Buddhism of Western converts, is naturally enough taking the flavor of the liberal democracies where it landed. The new Buddhists bring with them their comfort with democratic forms and their social activism, thus engaged Buddhism is much stronger in Western Buddhist communities than it ever had been in Asia, where it hardly existed in the past. Indeed, in the opinion of Robert Aitken Roshi, American Zen teacher, scholar, and one of the founding fathers of the engaged

Buddhist movement, "We do not find Buddhist social movements developing until the late nineteenth century, under the influence of Christianity and Western ideas generally."[6] In regard to Japan, Masaharu Anesaki (1873–1949), the Japanese historian who lived through the transition to modernity, agreed. He noted that modern ideas like rights were introduced from the West, particularly by missionaries, as were modern practices, like religious groups doing social reform work.[7]

Since there are no Buddhist blueprints for a political system, it is not surprising that Western Buddhism is moving to be as Western as Chinese Buddhism is Chinese in its self-governance and relations with the state. After all, since politics is of the relative, mundane level, there have been multitudes of ways that Buddhists have lived and governed themselves. Buddhists have generally fitted into the political and social systems of the places they settled. Thus many new Buddhists in the West have carried their native human rights tradition and social activism to their attempts to apply their new Buddhist faith in daily life. In reviewing a number of such admirable and brave initiatives by Buddhists in the struggle against racism and apartheid in South Africa, Darrel Wratten, lecturer in religious studies at the University of Cape Town, asked what made them "*distinctively Buddhist* examples of socially engaged practice." Although inspired by a critical interpretation of Buddhist principles, "their symbolic acts of opposition—a peace march, a vigil, and a fast—were not essentially incongruous with Christian Catholic or Protestant, or Muslim anti-apartheid activities employed in the struggle for a nonracist, nonsexist, and democratic South Africa."[8] Wratten's observations are perceptive and may be taken as an example of how Buddhists are shaping themselves to a new setting. Perhaps, it is not the form of action that makes it distinctively Buddhist; it is rather the motive (selfless giving) from an insight into the interdependence and inherent emptiness of all phenomena.

One of the most striking institutional manifestations of Western Buddhist activisim is the Master of Arts Program in Engaged Buddhism, which was established in 1995 at the Naropa Institute. The Naropa Institute is a Buddhist inspired postsecondary institution founded in Boulder, Colorado, by a Tibetan lama in the Karma Kagyu lineage, Chogyam Trungpa Rimpoche, in 1974. Its innovative programs are accredited by the North Central Association of Colleges and Schools. A blending of the academic study of Buddhism, meditation practice, and practical work in the streets on social problems, the director describes the program in engaged Buddhism as "blue-collar dharma."[9] Although grounded in Buddhism—students are required to sit a one-month long meditation retreat—it is open to students of all faiths. It has links with many different Buddhist activist organizations, including Sulak Sivaraksa's International Network of Engaged Buddhists.

Other uniquely Western contributions to Buddhism involve writing about engaged Buddhism and producing declarations and manifestos. Western Buddhists have written more on human rights in the last twenty-five years than all earlier Buddhists had done in twenty-five centuries. Buddhists in Asia very rarely made proclamations on matters of public interest, something that has very much been a part of Western religious and political activism. The United Nations Universal Declaration of 1948, for example, probably never would have appeared had it been left to Buddhist initiatives, although Buddhists countries did sign on.

A good example of how Western Buddhists' interests have driven the issue was the 1995 online conference on Buddhism and human rights sponsored by the *Journal of Buddhist Ethics* (another Western initiative.) Only one of the discussion papers was by an Asian Buddhist, and nearly all of the participants were from Europe and North America. Typically, those involved felt it important to produce a "Declaration of Interdependence,"[10] reprinted in chapter 13. This valuable document reflects the care and learning of the drafters. Interestingly, as a product of a primarily Western conference on Buddhism and human rights, the declaration makes no use of the term or concept of "rights." The preamble and the "whereas" clauses securely ground the matter in such fundamental Buddhist doctrines as compassion, nonharm, coconditioned arising, mutual dependency, no-self, and the dignity of human beings that comes from their potential of enlightenment. These core ideas of the dharma, which are foundational in all schools of Buddhists, led the conference to call for all governments and individuals to treat every person humanely and without discrimination in regard to the accidents of birth, and for all human beings to treat all sentient beings and the environment that sustains us with respect and nonharm. Such general principles neatly cohere with the political programs of Aung San Suu Kyi, the Dalai Lama, and basic dharma without calling on the imported notion of rights.

Part II
Human Rights
Resources in the
Buddhist Tradition

13

Sources Illustrative of Human Rights in the Buddhist Tradition

1. United Nations Universal Declaration of Human Rights, 1948

On December 10, 1948, the General Assembly of the United Nations adopted and proclaimed the Universal Declaration of Human Rights, the full text of which appears in the following pages. Following this historic act the Assembly called upon all member countries to publicize the text of the Declaration and "to cause it to be disseminated, displayed, read and expounded principally in schools and other educational institutions, without distinction based on the political status of countries or territories."

Preamble

Whereas recognition of the inherent dignity and of the equal and inalienable rights of all members of the human family is the foundation of freedom, justice and peace in the world,

Whereas disregard and contempt for human rights have resulted in barbarous acts which have outraged the conscience of mankind, and the advent of a world in which human beings shall enjoy freedom of speech and belief and freedom from fear and want has been proclaimed as the highest aspiration of the common people,

Whereas it is essential, if man is not to be compelled to have recourse, as a last resort, to rebellion against tyranny and oppression, that human rights should be protected by the rule of law,

Whereas it is essential to promote the development of friendly relations between nations,

Whereas the peoples of the United Nations have in the Charter reaffirmed their faith in fundamental human rights, in the dignity and worth of the human person and in the equal rights of men and women and have determined to promote social progress and better standards of life in larger freedom,

Whereas Member States have pledged themselves to achieve, in cooperation with the United Nations, the promotion of universal respect for and observance of human rights and fundamental freedoms,

Whereas a common understanding of these rights and freedoms is of the greatest importance for the full realization of this pledge,

Now, Therefore THE GENERAL ASSEMBLY *proclaims* THIS UNIVERSAL DECLARATION OF HUMAN RIGHTS as a common standard of achievement for all peoples and all nations, to the end that every individual and every organ of society, keeping this Declaration constantly in mind, shall strive by teaching and education to promote respect for these rights and freedoms and by progressive measures, national and international, to secure their universal and effective recognition and observance, both among the peoples of Member States themselves and among the peoples of territories under their jurisdiction.

Article 1.

All human beings are born free and equal in dignity and rights. They are endowed with reason and conscience and should act towards one another in a spirit of brotherhood.

Article 2.

Everyone is entitled to all the rights and freedoms set forth in this Declaration, without distinction of any kind, such as race, colour, sex, language, religion, political or other opinion, national or social origin, property, birth or other status. Furthermore, no distinction shall be made on the basis of the political, jurisdictional or international status of the country or territory to which a person belongs, whether it be independent, trust, non-self-governing or under any other limitation of sovereignty.

Article 3.

Everyone has the right to life, liberty and security of person.

Article 4.

No one shall be held in slavery or servitude; slavery and the slave trade shall be prohibited in all their forms.

Article 5.

No one shall be subjected to torture or to cruel, inhuman or degrading treatment or punishment.

Article 6.

Everyone has the right to recognition everywhere as a person before the law.

Article 7.

All are equal before the law and are entitled without any discrimination to equal protection of the law. All are entitled to equal protection against any discrimination in violation of this Declaration and against any incitement to such discrimination.

Article 8.

Everyone has the right to an effective remedy by the competent national tribunals for acts violating the fundamental rights granted him by the constitution or by law.

Article 9.

No one shall be subjected to arbitrary arrest, detention or exile.

Article 10.

Everyone is entitled in full equality to a fair and public hearing by an independent and impartial tribunal, in the determination of his rights and obligations and of any criminal charge against him.

Article 11.

(1) Everyone charged with a penal offence has the right to be presumed innocent until proved guilty according to law in a public trial at which he has had all the guarantees necessary for his defence.

(2) No one shall be held guilty of any penal offence on account of any act or omission which did not constitute a penal offence, under national or international law, at the time when it was committed. Nor shall a heavier

penalty be imposed than the one that was applicable at the time the penal offence was committed.

Article 12.

No one shall be subjected to arbitrary interference with his privacy, family, home or correspondence, nor to attacks upon his honour and reputation. Everyone has the right to the protection of the law against such interference or attacks.

Article 13.

(1) Everyone has the right to freedom of movement and residence within the borders of each state.

(2) Everyone has the right to leave any country, including his own, and to return to his country.

Article 14.

(1) Everyone has the right to seek and to enjoy in other countries asylum from persecution.

(2) This right may not be invoked in the case of prosecutions genuinely arising from non-political crimes or from acts contrary to the purposes and principles of the United Nations.

Article 15.

(1) Everyone has the right to a nationality.

(2) No one shall be arbitrarily deprived of his nationality nor denied the right to change his nationality.

Article 16.

(1) Men and women of full age, without any limitation due to race, nationality or religion, have the right to marry and to found a family. They are entitled to equal rights as to marriage, during marriage and at its dissolution.

(2) Marriage shall be entered into only with the free and full consent of the intending spouses.

(3) The family is the natural and fundamental group unit of society and is entitled to protection by society and the State.

Article 17.

(1) Everyone has the right to own property alone as well as in association with others.

(2) No one shall be arbitrarily deprived of his property.

Article 18.

Everyone has the right to freedom of thought, conscience and religion; this right includes freedom to change his religion or belief, and freedom, either alone or in community with others and in public or private, to manifest his religion or belief in teaching, practice, worship and observance.

Article 19.

Everyone has the right to freedom of opinion and expression; this right includes freedom to hold opinions without interference and to seek, receive and impart information and ideas through any media and regardless of frontiers.

Article 20.

(1) Everyone has the right to freedom of peaceful assembly and association.

(2) No one may be compelled to belong to an association.

Article 21.

(1) Everyone has the right to take part in the government of his country, directly or through freely chosen representatives.

(2) Everyone has the right of equal access to public service in his country.

(3) The will of the people shall be the basis of the authority of government; this will shall be expressed in periodic and genuine elections which shall be by universal and equal suffrage and shall be held by secret vote or by equivalent free voting procedures.

Article 22.

Everyone, as a member of society, has the right to social security and is entitled to realization, through national effort and international cooperation and in accordance with the organization and resources of each State, of the economic, social and cultural rights indispensable for his dignity and the free development of his personality.

Article 23.

(1) Everyone has the right to work, to free choice of employment, to just and favourable conditions of work and to protection against unemployment.

(2) Everyone, without any discrimination, has the right to equal pay for equal work.

(3) Everyone who works has the right to just and favourable remuneration ensuring for himself and his family an existence worthy of human dignity, and supplemented, if necessary, by other means of social protection.

(4) Everyone has the right to form and to join trade unions for the protection of his interests.

Article 24.

Everyone has the right to rest and leisure, including reasonable limitation of working hours and periodic holidays with pay.

Article 25.

(1) Everyone has the right to a standard of living adequate for the health and well-being of himself and of his family, including food, clothing, housing and medical care and necessary social services, and the right to security in the event of unemployment, sickness, disability, widowhood, old age or other lack of livelihood in circumstances beyond his control.

(2) Motherhood and childhood are entitled to special care and assistance. All children, whether born in or out of wedlock, shall enjoy the same social protection.

Article 26.

(1) Everyone has the right to education. Education shall be free, at least in the elementary and fundamental stages. Elementary education shall be compulsory. Technical and professional education shall be made generally available and higher education shall be equally accessible to all on the basis of merit.

(2) Education shall be directed to the full development of the human personality and to the strengthening of respect for human rights and fundamental freedoms. It shall promote understanding, tolerance and friendship among all nations, racial or religious groups, and shall further the activities of the United Nations for the maintenance of peace.

(3) Parents have a prior right to choose the kind of education that shall be given to their children.

Article 27.

(1) Everyone has the right freely to participate in the cultural life of the community, to enjoy the arts and to share in scientific advancement and its benefits.

(2) Everyone has the right to the protection of the moral and material interests resulting from any scientific, literary or artistic production of which he is the author.

Article 28.

Everyone is entitled to a social and international order in which the rights and freedoms set forth in this Declaration can be fully realized.

Article 29.

(1) Everyone has duties to the community in which alone the free and full development of his personality is possible.

(2) In the exercise of his rights and freedoms, everyone shall be subject only to such limitations as are determined by law solely for the purpose of securing due recognition and respect for the rights and freedoms of others and of meeting the just requirements of morality, public order and the general welfare in a democratic society.

(3) These rights and freedoms may in no case be exercised contrary to the purposes and principles of the United Nations.

Article 30.

Nothing in this Declaration may be interpreted as implying for any State, group or person any right to engage in any activity or to perform any act aimed at the destruction of any of the rights and freedoms set forth herein.

Source: United Nations Organization, 50th Anniversary Edition of the Universal Declaration.

2. The Law of Karma, From the Larger Pure Land Sutra, Excerpts

The Larger Pure Land Sutra, in Sanskrit—the larger Sukhavativyuha Sutra, is from the Pure Land Mahayana strain of Buddhism out of India.

Numerous Sanskrit manuscript copies have survived. One of the earlier Mahayana Sutras dates from perhaps around the beginning of the Common Era and is extremely popular in China and Japan. It was first translated into Chinese in the second half of the second century C.E., and there are five extant Chinese versions.

The sections below were chosen to illustrate the law of karma, one of the central Buddhist ideas. The iron law is that bad acts lead to bad effects in this life or in the next life, perhaps even warranting a long period of misery in a burning hell. The good news is that one can overcome bad karma by following the precepts, avoiding evil acts, and doing good ones. Just as bad leads to bad, so good leads to good. This is the natural law of karma.

> *From I.39* [The Buddha said to Maitreya], "Between heaven and earth, the five realms are clearly distinguishable. They are vast and deep, extending boundlessly. In return for good or evil deeds, happiness or misery ensues. The result of one's karma must be borne by oneself alone and no one else can take one's place. This is the natural law. Misfortune follows evil deeds as their retribution, which is impossible to avoid. Good people do good deeds, and so enjoy pleasure after pleasure and proceed from light to greater light. Evildoers commit crimes, and so suffer pain after pain and wander from darkness to deeper darkness. No one, except the Buddha knows this completely. Even though someone admonishes and teaches them, very few believe; and so the cycles of birth-and-death never cease and the evil paths continue endlessly. The karmic consequences for such worldly people cannot be described in detail.
>
> Hence, because of the natural working of karma, there are innumerable kinds of suffering in the three evil realms through which wicked beings must pass, life after life, for many [immeasurably long time spans], with no end in sight. It is indeed difficult for them to gain release, and the pain they must undergo is indescribable. This is called the fifth great evil, the fifth suffering and the fifth burning. The afflictions are such that they are comparable to a huge fire burning people alive.
>
> If, in the midst of this, one controls one's thoughts with single-mindedness, does worthy deeds with proper demeanour, mindfully recollects, harmonizes words and deeds, acts with sincerity, utters true words, speaks from the heart, commits no evil, and performs only good, then with the merit and virtue acquired one reaches emancipation and is able to escape from this world, be reborn in heavenly realms, and finally reach Nirvana. This is the fifth great good."

From I.40 [The Buddha said to Maitreya], "The law of karma operates like a net stretched everywhere; in its meshes, it inevitably catches all offenders. The net woven of large and small ropes covers the whole world, from top to bottom, and those caught in it feel utterly helpless and tremble in fear. This net has been in existence from of old. How painful and heart-rending!"

. . . The Buddha continued, "You and other [gods] and humans of the present and people of future generations, having received the Buddha's teachings, should reflect upon them, and while following them, should remain upright in thought and do virtuous deeds. Rulers should abide by morality, reign with beneficence and decree that everyone should maintain proper conduct, revere the sages, respect men of virtue, be benevolent and kind to others, and take care not to disregard the Buddha's teachings and admonitions. All should seek emancipation, cut the roots of Samsara and its various evils, and so aspire to escape from the paths of immeasurable sorrow, fear and pain in the three evil realms."

SOURCE: Hisao Inagaki in collaboration with Harold Stewart, *The Three Pure Land Sutras: A Study and Translation from Chinese* (Kyoto: Nagata Bunshodo, 1995).

3. KARMA AND HUMAN INEQUALITY (COMPLETE)

IN THE AFTERMATH of Alexander the Great's conquest of India, there were a number of small independent states in Northern India ruled by Greek kings. The Questions of King Milinda is a compendium of Theravada doctrines, in the form of a series of dialogues between a learned Buddhist monk, Nagasena, and a Greek-Indian king, Milinda. They were composed in written form sometime in the early centuries of the Common Era.

Said the king, "[Venerable] Nagasena, what is the reason that men are not all alike, but some long-lived and some short-lived, some healthy and some sickly, some handsome and some ugly, some powerful and some weak, some rich and some poor, some of high degree and some of low degree, some wise and some foolish?"

Said the elder, "Your majesty, why are not trees all alike, but some sour, some salt, some bitter, some pungent, some astringent, some sweet?"

"I suppose, [Venerable,] because of a difference in the seed."

"In exactly the same way, your majesty, it is through a difference in their karma that men are not all alike, but some long-lived and some short-lived, some healthy and some sickly, some handsome and some ugly, some powerful and some weak, some rich and some poor, some of high degree and some of low degree, some wise and some foolish. More over, your majesty The Blessed One has said as follows: 'All beings O youth, have karma as their portion; they are heirs of their karma; they are sprung from their karma; their karma is their kinsman; their karma is their refuge; karma allots beings to meanness or greatness.'"

"You are an able man, [Venerable] Nagasena."

SOURCE: Henry Clarke Warren, *Buddhism in Translations* (Cambridge, MA: Harvard University Press, 1900), pp. 214–215.

4. CALAMITY IS THE RESULT OF ONE'S OWN KARMA

THE *DHAMMAPADA* IS one of the most popular of the Pali scriptures in the Theravada canon. It dates from the first century before the Common Era. Buddhaghosa is the most influential Theravada authority and commentator, who worked in Sri Lanka in the Pali language in the fifth century of the Common Era.

> Who striketh him that striketh not,
> And harmeth him that harmeth not,
> Shall quickly punishment incur,
> Some one among a list of ten.
>
> Or cruel pain, or dread old age
> And failure of the vital powers,
> Or some severe and dread disease,
> Or madness him shall overtake.
>
> Or from the king calamity,
> Or calumny shall be his lot;
> Or he shall see his kinsfolk die,
> Or all his wealth shall disappear.

Or conflagrations shall arise
And all his houses sweep away;
And when his frame dissolves in death,
In hell the fool shall be reborn.

SOURCE: Translated from the *Dhammapada,* and from Buddhaghosa's commentary on verse 137 by Henry Clarke Warren, *Buddhism in Translations* (Cambridge, MA: Harvard University Press, 1900).

5. LORD BUDDHA'S FIRST SERMON, THE FOUR NOBLE TRUTHS (EXCERPT)

ONE OF THE fundamental texts of Buddhism, this sermon contains doctrines which all schools agree to be central to the dharma. In this passage "Tathagata" is an epithet for the Buddha, meaning "He who has gone or come in this fashion," that is, one who has successfully broken the bonds to the world of becoming. It is from the Pali canon, dating in written form to the first century before the Common Era.

Thus have I heard. The Blessed One was once living in the Deer Park at . . . (the Resort of Seers) near . . . (Benares). There he addressed the group of five [monks.]

"[Monks], these two extremes ought not to be practised by one who has gone forth from the household life. What are the two? There is devotion to the indulgence of sense-pleasures, which is low, common, the way of ordinary people, unworthy and unprofitable; and there is devotion to self-mortification, which is painful, unworthy and unprofitable.

"Avoiding both these extremes, the Tathagata has realized the Middle Path: it gives vision, it gives knowledge, and it leads to calm, to insight, to enlightenment, to nirvana. And what is that Middle Path? It is simply the Noble Eightfold Path, namely, right view, right thought, right speech, right action, right livelihood, right effort, right mindfulness, right concentration. This is the Middle Path realized by the Tathagata, which gives vision, which gives knowledge, and which leads to cairn, to insight, to enlightenment, to nirvana.

"The Noble Truth of suffering . . . is this: Birth is suffering; aging is suffering; sickness is suffering; death is suffering; sorrow and lamentation, pain, grief and despair are suffering; association with the unpleasant is suffering; dissociation from the pleasant is suffering; not to get what one wants is suffering—in brief, the five aggregates of attachment are suffering.

"The Noble Truth of the origin of suffering is this: It is this thirst (craving) which produces re-existence and re-becoming, bound up with passionate greed. It finds fresh delight now here and now there, namely, thirst for sense-pleasures; thirst for existence and becoming; and thirst for non-existence (self-annihilation).

"The Noble Truth of the Cessation of suffering is this: It is the complete cessation of that very thirst, giving it up, renouncing it, emancipating oneself from it, detaching oneself from it.

"The Noble Truth of the Path leading to the Cessation of suffering is this: It is simply the Noble Eightfold Path, namely right view; right thought; right speech, right action; right livelihood; right effort; right mindfulness; right concentration."

SOURCE: *Samyutta Nikaya*, 56.11, from Walpola Rahula, *What the Buddha Taught*, 2nd ed. (New York: Grove Press, 1974). Reprinted by permission of Grove/ Atlantic, Inc.

6. "THE FIVE WONDERFUL PRECEPTS" (COMPLETE)

THE FIVE PRECEPTS are the basic rules for living that are supposed to guide all Buddhists, and which are the foundation for social and individual morality. First, consider the sparse version that is preserved in the Theravada scriptures:

"I undertake to observe the rule to abstain from taking life; to abstain from taking what is not given; to abstain from sensuous misconduct; to abstain from false speech; to abstain from intoxicants as tending to cloud the mind."

SOURCE: Edward Conze, ed. and trans., *Buddhist Scriptures* (Harmondsworth, Middlesex: Penguin, 1959), p. 70. Reprinted by permission of the publisher.

For comparison, here is the expanded contemporary version penned by Thich Nhat Hahn,* one of the founders of engaged Buddhism. It addresses modern problems and more clearly draws in social and ecological issues. Note that both expressions of the basic moral law take the form of vows for individuals, vows to live compassionately and unselfishly for others. These duties are undertaken not because others have rights to them, but because they are the skillful things to do.

First Precept

Aware of the suffering caused by the destruction of life, I vow to cultivate compassion and learn ways to protect the lives of people, animals, plants, and minerals. I am determined not to kill, not to let others kill, and not to condone any act of killing in the world, in my thinking, and in my way of life.

Second Precept

Aware of the suffering caused by exploitation, social injustice, stealing, and oppression, I vow to cultivate loving kindness and learn ways to work for the well-being of people, animals, plants, and minerals. I vow to practice generosity by sharing my time, energy, and material resources with those who are in real need. I am determined not to steal and not to possess anything that should belong to others. I will respect the property of others, but I will prevent others from profiting from human suffering or the suffering of other species on Earth.

Third Precept

Aware of the suffering caused by sexual misconduct, I vow to cultivate responsibility and learn ways to protect the safety and integrity of individuals, couples, families, and society. I am determined not to engage in sexual relations without love and a long-term commitment. To preserve the happiness of myself and others, I am determined to respect my commitments and the commitments of others. I will do everything in my power to protect children from sexual abuse and to prevent couples and families from being broken by sexual misconduct.

Fourth Precept

Aware of the suffering caused by unmindful speech and the inability to listen to others, I vow to cultivate loving speech and deep listening in order to bring joy and happiness to others and relieve others of their suffering. Knowing that words can create happiness or suffering, I vow to learn to speak truthfully, with words that inspire self-confidence, joy, and hope. I am determined not to spread news that I do not know to be certain and not to criticize or condemn things of which I am not sure. I will refrain from uttering words that can cause division or discord, or that can cause the family or the community to break. I will make all efforts to reconcile and resolve all conflicts, however small.

Fifth Precept

Aware of the suffering caused by unmindful consumption, I vow to cultivate good health, both physical and mental, for myself, my family, and my society by practicing mindful eating, drinking, and consuming. I vow to ingest only items that preserve peace, well-being, and joy in my body, in my consciousness, and in the collective body and consciousness of my family and society. I am determined not to use alcohol or any other intoxicant or to ingest foods or other items that contain toxins, such as certain TV programs, magazines, books, films, and conversations. I am aware that to damage my body or my consciousness with these poisons is to betray my ancestors, my parents, my society, and future generations. I will work to transform violence, fear, anger, and confusion in myself and in society by practicing a diet for myself and for society. I understand that a proper diet is crucial for self-transformation and for the transformation of society.

SOURCE: Thich Nhat Hahn et al., *For a Future to Be Possible: Commentaries on the Five Wonderful Precepts* (Berkeley, CA: Parallax Press, 1993). Reprinted by permission of Parallax Press (*www.parallax.org*).

7. *SIGALAKA SUTTA*: BUDDHA'S ADVICE TO LAY PEOPLE (EXCERPTS)

THIS VERY IMPORTANT sermon shows how practical some of the Buddha's teaching was, especially when he was addressing laymen and laywomen. The first section, not included here maintained that following the Buddhist moral precepts, purifying one's motives, and living a clean and industrious life will pay off with great benefits here and now to the householder, and will lead to good karma and a better rebirth in the future. Verses 27–33, included below, reinterpret the proper protection of the six directions, away from ritual to practical moral behavior here and now. In this very famous section, six ideal human relationships for the householder are laid out. Each of them of them involves a hierarchical dyad with each party to attend to his or her duties in regard to the other. These duties are rooted in Buddhist virtues, not rights.

27. [Buddha is speaking.] "And how, householder's son, does the Ariyan disciple protect the six directions? These six things are to be regarded as the six directions. The east denotes mother and father. The south denotes teachers. The west denotes wife and children. The north denotes friends and companions. The nadir denotes servants, workers and helpers. The zenith denotes ascetics and Brahmins.

28. "There are five ways in which a son should minister to his mother and father as the eastern direction. [He should think:] 'Having been supported by them, I will support them. I will perform their duties for them. I will keep up the family tradition. I will be worthy of my heritage. After my parents' deaths I will distribute gifts on their behalf.' And there are five ways in which the parents, so ministered to by their son as the eastern direction, will reciprocate: they will restrain him from evil, support him in doing good, teach him some skill, find him a suitable wife and, in due time, hand over his inheritance to him. In this way the eastern direction is covered, making it at peace and free from fear.

29. "There are five ways in which pupils should minister to their teachers as the southern direction: by rising to greet them, by waiting on them, by being attentive, by serving them, by mastering the skills they teach. And there are five ways in which their teachers, thus ministered to by their pupils as the southern direction, will reciprocate: they will give thorough instruction, make sure they have grasped what they should have duly grasped, give them a thorough grounding in all skills, recommend them to their friends and colleagues, and provide them with security in all directions. In this way the southern direction is covered, making it at peace and free from fear.

30. "There are five ways in which a husband should minister to his wife as the western direction: by honouring her, by not disparaging her, by not being unfaithful to her, by giving authority to her, by providing her with adornments. And there are five ways in which a wife, thus ministered to by her husband as the western direction, will reciprocate: by properly organizing her work, by being kind to the servants, by not being unfaithful, by protecting stores, and by being skillful and diligent in all she has to do. In this way the western direction is covered, making it at peace and free from fear.

31. "There are five ways in which a man should minister to his friends and companions as the northern direction: by gifts, by kindly words, by looking after their welfare, by treating them like himself, and by keeping

his word. And there are five ways in which friends and companions, thus ministered to by a man as the northern direction, will reciprocate: by looking after him when he is inattentive, by looking after his property when he is inattentive, by being a refuge when he is afraid, by not deserting him when he is in trouble, and by showing concern for his children. In this way the northern direction is covered, making it at peace and free from fear.

32. "There are five ways in which a master should minister to his servants and workpeople as the nadir: by arranging their work according to their strength, by supplying them with food and wages, by looking after them when they are ill, by sharing special delicacies with them, and by letting them off work at the right time. And there are five ways in which servants and workpeople, thus ministered to by their master as the nadir, will reciprocate: they will get up before him, go to bed after him, take only what they are given, do their work properly, and be bearers of his praise and good repute. In this way the nadir is covered, making it at peace and free from fear.

33. "There are five ways in which a man should minister to ascetics and Brahmins as the zenith; by kindness in bodily deed, speech and thought, by keeping open house for them, by supplying their bodily needs. And the ascetics and Brahmins, thus ministered to by him as the zenith, will reciprocate in six ways: they will restrain him from evil, encourage him to do good, be benevolently compassionate towards him, teach him what he has not heard, and point out to him the way to heaven. In this way the zenith is covered, making it at peace and free from fear." Thus the Lord spoke.

SOURCE: Maurice Walshe, trans., *Thus Have I Heard: The Long Discourses of the Buddha: Digha Nikaya* (London: Wisdom Publications, 1987). This selection is from the *Digha Nikaya*, iii, vv 180–191.

8. SUTRA ON THE PRACTICE OF UNIVERSAL LOVE (EXCERPT)

BUDDHIST TEACHINGS AND practices are not at all restricted to the intellect. This core practice, taught by the Buddha and retained in all the major divisions of the tradition, is one designed to cultivate feelings of love and goodwill towards all beings in the world. The version presented here was translated from the Pali canon.

He who is skilled in good and who wishes to attain that state of Calm should act (thus):

He should be able, upright, perfectly upright, compliant, gentle, and humble.

Contented, easily supported, with few duties, of simple livelihood, controlled in senses, discreet, not impudent, he should not be greedily attached to families.

He should not commit any slight wrong such that other wise men might censure him, (Then he should cultivate his thoughts thus:)

May all beings be happy and secure; may their minds be contented.

Whatever living beings there may be—feeble or strong, long (or tall), stout, or medium, short, small, or large, seen or unseen, those dwelling far or near, those who are born and those who are yet to be born—may all beings, without exception, be happy-minded!

Let not one deceive another nor despise any person whatever in any place. In anger or ill will let not one wish any harm to another.

Just as a mother would protect her only child even at the risk of her own life, even so let one cultivate a boundless heart towards all beings.

Let one's thoughts of boundless love pervade the whole world—above, below and across—without any obstruction, without any hatred, without any enmity.

Whether one stands, walks, sits or lies down, as long as one is awake, one should maintain this mindfulness. This, they say, is the Sublime State in this life.

Not failing into wrong views, virtuous and endowed with Insight, one gives up attachment to sense-desires. Verily such a man does not return to enter a womb again.

SOURCE: *Suttanipata*, 1.8 in Walpola Rahula, *What the Buddha Taught*, 2nd ed. (New York: Grove Press, 1974), pp. 97–98. Reprinted by permission of Grove/ Atlantic, Inc.

9. THE HEART SUTRA (COMPLETE)

CALLED THE HEART Sutra because it is believed to contain the heart of the Mahayana message, it is often chanted in services. This sermon was preached not by Lord Buddha, but by the great Bodhisattva, Avalokitesvara, while he was in the deepest stages of meditative insight. Sariputra, the hearer of the sermon was considered to be the most learned of all of Buddha's disciples, but in Mahayana literature, he is a stock figure, representing a student who knows all the answers on the quizzes but has not taken the teachings to heart. This sermon was composed from 150–350 in the Common Era in India.

This sutra undercuts all certainties, even and especially Buddhist doctrines. From the viewpoint of absolute wisdom, all attainments along the Buddhist path are only relative, and to hold on to them as absolute is an impediment to full enlightenment. This sutra in part is a warning against taking anything in the phenomenal world as fixed.

The headings are not in the original text; Edward Conze, the translator, supplied them.

I. The invocation

Homage to the Perfection of Wisdom, the lovely, the holy!

II. The prologue

Avalokita, the holy Lord and Bodhisattva, was moving in the deep course of the wisdom which has gone beyond. He looked down from on high, he beheld but five heaps, and he saw that in their own-being they were empty.

III. The dialectics of emptiness. First stage

Here, O Sariputra, form is emptiness, and the very emptiness is form; emptiness does not differ from form, form does not differ from emptiness; whatever is form, that is emptiness, whatever is emptiness, that is form. The same is true of feelings, perceptions, impulses, and consciousness.

IV. The dialectics of emptiness. Second stage

Here, O Sariputra, all dharmas are marked with emptiness; they are not produced or stopped, not defiled or immaculate, not deficient or complete.

V. The dialectics of emptiness. Third stage

IN THIS SECTION, basic categories of *buddhadharma* are negated, including the Four Noble Truths.

Therefore, O Sariputra, in emptiness there is no form, nor feeling, nor perception, nor impulse, nor consciousness; no eye, ear, nose, tongue, body, mind; no forms, sounds, smells, tastes, touchables or objects of mind; no sight-organ-element and so forth, until we come to: no mind-consciousness-element; there is no ignorance, no extinction of ignorance, and so forth, until we come to: there is no decay and death, no extinction of decay and death; there is no suffering, no origination, no stopping, no path; there is no cognition, no attainment, and no non-attainment.

VI. The concrete embodiment and practical basis of emptiness

Therefore, O Sariputra, it is because of his indifference to any kind of personal attainment that a Bodhisattva, through having relied on the perfection of wisdom, dwells without thought-coverings. In the absence of thought-coverings he has not been made to tremble, he has overcome what can upset, and in the end he attains to Nirvana.

VII. Full emptiness is the basis also of Buddhahood

All those who appear as Buddhas in the three periods of time fully awake to the utmost, right and perfect enlightenment because they have relied on the perfection of wisdom.

VIII. The teaching brought within reach of the comparatively unenlightened

Therefore one should know the Prajnaparamita as the great spell, the spell of great knowledge, the utmost spell, the unequalled spell, allayer of all suffering, in truth—for what could go wrong? By the Prajnaparamita has this spell been delivered. It runs like this: Gone, Gone, Gone beyond. Gone altogether beyond, O what an awakening. All Hail!

This completes the Heart of Perfect Wisdom.

SOURCE: Edward Conze, ed. and trans., *Buddhist Scriptures* (Harmondsworth, Middlesex: Penguin, 1959). Reprinted by permission of the publisher.

10. Santideva, "The Selfless Aspiration of the Bodhisattva Path" (Excerpt)

These are the first sixteen verses of chapter three of Santideva's *Bodhicaryavatara*, written in Sanskrit as a guide to the Bodhisattva path. It probably dates to the early middle years of the eighth century C.E. Santideva was one of the finest writers in the Indian Mahayana tradition and was attached to the great Buddhist university at Nalanda in North India.

The Bodhisattva is one of the defining figures of the Mahayana Buddhist tradition, and these verses express the aspirations that arise when one begins to cultivate the mind of enlightenment. He or she resolves to bring all creatures, all sentient beings, to enlightenment by sacrificing his or her own interests. This great vow precludes any idea of proclaiming or protecting one's "rights." Everything—one's body, feelings, and accumulated merits—is freely donated for the progress of others on the path to perfection.

I rejoice with delight at the good done by all beings, which abates the suffering of hell. May those who are suffering abide in happiness.

I rejoice at the deliverance of embodied beings from the suffering of cyclic existence. I rejoice at the Bodhisattva- and Buddha-nature of the Saviours.

I also rejoice at the resolutions of the Teachers, which are oceans bearing happiness to every being, bestowing well-being on all creatures.

Holding my bands together in reverence, I beseech the perfect Buddhas in every direction, "Set up the light of the Dharma for those falling into suffering in the darkness of delusion."

Holding my hands together in reverence, I implore the Conquerors who wish to leave cyclic existence, "Remain for endless aeons. Do not let this world become blind!"

With the good acquired by doing all this as described, may I allay all the suffering of every living being.

I am medicine for the sick. May I be both the doctor and their nurse, until the sickness does not recur.

May I avert the pain of hunger and thirst with showers of food and drink. May I become both drink and food in the intermediate aeons of famine.

May I be an inexhaustible treasure for impoverished beings. May I wait upon them with various forms of offering.

See, I give up without regret my bodies, my pleasures, and my good acquired in all three times, to accomplish good for every being.

Abandonment of all is Enlightenment and Enlightenment is my heart's goal. If I must give up everything, better it be given to sentient beings.

I make over this body to all embodied beings to do with as they please. Let them continually beat it, insult it, and splatter it with filth.

Let them play with my body; let them be derisive and amuse themselves. I have given this body to them, what point has this concern of mine?

Let them have me do whatever brings them pleasure. Let there never be harm to anyone on account of me.

Should their mind become angry or displeased on account of me, may even that be the cause of their always achieving every goal.

Those who will falsely accuse me, and others who will do me harm, and others still who will degrade me, may they all share in Awakening.

SOURCE: Santideva, *The Bodhicaryavatara*, trans. Kate Crosby and Andrew Skilton (Oxford: Oxford University Press, 1995), chapter 3, verses 1–16.

11. ASOKA, "THE IDEAL BUDDHIST KING," ROCK EDICT XIII (COMPLETE)

KING ASOKA, RULER of the Mauryan Empire in India (r. c. 269–232 B.C.E.), is remembered in Buddhist history and legend as the greatest of all

Buddhist monarchs and has become the model for good governance. Priyadarsi, "Beloved of the Gods," is one of the epithets by which he referred to himself.

The Kalinga country was conquered by King Priyadarsi, Beloved of the Gods, in the eighth year of his reign. One hundred and fifty thousand persons were carried away captive, one hundred thousand were slain, and many times that number died.

Immediately after the Kalingas had been conquered, King Priyadarsi became intensely devoted to the study of Dharma, to the love of Dharma, and to the inculcation of Dharma.

The Beloved of the Gods, conqueror of the Kalingas is moved to remorse now. For he has felt profound sorrow and regret because the conquest of a people previously unconquered involves slaughter, death, and deportation.

But there is a more important reason for the King's remorse. The Brahmanas and Sramanas [the priestly and ascetic orders] as well as the followers of other religions and the householders—who all practiced obedience to superiors, parents, and teachers, and proper courtesy and firm devotion to friends; acquaintances, companions, relatives, slaves, and servants—all suffer from the injury, slaughter, and deportation inflicted on their loved ones. Even those who escaped calamity themselves are deeply afflicted by the misfortunes suffered by those friends, acquaintances, companions, and relatives for whom they feel an undiminished affection. Thus all men share in the misfortune, and this weighs on King Priyadarsi's mind.

[Moreover, there is no country except that of the Yonas (that is, the Greeks) where Brahmin and Buddhist ascetics do not exist] and there is no place where men are not attached to one faith or another.

Therefore, even if the number of people who were killed or who died or who were carried away in the Kalinga war had been only one one-hundredth or one one-thousandth of what it actually was, this would still have weighed on the King's mind.

King Priyadarsi now thinks that even a person who wrongs him must be forgiven for wrongs that can be forgiven.

King Priyadarsi seeks to induce even the forest peoples who have come under his dominion [that is, primitive peoples in the remote sections of the conquered territory] to adopt this way of life and this ideal. He reminds them, however, that he exercises the power to punish, despite his repentance, in order to induce them to desist from their crimes and escape execution.

For King Priyadarsi desires security, self-control, impartiality, and cheerfulness for all living creatures.

King Priyadarsi considers moral conquest [that is, conquest by Dharma] the most important conquest. He has achieved this moral conquest repeatedly both here and among the peoples living beyond the borders of his kingdom, even as far away as six hundred yojanas [about three thousand miles], where the [Greek] king Antiyoka rules [Syria], and even beyond Antiyoka in the realms of the four kings [of Egypt, Macedonia, Cyrene, and Epirus], and to the south among the Cholas and Painjyas [in the southern tip of the Indian peninsula] as far as Ceylon.

Here in the King's dominion also, among the Yonas [inhabitants of a northwest frontier province, probably Greeks] and the Kambojas [neighbors of the Yonas], among the Nabhakas and Nabhapankvis [who probably lived along the Himalayan frontier], among the Bhojas and Paitryaniikas, among the Andhras and Paulindas [all peoples of the Indian peninsula], everywhere people heed his instructions in Dharma.

Even in countries which King Priyadarsi envoys have not reached, people have heard about Dharma and about his Majesty's ordinances and instructions in Dharma, and they themselves conform to Dharma and will continue to do so.

Wherever conquest is achieved by Dharma, it produces satisfaction. Satisfaction is firmly established by conquest by Dharma [since it generates no opposition of conquered and conqueror]. Even satisfaction, however, is of little importance. King Priyadarsi attaches value ultimately only to consequences of action in the other world.

This edict on Dharma has been inscribed so that my Sons and great-grandsons who may come after me should not think new conquests worth achieving. If they do conquer, let them take pleasure in moderation and mild punishment. Let them consider moral conquest the only true conquest.

This is good, here and hereafter. Let their pleasure be pleasure in morality. For this alone is good, here and hereafter.

Source: N. A. Nikam and Richard McKeon, ed. and trans., *The Edicts of Asoka* (Chicago: University of Chicago Press, 1959).

12. KING MONGKUT OF SIAM (R. 1851–1868), "PROCLAMATION CONCERNING RELIGIOUS FREEDOM AND SUPERSTITION" (EXCERPTS)

THIS LAW ILLUSTRATES King Mongkut's tolerance and moderation in religious matters and shows how he was concerned with protecting the interests of the sangha.

> Whereas no just ruler restricts the freedom of His people in the choice of their religious belief, wherewith each man hopes to find strength and salvation in his last hour as well as the future beyond;
>
> And whereas there are many precepts common to all religions, such for instance as the injunctions not to kill, nor steal, nor commit adultery, nor speak falsehood, nor partake of intoxicating liquor, and the advice to forbear anger, to be kind and truthful, to practise gratitude and generosity and to demonstrate innumerable other merits which mankind of whatever race and language holds to be good, true and righteous;
>
> Wherefore, in the exercise of the said freedom of religion some persons do commit acts which are inconsistent with polity, although such acts may appear to be praiseworthy in the eyes of those who are about to lose their mind, having been led to believe in the merit of such acts by reports and hearsay or by the scattered brain and aberrant sermon of some priest unlearned in the Holy Tripitaka [scripture], whose mind is about to go as well; such, for instance, as the acts of committing oneself to the fire in worship of the Triple Gems, or presenting one's severed head as token of veneration to the Buddha, of offering one's blood collected from self-inflicted wounds as burning oil for the temple lamp, and others, which are performed to the surprise and consternation of the Government.

THERE FOLLOWS A section detailing some recent offenses of the sort mentioned in the paragraph above.

> For the reason above stated no person shall be permitted, as from now on, to commit himself to the fire in worship, nor to behead himself in the act of veneration, nor to inflict wounds on himself for the purpose of supplying the temple fire with fuel. Should any of such acts be about to be committed in the presence of any person, it shall be his duty to prevent the commission thereof. The same shall apply to cases of suicide by hanging and drowning. Should the person in whose presence such an act of self de-

struction is about to be committed be unable to prevent the commission thereof, either because he is alone and powerless or because he fears whatever the weapon used by the would-be suicide, it shall be his duty to raise an alarm and call others to help. A person in whose presence the said act shall have been committed, who shall have failed to prevent the commission of the same by neglect or sympathy, shall be fined by the amount prescribed in the measurement.

THE FOLLOWING SECTION of this proclamation was preceded by a description of how some widows, spinsters, or divorced women were seducing monks or enticing them to leave the order.

Be this, therefore, given as a warning, that His Majesty is firmly resolved to preserve the purity of the Holy Order, so that it may continue to be a help and guidance to His people, for whom He ever wishes a long life in coolness and felicity. Be it hereby declared, therefore, that henceforth any woman charged with the crime of fornication with a priest, or any priest charged with the like crime with a woman being divorced from her husband, a widow or a spinster, upon the said woman or priest being found guilty, punishment shall be within the measurement of [15 km] of the place where the crime shall have been committed—whoever knowingly shall have neglected to interrupt the commission thereof, or failed to prefer charges against the offenders, shall be penalized to clear the monastery of wild growth or to remove bricks and lime for the purpose of charitable construction within the area under the measurement, to such an extent as may be deemed suitable. However, within a period of 15 days as from today's date, should any culprit to the crime of fornication confess his or her crime, pardon will be granted. Otherwise, upon a charge preferred against him or her being provided, grave punishment under the law of [vinaya] will be [inflicted] upon the offender, and the accomplice, being a priest or layman as above referred to, will be penalised to perform half the labour to which the offender is sentenced.

Given in the Year of the Horse, being the completing year of the Decade.

SOURCE: M. R. Seni Pramoj and M. R. Kukrit Pramoj, eds., A King of Siam Speaks (Bangkok: The Siam Society, 1987).

13. LORD BUDDHA RULES THAT SLAVES MAY NOT BE ADMITTED TO THE ORDER OF MONKS (COMPLETE)

THIS SELECTION COMES from the *Vinaya*, the part of the Buddhist canon that records the rules and the case law laid down by Lord Buddha that governs the life of monks and nuns. This particular passage comes from a section where a number of categories of people are denied the possibility of ordination. They include those physically infirm with leprosy, boils, consumption, and fits as well as soldiers, fugitives from the law, scourged or branded criminals, debtors, under-aged persons, and slaves. In general, the reason was to discourage the use of ordination to avoid one's social responsibilities, which shirking caused public outrage and the ensuing loss of support through donations. It was also necessary not to abuse the protection afforded by the powerful King of Magadha.

At that time a slave ran away and was ordained with the [monks]. When his masters saw him they said: "There is our slave; come, let us lead him away (back to our house)." But some people replied: "Do not say so, Sirs." A decree has been issued by the Magadha king Seniya Bimbisara: "No one is to do any harm to those who are ordained with the [Buddhist wanderers]; well taught is their doctrine; let them lead a holy life for the sake of the complete extinction of suffering."

People were annoyed, murmured, and became angry: "Indeed these [Buddhist wanderers] are secure from anything; it is not allowed to do any thing to them. How can they ordain a slave?"

They told this thing to the Blessed One.

"Let no slave, O [monks], receive the . . . ordination. He who confers the . . . ordination (on a slave), is guilty of a minor offence."

SOURCE: T. W. Rhys Davids and Hermann Oldenberg, trans., *Vinaya Texts in Sacred Books of the East*, vol. 13 (Oxford: Oxford University Press, 1881; reprint, Delhi: Motilal Banarsidass, 1966). This is from the *Mahavagga*, I.47.

14. Slavery in Siam (1), "The Wives and Children of an Executed Noble Enslaved" (Excerpt from the Chronicles of Nagara)

The following incident, which occurred sometime before C.E. 1493, shows both the absolute nature of the king's authority and one way that enslavement could occur. In this incident, a noble used a ruse to thwart the king's desire to take the noble's daughter as a wife.

> A royal command arrived, demanding that [Sir] Indara present his daughter to the king.
>
> Sir Indara sent the daughter of an elephant doctor instead, and the elephant doctor accompanied her. The elephant doctor reported to the king that Sir Indara had not sent his own daughter to be presented. The king had a royal commissioner . . . take the elephant doctor and his daughter and go and investigate the allegations of the elephant doctor. . . . Interrogated, Sir Indara admitted the truth as the elephant doctor had reported it. So [the royal commissioner] took the written report of his testimony under oath and reported it to the king, as he had been commanded. The king had Sir Indara beaten [to death] by the Nun's Landing gate, and had his children and wives brought in as [royal] slaves.

Since it was forbidden to shed the blood of nobility, Sir Indara was executed by being beaten to death.

Source: David K. Wyatt, *The Crystal Sands: The Chronicles of Nagara Sri Dharrmaraja*, Data Paper Number 98 (Ithaca, NY: Southeast Asia Program, Cornell University, 1975).

15. Slavery in Siam (2), Mongkut, King of Siam: "Proclamation of the Royal Decree Regarding Husbands Selling Wives, Parents Selling Children," March 21, 1868 (Complete)

This proclamation from the end of the reign of King Mongkut, Rama IV, of Siam shows his tendency to modernize and liberalize the laws of his kingdom. An absolute monarch in the Buddhist mold, Mongkut constantly strived to live and govern by the traditional virtues of a king. While this document represents a considerable step towards the liberation of women and children from absolute patriarchal controls, it did not abolish the institution of slavery altogether. The provisions of the new law show how debt bondage worked in Siam. The advance is that the wives and children over fifteen years old must consent to their being sold into bondage. Younger children can still be sold for the benefit of their parents.

Proclaimed on Saturday the 13th of the waning moon, of the 4th month of the year of the Rabbit.

It is hereby proclaimed to His Majesty's high and lower officials, both on the spear-side and distaff-side, to His Majesty's subjects, both in the city and outside the city. Let it be known that on Thursday, the 14th day of the waning moon of the 2nd month in the year of the Rabbit. Mrs. Chan has presented a petition to His Majesty accusing Mr. Lam, who was her husband, that he put her name up for sale to noted person, without her knowing anything about it.

When this fact was brought to His Majesty's knowledge His Majesty decided that the fact that a husband posted the name of his wife for sale without her knowledge, did not mean that she should be regarded as a slave. His Majesty did not know what former laws regarding the matter had specified, so on Tuesday, the 10th day of the waning moon of the 3rd month in the year of the Rabbit, the 9th year, His Majesty wrote a memorandum asking Phra Indradeb to present this case to the Juridical Group, asking them about the previous law. The Juridical Group reported the relevant law as follows: If a husband, a parent or a slave-owner puts the name of a wife, an off-spring or a slave into a sale deed, it is decreed that the former party has the right, with or without the knowledge of the latter party. Putting the name of a person into the sale deed is within the right according to law, because the husband, the parent and the slave owner are free. Another clause of the law stipulates that a wife or an off-spring has no right to put the name of a husband, or a parent into a sale deed, because a wife or an off-spring is not free, and is subservient to the husband or parent. Thus decreed the previous law.

In considering the previous law, it seems to His Majesty that a woman is like a buffalo a man a human being. Because of its unfairness, he orders the previous law be abolished. It is hereby decreed that, if a husband desires to put the name of his wife in a sale deed, provided that the wife is not a slave wife for whom the husband possesses a bill of sale he can do so only if the wife agrees, and signs her name or puts her mark in agreement with full knowledge of the writer of the deed and the witness, in which case she becomes slave. If the wife does not consent, or if the husband arbitrarily put her name for sale, without any witness, then it is not considered a valid sale. But if a wife lives with her husband without any divorce or separation, and the husband puts the name of his wife in to a sale deed and then flees, the buyer can ask the authorities to hold the wife as a hostage until the husband can be found and judged by the authorities. If the wife consents to act as hostage for the husband and pay for his interest, and if she later consents to be a slave and puts her mark to a deed, she can be taken as a slave. If she does not consent, she can only be held as a hostage in the court of law, and she cannot be held as a slave. If the wife has previously separated (or divorced) from her husband and the husband has fled, or if her name is in the sale deed without her knowledge or if the husband has already sold his wife as a slave to somebody else, and she has consented to be a slave of the owner, she cannot be held as a hostage. Only the guarantor can be arrested. This causes trouble only to those who believe in the old law which assumes that a woman is a buffalo while a man is a human being. If the wife is a slave having her set price and her sale-deed has not yet been destroyed by her husband allowing her to be free, she is still a slave. The name of a slave, whether she is a wife or not, can be put in a sale-deed at any price by her owner, whether he is her husband or not, on condition that her old sale-deed be handed to the new owner. A slave-wife is different from a slave who has not become a wife at the time of her owner's death. A slave-wife inherits some small portion of the husband's property, or her husband's debtor must decrease her sale price by 10 or 12 or 15 or whatever is supposed to be the late husband's bequest to his slave-wife.

- If the husband sells his slave-wife or the owner sells his slave for more than is stated in the previous sale-deed, it can be done provided the slave woman puts her mark to show her consent on the paper. If she does not consent, only the exact sum of her previous sale price is considered as valid, the recent seller must be ordered to return the excess money.

- If the former owner puts an absent slave's name for sale whether she is his wife or not, he has right to ask for her previous sale price, plus interest, from the buyer whenever the slave has been found.

- If the parents put a child under 15 years old up for sale, it can be sold with or without the child's sign mark in agreement.

- But if the parents are divorced or separated and the child lives with either party, the child cannot be sold. If this happens the money must be returned and the guarantor cannot hold the child.

- If the child whether male or female is over 15 years old his parents cannot sell him (her) unless he (she) puts his or her mark on the deed in the presence of witnesses.

- The same thing applies to the case of a non-slave wife. If her parents flee but she still remains in her parents' home, she can be arrested as a hostage by the court. She will become a slave only if she consents to put her mark on an agreement to become a slave in payment for her parents' debt. Without her consent she can be held only as hostage by the court until her parents have been found. But if she does not reside in her parents' home, the buyer cannot hold her as hostage. The guarantor must be responsible.

- If the seller dies, his heirs whether they be a husband or wife or children or relative must be responsible for his debts.

- If a wife sells her husband who is her slave according to a bill of sale, it is a slave case; the husband and wife relationship cannot be considered.

- If a wife sells her husband, if children sell their parents, if brothers sell sisters and vise versa, if friends sell friends; these can be legally done only with the consent of the party being sold, and shown by putting up his mark on the agreement in the presence of witnesses.

- An orphan between the ages of 7 years to 15 years, and brought up by adopted parents, can be sold if nobody challenges his adoption rights, because the child has the right to inherit from his adopted parents, but if he is over 15 years old he can be sold only on his own consent.

- A child between the ages of 7 years to 15 years, who is brought up by somebody (but not adopted), cannot be sold without the child's consent because he has no right to inherit.

Let the judges and the juries conduct their proceedings according to this proclaimed law. If anybody still acknowledges the old law as valid he will be punished.

Source: Chattip Nartsupha and Suthy Prasartset, *The Political Economy of Siam, 1851–1910* (Bangkok: The Social Science Association of Thailand, 1981.)

16. Chulalongkorn, King of Siam: "The Act Fixing the Redemption Age of the Offspring of Slaves," August 21, 1874 (Complete)

This important act came very early in the reign of Mahachulalongkorn after his period of regency ended and was his first step in the gradual abolition of slavery in the Kingdom of Siam. The new king was moving in the direction towards liberation and modernization that his father, King Mongkut, had begun. The effect of this act was to abolish the traditional old redemption price scheme, as detailed below, by one that reduced the cost of buying the freedom of a slave's offspring to zero when the person reached the age of twenty-one.

May You Prosper. Entered Chullasakrat 1236, Ninth Month, Ninth Day of the Waxing Moon . . .

Phrabat Somdet Phra Chao Yuhua Somdet Phra Paramintr Maha Chulalongkorn Bodindarathepya Mahamongkut Burutyaratana Ratrawiwong Warutamapongse Boripatr Worakattaya Rajanikrodom Jaturanta Borommaha Chakrapadiratsangkas Borom Dhammik Maharajathirat Boromnath Bopitr Phra Chullachomkhlao Chao Paendin Sayam, Rarna V in the Dynasty which established and has maintained the Throne . . . at Krungthep Mahanakhon Arnorn Ratanakosin Nahinthayuthya Mahadilokphop Noparat Rajthani Burirom Udoniratnives Nahasathan, which is the great city of the Kingdom of Siam throughout the North and South. He is also the sovereign lord of neighboring dependent countries, namely, Laos, Karen, Malaya and others. He is a person of Great Virtue.

His Majesty Proceeded to the Sommati Dhevarajubut Throne Hall east of Dusit Throne Hall, and was seated on the ornate throne facing the southern direction, surrounded by an assembly of his advisers seated in audience according to their respective ranks. His Majesty made reference to the country's ancient customs, saying that if any of them have brought progress, benefit and justice, to the country he is desirous of maintaining and promoting them to be ever more progressive and to let them remain in use forever. If any customs have not brought progress to the people of the city, and have not been beneficial or just, he wants to abolish them. But the abolition must proceed slowly so as to make matters orderly up to the time until the reform is complete.

Under the old laws, enacted by the ancient kings in accordance with Phra Dhammasat Scripture, there are seven categories of (slaves), namely: debt slave; the offspring of a slave born in the household of the slave-owner; a slave given away by the parents; a slave donated by its owner; a slave secured from redress of trouble; a slave supported during a time of famine; a slave taken in a war. These seven categories of slaves are regarded as slaves by the law of the land. If they have no money to pay the slave-owner to redeem themselves, there is no chance for them to be released from servitude and to become free.

As for the offspring born to these seven categories of slaves, from the moment they come out from the womb and open their eyes, they are counted as debt slaves, unredeemable even if they reach the age of 100. That is, their age is counted from one month, two months, three months each of which has a price of 6 baht for a male and 1 for a female. For a male slave, between the age of 26 to 40, his full price is 14 tamleung; for a female slave, between the age of 21 to 30, her full price is set at 12 tamleung. If a male slave is over 40 years old, and female over 30 years old, the redemption price is gradually reduced until the age of 100 when the male slave still has a price of 1 tamleung and a female, 3 baht. Their redemption price is never completely nil. This has been a custom which has persisted to the present. It looks as if no kindness is shown to the slaves' offspring at all. The offspring of the slaves are born innocent; they knew and saw nothing. If the parents have committed evil things, why have they also turned their offspring into slaves who will remain as such until their death, only to receive punishment for the sins of their parents? They should not be enslaved throughout their life.

However, if the King takes action to abolish slavery of the slaves' offspring, once and for all, those slave-owners who have no kindness will not allow the mothers to take care of their children. The slave-owners will see that the offspring of their slaves bring no benefit to them. The slave-owners will send away the slaves who are the parents to work for them in another place and will not allow them to take care of the children. A great number of these children will die because of this kind of mistreatment by the slave-owners. It is therefore necessary to give the slave-owners some leeway, but at the same time give the offspring of slaves the specific date, after which they will be free. Once the male offspring of the slaves are freed, they will be able to seek employment and earn their living, to be taught some useful trade or to be ordained as novices and priests. If the freed slaves are female, they can have husbands and children and seek opportunities to earn their living. It is only through this way that progress can be brought to the people of Siam.

His Majesty therefore orders his advisers to-enact a Royal Decree and announce it to members of the Royal Family, officials of all ministries for both military and civilian affairs, and to all the people in Bangkok, and in the first, second and third-class provinces in the North and South, that Chullasakrat 1230, the Year of the Dragon, Samrithsok, is the year of the Coronation of His Majesty the King, the Most Auspicious Year. His Majesty hereby declares this year of the Dragon, Samrithsok, as the year in which the Act Concerning the Offspring of Slaves shall be enforced from now on.

Source: Chattip Nartsupha and Suthy Prasartset, *The Political Economy of Siam, 1851–1910* (Bangkok: The Social Science Association of Thailand, 1981).

17. Monastic Slavery in Siam (1): "A Donation of Slaves to Maintain Temple at Nagara Sri Dharrmaraja" in Southern Siam, from a document of the early Ayutthyan period, c. c.e. 1400 [?] (Excerpt)

This document shows how it was customary to donate slaves to provide their services as tax collectors in perpetuity to maintain a temple after is was built or reconstructed. By such a donation of bound labor to a temple, the giver received great religious merit, and such generosity towards the Buddhist establishment was expected of nobles.

When he had ordered people to build villages and work the rice fields, the ruler then had the Great Reliquary [re-]constructed. He had the people of [various districts] assist in the building of the Great Reliquary in

Nagara Sri Dharrmaraja until it was completed. [The Official] sent tribute and presented it, and the King came on elephant to Pan Sahban. [The Official] made obeisance before the King and said, "I have put my country in order, and Nagara Sri Dharrmaraja is completed. I have completed the construction of the Great Reliquary, and I present these good works as donations to Your Majesty." The King was pleased with [the Official, who] begged leave to present to the king 3 men, 3 women, and 100 men in the retinue of the three men and three women, and asked that the king accept the children and grandchildren of these 3 men and 3 women as his agents for the collection of the [taxes]; and he pledged these three men and three women to be servants forever after. The King was pleased to have [the treasurer] register the names of the three men and three women, that they might be recognized and recalled in the future. . . .

The official gave three of his relatives: Yu, his younger brother, U and Ku, two nephews or grandsons, and their wives. The following paragraph records the bondage in perpetuity of their descendents. (ed)

[The Official] in respectful audience [with the King] said, "When in the future Your Majesty's servant U has descendents, please allow them, whether male or female, to become your Majesty's servants, and bestow them as slaves upon the monks and monasteries, that they may continuously build up royal good works for the [merit of the] King in the future. When in the future your servant Yu has descendents, may Your Majesty be pleased to employ them to work with elephants for Your Majesty. [Furthermore,] when your servant Yu has descendents, may Your Majesty be pleased to accept them as Your Majesty's volunteer [soldiers] from that time forward. May Your Majesty have mercy upon poor human creatures, I respectfully submit to Your Majesty." The King was pleased to reply, "The three men and three women whom you have presented me I entrust first to you. Whenever any public business arises in future, have these three men and three women report to me." Having been given leave to present . . . a royal granddaughter, they then took leave of the king and returned to Nagara Sri Dharrmaräja.

When [The Official] died, the king had U, Ku, and Yu come to pay their respects to him, and requested of them the [tax] in silver . . . payable to the royal treasury.

Source: David K. Wyatt, *The Crystal Sands: The Chronicles of Nagara Sri Dhar-rmaraja*, Data Paper Number 98 (Ithaca, NY: Southeast Asia Program, Cornell University, 1975), pp. 115–117.

18. Monastic Slavery in Siam (2): "Report on Monastic Slaves from his Official to the King of Nagara Sri Dharrmaraja," 1628 (Excerpts)

This report is another example of how monastery slaves were used in traditional Siam and illustrates how it was the king's duty to be informed about and to regulate the activities of the monastic sangha. In this case, the slaves were used to clear new fields, to farm established land, to work in construction, to maintain religious images, and to take up arms in defense of the temple complexes.

[The Official] then reported to him on religious and monastic affairs and the appointment of patriarchs, and presented the petition and the great register of all the monks, and reported concerning the request for true deeds to land for the monastery slaves of all the monks, on which they could plant gardens and fields for the monasteries, for the Buddha image rooms, and for all the monks. His Majesty had [a clerk] take down his orders. [The Official] had a register compiled of all lands on both sides of the sea and land granted to the monks on which their slaves could plant gardens and fields for the Buddha image rooms and the monks in [1628 C.E.]. . . .

All these nine monasteries were dependent on . . . the abbot of [Elephant Landing], the royal monastery; together with the village and slaves of hmo Jaiya at the Traimit Plain on the White Sands. These slaves of hmo Jaiya and their sons and grandsons, being followers and temple slaves, had built up 823 pin of demarcated rice-fields. . . . They repaired the Buddha images [and temple buildings] thus did [the] King and [his nobles] donate and build [two temple complexes] to be the royal monasteries over all the [other] monasteries. Were the enemy to come to seize . . . Nagara, [the] King would consult with [his advisor], and then order the governing officials and all the temple slaves they controlled to go out and assist in defending against the enemy all along the walls, to prevent them from entering to damage the Holy Reliquary or the gold and silver Buddha images which [the] King had cast.

SOURCE: David K. Wyatt, *The Crystal Sands: The Chronicles of Nagara Sri Dharrmaraja*, Data Paper Number 98 (Ithaca, NY: Southeast Asia Program, Cornell University, 1975), pp. 136 and 158.

19. SULAK SIVARAKSA, "BUDDHISM AND THAI POLITICS" (EXCERPTS)

SULAK SIVARAKSA, THAILAND's leading Buddhist social activist, sometimes refers to himself as a "radical conservative," which this essay shows to be true. He combines traditional Buddhist concepts of governance, such as having a righteous ruler who embodies the precepts and virtues of Buddhism, along with a radical concern for social justice, ecological stewardship, and economic self-sufficiency. His distrust of multinational companies and powerful first world nations is coupled with equal scorn for homegrown, self-seeking, and venal political leaders.

. . . To me . . . politics has something to do with the rulers and the ruled. It is a framework where justice, peace, mercy, decency, friendliness and basic human rights can be conducted. Politics on the one hand gives powers and legitimation to the rulers to use a set of laws to run the country in the name of, or for the benefit of, the people who are being ruled. On the other hand, if the people refuse that authority or question that legitimacy, the rulers have no right to rule any more.

My last statement is a basic Buddhist concept concerning national polity. It was quoted by Mongkut, the first "modern" Siamese King to open his country to the West in the 1850s. Many regard this open door policy as a safeguard to our independence, whereas all our neighbors were subjugated to the great Western, powers in the nineteenth century.

Since Mongkut, all the Thai kings including the present reigning monarch proclaim these first words on coronation: "We will rule righteously." The implication is that if the rulers do not rule righteously, they can be removed from their position of authority by the people, who are being ruled. Although this rarely happens, the people's praises and grievances must be taken into consideration. . . .

In olden times, Thai rulers relied mostly, but not exclusively, on Buddhism to make the people accept their authority. The theory of *dhammaraja* or righteous king and *cakkavadin*, the universal ruler or righteous emperor, adopted from Brahminism since the time of Emperor Asoka, was used as a national polity.

Two Buddhist arguments were used to justify the rulers: (1) they had done such good deeds in the past, or in their past lives, that they were fit to rule and enjoy more power than ordinary people. However, (2) they had to rule righteously, according to a prescribed Buddhist moral conduct for rulers, lest the people remove them from authority.

. . . Buddhism regards politics as a necessary evil in which the rulers and the ruled must not exploit one another. Nor should they exploit other beings, namely animals, spiritual beings like gods and ghosts, as well as mountains, trees, lands, air and water.

That of course is ideal. In the reality of Siam or other South and Southeast Asian countries which claimed to be Buddhist kingdoms before the colonial period, the kings might not be that righteous, but they had to try to be for two reasons: (1) they on the whole were believers in Buddhism, and (2) their authority had to be supported by the Sangha or Buddhist brotherhood, which could relate to the court as well as commoners all over the kingdom. . . .

Since the age of the colonial masters, we have had new gurus from the West, who were not necessarily white men but our own nationals who have been educated abroad or who believed in Western progress or models of development. These new gurus, who are professors, teachers, writers, administrators and advisors to government, have now taken the role that the Sangha used to play. By and large, they are non-believers in the lofty teachings of the Buddha. Of course, they pay lip service to Buddhism and adhere to Buddhist ceremonies and traditional etiquette. Even worse they think they understand and know Buddhism. The Buddha said those who do not know, yet think they know, are the most difficult ones to be redeemed. . . .

In the case of Siam, our rulers since at least 1947 have been the military, which has used democracy for window dressing every now and again to please Western powers, which to us are still very important. By virtue of following the West blindly, our rulers use Buddhism and the Sangha merely to justify their policies and actions, despite the fact that they are unrighteous and against all basic teachings of the Buddha. . . .

Worse than that is our Sangha, which lost its leadership, and was replaced by the new Western trained educated elites. Now the Sangha is being used effectively by the military, the bureaucracy, the industrialists and commercial sectors, who combine to suck everything out of the people, as well as from Mother Earth—in the name of development or progress.

Another factor which we must not forget is that since the time of King Mongkut, politics does not mean only national sovereignty anymore. While the colonial masters have gone, we now have the superpowers, the multinational corporations and the World Bank, which are more powerful politically and economically than any state as small as Siam. Economics or money and material benefits have nowadays replaced religious norms for most people. . . .

We, the lay Western educated, together with some leading members of ecclesiastics in the monkhood should be brave enough to point out and to denounce the unrighteousness of the rulers, who spend the poor tax payer's money on armaments and the material well-being of the rich—in the name of the poor. It is our rulers who collaborate with the superpowers and the multinational corporations to exploit our peasants and labourers. Hence we now have more prostitutes than monks and more child malnutrition than hitherto known in the history of Siam—the "rice bowl of Asia."

By pointing out that the ruling elites are not sacred, are not better, morally, spiritually, or intellectually, than the commoners, we must not make the common people despair, but make them proud of their national and local heritage, so that they will not be trapped by consumerism and the mass media which lead the people to belittle themselves in a universal culture of Coca Cola, fast food and all the benefits that the drug companies and high technology can offer. . . .

In this day and age, to be a Buddhist and to fight non-violently for social justice, and peace and decency, one cannot only look back to the essential teaching of the Buddha and one's own national heritage. One must indeed find good friends beyond one's national boundary and one's religious affiliation. . . .

As a Buddhist, I feel that we should really get our grassroots (or *riceroots*) together—using our friendship through our different religious and cultural traditions—yet with the common bonds for peace and justice so that we shall be more and more aware of the wickedness and hypocrisy of the rulers. Common people must realize that the rulers in most lands have lost moral legitimacy to rule any country in the name of the people.

Although the rulers may cling to the state machinery, the common people must be able to use religion and morality to rule themselves more effectively without waiting for the next millennium or life to come.

This may be easier said than done, but in a country like Siam we must start doing this now before our country becomes as hopeless as the USA, USSR or some great European countries.

Yet in those great countries, there are people who realize that the First World is exploiting us in Third World. It is these people who really are our good friends and if good friends are together, we can perhaps do something meaningful for our mutual problems—the safety of this planet, and its natural habitats in the near future, for example.

To me, this is the essence of the Buddhist message as applied to any state or beyond, using my own country and my own experiences as examples to share some very vital issues with you all.

SOURCE: First published in *Asian Action* (March-April 1986), the journal of the Asian Cultural Forum on Development (ACFOD). Reprinted in Sulak Sivaraksa, *A Socially Engaged Buddhism* (Bangkok: Thai Inter-Religious Commission for Development, 1988). Reprinted by permission.

20. BUDDHIST HYMN FROM THE DALIT COMMUNITY OF INDIA, C. 1956 (COMPLETE)

DR. AMBEDKAR LED some half million people from his untouchable community in India to convert to Buddhism in 1956. On converting, the community rejected its old labels and took on Dalit as their name. The community has continued on its new path since the founder's death a few weeks after the mass conversion. This hymn reflects the practical this-worldly motivation for their change of religion and is typical of the material found in cheap songbooks sold throughout the new Buddhist fellowship.

The Awakened Torch of Life

By Rajananda Gadapyle

The light of enthusiasm is spread everywhere and the teaching of
  Buddha is happy.
The evil days of slavery are gone and the sorrowful songs gone.
Bhim [Dr. Ambedkar's nickname] gave us the great hymn, "I go for
  refuge to the Buddha,"
And by attaining the perfection of this hymn we become the riders
  of our own chariot.

The torch of revolution is burning in every heart.
A Buddhist life is smitten with humanity.
He [Buddha or Ambedkar?] turned the wheel of revolution.
He died the maker of an age.
All the ten directions give praise,
India gives praise.

SOURCE: Eleanor Zelliot, *From Untouchable to Dalit: Essays on the Ambedkar Movement* 2nd ed. (Delhi: Manohar, 1996). Reprinted by permission.

21. DECLARATION OF THE LEVELERS ASSOCIATION, MARCH 3, 1922 (COMPLETE)

IN FEUDAL JAPAN, there had long been groups of hereditary outcastes, who were restricted to the lowest and dirtiest jobs and who were isolated from the rest of society. In 1871, as part of the Meiji program of modernization, it was declared illegal to discriminate against the now former outcastes, called burakumin. When things did not get markedly better, the burakumin formed an association to help themselves in 1922. This declaration shows that socialism, Buddhism, and Christianity influenced them.

Declaration of the Levelers Association
Adopted and proclaimed on 3 March 1922

Burakumin throughout the country unite!
Long suffering brothers:
In the past half century, reform undertakings on our behalf by many people in various ways have not yielded any appreciable results. This should be taken as divine punishment for permitting others as well as ourselves to debase our human dignity. Previous movements, though seemingly motivated by compassion, actually degraded many of our brothers. Therefore, it is necessary for us to organize a new collective movement through which we shall liberate ourselves by our own effort and self-respect.
Brothers—our ancestors pursued liberty and equality, and practiced these principles. But they became the victims of a contemptible system

developed by a despicable ruling class. They became the manly martyrs of industry. In recompense for their work in skinning animals, they were skinned alive. For tearing out the animals' hearts, their own warm hearts were ripped out. They were spat at with ridicule. Yet all through these cursed nights of evil dreams, their human blood has kept on flowing. We, who have been born of this blood, are trying to become divine. The time has come when the oppressed shall throw off the brandmark of martyrdom. The martyr's crown of thorns shall receive blessing.

We, who know how cruel and cold it is to be discriminated against, must not use unrespectable words and cowardly behavior to retaliate against the ordinary human being. To do so would be to discredit our ancestors who died for freedom and to desecrate humanity. Therefore we should work passionately for human rights and seek the light of true humanity.

Let there be warmth in the hearts of people, and let there be light upon all mankind. In this, the Levelers Association is born.

SOURCE: Buraku Liberation Research Institute, *Long-Suffering Brothers and Sisters, Unite! The Buraku Problem, Universal Human Rights and Minority Problems in Various Countries* (Osaka: Buraku Liberation Research Institute, 1981).

22. Aung San Suu Kyi: "In Quest of Democracy" (Excerpts)

THIS WAS PART of a projected book on human rights and democracy in honor of her late father, which Aung San Suu Kyi was unable to complete after her house arrest in July 1989. It gives the Buddhist basis for good government, based on the Agganna Sutra and the Ten Virtues of a King, which are explained in some detail.

Opponents of the movement for democracy in Burma have sought to undermine it by on the one hand, casting aspersions on the competence of the people to judge what was best for the nation and on the other condemning the basic tenets of democracy as un-Burmese. There is nothing new in Third World governments seeking to justify and perpetuate authoritarian rule by denouncing liberal democratic principles as alien: By implication they claim for themselves the official and sole right to decide what does or does not conform to indigenous cultural norms. . . .

As soon as the movement for democracy spread out across Burma there was a surge of intense interest in the meaning of the word "democracy," in its history and its practical implications. . . .

There was a spontaneous interpretative response to such basic ideas as representative government, human rights and the rule of law. The privileges and freedoms which would be guaranteed by democratic institutions were contemplated with understandable enthusiasm. . . .

Why has Burma with its abundant natural and human resources failed to live up to its early promise as one of the most energetic and fastest-developing nations in South-east Asia? International scholars have provided detailed answers supported by careful analyses of historical, cultural, political and economic factors. The Burmese people, who have had no access to sophisticated academic material, got to the heart of the matter by turning to the words of the Buddha on the four causes of decline and decay: failure to recover that which had been lost, omission to repair that which had been damaged, disregard of the need for reasonable economy, and the elevation to leadership of men without morality or learning. Translated into contemporary terms, when democratic rights had been lost to military dictatorship sufficient efforts had not been made to regain them, moral and political values had been allowed to deteriorate without concerted attempts to save, the situation, the economy had been badly managed, and the country had been ruled by men without integrity or wisdom. A thorough study by the cleverest scholar using the best and latest methods of research could hardly have identified more correctly or succinctly the chief causes of Burma's decline since 1962. . . .

The Buddhist view of world history tells that when society fell from its original state of purity into moral and social chaos a king was elected to restore peace and justice. The ruler was known by three titles: *Mahasammata*, "because he is named ruler by the unanimous consent of the people"; *Khattjya* "because he has dominion over agricultural land"; and *Raja*, "because he wins the people to affection through observance of the *dhamma* (virtue, justice, the law)". The agreement by which their first monarch undertakes to rule righteously in return for a portion of the rice crop represents the Buddhist version of government by social contract. The *Mahasammata* follows the general pattern of Indic kingship in South-east Asia. This has been criticized as antithetical to the idea of the modern state because it promotes a personalized form of monarchy lacking the continuity inherent in the western abstraction of the king as possessed of both a body politic and a body natural. However, because the *Mahasammata* was chosen by popular consent and required to govern in accordance with just laws, the concept of government elective and *sub lege* is not alien to traditional Burmese thought.

The Buddhist view of kingship does not invest the ruler with the divine right to govern the realm as he pleases. He is expected to observe the Ten Duties of Kings, the Seven Safeguards against Decline, the Four Assistances to the People, and to be guided by numerous other codes of conduct such as the Twelve Practices of Rulers, the Six Attributes of Leaders, the Eight Virtues of Kings and the Four Ways to Overcome Peril. There is logic to a tradition which includes the king among the five enemies or perils and which subscribes to many sets of moral instructions for the edification of those in positions of authority. The people of Burma have had much experience of despotic rule and possess a great awareness of the unhappy gap that can exist between the theory and practice of government.

The Ten Duties of Kings are widely known and generally accepted as a yardstick which could be applied just as well to modern government as to the first monarch of the world. The duties are: liberality, morality, self-sacrifice, integrity, kindness, austerity, non-anger, non-violence, forbearance and non-opposition (to the will of the people). . . .

The tenth duty of kings, non-opposition to the will of the people (*avirodha*), tends to be singled out as a Buddhist endorsement of democracy, supported by well-known stories from the *Jakatas*. Pawridasa, a monarch who acquired an unfortunate taste for human flesh, was forced to leave his kingdom because he would not heed the people's demand that he should abandon his cannibalistic habits. A very different kind of ruler was the Buddha's penultimate incarnation on earth, the pious King Vessantara. But he too was sent into exile when in the course of his strivings for the perfection of liberality he gave away the white elephant of the state without the consent of the people. The royal duty of non-opposition is a reminder that the legitimacy of government is founded on the consent of the people, who may withdraw their mandate at any time if they lose confidence in the ability of the ruler to serve their best interests.

By invoking the Ten Duties of Kings the Burmese are not so much indulging in wishful thinking as drawing on time-honoured values to reinforce the validity of the political reforms they consider necessary: It is a strong argument for democracy that governments regulated by principles of accountability, respect for public opinion and the supremacy of just laws are more likely than an all-powerful ruler or ruling class, uninhibited by the need to honour the will of the people, to observe the traditional duties of Buddhist kingship. Traditional values serve both to justify and to decipher popular expectations of democratic government.

II

. . . It was predictable that as soon as the issue of human rights became an integral part of the movement for democracy the official media should start ridiculing and condemning the whole concept of human rights, dubbing it a western artifact alien to traditional values. It was also ironic—Buddhism, the foundation of traditional Burmese culture, places the greatest value on man, who alone of all beings can achieve, the supreme state of Buddha-hood. Each man has in him the potential to realize the truth through his own will and endeavour and to help others to realize it. Human life therefore is infinitely precious. "Easier is it for a needle dropped from the abode of Brahma to meet a needle stuck in the earth than to be born as a human being." . . .

It is a puzzlement to the Burmese how concepts which recognize the inherent dignity and the equal and inalienable rights of human beings, which accept that all men are endowed with reason and conscience and which recommend a universal spirit of brotherhood, can be inimical to indigenous values. It is also difficult for them to understand how any of the rights contained in the thirty articles of the Universal Declaration of Human Rights can be seen as anything but wholesome and good. That the declaration was not drawn up in Burma by the Burmese seems an inadequate reason, to say the least, for rejecting it, especially as Burma was one of the nations which voted for its adoption in December 1948. If ideas and beliefs are to be denied validity outside the geographical and cultural bounds of their origin, Buddhism would be confined to north India, Christianity to a narrow tract in the Middle East and Islam to Arabia. . . .

From the beginning Burma's struggle for democracy has been fraught with danger. A movement which seeks the just and equitable distribution of powers and prerogatives that have long been held by a small elite determined to preserve its privileges at all costs is likely to be prolonged and difficult. Hope and optimism are irrepressible but there is a deep underlying premonition that the opposition to change is likely to be vicious. Often the anxious question is asked: will such an oppressive regime really give us democracy? And the answer has to be: democracy, like liberty, justice and other social and political rights, is not 'given', it is earned through courage, resolution and sacrifice. . . .

The words "law and order" have so frequently been misused as an excuse for oppression that the very phrase has-become suspect in countries: which have known authoritarian rule. Some years ago a prominent Burmese author wrote an article on the notion of law and order as expressed by the official term *nyein-wut-pi-pyar*. One by one he analysed the words, which literally mean "silent-crouched-crushed-flattened", and concluded that the whole made for an undesirable state of affairs, one which militated against the emergence of an articulate, energetic, progressive citizenry. There is no intrinsic virtue to law and order unless "law" is equated with justice and "order" with the discipline of a people satisfied that justice has been done. Law as an instrument of state oppression is a familiar feature of totalitarianism. Without a popularly elected legislature and an independent judiciary to ensure due process, the authorities can enforce as "law" arbitrary decrees that are in fact flagrant negations of all acceptable norms of justice. . . . The Buddhist concept of law is based on *dhamma*, righteousness or virtue, not on the power to impose harsh and inflexible rules on a defenceless people. The true measure of the justice of a system is the amount of protection it guarantees to the weakest. . . .

Thus to provide the people with the protective coolness of peace and security, rulers must observe the teachings of the Buddha. Central to these teachings are the concepts of truth, righteousness and loving kindness. It is government based on these very qualities that the people of Burma are seeking in their struggle for democracy. . . .

The people of Burma want not just a change of government but a change in political values. The unhappy legacies of authoritarianism can be removed only if the concept of absolute power as the basis of government is replaced by the concept of confidence as the mainspring of political authority: the confidence of the people in their right and ability to decide the destiny of their nation, mutual confidence between the people and their leaders and, most important of all, confidence in the principles of justice, liberty and human rights. . . . In their quest for democracy the people of Burma explore not only the political theories and practices of the world outside their country but also the spiritual and intellectual values that have given shape to their own environment. . . .

The quest for democracy in Burma is the struggle of a people to live whole, meaningful lives as free and equal members of the world community. It is part of the unceasing human endeavour to prove that the spirit of man can transcend the flaws of his own nature.

SOURCE: Aung San Suu Kyi, *Freedom from Fear and Other Writings*, 2nd ed. (London: Penguin, 1995). Reprinted by permission.

23. THE 14TH DALAI LAMA, "HUMAN RIGHTS AND UNIVERSAL RESPONSIBILITY" (COMPLETE)

THIS IS ONE of the clearest statements on human rights and Buddhism made by the Dalai Lama. Delivered at the United Nations World Conference on Human Rights, on June 15, 1993, in Vienna, Austria.

Our world is becoming smaller and ever more interdependent with the rapid growth in population and increasing contact between people and governments. In this light, it is important to reassess the rights and responsibilities of individuals, peoples and nations in relation to each other and to the planet as a whole. This World Conference of organizations and governments concerned about the rights and freedoms of people throughout the world reflects the appreciation of our interdependence.

No matter what country or continent we come from we are all basically the same human beings. We have the common human needs and concerns. We all seek happiness and try to avoid suffering regardless of our race, religion, sex or political status. Human beings, indeed all sentient beings, have the right to pursue happiness and live in peace and in freedom. As free human beings we can use our unique intelligence to try to understand ourselves and our world. But if we are prevented from using our creative potential, we are deprived of one of the basic characteristics of a human being. It is very often the most gifted, dedicated and creative members of our society who become victims of human rights abuses. Thus the political, social, cultural and economic developments of a society are obstructed by the violations of human rights. Therefore, the protection of these rights and freedoms are of immense importance both for the individuals affected and for the development of the society as a whole.

It is my belief that the lack of understanding of the true cause of happiness is the principal reason why people inflict suffering on others. Some people think that causing pain to others may lead to their own happiness or that their own happiness is of such importance that the pain of others is of no significance. But this is clearly shortsighted. No one truly benefits from causing harm to another being. Whatever immediate advantage is gained at the expense of someone else is short-lived. In the long run causing others misery and infringing upon their peace and happiness creates anxiety, fear and suspicion for oneself.

The key to creating a better and more peaceful world is the development of love and compassion for others. This naturally means we must develop concern for our brothers and sisters who are less fortunate than we are. In this respect, the non-governmental organizations have a key role to play. You not only create awareness for the need to respect the rights of all human beings, but also give the victims of human rights violations hope for a better future.

When I travelled to Europe for the first time in 1973, I talked about the increasing interdependence of the world and the need to develop a sense of universal responsibility. We need to think in global terms because the effects of one nation's actions are felt far beyond its borders. The acceptance of universally binding standards of Human Rights as laid down in the Universal Declaration of Human Rights and in the International Covenants of Human Rights is essential in today's shrinking world. Respect for fundamental human rights should not remain an ideal to be achieved but a requisite foundation for every human society.

When we demand the rights and freedoms we so cherish we should also be aware of our responsibilities. If we accept that others have an equal right to peace and happiness as ourselves, do we not have a responsibility to help those in need? Respect for fundamental human rights is as important to the people of Africa and Asia as it is to those in Europe or the Americas. All human beings, whatever their cultural or historical background, suffer when they are intimidated, imprisoned or tortured. The question of human rights is so fundamentally important that there should be no difference of views on this. We must therefore insist on a global consensus not only on the need to respect human rights world wide but more importantly on the definition of these rights.

Recently some Asian governments have contended that the standards of human rights laid down in the Universal Declaration of Human Rights are those advocated by the West and cannot be applied to Asia and others parts of the Third World because of differences in culture and differences in social and economic development. I do not share this view and I am convinced that the majority of Asian people do not support this view either, for it is the inherent nature of all human beings to yearn for freedom, equality and dignity, and they have an equal to achieve that. I do not see any contradiction between the need for economic development and the need for respect of human rights. The rich diversity of cultures and religions should help to strengthen the fundamental human rights in all communities. Because underlying this diversity are fundamental principles that bind us all as members of the same human family. Diversity and traditions can never justify the violations of human rights. Thus discrimination of persons from a different race, of women, and of weaker sections of society may be traditional in some regions, but if they are inconsistent with universally recognized human rights, these forms of behavior must change. The universal principles of equality of all human beings must take precedence.

It is mainly the authoritarian and totalitarian regimes who are opposed to the universality of human rights. It would be absolutely wrong to concede to this view. On the contrary, such regimes must be made to respect and conform to the universally accepted principles in the larger and long term interests of their own peoples. The dramatic changes in the past few years clearly indicate that the triumph of human rights is inevitable.

There is a growing awareness of peoples' responsibilities to each other and to the planet we share. This is encouraging even though so much suffering continues to be inflicted based on chauvinism, race, religion, ideology and history. A new hope is emerging for the downtrodden, and people everywhere are displaying a willingness to champion and defend the rights and freedoms of their fellow human beings.

Brute force, no matter how strongly applied, can never subdue the basic human desire for freedom and dignity. It is not enough, as communist systems have assumed, merely to provide people with food, shelter and clothing. The deeper human nature needs to breathe the precious air of liberty. However, some governments still consider the fundamental human rights of its citizens an internal matter of the state. They do not accept that the fate of a people in any country is the legitimate concern of the entire human family and that claims to sovereignty are not a license to mistreat one's citizens. It is not only our right as members of the global human family to protest when our brothers and sisters are being treated brutally, but it is also our duty to do whatever we can to help them.

Artificial barriers that have divided nations and peoples have fallen in recent times. With the dismantling of Berlin wall the East–West division which has polarized the whole world for decades has now come to an end. We are experiencing a time filled with hope and expectations. Yet there still remains a major gulf at the heart of the human family. By this I am referring to the North-South divide. If we are serious in our commitment to the fundamental principles of equality, principles which, I believe, lie at the heart of the concept of human rights, today's economic disparity can no longer be ignored. It is not enough to merely state that all human beings must enjoy equal dignity. This must be translated into action. We have a responsibility to find ways to achieve a more equitable distribution of world's resources.

We are witnessing a tremendous popular movement for the advancement of human rights and democratic freedom in the world. This movement must become an even more powerful moral force, so that even the most obstructive governments and armies are incapable of suppressing it. This conference is an occasion for all of us to reaffirm our commitment to this goal. It is natural and just for nations, peoples and individuals to demand respect for their rights and freedoms and to struggle to end repression, racism, economic exploitation, military occupation, and various forms of colonialism and alien domination. Governments should actively support such demands instead of only paying lip service to them.

As we approach the end of the Twentieth Century, we find that the world is becoming one community. We are being drawn together by the grave problems of over population, dwindling natural resources, and an environmental crisis that threaten the very foundation of our existence on this planet. Human rights, environmental protection and great social and economic equality, are all interrelated. I believe that to meet the challenges of our times, human beings will have to develop a greater sense of universal responsibility. Each of us must learn to work not just for one self, one's own family or one's nation, but for the benefit of all humankind. Universal responsibility is the key to human survival. It is the best foundation for world peace.

This need for co-operation can only strengthen humankind, because it helps us to recognize that the most secure foundation for a new world order is not simply broader political and economic alliances, but each individual's genuine practice of love and compassion. These qualities are the ultimate source of human happiness, and our need for them lies at the very core of our being. The practice of compassion is not idealistic, but the most effective way to pursue the best interests of others as well as our own. The more we become interdependent the more it is in our own interest to ensure the well-being of others.

I believe that one of the principal factors that hinder us from fully appreciating our interdependence is our undue emphasis on material development. We have become so engrossed in its pursuit that, unknowingly, we have neglected the most basic qualities of compassion, caring and cooperation. When we do not know someone or do not feel connected to an individual or group, we tend to overlook their needs. Yet, the development of human society requires that people help each other.

I, for one, strongly believe that individuals can make a difference in society. Every individual has a responsibility to help more our global family in the right direction and we must each assume that responsibility. As a Buddhist monk, I try to develop compassion within myself, not simply as a religious practice, but on a human level as well. To encourage myself in this altruistic attitude, I sometimes find it helpful to imagine myself standing as a single individual on one side, facing a huge gathering of all other human beings on the other side. Then I ask myself, "Whose interests are more important?" To me it is quite clear that however important I may feel I am, I am just one individual while others are infinite in number and importance.

Thank you

SOURCE: The Government of Tibet in Exile Web Site, www.tibet.com/DL/vienna.html.

24. THE DRAFT CONSTITUTION OF TIBET, ADOPTED BY THE GOVERNMENT IN EXILE, 1963 (EXCERPTS)

IN THIS DOCUMENT, the fourteenth Dalai Lama's concerns for reforming Tibet's society to bring it into line with the modern democracies of the world are obvious. The Constitution is very much in accord with the 1948 United Nations Universal Declaration of Human Rights.

Preamble (Complete)

WHEREAS it has become increasingly evident that the system of government which has hitherto prevailed in Tibet has not proved sufficiently responsive to the present needs and future development of the people

AND WHEREAS it is deemed desirable and necessary that the principle of justice, equality and democracy laid down by the Lord Buddha should be reinforced and strengthened in the government of Tibet

AND WHEREAS it is deemed essential that the people of Tibet should have a more effective voice in shaping their destiny

NOW, THEREFORE, His Holiness the Dalai Lama has been pleased to ordain, and it is hereby ordained as follows:

Chapter II (Complete)

Fundamental Rights and Duties

Equality before the Law—Article 8. All Tibetans shall be equal before the law and the enjoyment of the rights and freedoms set forth in this Chapter shall be secured without discrimination on any ground such as sex, race, language, religion, social origin, property, birth or other status.

Right to Life, Liberty and Property—Article 9. No person shall be deprived of life, liberty or property without due process of law.

Right to Life—Article 10. Every person shall have the right to life, provided that deprivation of life shall not be deemed to contravene this Article when it results from the use of force which is no more than absolutely necessary (a) in defence of any person from unlawful violence, (b) in order to effect a lawful arrest or to prevent the escape of a person lawfully detained or (c) in action lawfully taken for the purpose of quelling a riot or insurrection.

Right to Liberty—Article 11(1) No person who is arrested shall be detained in custody without being informed, as soon as may be, of the grounds for such arrest, nor shall he be denied the right to consult and to be defended by a legal practitioner of his choice and to have adequate time and facilities for the preparation of his defence.

(2) Every person who is arrested and detained in custody shall be produced before the nearest court having jurisdiction within a period of twenty-four hours of such arrest excluding the time necessary for the journey from the place of arrest to the court of the magistrate and no such person shall be detained in custody beyond the said period without the authority of a magistrate.

(3) Every person who has been arrested or detained in contravention of this provision of this Article shall have an enforceable right to compensation.

Safeguards in Judicial Proceedings—Article 12. (1) Every person shall be entitled to a fair and public hearing within a reasonable time by an independent and impartial tribunal established by law. Judgement shall be pronounced publicly but the press and public may be excluded from all or part of the trial in the interests of public morality, public order or national security where the interests of juveniles or the protection of the private life of the parties so require, or to the extent strictly necessary in the opinion of the court in special circumstances where publicity would prejudice the interests of justice.

(2) Every person charged with a criminal offence shall be presumed innocent until proved guilty according to law.

(3) Every person charged with a criminal offence shall have the free assistance of (a) a legal practitioner, when the interests of justice so require, if he has not sufficient means to pay and (b) an interpreter, if he cannot understand or speak the language used in court.

Protection in respect of Conviction for Offences—Article 13. (1) No person shall be convicted of any offence except for violation of a law in force at the time of commission of the act charged as an offence, nor be subjected to a penalty greater than that which might have been inflicted under the law in force at the time of the commission of the offence.

(2) No person shall be prosecuted and punished for the same offence more than once.

(3) No person accused of any offence shall be compelled to be a witness against himself.

Prohibition of Inhuman Treatment—Article 14. No person shall be subjected to torture or to inhuman or degrading treatment or punishment.

Prohibition of Slavery and Forced Labour—Article 15. (1) No one shall be held in slavery or be required to perform forced or compulsory labour.

(2) For the purpose of this Article, the term "forced or compulsory labour" shall not include (a) any work required to be done in the course of detention under the sentence of a court of law, (b) any service exacted in case of an emergency or calamity threatening the life or well-being of the community, (c) any service of a military character or (d) any work or service which forms part of the normal civic obligations of a nation.

Prohibition of Employment of Children—Article 16. No child below the age of fourteen years shall be employed to work in any factory or mine or engaged in any other hazardous employment.

Religious Freedom—Article 17. (1) All religious denominations are equal before the law.

(2) Every Tibetan shall have the right to freedom of thought, conscience and religion. The right includes freedom to openly believe, practice, worship and observe any religion either alone or in community with others.

(3) Freedom to manifest one's religion or beliefs and to deal with any matter relating to religious or charitable purpose either alone or in community with others shall be subject only to such limitations as are prescribed by law and are necessary in the interests of public safety, for the

protection of public order, health or morals, or for the protection of the rights and freedoms of others.

Other Fundamental Freedoms—Article 18. Subject to any law imposing reasonable restrictions in the interests of the security of the State, public order, health or morality, all citizens shall be entitled to:

(a) freedom of speech and expression;

(b) assemble peaceably and without arms;

(c) form associations or unions;

(d) move freely throughout the territories of Tibet;

(e) the right to a passport to travel outside those territories;

(f) reside and settle in any part of Tibet;

(g) acquire, hold and dispose of property;

(h) practise any profession or carry on any occupation, trade or business.

Right to Property—Article 19. No person shall be deprived of his property save by authority of law and for public purpose on payment of just compensation.

The Right to Vote—Article 20. All Tibetans, men and women, who have attained the age of eighteen and above shall have the right to vote. The vote shall be personal, equal, free, and secret, and its exercise shall be deemed to be a civic obligation.

Disqualification of Vote—Article 21. (1) A person shall be disqualified to vote if he is of unsound mind and stands so declared by a competent court.

(2) A person shall not have the right to vote if he is so disqualified by any law.

Right to hold Office—Article 22. All Tibetans of either sex shall have the right to hold public offices, whether elective or otherwise, on conditions of equality in accordance with the requirements of law.

Obligations of Nationals—Article 23. All Tibetans shall fufil the following constitutional obligations:

(a) bear true allegiance to the State of Tibet;

(b) faithfully comply with and observe the Constitution and the laws of the State;

(c) to pay taxes imposed by the State in accordance with the laws; and

(d) perform such obligations as may be imposed by law in the event of a threat to national security or other public calamity.

Enforcement of Rights—Article 24. Every citizen whose rights and freedoms as set forth in this Chapter are violated shall have the right to approach the Supreme Court. Regional Courts and such other courts as the National Assembly may by a law designate for the enforcement of those rights and freedoms enumerated in this Chapter and the court shall be entitled to pass such orders as are necessary to protect those rights.

Excerpt from Chapter V, Of Executive Government:

Council of Regency—Article 36 (complete). (1) There shall be Council of Regency to exercise executive powers in the following circumstances:

(a) until such period as the reincarnate Dalai Lama becomes of age to assume the powers of his predecessors;

(b) until such period as His Holiness the Dalai Lama has not assumed the powers of his predecessors;

(c) in case of any disability which prevents His Holiness the Dalai Lama from exercising his executive functions;

(d) in case of the absence of His Holiness the Dalai Lama from the State;

(e) when the National Assembly, by majority of two-thirds of its total members in consultation with the Supreme Court, decides that in the highest interests of the State it is imperative that the executive functions of His Holiness the Dalai Lama shall be exercised by the Council of Regency.

SOURCE: Roger Hicks and Ngakpa Chogyam, *Great Ocean: An Authorised Biography of the Dalai Lama* (Longmead, Dorset: Element Books, 1984).

25. "DECLARATION OF INTERDEPENDENCE" BY THE ONLINE CONFERENCE ON BUDDHISM AND HUMAN RIGHTS, OCTOBER 1–14, 1995, SPONSORED BY THE *JOURNAL OF BUDDHIST ETHICS* (COMPLETE)

THE PARTICIPANTS IN the Online Conference on Buddhism and Human Rights felt that the importance of the topic and the considerable amount of work that went into the conference warranted the preparation of this declaration. It took into account the formal papers presented as well as the voluminous comments made by those who took part in the discussions. Dr. Peter Harvey shepherded its production, which was no easy task.

Preamble

Those who have the good fortune to have a "rare and precious human rebirth," with all its potential for awareness, sensitivity, and freedom, have a duty to not abuse the rights of others to partake of the possibilities of moral and spiritual flourishing offered by human existence. Such flourishing is only possible when certain conditions relating to physical existence and social freedom are maintained. Human beings, furthermore, have an obligation to treat other forms of life with the respect commensurate to their natures.

To repress our basic sympathy by abusing other sentient beings, human or otherwise, cripples our own potential, and increases the amount of suffering in the world for both others and ourselves. The doctrine of Conditioned Arising shows that our lives are intertwined, and abusing others can only be done when we are blind to this fact. As vulnerable beings in a conditioned world, our mutual dependency indicates that whatever can be done to reduce suffering in the world should be done.

The Buddhist teaching that we lack an inherently existing Self (*anatman*) shows that suffering does not really "belong" to anyone. It arises, in the life-stream of various sentient beings. To try and reduce it in "my" stream at the expense of increasing it in another life-stream is folly, both because this will in fact bring more suffering back to me (karma), and because it depends on the deluded notion that "I" am an inviolable entity that is not dependent and can treat others as if only *they* are limited and conditioned.

Whereas in its teachings Buddhism recognizes:

1. The interdependency of all forms of life and the reciprocal obligations which arise from it, such as the duty to repay the kindness of those who in previous lives may have been our parents, relatives and friends;
2. The need for universal compassion for sentient beings who are all alike in that they dislike pain and wish for happiness;
3. The inalienable dignity which living creatures possess by virtue of their capacity to achieve enlightenment in this life or in the future;

The Conference affirms:

1. Every human being should be treated *humanely* both by other individuals and governments in keeping with the Buddhist commitment to non-violence (*ahimsa*) and respect for life.

2. Every human being must be treated *equally* and without discrimination on grounds of race, nationality, religion, sex, color, age, mental ability, or political views.
3. Human beings have obligations to other sentient beings and to the environment that all depend on for life and flourishing, now and in the future. Accordingly, humans have an obligation to present and future generations to protect the environment they share with other sentient beings, and to avoid causing direct or indirect harm to other forms of sentient life.

Dated: 14 October 1995

SOURCE: Damien Keown, Charles Prebish, and Wayne Husted, eds., *Buddhism and Human Rights* (Richmond, Surrey: Curzon Press, 1998). Also available in the *Journal of Buddhist Ethics*, under Online Conferences. Reprinted by permission.

14

BIOGRAPHICAL SKETCHES OF HUMAN RIGHTS LEADERS IN THE BUDDHIST TRADITION

Ambedkar, Bhimrao Ramji (1891–1956)

Leader of the untouchable community of India in the years of struggle that led to independence from Britain, converted to Buddhism for human rights. His father was an officer in the British Indian Army, a singular position for a member of the Mahar untouchable caste, who according to Hindu traditions should be restricted to the most humble, menial, and filthy jobs available. B. R. Ambedkar, M.A., Ph.D., D.Sc., LL.D., D. Litt., Barrister at Law, was a brilliant student who amassed more degrees than any other Indian of his time. Having secured a scholarship from a generous maharaja, he graduated from a college in India and then studied at Columbia University, where he received an M.A. and Ph.D. He later earned the M.Sc. and D.Sc. from the University of London, and was admitted to the bar in London after studying at Gray's Inn. On returning to India in the 1920s, he discovered that his education did not spare him the indignities due to one of his low birth. Dr. Ambedkar joined the Congress Party, working with Gandhi toward independence, but he and Gandhi disagreed on the matter of caste. In 1935, Ambedkar declared that he was giving up on Hinduism and would seek out another religion, one that would free his community from their disadvantages. In 1955, only six weeks before his death, after much study and offers from Christians, Sikhs, and Moslems, Ambedkar, along with a half million of his fellow caste members, converted to Buddhism. The fledgling Buddhist community has survived and developed reasonably well. His writings on Buddhism focus on the practical social benefits of the dharma and controversially reinterpret many basic doctrines. Before independence in 1947 Ambedkar chaired the group that drafted the Indian Constitution, which under his influence established a secular state with strong protections for civil liberties, for the untouchables, and for minority communities, which protections proved much easier to proclaim than to implement. See also the biographical sketches on Dharmachari Lokamitra* and Sangharakshita.* **Work:** *The Buddha and His Dhamma*, 2nd ed. (Bombay: Siddharta Publications, 1974). **Suggested Reading:** Christopher S. Queen, "Dr. Ambedkar and the Hermeneutics of Buddhist Liberation," in Christopher S. Queen and Sallie B. King, *Engaged Buddhism: Buddhist Liberation Movements in Asia* (Albany: State University of New York Press, 1996).

Ananda Mahidol: See Rama VIII.

Ariyaratne, A. T. (1931–   )

Sri Lankan educator and social activist, founder of the Sarvodaya Shramadana movement in Sri Lanka in 1958. This movement, inspired by Gandhi's notion of *sarvodaya*, "the well-being of all" through community action, relies on the voluntary donation of effort (*shramadana*). It is based on Dr. Ariyaratne's vision of Sri Lanka's idealized village life in the past and Angarika Dharmapala's* "Protestant Buddhism," a religion of activity in the world to improve the life of the people. It began in 1958 with work camps for student volunteers, who labored to improve destitute villages, and is run from Nalanda College in Colombo, where Dr. Ariyaratne was an instructor. Since then there have been thousands of local self-help development programs sponsored in villages and communities in Sri Lanka with the end of transforming society by transforming individuals through Buddhist values and practices. Although controversial for its interpretation of Buddhism and questioned about the practical benefits actually attained, Sarvodaya has become very well known and has attracted considerable aid from international donors. Recently the organization has turned more of its efforts to working to resolve the bloody intercommunal conflicts that have devastated the country since 1971. Generally speaking Sarvodaya has spoken out to protect the Tamil minority and has endeavored to find solutions for the violence, sometimes incurring the displeasure of the government. He remains a director. **Work:** *Collected Works*, vols. I–V (Moratuwa, Sri Lanka Sarvodaya Research Institute, 1978–1991). **Suggested Readings:** George D. Bond, "A. T. Ariyaratne and Sarvodaya Shramadana Movement in Sri Lanka," in Christopher S. Queen and Sallie B. King, *Engaged Buddhism: Buddhist Liberation Movements in Asia* (Albany: State University of New York Press, 1996); Joanna Macy, *Dharma and Development* (West Hartford, CT: Kumarian Press, 1983).

Aung San Suu Kyi, Daw (1945–   )

Daughter of Aung San, Burma's foremost leader in the struggle for independence from Britain, Nobel Laureate, and leader of the prodemocracy movement in Burma since 1988. For details see chapter 6.

Bandaranaike, S.W.R.D. (1899–1959)

S.W.R.D. Bandaranaike, Sri Lankan patriot and politician, active in the campaigns to attain freedom from British Colonial rule and prime minister of Sri Lanka (1956–1959.) Of the highest caste and educated at an elite Roman Catholic college in Colombo, he placed third in the entire British Empire in the senior Cambridge examination. Educated at Oxford, he became secretary of the prestigious Oxford Union in 1923. He was called to the bar in England and entered politics on his return to Ceylon in 1927, holding cabinet offices in the State Council under British rule. In 1937 he reconverted to Buddhism and founded a Buddhist revivalist political party influenced by followers of Dharmapala.*

Bandaranaike was a cabinet minister in the first parliament of independent Sri Lanka in 1947. Leaving the ruling party, he became leader of the opposition, and as head of his newly formed party, a union of four socialist parties, swept the elections of 1956 with the help of the Buddhist Front. Bandaranaike promised to see that that the place of Buddhism would be recognized officially and that Sinhalese, which is spoken by the Buddhist majority, would become the official language of the country. Many radical political monks worked in his election campaign.

While the passing of the Sinhalese only bill was a great blow to the Tamil minority, whose language rights had been protected, Bandaranaike passed bills to eliminate caste discrimination, and began to implement socialist measures, establishing a ten-year plan for a centralized economy.

Things did not go smoothly, and there were widespread anti-Tamil riots in 1958, with thousands being murdered before the prime minister was able to bring things under control again. When he changed his position on the Tamil language in 1958, many of his Buddhist supporters were enraged. During the election campaign of 1959, the Venerable Mapitagama Buddharakkhita, a leading political monk, organized an assassination plot against the prime minister. On the morning of September 25, 1959, the monk Talduwe Somarama called on Bandaranaike at his residence and shot him in the stomach as the politician was paying obeisance to his religious guest. He died the next day from the wound. Since then, the struggle between the Buddhist majority and the Tamil minority has continued its bloody course, with political monks continuing to support the suppression of Tamil interests in the name of Buddhism. Of course, other Buddhist voices have spoken out in favor of tolerance, compromise, and protection of Tamil interests.

See the biographical entries for his wife, Sirimavo Bandaranaike,* and his daughter, Chandrika Bandaranaike Kumaratunga,* both of whom became the elected political leaders of Sri Lanka.

Works: *The Government and the People: A Collection of the Speeches of S.W.R.D. Bandaranaike* (Colombo, Ceylon: Government Press, 1959); *Towards a New Era, Selected Speeches of S.W.R.D. Bandaranaike* (Colombo, Ceylon: Government Press, 1961). **Suggested Reading:** Heinz Bechert, "S.W.R.D. Bandaranaike and the Legitimation of Power through Buddhist Ideals," in Bardwell L. Smith, ed., *Religion and Legitimation of Power in Thailand, Laos, and Burma* (Chambersburg, PA: Anima Books, 1978).

Bandaranaike, Sirimavo (1916–2000)

Wife of the Sri Lankan Prime Minister, S.W.R.D. Bandaranaike, who was assassinated by a Buddhist monk in 1959, Mrs. Bandaranaike took over the leadership of the party and won the election of 1960, becoming the first ever female prime minister of a nation. She was born into a wealthy family of the highest caste and received an English language education at a Roman Catholic school in Sri Lanka but retained her Buddhist faith. Until the death of her husband, her life was that of wife and mother in a powerful family, with no experience in politics.

However, she became a strong campaigner and forceful leader, after the party convinced her to run. Her first term was from 1960 to 1965, when she lost decisively. Winning again in 1970, she held office until 1977. In office she was noted for her strong socialist positions and for firmly supporting the radical Buddhist nationalists against the Tamils, thus continuing the legacy of her late husband. She suspended civil rights to put down armed resistance from several groups and made Buddhism the state religion. Her economic programs left the country impoverished. She was expelled from parliament in 1980 and stripped of her civil rights for alleged corruption and abuse of office. In 1994, her party was once again successful under the leadership of her daughter, Chandrika Bandaranaike Kumaratunga, who became president of the country under the new constitution. President Kumaratunga then appointed her mother to the then largely ceremonial role of prime minister, which she held from 1994 until failing health forced her to resign shortly before her death in 2000.

To quote from her obituary:

> The Bandaranaikes—husband and widow—unquestionably broke the stifling colonial ethos of the English-speaking elite, and restored dignity and a rightful place to the Sinhalese majority. But it was done largely by exploiting their chauvinism, and at the expense of the Tamils, not least because Mrs. Bandaranaike, like most Sinhalese, had little concept of her island as a multi-ethnic whole. If a country may be judged by how it treats its minorities, the failure to treat them properly in Sri Lanka has carried a fearsome price, which even yet has not been fully paid.

See the biographical entries for her husband, S.W.R.D. Bandaranaike,* and daughter, Chandrika Bandaranaike Kumaratunga.* **Suggested Reading:** "Obituary," *Guardian* October 11, 2000.

Bhumipol (also transliterated Bhumibol) Adulyadej: See Rama IX.

Buddhadasa Bhikkhu (1906–1993)

Thai Buddhist monk (bhikkhu), influential teacher, writer, and organizer with strong local and international following. His writings are highly original for a Thai cleric in that they reflect interests in religious ideas outside the Theravada tradition. He used Zen and the Christian Bible, for example. Buddhadasa's monastic career also showed a certain independence in that he did not seek advancement through the ecclesiastical ranks. Rather in 1932 he established himself in a quiet corner of southern Thailand, where he devoted himself to contemplation, study, and writing. Over the years, his retreat, Suan Mokh (garden of liberation), attracted lay and monastic disciples and grew into an independent dharma center and monastery not integrated into the national hierarchy. His teachings emphasize the interconnection of all aspects of human and natural life under the principles of Buddhist dharma. He stressed the importance of the elimination of suffering in both the individual and social sphere with the goal of true peace, and taught that Buddhism was consistent with democracy (understood as inner freedom), socialism (as nonattachment and sharing), and dictatorship (understood as a powerful ruler with the ten virtues of a Buddhist ruler). All this led to his controversial solution for the political problems of Thailand of "dictatorial dharmic socialism," arguing that liberal democracy was inconsistent with Buddhist traditions and brought as many problems as it did solutions. His voluminous works are highly influential with the educated elite Buddhists of Thailand such as Sulak Sivaraksa* and many have been translated and read widely abroad. **Work:** *Handbook for Mankind*, trans. Roderick Bucknell (Bangkok: Buddhadasa Foundation, 1989). **Suggested Reading:** Peter Jackson, *Buddhadasa: A Buddhist Thinker for the Modern World* (Bangkok: Siam Society, 1988).

Chulalongkorn or Mahachulalongkorn: See Rama V.

Thirteenth Dalai Lama (1876–1933)

Like all Dalai Lamas, believed to be an incarnation of the Bodhisattva Avalokitesvara, head of the Gelugpa sect and ruler of Tibet from 1895–1933. See chapter 11 for details.

Fourteenth Dalai Lama (1935–   )

Like all Dalai Lamas, believed to be an incarnation of the Bodhisattva Avalokitesvara, head of the Gelugpa sect and last traditional ruler of Tibet (1950–1959, currently heads the Tibet Government in Exile, and Nobel Peace Laureate in 1989. See chapter 11 for details.

Dharmapala, Angarika (1864–1933)

Sri Lankan "Protestant Buddhist" who worked for religious and political freedom against the British. Born as Don David Hevavitarana to a middle-class family in Colombo, the capital of the British Ceylon, now

Sri Lanka, he was educated at English-language Roman Catholic and Anglican schools, since at the time there were no Buddhist schools available. In later life he stressed how little he thought of his Anglican schoolmasters, because not only did they drink whiskey and eat meat, they also killed birds for sport. The contrast with the Buddhist monks, who practiced nonharm and abstained from all strong drink, reinforced his Buddhist faith. He met Col. Henry Steel Olcott* and Mme. Helena Blavasky, cofounders of the Theosophist Society, on their first visit to Ceylon, and worked closely with them until 1898, when they parted ways after a quarrel. He was widely traveled, in 1889 being the first Sri Lankan Buddhist to contact the Buddhists in Japan, and represented Buddhism at the Congress of World Religions held in conjunction with the Chicago World's Fair in 1893, where his speech attracted considerable attention.

In 1881 he adopted his new name, Dharmapala, which means "defender of the dharma" and invented a new title and status, which he then assumed, that of Anagarika, or "homeless," a descriptive term used for the monks of Sri Lanka. In his case, it represented a state between the monk and the layman. He did not seek ordination until shortly before his death in 1933, but took as an Anagarika the eight vows of abstention from killing, sexual activity, taking alcohol, and the like. He wore white instead of the monk's saffron, and he did not shave his head. In this way he was free from both the cares of the world and the discipline of the organized sangha. He fought for Buddhism and Singhalese culture against British imperialism, campaigned for the refurbishment and Buddhist control of the Buddhist monuments in India, and was a tireless proponent for a new style of "Protestant Buddhism," which has had enormous influence in Theravada countries. **Work:** Ananda Guruge, ed., *Return to Righteousness: A Collection of Speeches, Essays, and Letters of Anagarika Dharmapala* (Colombo, Ceylon, 1965). **Suggested Reading:** Richard Gombrich, *Theravada Buddhism: A Social History from Ancient India to Modern Colombo* (London: Routledge and Kegan Paul, 1988), ch. 7.

Kabilsingh, Chatsumarn (1944–)

Thai Buddhist scholar, feminist, and campaigner for the establishment of a Thai order of nuns, daughter of Voramai Kabilsingh,* pioneer Thai Buddhist nun. Chatsumarn received her bachelor's degree and doctorate at universities in India and her master's in Canada. For many years she taught religious studies at Thamassat University at Bangkok. Her many publications are mostly in the area of engaged Buddhism with a particular concern for women's issues. She served as the president of Sakyadhita, an international organization for Buddhist women, from 1991 to 1995. After taking early retirement from her university job, in February 2001, and renouncing married life, Chatsumarn received ordination in the newly revived Theravada order of nuns in Sri Lanka, and received full ordination in February 2003 in the same lineage. She now resides in the temple founded by her mother in 1957. Since there has never been an order of fully ordained nuns in Thailand, and since the male (of course) hierarchy of the sangha does not recognize the validity of the ordination of the Thai females, there has been a large controversy over the new order. Her name as a nun is Dhamma-ananda, "bliss in the dharma." **Work:** Chatsumarn Kabilsingh, *Thai Women in Buddhism* (Berkeley, CA: Parallax Press, 1991). **Suggested Readings:** Nancy J. Barnes, "Buddhist Women and the Nun's Order in Asia," in Christopher S. Queen and Sallie B. King, *Engaged Buddhism: Buddhist Liberation Movements in Asia* (Albany: State University of New York Press, 1996); Stephen Batchelor, "Chatsumarn Kabilsingh," in E. B. Findly, ed., *Women's Buddhism Buddhism's Women* (Boston: Wisdom Publications, 2000).

Kabilsingh, Voramai (1908–   )

Pioneer Thai Buddhist nun, founder of the first temple in the country for women, schoolteacher, wife, and mother of Chatsumarn Kabilsingh.* As a young woman, she learned martial arts and participated in a bicycle trek from Bangkok to Singapore, highly unusual activities for the time and place. Thailand has never had an order of fully ordained nuns, but does have an order for laywomen, who take the vows for a novice, wear white robes rather than the saffron of monks, and live lives of service to the sangha. Such a woman has the title of *mae ji*. In 1956, Voramai took the eight *mae ji* vows, but took on yellow robes to emphasize that her aspirations were higher. In 1957 she founded a temple for women to practice Buddhism in Nakhonpathom, not far from Bangkok. Her temple sponsored a school, an orphanage, and many other good works and published journals and ran religious retreats for its many supporters. When sangha authorities and the Department of Religious Affairs objected, the sangha council of elders ruled in her favor. However, when she sought and received full ordination in 1971 as a nun in Taiwan in a Mahayana lineage, the Thai sangha refused to accept her into the Thai Buddhist structure, although she is recognized as a Chinese nun. Her name as a nun is Ta Tao, which in Chinese means "great way." Her daughter, Chatsumarn has continued the struggle for the establishment of a Thai order of nuns. **Suggested Readings:** Chatsumarn Kabilsingh, *Thai Women in Buddhism* (Berkeley, CA: Parallax Press, 1991), pp. 48–53; Stephen Batchelor, "Voramai Kabilsingh," in E. B. Findly, ed., *Women's Buddhism Buddhism's Women* (Boston: Wisdom Publications, 2000).

Kitthiwuttho, Bhikku (1936–   )

Thai monk, ordained in 1957, successful leader of mass Buddhist movements, and controversial campaigner against democratic elements. See chapter 7 for details.

Kumaratunga, Chandrika Bandaranaike (1945–   )

Daughter of two prime ministers of Sri Lanka, her father, S.W.R.D. Bandaranaike (1899–1959), and her mother Sirimavo Bandaranaike (1916–2000), Mrs. Kumaratunga was elected president in 1994, under a new constitution which gave considerable powers to the office of the president. She inherited a country that had been in turmoil for some forty years, with serious civil war raging between the Tamil Hindu minority and the Sinhalese Buddhist majority for more than twenty years. The economy also was in shambles. In large part the problems of the country could be placed on her parents, whose support for a centralized socialist planned economy and for imposing Buddhist hegemony on the entire country had worked out very badly. She has tried to find ways to recognize the aspirations of the Tamils and to rebuild the economy, but has not yet been successful. In 1988, her film star and politician husband was killed in a political assassination, as was her father in 1959. She survived a suicide bombing in 1999 during an election where she was reelected. See the biographical entries for her father, S.W.R.D. Bandaranaike,* and mother, Sirimavo Bandaranaike.*

Lert-Lah: See Rama II.

Lokamitra, Dharmachari (1947–   )

British born as Jeremy Goody, ordained in the Western Buddhist Order in 1974, and tireless worker for human rights in India. Since 1977 he has dedicated himself to working with the Trailokya Bauddha Mahasangha Sahayaka Gana, or TBMSG, the Ambedkarite ex-untouchable Buddhist community in India. Due to Indian immigration rules and to the difficulty of living in untouchable communities, Lokamitra is the main Western Buddhist who has helped the TBMSG on the ground. There have been great successes in education, medical services, and community development that emphasizes self-reliance and economic cooperation. Since the TBMSG has grown and matured, the leadership is now nearly all local ex-untouchables, and Lokamitra has become only an advisor. See also the biographical sketches on Ambedkar* and Sangharakshita.* **Suggested Reading:** Alan Sponberg, "TBMSG: A Dhamma Revolution in Contemporary India," in Christopher S. Queen and Sallie B. King, *Engaged Buddhism: Buddhist Liberation Movements in Asia* (Albany: State University of New York Press, 1996).

Mahachulalongkorn or Chulalongkorn: See Rama V.

Mongkut: See Rama IV.

Nang Klao: See Rama III.

Ne Win, U (1911–2002)

Burmese military leader in the struggle against British imperialism and Japanese occupation, military dictator of Myanmar (1962–1988), noted for repressive rule and destruction of the economy. For details, see chapter 6.

Nhat Hanh, Thich (1926–   )

Vietnamese Zen monk and Zen master, peace activist, Buddhist innovator, writer of some 100 books, and religious organizer. Thich Nhat Hahn has been in exile from Vietnam since 1966, first banned by the pro-American South Vietnamese regime and now by the Communists. He became a novice monk at the age of seventeen, and received full ordination in 1949 in a Vietnamese school of Buddhism, which synthesizes Theravada and Zen traditions. Vietnam had been embroiled in war since the early 1940s, having been drawn into World War II when occupied by the Japanese, then in a war of liberation against the French Colonial regime, and after that a civil war, involving American support for anticommunist forces in the 1960s and 1970s. Moved by the suffering of his nation, Nhat

Hanh was active as a leader of Buddhist activists from the 1950s on. He is credited with having coined the phrase "engaged Buddhism" and has consistently taught that Buddhist practice and belief must lead to day-to-day action in the world for nonviolence and nonexploitation in all social interchange. It was his Unified Buddhist Church of Vietnam that led popular demonstrations that nearly toppled the American dominated regime in the South from 1963 to 1966. This struggle saw some monks immolate themselves to draw the world's attention to the suffering of their countrymen, and it ended with a brutal military suppression of the Buddhist activists. Nhat Hanh escaped assassination and fled into exile, where he has remained since 1966, still actively working for peace and decency according to Buddhist principles in Vietnam and worldwide. His organization is headquartered in Southern France with branches and many followers around the globe. **Works:** *The Miracle of Mindfulness: A Manual on Meditation* (Boston: Beacon Press, 1981); *Interbeing: Commentaries on the Tiep Hien Precepts*, Fred Eppsteiner, ed. (Berkeley CA: Parallax Press, 1987). **Suggested Reading:** Sallie B. King, "Thich Nhat Hanh and the Unified Buddhist Church: Nondualism in Action," in Christopher S. Queen and Sallie B. King, *Engaged Buddhism: Buddhist Liberation Movements in Asia* (Albany: State University of New York Press, 1996).

Nu, U (1907–1995)

First prime minister of Burma (1948–1956), deposed by the military in his second term (1960–1962), he made Buddhism the state religion. See chapter 6 for details.

Olcott, Col. Henry Steel (1832–1907)

American soldier, founder of the Theosophist Society with Madame Helena Blavasky in 1875, convert to Buddhism, and patron of "Protestant Buddhism." Raised as a Presbyterian in New Jersey, Olcott worked as a journalist in New York City and served in the American Army in the Civil War, rising to the rank of colonel. Olcott, like many Americans in the era, became interested in spirituality and eastern religions. The Theosophist Society that he cofounded remains in operation today. In 1879, he and Mme. Blavasky moved with the headquarters of the Society to India, and in 1880, he made his first visit to Sri Lanka, then the British colony of Ceylon. One of the first Americans and Westerners to convert to Buddhism, he soon began campaigning on behalf of the Buddhists in Ceylon against the Christian missionaries and educators, who were trying to replace traditional values with Western ones. Olcott invented a Buddhist flag, which now has been adopted by Buddhists around the world, to inspire the faithful. He also wrote a Buddhist catechism, based on his understanding of the essential teachings of the faith, founded Buddhist schools, inspired the foundation of the YMBA and YWBA, started the custom of setting Buddhist words to Christian hymns, invented Vesak cards to celebrate the major Buddhist religious holiday, and was a formidable worker on behalf of Buddhist interests for the rest of his life. His version of Buddhism was moralistic, socially active, and scorned popular rites and practices that he believed were not in the spirit of "original Buddhism." His version of "Protestant Buddhism" inspired his Sinhalese disciple Angarika Dharmapala (1864–1933),* who led Sri Lanka's elite Buddhists in their struggle for cultural, intellectual, and political independence. **Works:** Autobiography, *Old Diary Leaves*, 6 vols. (1895–1935; reprint, Adyar, India: Theosophical Publishing House, 1972–1975); *Buddhist Catechism* (Colombo, Ceylon: Theosophical Society, Buddhist Section, 1881). **Suggested Reading:** Stephen Prothero, *The White Buddhist: The Asian Odyssey of Henry Steel Olcott* (Bloomington: Indiana University Press, 1996).

Prajadhipok: See Rama VII.

Rama I (1737–1809)

First king of the Chakri dynasty, which remains the royal house of Siam (Thailand), ruled in Bangkok which he founded, from 1782 to 1809. His royal name was Yodfah Chulaloke. Since the Siamese kings are understood to be incarnations of the Hindu god Rama, the Chakris are generally referred to as Rama with a number denoting their order in the dynasty. Yodfah was born in 1737 in Ayutthya to a high noble family. After a typical education and serving for a time as a monk, he entered government service, becoming governor of a province. As governor he was away from the capital when it fell to the Burmese in 1767 and joined Taksin* to defeat the Burmese and later served as a general under King Taksin. As a general, he was called Chao Phrya Chakri, which explains the name of the dynasty. Rama I was chosen king by those who usurped

Taksin, and Rama I ordered Taksin's execution. In matters religious, Rama I restored the monks wrongly removed by his predecessor, took the first steps to bring the sangha under centralized bureaucratic control, assured that the scriptures were kept intact, and welcomed Christian missionaries to return. He was a good administrator, codifying the laws of the kingdom and improving the lot of slaves, and was a noted poet and composer. In foreign affairs, he encouraged trade with the West although troubled by British imperialism in the South. Rama I fought them all his Buddhist neighbors, repelling Burmese incursions to the west and maintaining and extending Siamese holdings in the north in Indochina. The original beautiful layout of Bangkok was his responsibility as are many of the exquisite buildings. **Work:** *Ramakien.* **Suggested Reading:** M. L. Manich Jumsai, *Popular History of Thailand* 3rd ed. (Bangkok: Chalermnit 1993), pp. 410–437.

Rama II (1767–1826)

Second king of the Chakri dynasty, ruled 1809 to 1824, Lert-Lah was the fourth son of Rama I. In the first months of his regime, the Burmese attempted to overrun Siam again, but were successfully repulsed. The Burmese turned their attention to rebels on their borders with India, which precipitated the Anglo-Burmese wars and put an end to any Burmese military threats to Siam. In a time of relative peace, Rama II was able to devote himself to his literary and artistic interests designing temples. He is credited with carving a famous set of temple doors and composing a number of classical dance dramas. He was also a lavish patron of the arts. He increased foreign trade, brought in Chinese immigrants to help develop the country, and reestablished close religious ties with the Theravada Buddhists of Ceylon (Sri Lanka). **Work:** *Sang Thong: A Dance Drama from Thailand,* trans. and intro. by Fern S. Ingersoll (Rutland, VT: C. E. Tuttle Co., 1973). **Suggested Reading:** B. J. Terwiel, *A History of Modern Thailand 1762–1942* (St. Lucia: University of Queensland Press, 1983).

Rama III (1788–1851)

Nang Klao, who ruled from 1824 to 1851, the last traditional Siamese monarch in the ancient mode. He was the son of a minor wife of Rama II.

Although he sought to avoid the unequal treaties that other Asian nations had been forced to sign, he did grant certain trading advantages to Great Britain and the United States. Furthermore, during his years, Britain won considerable power over Siamese vassal states in Malaya. He increased Siamese suzerainty in Indochina through military action and continued the Chakri tradition of religious and artistic patronage. He was a writer, though not of the same rank as his father. **Suggested Reading:** M. L. Manich Jumsai, *Popular History of Thailand* 3rd ed. (Bangkok: Chalermnit, 1993), pp. 410–437.

Rama IV (1804–1868)

Mongkut, the best-known and most respected Siamese king in the West (r. 1851–1858). See chapters 5 and 7 for details.

Rama V (1853–1910)

Chulalongkorn, or Mahachulalongkorn, "the great Chulalongkorn," most beloved King of Siam (r. 1873–1910). See chapters 5 and 7 for details.

Rama VI (1881–1925)

King Vajiravudh, the last successful absolute monarch of Siam reigned 1910 to 1925. Rama VI was the first Thai king to be educated in the West, having spent nine years in England at Oxford and at Sandhurst where he received a military education, including service in the British army. Vajiravudh continued in the reforming and modernizing tradition of his father and grandfather. He was a strong patriot and formulated the three-pillar doctrine that remains the foundation of Thai political ideology: namely, that the people, the monarch, and the Buddhist religion are interdependent strands that together are the essence of the nation. As so many of the Chakri monarchs, Vajiravudh was an accomplished writer, pioneering the novel form in the Thai language, writing more than fifty plays, much poetry, and translating some of the works of Shakespeare into Thai—translations that are still read today. He was a great patron of the arts and architecture and enthusiastic about the values of education, founding Chulalongkorn University in Bangkok and making primary education free and compulsory throughout the kingdom. In 1917 he brought Thailand into World War I on the side of the British and French, and Thailand was rewarded in the treaties by the abolition of all extraterritorial rights to foreigners in Thailand and by the elimination of unequal trading agreements. Two major criticisms can be levelled against his rule: He refused to entertain the idea of any constitutional limitations on his powers, which some of his Western-educated countrymen were beginning to desire, and his high spending habits left a considerable debt to be dealt with by his successor. **Suggested Reading:** Walter Francis Vella, *Chaiyo! King Vajiravudh and the Development of Thai Nationalism* (Honolulu: University Press of Hawaii, 1978).

Rama VII (1893–1941)

Prajadhipok, the king who lost absolute powers in Siam, the seventy-sixth child of King Chulalongkorn, and the only son born of the queen to survive. He was educated in England and went to military college in France. When he took the throne in 1925, the country was in great financial trouble, and he responded by cutting back services in all government departments and by managing the finances of the country very carefully. Many remember his years in power as perhaps the time of the best ever administration in the country, although others dismiss him as reactionary and indecisive. He was a well-traveled, modest man, who encouraged religious tolerance, and who worked very hard on behalf of the nation. His literary output was restricted to a few introductions to the works of others. In June of 1932, a group of military officers overthrew the absolute monarchy in a relatively bloodless coup. The impetus came mainly from a group of those Thais who had studied abroad and who believed that the financial and social problems of the country were due to its having an absolute monarchy rooted in antiquity and therefore ill suited to cope with modernity. Under the name of the People's Party, the new leaders invited Rama VII to continue as head of state as a constitutional monarch with little direct power. He agreed to the new constitution late in 1932, but abdicated in March 1935 arguing that the People's Party had assumed absolute authority and was ignoring its promises to foster democracy. From 1934 until his death in 1941, he lived in England. **Suggested Readings:** Benjamin A. Batson, *The End of the Absolute Monarchy in Siam* (Singapore: Oxford University Press, 1984); Nigel J. Brailey, *Thailand and the Fall of Singapore: A Frustrated Asian Revolution* (Boulder, CO: Westview Press, 1986).

Rama VIII (1925–1946)

Prince Ananda Mahidol, the nephew of Rama VII, was a schoolboy in Lausanne, Switzerland, when the Thai parliament chose him to succeed his uncle. As an absent child, he could not interfere with the interests of those brought into power by the Democracy Revolution of 1932. He stayed in Europe throughout a tumultuous period of coups, new constitutions, and the Japanese occupation, returning to Bangkok only in 1946, for a visit. During that visit, he died in the Royal Palace of gunshot wounds, which have never been explained to everyone's satisfaction. **Suggested Reading:** M. L. Manich Jumsai, *Popular History of Thailand*, 3rd ed. (Bangkok: Chalermnit, 1993), pp. 572–574.

Rama IX (1927–   )

Current King of Thailand, born in Cambridge, Massachusetts, while his father was at Harvard Medical School, King Bhumipol (also transliterated Bhumibol) Adulyadej, the brother of Rama VIII, succeeded to the throne in 1946. It was not until the period after 1958 that the royal family began to regain some real influence after the 1932 Democracy Revolution. Although presumably a constitutional monarch with no real political power, in fact, Rama IX has tremendous authority in Thailand. This comes in large part from the three-pillar ideology that dominates popular Thai thought, the belief that the king, Buddhism, and the people together support each other in creating and sustaining a strong and free Thai nation. But ideology alone would not be enough to explain his enormous popularity and power, which comes from his personal prestige as a king who embodies the traditional ten virtues of a Buddhist monarch. He and Queen Sirikit are visibly very active in educational, welfare, development, cultural, and religious projects. On two notable occasions, in 1973 and 1992, the king intervened to stop the army from slaughtering prodemocracy demonstrators, which each time led to the downfall of a military government and the restoration of a more progressive regime. On the other hand, during much of his reign, he has worked quietly and apparently cooperatively with repressive regimes. King Bhumipol is recognized as a jazz composer and saxophonist, who often invites visiting musicians to the palace for a chance to play together. **Suggested Readings:** Anand Panyarachun, ed., *Thailand: King Bhumibol Adulyadej: The Golden Jubilee, 1946–1996* (Bangkok: Asia Book Company, 1996); Nigel J. Brailey, *Thailand and the Fall of Singapore: A Frustrated Asian Revolution* (Boulder, CO: Westview Press, 1986).

Sangharakshita (1925–)

A major figure in engaged Buddhism in the West and for the ex-untouchable Buddhist community in India, born as Dennis Lingwood in South London, to a working-class English family and was raised in the Anglican tradition. After reading the *Diamond Sutra*, at the age of sixteen, Lingwood self-converted to Buddhism Drafted into the British Army in World War II, Lingwood was stationed in Sri Lanka, Singapore, and India, where at the end of the war, he simply wandered off AWOL to take up the life of a mendicant seeker. In 1949 he ordained as a novice monk in the Burmese Theravada tradition, taking full ordination in 1950. His monastic name, Sangharakshita, means "protected by the sangha." He continued as a monk in India for more than twenty years and in the 1950s received initiations and many teachings from refugee Tibetan Buddhist masters in the Vajrayana tradition. A prolific author, with more than forty books to his credit, Sangharakshita is a religious innovator, who bridges East and West in his style of Buddhism, which emphasizes practical work in the world, study, and traditional contemplative practices. In India he was a major influence in bringing Ambedkar* and his fellow untouchables to the Buddhist fold. Returning to England, he founded the Friends of the Western Buddhist Order in 1967 and the Western Buddhist Order in 1968, very influential Western Buddhist movements with branches in many countries. The allied Trailokya Bauddha Mahasangha Sahayaka Gana, or TBMSG, in India has undertaken to sustain the Ambedkarite Buddhist community, which has grown to perhaps six million or more members. See also the biographical sketch on Lokamitra.* **Work:** Sangharakshita, *The History of My Going for Refuge* (Glasgow: Windhorse, 1988). **Suggested Readings:** Subhuti, *Bringing Buddhism to the West: A Life of Sangharakshita* (Birmingham: Windhorse, 1996); Alan Sponberg, "TBMSG: A Dhamma Revolution in Contemporary India," in Christopher S. Queen, and Sallie B. King, *Engaged Buddhism: Buddhist Liberation Movements in Asia* (Albany: State University of New York Press, 1996).

Sivaraksa, Sulak (1933–)

Controversial lay-Buddhist writer, publisher, and reformer in Thailand, or Siam, as he would insist, nominated for the Nobel Peace Prize in 1993 and 1994, winner of the Right Livelihood Award in 1995. See chapter 5 for details.

Taksin (1734–1782)

Taksin of Thonburi reigned as King of Siam from 1768 to 1782. Born into the influential Sin family during the Ayutthyan period, he was raised by the prime minister as an adopted son, receiving his education at a monastery, and, like most young Siamese young men, served for a while as a monk. After his religious training, he continued to serve the king, rising to the position of governor of the province of Tak, thus the name he is known by—Taksin. Later in 1767, he commanded troops in the war against the Burmese invaders, fleeing the capital with five hundred men when he saw how badly run the defense was. After Ayutthya fell, Taksin rallied the people in the provinces, and defeated the Burmese in 1768, whereupon he was crowned King and established his capital in Thonburi, across the river from where Bangkok was later built. Taksin was an excellent military leader and spent the next eleven years in difficult campaigns consolidating Siam's position in regard to Burma and its neighbours on its northern boundaries. It is interesting that all of the rulers involved in these wars were Buddhists. Taking on the duties of Buddhist monarch, he worked hard to see that the sangha was purged of those monks who had violated their vows in the years of chaos. In his last years, Taksin became very concerned with his own religious status, believing that he had attained supernormal powers through Buddhist meditation. He offended the people by demanding that the monks defer to him as their spiritual superior and severely punished those who insisted, correctly, that monks must never bow to laymen according to the rules that Lord Buddha established. He also expelled Christian missionaries and persecuted some Siamese converts. In the end, he was deposed and executed for his excesses with many of his subjects, and later writers believed he had gone mad. **Suggested Reading:** B. J. Terwiel, *A History of Modern Thailand 1762–1942* (St. Lucia: University of Queensland Press, 1983).

Vajiravudh: See Rama VI.

Victoria, Brian Daizen (1939–)

American Buddhist scholar, Soto Zen Priest, and spiritual gadfly. Brian Victoria went to Japan as a Methodist missionary in 1961, and with the encouragement of the church immersed himself in Buddhism to help better understand his mission field. Attracted to Buddhism in part because of its reputation as a peace-loving and nonviolent faith, he converted and was ordained as a priest in the Soto sect of Zen in 1964. During the Vietnam war, he was active in antiwar protests, wearing his robes, although the Soto hierarchy let it be known that they would have preferred no political activity on his part. In 1975 he was deported from Japan for antigovernment activities, the first of six times in five different Asian countries he was asked to leave for political activism. In the 1970s he became interested in Zen Buddhists' involvement in formulating the militaristic ethos that led to Japan's imperial misadventures in Asia and in Buddhist support for the war effort. The first fruits of these researches were *Zen at War* (1997), where he meticulously documented how D. T. Suzuki and other Zen intellectuals and leaders drafted the blueprints for an ultrapatriotic religious-based war machine. As a direct result of the interest and self-reflection generated by this book, several of Japan's largest Zen organizations have issued detailed public apologies for their bellicose mistakes. Victoria commented, "This is one of the relatively rare cases where an historian has been given the opportunity to help make history. It is a reminder that we academics are not people who sit in ivory towers but people who can make a difference." In February 2003, *Zen War Stories*, on the same theme, was published. Currently he is a senior lecturer in the Centre for Asian Studies at the University of Adelaide, Australia. **Works:** *Zen at War* (New York: Weatherhill, 1997); *Zen War Stories* (Richmond, Surrey: Curzon Press, 2003). **Suggested Readings:** University of Adelaide, Media Release, April 23, 2002; Christopher Stephens, "Zen's Holy War," *Kansai Times* (April 2003).

Vo Van Ai (1938–   )

Vietnamese writer and activist, in exile in Paris, spokesman for the Unified Buddhist Church of Vietnam, founder and president of Action for Democracy in Vietnam and of the Vietnam Council on Human Rights. Vo Van Ai was active in the independence movement against the French and became an opponent of the American-backed regimes in South Vietnam. Since 1964 he has worked outside the country on behalf of the Unified Buddhist Church of Vietnam for peace, religious freedom, and human rights in his homeland. He edits a Vietnamese journal, *Quê Me*, published in Paris since 1976, which focuses on democracy, human rights, and cultural issues.

Yodfah Chulaloke: See Rama I.

NOTES

Chapter 1. A Brief Overview

1. Donald S. Lopez Jr., ed., "Introduction," in *Buddhism in Practice* (Princeton, NJ: Princeton University Press, 1995), p. 3.

2. Robert A. F. Thurman, "Human Rights and Human Responsibilities: Buddhist Views on Individualism and Altruism," in Irene Bloom, J. Paul Martin, and Wayne L. Proudfoot, eds., *Religious Diversity and Human Rights* (New York: Columbia University Press, 1996).

3. Lopez, "Introduction," p. 3.

4. See chapter 13.

5. See the section on Sri Lanka in the Annotated Bibliography for a guide to the religious war that is raging there now.

Chapter 2. Are There Human Rights in Buddhism?

1. Damien Keown, "Are There Human Rights in Buddhism?" in Damien Keown, Charles Prebish, and Wayne Husted, eds., *Buddhism and Human Rights* (Richmond, Surrey: Curzon Press, 1998), p. 15.

2. Damien Keown, *The Nature of Buddhist Ethics* (New York: St. Martin's Press, 1992) and Damien Keown, *Buddhism and Bioethics* (London: Macmillan, 1995).

3. Sulak Sivaraksa, "Buddhist Ethics and Modern Politics: A Theravada Viewpoint," in Charles Wei-hsun Fu and Sandra A. Wawrytko, eds., *Buddhist Ethics and Modern Society: An International Symposium* (Westport, CT: Greenwood Press, 1991), p. 163.

4. Lily de Silva, "The Scope and the Contemporary Significance of the Five Precepts," in Fu and Wawrytko, *Buddhist Ethics*, pp. 146–147.

5. Peter D. Junger, "Why the Buddha Has No Rights," in Keown, Prebish, and Husted, *Buddhism and Human Rights*, p. 53.

6. Maseo Abe, "Religious Tolerance and Human Rights: A Buddhist Perspective," in Leonard Swidler, *Religious Liberty and Human Rights* (Philadelphia: Ecumenical Press, 1986), p. 202.

7. Keown, "Human Rights," p. 22.

8. Soraj Hongladarom, "Buddhism and Human Rights in the Thoughts of Sulak Sivaraksa and Phra Dammapidok (Prayudh Prayutto)," in Keown, Prebish, and Husted, *Buddhism and Human Rights*, p. 97.

9. Peter Harvey, *An Introduction to Buddhist Ethics: Foundations, Values and Issues* (Cambridge: Cambridge University Press, 2000), pp. 36–37, 118–122.

10. Morton E. Winston, "Understanding Human Rights," in Morton E. Winston, ed., *The Philosophy of Human Rights* (Belmont, CA: Wadsworth Publishing Company, 1989), p. 7.

11. J. M. Finnis, *Natural Law and Natural Rights*, Clarendon Law Series, H.L.A. Hart, ed. (Oxford: Oxford University Press, 1980), p. 205. Keown ("Human Rights," pp. 19–20) uses Finnis's definition as well.

12. David Chappell, "Buddhist Peace Principles," in David Chappell, ed., *Buddhist Peacework: Creating Cultures of Peace* (Boston: Wisdom Publications, 1999), p. 211.

13. Young-Sun Chung, "Asian Values and Challenges to Universal Human Rights," *Peace Forum* 15:27 (1999).

14. Wapola Rahula, *What the Buddha Taught*, 2nd ed. (New York: Grove Press, 1974), p. 32.

15. Keown, "Human Rights," pp. 15–18.

16. *Journal of Buddhist Ethics* 3 (1996).

17. Craig K. Ihara, "Why There Are No Rights in Buddhism: A Reply to Damien Keown," and Peter D. Junger, "Why the Buddha Has No Rights," both in Keown, Prebish, and Husted, *Buddhism and Human Rights*.

18. "Introduction," in Keown, Prebish, and Husted, *Buddhism and Human Rights*, p. vi.

19. Keown, *Buddhism and Bioethics*, p. xiv.

20. Keown, "Human Rights," p. 26.

21. Ibid., p. 17.

22. Rita Gross, "Karma and Social Justice," *World Faiths Encounter* 29 (2001); see also Brian Victoria, *Zen at War* (New York: Weatherhill, 1997), pp. 171–172.

23. Rahula, *What the Buddha Taught*; Gunapala Dharmasiri, *A Buddhist Critique of the Christian Conception of God* (Antioch, CA: Golden Leaves, 1988).

24. Keown, *The Nature of Buddhist Ethics*, p. 232, takes the opposite position.

25. Harvey, *Introduction*, p. 51.

26. Hema Goonatilake, "Women and Family in Buddhism," in Sulak Sivaraksa, ed., *Buddhist Perception for Desirable Societies in the Future* (Bangkok: The Inter-Religious Commission for Development, 1992), p. 235.

27. Harvey, *Introduction*, p. 16.

28. Ven. P. A. Payutto [Phra Prayudh Payutto], *Buddhist Economics: A Middle Way for the Market Place*, trans. Dhammavijaya and Bruce Evans (Bangkok: Buddhadhamma Foundation, 1994), p. 21.

29. P. A. Payutto [Phra Prayudh Payutto], A *Constitution for Living: Buddhist Principles for a Fruitful and Harmonious Life*, trans. Bruce Evans (Bangkok: Buddhadhamma Foundation, 1996), p. viii.

30. P. A. Payutto [Phra Prayudh Payutto], *Phuttavithii Kae Panha Phua Satawad Thii 21* [A Buddhist Solution for the Twenty-first Century] (Bangkok: Sahathammik, 1994), pp. 13–15, translated into English and cited in Soraj Hongladarom, "Buddhism and Human Rights," p. 105.

31. Payutto, *Constitution*, p. viii. He is somewhat more positive about human rights in Phra Debvedi [Phra Prayudh Payutto], *Freedom: Individual and Social* (Bangkok: Buddhadhamma Foundation, 1987), pp. 21 and 27.

32. Payutto, *Constitution*, p. vii.

33. Payutto, *Buddhist Economics*, pp. 56–57.

34. Ibid., p. 33.

35. Ibid., p. 34.

36. Ibid., pp. 55–56.

37. Bhikku P. A. Payutto [Phra Prayudh Payutto], *Good, Evil and Beyond: Kamma in the Buddha's Teaching* (Bangkok: Buddhadhamma Foundation, 1993), p. 69.

38. Chapter 13, document 5.

39. Keown, "Human Rights," pp. 24ff.

40. Rahula, *What the Buddha Taught*, p. 23.

41. Keown, "Human Rights," p. 28. Keown was arguing against Kenneth Inada, Distinguished Professor Emeritus at the State University of New York, a pioneer Buddhist scholar, who in a very early article tried to ground human rights on the first two Holy Truths: Kenneth Inada, "The Buddhist Perspective on Human Rights," in Arlene Swidler, ed., *Human Rights in Religious Traditions* (New York: Pilgrim Press, 1982).

42. L.P.N. Perera, *Buddhism and Human Rights: A Buddhist Commentary on the Universal Declaration of Human Rights* (Colombo, Sri Lanka: Karunaratne and Sons, 1991), p. 21.

43. Ibid., p. 24.

44. Keown, "Human Rights," pp. 29–30.

45. Ibid., p. 41 n54.

46. Ibid., pp. 30–34.

47. Ibid., p. 22.

48. Ibid., pp. 31–33.

49. Ihara, "Why There Are No Rights in Buddhism," pp. 45–46.

50. Ibid., p. 44.

51. Keown, "Human Rights," pp. 20–22.

52. Sigalaka Sutta (chapter 13, document 7).

53. Ihara, "Why There Are No Rights in Buddhism," p. 49.

54. Keown, "Human Rights," p. 53.

55. Ibid., p. 33.

56. Keown is aware of these texts. See Keown, *Nature of Buddhist Ethics*, ch. 6.

57. Junger, "Why the Buddha Has No Rights," p. 86. Keown agrees on this point.

58. Ibid., pp. 65–66.

59. Ibid., p. 65.

60. Harvey, *Introduction*, p. 36.

61. Derek S. Jeffreys, "Does Buddhism Need Human Rights," in Christopher Queen, Charles Prebish, and Damien Keown, eds., *Action Dharma: New Studies in Engaged Buddhism* (London: RoutledgeCurzon, 2003), p. 282.

62. Robert A. F. Thurman, "Human Rights and Human Responsibilities: Buddhist Views on Individualism and Altruism," in Irene Bloom, J. Paul Martin, and Wayne L. Proudfoot, eds., *Religious Diversity and Human Rights* (New York: Columbia University Press, 1996), p. 96.

63. Ibid., pp. 96–97.

64. Ibid., pp. 90–91.

65. Ibid., p. 97.

66. Ibid., p. 112.

67. Kenneth Inada, "A Buddhist Response to the Nature of Human Rights," in Keown, Prebish, and Husted, *Buddhism and Human Rights*, pp. 1–13. It was first published in Claude E. Welch Jr. and Virginia A. Leary, eds., *Asian Perspectives on Human Rights* (Boulder, CO: Westview Press, 1990).

68. Inada, "Buddhist Response," p. 4.

69. Ibid., pp. 11–12.

70. Ibid., p. 3.

Chapter 3. Human Rights as Skillful Means

1. Santideva, *The Bodhicaryavatara*, trans. Kate Crosby and Andrew Skilton (Oxford: Oxford University Press, 1995), 10:2.

2. Ibid., 10:55–56.

3. See the Heart Sutra (chapter 13, document 9).

4. Jataka 431. Jatakas 66 and 251 are similar.

5. E. B. Cowell, ed., *The Jataka or Stories of the Buddha's Former Births*, vol. 3 (Cambridge: Cambridge University Press, 1895; reprint, London: Pali Text Society, 1957), p. 296.

6. John Garrett Jones, *Tales and Teachings of the Buddha: The Jataka Stories in Relation to the Pali Canon* (London: George Allen and Unwin, 1979), pp. 61ff.

7. Peter Harvey, *An Introduction to Buddhist Ethics: Foundations, Values and Issues* (Cambridge: Cambridge University Press, 2000), p. 255.

8. Jones, *Tales*, p. 136.

9. Jataka 313; Cowell, *Jataka*, vol. 3, pp. 27–28.

10. Jones, *Tales*, p. 132.

11. Jataka 547; Cowell, *Jataka*, vol. 6, p. 250.

12. Cowell, *Jataka*, vol. 6, p. 279.

13. Ibid., p. 283.

14. Jones, *Tales*, p. 134.

15. Cowell, *Jataka*, vol. 6, p. 304.

16. Jataka 499; Cowell, *Jataka*, vol. 6, p. 251.

17. Cowell, *Jataka*, vol. 4, p. 254.

18. His Holiness Tenzin Gyatso, the Fourteenth Dalai Lama of Tibet, *Kindness, Clarity, and Insight*, J. Hopkins and E. Napper, eds. (Delhi: Motilal Banarsidass, 1997; first published Ithaca, NY: Snowlion, 1984), pp. 108 and 111.

19. Michael Pye, *Skilful Means: A Concept in Mahayana Buddhism* (London: Duckworth, 1978); Damien Keown, *The Nature of Buddhist Ethics* (New York: St. Martin's Press, 1992), pp. 157–163 and 185–191; D. T. Suzuki, *Outlines of Mahayana Buddhism* (New York: Schocken, 1963; first published in London: 1907), pp. 298–299.

20. Burton Watson, trans., *The Lotus Sutra* (New York: Columbia University Press, 1993), p. 57.

21. Watson, *Lotus*, p. 58.

22. Dalai Lama, *Kindness*, p. 109.

23. Ibid., p. 108.

24. Harvey, *Introduction*, pp. 134–142; Keown, *Nature of Buddhist Ethics*, pp. 145–146 and 152–157.

25. Keown, *Nature of Buddhist Ethics*, pp. 157–160.

26. Craig K. Ihara, "Why There Are No Rights in Buddhism: A Reply to Damien Keown," in Damien Keown, Charles Prebish, and Wayne Husted, eds., *Buddhism and Human Rights* (Richmond, Surrey: Curzon Press, 1998), pp. 49–50.

27. David W. Chappell, "Buddhist Peace Principles," in David Chappell, ed., *Buddhist Peacework: Creating Cultures of Peace* (Boston: Wisdom Publications, 1999), pp. 211–212.

28. Ihara, "Why There Are No Rights in Buddhism," p. 51 n21.

29. Donald K. Swearer, "'Rights' Because of Intrinsic Nature or 'Responsibilities' Because of Mutual Interdependence?" in Amy Morgante, ed., *Buddhist Perspectives on the Earth Charter* (Boston: Boston Research Center for the 21st Century, 1997), p. 87.

30. Swearer, "Rights," p. 89.

31. Bhikku Nanamoli and Bhikku Bodhi, *The Middle Length Discourses of the Buddha: A Translation of the Majjhima Nikaya*, 2nd ed. (Boston: Wisdom Publications, 2001), Sutta 63.

32. James E. Deitrick, "Engaged Buddhist Ethics: Mistaking the Boat for the Shore," in Christopher Queen, Charles Prebish, and Damien Keown, eds., *Action Dharma: New Studies in Engaged Buddhism* (London: RoutledgeCurzon, 2003), thinks that engaged Buddhist ethical theory, as it has developed currently, is not "basically Buddhist" but is hopeful that it can evolve into something metaphysically closer.

33. Ananda Wickremeratne, *Buddhism and Ethnicity in Sri Lanka: A Historical Analysis* (Delhi: International Centre for Ethnic Studies [Kandy, Sri Lanka] in association with Vikas Publishing House, 1995), p. xxxv.

Chapter 4. State, Society, and the Buddhist Order

1. Richard F. Gombrich, *Theravada Buddhism: A Social History from Ancient Benares to Modern Colombo* (London: Routledge and Kegan Paul, 1988), p. 30.

2. Maurice Walshe, trans., *Thus Have I Heard: The Long Discourses of the Buddha: The Digha Nikaya* (London: Wisdom Publications, 1987), Sutta 16, v. 1.4.

3. Ibid., Sutta 27, v. 20.

4. Ibid., Sutta 26, v. 5.

5. E. B. Cowell, ed., *The Jataka or Stories of the Buddha's Former Births*, vol. 5 (Cambridge: Cambridge University Press, 1905; reprint, London: Pali Text Society, 1957), p. 200.

6. P. A. Payutto [Phra Prayudh Payutto], *A Constitution for Living: Buddhist Principles for a Fruitful and Harmonious Life*, trans. Bruce Evans (Bangkok: Buddhadhamma Foundation, 1996), pp. 22–23.

7. Asvaghosa, *Buddhacarita: or Acts of the Buddha*, trans. E. H. Johnston (1936; reprint, Delhi: Motilal Banarsidass, 1972), p. 26.

8. Thanisarro Bhikkhu, trans., *Anguttara Nikaya*, V. 177, www.accesstoinsight.org/canon/anguttara (November 20, 2002).

9. T. W. Rhys Davids and Hermann Oldenberg, trans., *Vinaya Texts*, in *Sacred Books of the East* (SBE), vols. 13, 17, and 20 (Oxford: Clarendon Press, 1881–1885; reprint, Delhi: Motilal Banarsidass, 1966), Mahavagga, VI. 31, *SBE*, vol. 17, pp. 108–117.

10. Ven. P. A. Payutto [Phra Prayudh Payutto], *Buddhist Economics: A Middle Way for the Market Place*, 2nd ed., trans. Dhammavijaya and Bruce Evans (Bangkok: Buddhadhamma Foundation, 1994), p. 83.

11. Bhikkhu, *Anguttara Nikaya*, V. 177.

12. Davids and Oldenberg, *Vinaya Texts*, SBE, vol. 13, pp. 194–196.

13. Ibid., vol. 13, p. 43.

14. *Digha Nikaya*, Sutta I, v 1.17.

15. Gombrich, *Theravada Buddhism*, pp. 78 and 81.

16. Eugene Watson Burlingame, trans., *Buddhist Legends Translated from the Original Pali Text of the Dhammapada Commentary* (1921; reprint, London: Pali Text Society, 1969), vol. 3, pp. 70–72.

17. Dorothy H. Fickle, *Images of the Buddha in Thailand* (Singapore: Oxford University Press, 1989), pp. 79–81.

18. Gombrich, *Theravada Buddhism*, p. 82.

19. Ibid., pp. 131–136.

20. N. A. Nikam and Richard McKeon, eds. and trans., *The Edicts of Asoka* (Chicago: University of Chicago Press, Phoenix Books, 1966), Rock Edict XI, and IX, pp. 45–46.

21. Gombrich, *Theravada Buddhism*, pp. 130 and 83.

22. Nikam and McKeon, *Edicts*, Kalinga Edict I, p. 63.

23. Ibid., Rock Edict II, p. 64, Pillar Edict VII, p. 64.

24. Ibid., Kalinga Edict I, pp. 61–62.

25. Ibid., Rock Edict V, p. 59.

26. Ibid., Pillar Edict VII, pp. 33–35.

27. Ibid., Rock Edict VIII, p. 37.

28. Ibid., Rock Edict VII, p. 51.

29. Ibid., Rock Edict XII, p. 51.

30. Ibid., Babra Rock Edict, p. 67, and Sanchi Pillar Edict, pp. 67–68.

31. Ibid., Babra Rock Edict, pp. 66–67.

32. Ibid., Sanchi Pillar Edict, pp. 67–68, and Sarnath Pillar Edict, p. 68.

33. Gombrich, *Theravada Buddhism*, pp. 132–133.

34. Robert Thurman, "Human Rights and Human Responsibilities: Buddhist Views on Individualism and Altruism," in Irene Bloom, J. Paul Martin, and Wayne L. Proudfoot, eds., *Religious Diversity and Human Rights* (New York: Columbia University Press, 1996), pp. 99–100.

35. Thurman, "Human Rights," p. 102.

Chapter 5. Buddhism and Human Rights in Thailand

1. Somboon Suksamran, *Buddhism and Politics in Thailand: A Study of Socio-Political Change and Political Activism of the Thai Sangha* (Singapore: Institute of Southeast Asian Studies, 1982), p. 12.

2. Suksamran, *Buddhism and Politics*, p. 56.

3. Nigel J. Brailey, *Thailand and the Fall of Singapore: A Frustrated Asian Revolution* (Boulder, CO: Westview Press, 1986), p. 219.

4. Somboon Suksamran, *Political Buddhism in Southeast Asia: The Role of the Sangha in the Modernization of Thailand* (London: C. Hurst, 1977), p. 67.

5. Craig J. Reynolds, ed., *Thai Radical Discourse: The Real Face of Thai Feudalism Today* (Ithaca: Cornell University Southeast Asia Program, 1987), pp. 24ff.

6. Revolutionary Councils' Announcement No. 8 (October 20, 1958), quoted in Suksamran, *Buddhism and Politics*, p. 44.

7. Modified from Suksamran, *Political Buddhism*, pp. 67–68.

8. Ibid., pp. 70–108.

9. Somboon Suksamran, "A Buddhist Approach to Development: The Case of 'Development Monks' in Thailand," in Lim Teck Ghee, ed., *Reflections on Development in Southeast Asia* (Singapore: Institute of Southeast Asian Studies, 1988), pp. 42–43.

10. Suksamran, *Buddhism and Politics*, p. 71.

11. Suksamran, *Political Buddhism*, p. 114.

12. Suksamran, *Buddhism and Politics*, pp. 84ff.

13. Ibid., p. 107.

14. Ibid., p. 109.

15. Charles F. Keyes, "Political Crisis and Militant Buddhism in Contemporary Thailand," in Bardwell L. Smith, *Religion and Legitimation of Power in Thailand, Laos, and Burma* (Chambersburg, PA: Anima Books, 1978), p. 152.

16. Suksamran, *Buddhism and Politics*, pp. 80–83.

17. Keyes, "Political Crisis," pp. 147–164; Suksamran, *Buddhism and Politics*, pp. 91–99 and 132–157.

18. Suksamran, *Buddhism and Politics*, p. 95.

19. Ibid., p. 145.

20. Cited in Keyes, "Political Crisis," p. 152.

21. Translated by Suksamran, *Buddhism and Politics*, p. 150; for another version, see Keyes, "Political Crisis," p. 153.

22. Translated by Keyes, "Political Crisis," p. 153; for another version, see Suksamran, *Buddhism and Politics*, p. 150.

23. Suksamran, *Buddhism and Politics*, pp. 150–151; Keyes, "Political Crisis," p. 158.

24. Donald K. Swearer, "Sulak Sivaraksa's Buddhist Vision for Renewing Society," in Christopher S. Queen, and Sallie B. King, *Engaged Buddhism: Buddhist Liberation Movement in Asia* (Albany: State University of New York Press, 1996), pp. 201–204.

25. Keyes, "Political Crisis," p. 158.

26. Suksamran, *Buddhism and Politics*, p. 155.

27. Keyes, "Political Crisis," p. 159.

28. Suksamran, *Buddhism and Politics*, p. 157.

29. Keyes, "Political Crisis," p. 159.

30. Ibid., p. 160.

31. Donald K. Swearer, *The Buddhist World of Southeast Asia* (Albany: State University of New York Press, 1995), pp. 114–115.

32. Sulak Sivaraksa, *A Socially Engaged Buddhism* (Bangkok: Thai Inter-Religious Commission for Development, 1988), p. 8; Sulak Sivaraksa, "Buddhism and Human Rights in Siam," in Sulak Sivaraksa, ed., *Socially Engaged Buddhism for the New Millennium: Essays in Honour of Ven. Phra Dammapitaka (Bhikku P. A. Payutto [Phra Prayudh Payutto] on his 60th Birthday Anniversary* (Bangkok: Sathirakoses-Nagapradipa Foundation, 1999), p. 195.

33. This biographical sketch is based on Swearer, "Sulak Sivaraksa's Buddhist Vision," pp. 199–208, and personal observations in Thailand.

34. Ibid., p. 200–201.

35. Sulak Sivaraksa, "Buddhism and Thai Politics" in Sivaraksa, *A Socially Engaged Buddhism*, p. 42; see chapter 13 for excerpts from this article.

36. Sivaraksa, "Buddhism and Human Rights in Siam," p. 201. Sivaraksa's use of the term "evil" is somewhat unusual for a Buddhist, but the context makes it clear that he is referring to the eradication of the three poisons, hatred, greed, and delusion, that feed the flames of suffering in *samsara*.

37. Soraj Hongladarom, "Buddhism and Human Rights in the Thought of Sulak Sivaraksa and Phra Dhammapidok (Prayudh Payutto)," in Damien Keown, Charles Prebish, and Wayne Husted, eds., *Buddhism and Human Rights* (Richmond, Surrey: Curzon Press, 1998), pp. 101–102.

38. Sivaraksa, "Buddhism and Human Rights in Siam," pp. 202–205; for another account of this incident, see Swearer, "Sulak Sivaraksa's Buddhist Vision," pp. 196–198.

39. Sivaraksa, "Buddhism and Human Rights in Siam," p. 204.

40. Ibid., pp. 204–205.

41. Sulak Sivaraksa, "Being in the World: A Buddhist Ethical and Social Concern," unpublished paper presented at the conference, "Buddhism and Christianity: Toward the Human Future" at Berkeley in August 1987, cited in Robert Traer, "Buddhist Affirmations of Human Rights," *Buddhist Christian Studies* 8 (1988), p. 17.

Chapter 6. Buddhism, Democracy, and Human Rights: The Burmese Case Study

1. Melford E. Spiro, *Buddhism and Society: A Great Tradition and Its Burmese Vicissitudes* (New York: Harper and Row, 1970), pp. 378 and 379.

2. John P. Ferguson, "The Quest for Legitimation by Burmese Monks and Kings: The Case of the Shwegyin Sect (19th–20th Centuries)," in Bardwell L. Smith, ed., *Religion and Legitimation of Power in Thailand, Laos, and Burma* (Chambersburg, PA: Anima Books, 1978), p. 67.

3. E. Sarkisyanz, "Buddhist Backgrounds of Burmese Socialism," in B. L. Smith, *Religion and Legitimation*, p. 89.

4. Trevor Ling, *Buddhism, Imperialism and War* (London: George Allen and Unwin, 1979), p. 70.

5. Maung Htin Aung, *A History of Burma* (New York: Columbia University Press, 1967), pp. 266–267; John F. Cady, *A History of Modern Burma* (Ithaca, NY: Cornell University Press, 1959), p. 134, gives 45,000 as the number of troops involved.

6. Letters from Dr. Vinton, in Donald Mackenzie Smeaton, *The Loyal Karens of Burma* (London: Kegan Paul, Trench, 1887), pp. 11–13.

7. Spiro, *Buddhism and Society*, p. 383.

8. Ling, *Buddhism, Imperialism and War*, pp. 78–81.

9. Sir Charles Crosthwaite, *The Pacification of Burma* (London: Frank Cass, 1968), p. 39.

10. Spiro, *Buddhism and Society*, p. 383.

11. Crosthwaite, *Pacification*, p. 39.

12. Ling, *Buddhism, Imperialism and War*, pp. 72–73.

13. Cady, *History of Modern Burma*, pp. 169–170.

14. Aung San Suu Kyi, "Intellectual Life in Burma," in *Freedom from Fear and Other Writings*, 2nd ed. (London: Penguin, 1995), p. 130.

15. Donald Eugene Smith, *Religion and Politics in Burma* (Princeton, NJ: Princeton University Press, 1965), p. 111.

16. Ba Maw, *Breakthrough in Burma: Memoirs of a Revolution, 1939–1946* (New Haven: Yale University Press, 1968), ch. 4–6, for an insider's view of the B.I.A.

17. Angelene Naw, *Aung San and the Struggle for Burmese Independence* (Chiang Mai: Silkworm Books, 2001), p. 81.

18. Ba Maw, *Breakthrough*, p. 176.

19. Ibid., pp. 185 and 176.

20. Aung, *History of Burma*, p. 301.

21. E. Sarkisyanz, *Buddhist Backgrounds of the Burmese Revolution* (The Hague: Martinus Nijhoff, 1965), pp. 166–179 and 183–84.

22. Ling, *Buddhism, Imperialism and War*, p. 101.

23. Cady, *History of Modern Burma*, p. 465.

24. Ling, *Buddhism, Imperialism and War*, p. 101; see also, Cady, *History of Modern Burma*, p. 464.

25. Ling, *Buddhism, Imperialism and War*, p. 103.

26. Sarkisyanz, *Buddhist Backgrounds*, p. 185.

27. Ibid., p. 188.

28. Ibid., chs. XXV and XXVII.

29. D. E. Smith, *Religion and Politics*, pp. 241–242.

30. Ling, *Buddhism, Imperialism and War*, p. 123.

31. D. E. Smith, *Religion and Politics*, pp. 277–280.

32. John Badgley, "Burmese Ideology: A Comment," in Josef Silverstein, ed., *Independent Burma at Forty Years: Six Assessments* (Ithaca, NY: Southeast Asia Program, Cornell University, 1989), p. 68.

33. David I. Steinberg, "Neither Silver nor Gold: The 40th Anniversary of the Burmese Economy," in Silverstein, *Independent Burma at Forty Years*, p. 35.

34. Her deep familiarity with Gandhi is clear in Aung San Suu Kyi, "Intellectual Life in Burma" in *Freedom from Fear*, pp. 82–139.

35. Philip Kreager, "Aung San Suu Kyi and the Peaceful Struggle for Human Rights in Burma," in Aung San Suu Kyi, *Freedom from Fear*, p. 325.

36. Ibid., pp. 3–164.

37. Aung San was apparently no great advocate of human rights according to Laskiri Fernando, "The Burmese Road to Development and Human Rights," in Alice Tay, ed., *East Asia: Human Rights, Nation-Building, Trade* (Baden-Baden: Nomos Verlagsgesellschaft, 1999), p. 300.

38. Aung San Suu Kyi, "Speech to a Mass Rally at the Shwedagon Pagoda" [August 26, 1988] in Aung San Suu Kyi, *Freedom from Fear*, p. 193.

39. The name has been changed from SLORC to the much less ominous sounding "State Peace and Development Council," but the policies remain.

40. Chapter 13, document 22.

41. Ibid.

42. Aung San Suu Kyi and Alan Clements, *The Voice of Hope: Conversations: Aung San Suu Kyi with Alan Clements* (New York: Seven Stories Press, 1997), pp. 26–27.

43. Ibid., pp. 37 and 169.

44. Ibid., pp. 170–173.

45. Ibid., pp. 203–204.

46. Tin Maung Maung Than, "Sangha Reforms and Renewal of Sasana in Myanmar: Historical Trends and Contemporary Practice," in Trevor Ling, ed., *Buddhist Trends in Southeast Asia* (Singapore: Institute of Southeast Asian Studies, 1993).

47. Badgley, "Burmese Ideology," p. 72.

48. Tin Maung Maung, "Sangha Reforms," p. 25.

49. Bruce Matthews, "Buddhism under a Military Regime: The Iron Heel in Burma," *Asian Survey* 33:4 (April 1993), pp. 420–421.

50. Human Rights Watch, "Crackdown on Burmese Muslims," July 2002, available online at http://www.hrw.org; Matthews, "Buddhism under a Military Regime," p. 417.

51. Human Rights Watch, "Crackdown;" Human Rights Watch, "Burma: Rape, Forced Labor and Religious Persecution in Northern Arakan," *Human Rights Watch/Asia* 4:13 (May 7, 1992); Human Rights Watch, *World Report 1998*, "Burma," available online at http://www.hrw.org/worldreport/Asia-01.htm#P127_40364.

52. Human Rights Watch, "Crackdown," p. 3.

53. Matthews, "Buddhism under a Military Regime," p. 422.

54. Personal communications, May 2003, from NGO contacts in Burma.

55. D. E. Smith, *Religion and Politics*, p. 309.

56. Ibid., pp. 310–311.

57. L.P.N. Perera, *Buddhism and Human Rights: A Buddhist Commentary on the Universal Declaration of Human Rights* (Colombo: Karunaratne and Sons, 1991), p. 86.

58. Aung San Suu Kyi, "My Father" in Aung San Suu Kyi, *Freedom from Fear*, pp. 7–8.

59. Aung San Suu Kyi and Clements, *Voice of Hope*, p. 27.

60. Alan Clements and Leslie Kean, *Burma's Revolution of the Spirit: the Struggle for Democratic Freedom and Dignity*, foreword by His Holiness the Dalai Lama, preface by Sein Win (New York: Aperture, 1994), p. 69.

Chapter 7. Buddhism and Slavery

1. A. L. Basham, *The Wonder That Was India* (1954; reprint, New York: Grove Press, 1959), pp. 151–153; Dev Raj Chanana, *Slavery in Ancient India as Depicted in Pali and Sanskrit Texts* (New Delhi: People's Publishing House, 1960).

2. Maurice Walshe, trans., *Thus Have I Heard: The Long Discourses of the Buddha: The Digha Nikaya* (London: Wisdom, 1987), Sutta 2, vv. 35–36.

3. Ibid., Sutta 2, vv. 69–73.

4. Chanana, *Slavery*, p. 61.

5. Walshe, *Digha Nikaya*, Sutta 30, v. 2.4.

6. Ibid., Sutta 31, v. 27, (chapter 13, document 7).

7. Jonathan Silk in an unpublished paper, "The Problem of Slavery or Unfree Labor in Indian Buddhism," delivered at the American Academy of Religion, 1997, carefully reviewed both Theravada and Mahayana sources before coming to this tentative conclusion.

8. Leon Hurvitz, *Scripture of the Lotus Blossom of the Fine Dharma* (New York: Columbia University Press, 1976), p. 195.

9. See chapter 13, document 13.

10. Chanana, *Slavery*, pp. 53–57.

11. Walshe, *Digha Nikaya*, Sutta 2, v. 45.

12. Richard Gombrich, *Theravada Buddhism: A Social History from Ancient Benares to Modern Colombo* (London: Routledge and Kegan Paul, 1988), pp. 102–103.

13. Chanana, *Slavery*, p. 84.

14. N. A. Nikam and Richard McKeon, eds. and trans., *The Edicts of Asoka* (Chicago: University of Chicago Press, Phoenix Books, 1966), Pillar Edict VII, p. 34.

15. Ibid., Rock Edict XI, p. 45; Rock Edict IX, p. 46.

16. Ibid., Rock Edict XIII, (chapter 13, document 11).

17. Gombrich, *Theravada Buddhism*, pp. 169–170; Walpola Rahula, *History of Buddhism in Ceylon: The Anuradhapura Period, 3rd Century B.C.–10th Century A.C.*, 2nd ed. (Colombo, Ceylon: M. D. Gunasena, 1966), pp. 148–150.

18. Gombrich, *Theravada Buddhism*, p. 163.

19. Ibid., p. 163.

20. Rahula, *History*, pp. 261–262.

21. R. Lingat, *L'esclavage privé dans le vieux droit siamois (avec une traduction des anciennes lois siamoises sur l'esclavage)* (Paris: Les editions Domat-Montchrestien, 1931), pp. 3–7.

22. For the text of the 1805 law concerning slavery see Lingat, *L'esclavage*, pp. 293–358.

23. Jeremias van Vliet, *The Short History of the Kings of Siam*, trans. Leonard Andaya from a 1640 MS (Bangkok: The Siam Society, 1975), p. 83.

24. Akin Rabibhadana, "The Organization of Thai Society in the Early Bangkok Period, 1782–1874," Data Paper No. 74 (Ithaca, NY: Southeast Asia Program, Cornell University, 1969), pp. 113ff.

25. H. G. Quaritch Wales, *Ancient Siamese Government and Administration* (London: B. Quaritch, 1934; reprint, New York: Paragon, 1965), pp. 26 and 34–35.

26. Somboon Suksamran, *Buddhism and Politics in Thailand: A Study of Socio-Political Change and Political Activism of the Thai Sangha* (Singapore: Institute of Southeast Asian Studies, 1982), p. 17.

27. B. J. Terwiel, *A History of Modern Thailand: 1767–1942* (St. Lucia: University of Queensland Press, 1983), pp. 14–15.

28. B. J. Terwiel, "Bondage and Slavery in Early Nineteenth Century Siam," in Anthony Reid, *Slavery, Bondage, and Dependency in Southeast Asia* (St. Lucia: University of Queensland Press, 1983), pp. 127–128.

29. Lingat, *L'esclavage*, pp. 294–295.

30. Chapter 13, document 14.

31. J. B. Pallegoix, *Description du royaume Thai ou Siam*, 2 Vols. (Paris: Se vend au profit de la mission de Siam, 1854; reprint, Westmead, England: Gregg International, 1969), vol. I, p. 235. Terwiel ("Bondage," p. 129) notes that Pallegoix's estimate reflects the situation around the capital Bangkok and presents some evidence that the proportion of slaves may have been much smaller in the hinterland.

32. Andrew Turton, "Thai Institutions of Slavery," in James L. Watson, ed., *Asian and African Systems of Slavery* (Oxford: Basil Blackwell, 1980), p. 278.

33. Lingat, *L'esclavage*, p. 193.

34. Pallegoix, *Description*, I, pp. 233–234.

35. Sir John Bowering, *The Kingdom and People of Siam*, 2 vols. (Hong Kong: Government House, 1856; reprint, Oxford: Oxford University Press, 1969), vol. 1, pp. 123–124.

36. Bowering, *Kingdom*, vol. 1, p. 180.

37. James C. Ingram, *Economic Change in Thailand 1850–1970* (Stanford: Stanford University Press, 1971), pp. 60–61.

38. Turton, "Thai Institutions," p. 287, makes this interesting point about the contrast between Burmese and Siamese slave cultures. In order not to make this chapter too long, the Burmese situation will not be covered in any detail. For a general overview of slavery in Burma, see Bruno Lasker, *Human Bondage in Southeast Asia* (Chapel Hill: University of North Carolina Press, 1952), which confirms Turton's observation.

39. Lingat, *L'esclavage*, chapter 6, pp. 385–386, lists the relevant laws in an appendix.

40. Chattip Nartsupha and Suthy Prasartset, *The Political Economy of Siam, 1851–1910* (Bangkok: The Social Science Association of Thailand, 1981), p. 478. For the entire decree, see chapter 13, document 15.

41. Lingat, *L'esclavage*, pp. 95ff.

42. Abbot Low Moffat, *Mongkut, The King of Siam* (Ithaca, NY: Cornell University Press, 1960), p. 38.

43. Chattip and Prasartset, *Political Economy*, pp. 88–89.

44. James C. Ingram, *Economic Change in Thailand*, pp. 58–59.

45. Prachoom Chomchai, *Chulalongkorn the Great* (Tokyo: The Centre for East Asian Cultural Studies, 1965); M. L. Manich Jumsai, *Popular History of Thailand*, 3rd ed. (Bangkok: Chalermnit, 1993), pp. 529ff.

46. Prachoom, *Chulalongkorn*, ch. 4; and David K. Wyatt, *The Politics of Reform in Thailand: Education in the Reign of King Chulalongkorn* (New Haven: Yale University Press, 1969), pp. 52–61.

47. Prachoom, *Chulalongkorn*, p. 52.

48. See chapter 13, document 16.

49. Rabibhadana, "Organization," p. 112.

50. Lingat, *L'esclavage*, p. 265.

51. Prachoom, *Chulalongkorn*, p. 62.

52. Terwiel, "Bondage," p. 133.

53. Wyatt, *Politics*, pp. 28–29 and 37–38.

54. Walter E. J. Tips, *Gustave Rolin-Jaequemyns (Chao Phraya Aphai Raja) and The Belgian Advisers in Siam (1892–1902)* (Bangkok: Published by the Author, 1992), p. 212.

55. Tej Bunnang, *The Provincial Administration of Siam (1892–1915)* (Kuala Lumpur: Oxford University Press, 1977), p. 57. See also Turton, "Thai Institutions," pp. 280–283 and 291–292.

56. Kenneth Ch'en, *The Chinese Transformation of Buddhism* (Princeton, NJ: Princeton University Press, 1973), pp. 142–147.

57. Jacques Gernet, *les Aspects économiques du bouddhisme dans la société chinoise du V au X siècle* (Paris: École Française d'Extreme-orient, 1956), p. 99.

58. Ibid., pp. 77–78.

59. Ibid., p. 112.

60. Ibid., p. 136.

61. Emperor Wu-tsung, "Edict on the Suppression of Buddhism," in William Theodore de Bary, Wing-tsit Chan, and Burton Watson, eds., *Sources of Chinese Tradition* (New York: Columbia University Press, 1960), Vol. 1, pp. 380 and 381.

62. Ch'en, *Chinese Transformation*, p. 143.

63. Gernet, *Aspects économiques*, pp. 125–126.

64. Ibid., p. 110.

65. Ibid., pp. 68–69.

66. Peter Harvey, *An Introduction to Buddhist Ethics: Foundations, Values and Issues* (Cambridge: Cambridge University Press, 2000), pp. 188–189.

67. Damien V. Keown, "Are There Human Rights in Buddhism?" in Damien V. Keown, Charles S. Prebish, and Wayne R. Husted, eds., *Buddhism and Human Rights* (Richmond, Surrey: Curzon Press, 1998), p. 33.

68. Harvey, *Introduction*, p. 188.

69. Phra Nyanavarotama, *The Plan of Life* (Bangkok: Mahamakuta Rajavidyalaya Foundation, 2535/1992), p. 111.

70. Ibid., p. 112.

71. L.P.N. Perera, *Buddhism and Human Rights: A Buddhist Commentary on the Universal Declaration of Human Rights* (Colombo: Karunaratne and Sons, 1991), pp. 32–36. For the Declaration article see chapter 13, document 1.

72. As discussed in chapter 11.

73. Rebecca Redwood French, *The Golden Yoke: The Legal Cosmology of Buddhist Tibet* (Ithaca, NY: Cornell University Press, 1995), pp. 110–115 and 320–321.

74. Walshe, *Digha Nikaya*, Sutta 2, discussed above at the beginning of this chapter.

Chapter 8. Buddhism and Caste

1. Richard Gombrich, *Buddhist Precept and Practice: Traditional Buddhism in the Rural Highlands of Ceylon* (Delhi: Motilal Banarsidass, 1991), p. 354. Gombrich reviews the Pali scriptural references on caste, pp. 354–357. For another fine review, see Rahula Walpola, *History of Buddhism in Ceylon: The Anuradhapura Period, 3rd Century* B.C.–10th Century A.C., 2nd ed. (Colombo, Ceylon: M. D. Gunasena, 1966), pp. 233–237.

2. Maurice Walshe, trans., *Thus Have I Heard: The Long Discourses of the Buddha, The Digha Nikaya* (London: Wisdom Publications, 1987), p. 408.

3. Bhikku Nanamoli and Bhikku Bodhi, *The Middle Length Discourses of the Buddha: A Translation of the Majjhima Nikaya*, 2nd ed. (Boston: Wisdom Publications, 2001), *Majjhima Nikaya*, 11.177ff.

4. Gombrich, *Buddhist Precept*, p. 356. Y. Krishan argues that Buddha actually strengthened the caste system in India by the way he linked it to karma ("Buddhism and the Caste System," *The Journal for the International Association of Buddhist Studies* 9:1 [1996]).

5. Rahula, *History*, pp. 233–234.

6. Richard Gombrich and Gananath Obeyesekere, *Buddhism Transformed: Religious Change in Sri Lanka* (Princeton, NJ: Princeton University Press, 1988), p. 186; Gombrich, *Buddhist Precept*, pp. 147–148.

7. Kitsiri Malalgoda, *Buddhism in Sinhalese Society 1750–1900: A Study of Religious Revival and Change* (Berkeley: University of California Press, 1976), p. 88.

8. Michael Carrithers, *The Forest Monks of Sri Lanka: An Anthropological and Historical Study* (Delhi: Oxford University Press, 1983), pp. 160–161, 216.

9. Gombrich, *Buddhism Transformed*, p. 398.

10. Ibid., p. 373.

11. L.P.N. Perera, *Buddhism and Human Rights: A Buddhist Commentary on the Universal Declaration of Human Rights* (Colombo, Sri Lanka: Karunaratne and Sons, 1991), pp. 21–28.

12. Ian Neary, *Political Protest and Social Control in Pre-War Japan: The Origins of Buraku Liberation* (Manchester: Manchester University Press, 1989), p. 15; Buraku Liberation Research Institute, *Long-Suffering Brothers and Sisters, Unite! The Buraku Problem, Universal Human Rights and Minority Problems in Various Countries* (Osaka: Buraku Liberation Research Institute, 1981), p. 265.

13. Neary, *Political Protest*, p. 13; Herbert Passin, "Untouchability in the Far East," *Monumentica Nipponica* XI:3 (October 1955), pp. 32–33.

14. Neary, *Political Protest*, p. 25. The italics are Neary's.

15. Passin, "Untouchability," p. 35.

16. Takumi Ueda, "A Discriminated-Against Minority in Japan—The Present Situation of the Burakumin and the Buraku Liberation Movement," in Buraku Liberation Research Institute, *The Road to a Discrimination-Free Future* (Osaka: Buraku Liberation Research Institute, 1983), pp. 3–4.

17. George De Vos and Hiroshi Wagatsuma, *Japan's Invisible Race: Caste in Culture and Personality* (Berkeley: University of California Press, 1966), pp. 88–92.

18. Leslie D. Alldritt, "The *Burakumin*: The Complicity of Japanese Buddhism in Oppression and an Opportunity for Liberation," *Journal of Buddhist Ethics* 7 (2000), pp. 4–5.

19. Neary, *Political Protest*, p. 38.

20. Wagatsuma, *Japan's Invisible Race*, pp. 90–91.

21. Neary, *Political Protest*, pp. 68–69.

22. See chapter 13, document 21.

23. Neary, *Political Protest*, p. 90.

24. Wagatsuma, *Japan's Invisible Race*, p. 91.

25. William Bodiford, "Zen and the Art of Religious Prejudice: Efforts to Reform a Tradition of Social Discrimination," *Japanese Journal of Religious Studies* 23:1–2 (1996), pp. 14–15. Shows how the Buddhists did use karma and the precepts against killing to justify caste discrimination.

26. Toshinori Kasahara, "Shin Buddhism and the Buraku-min," Shin Dharma Net, available online at http://www.shindharmanet.com/writings/burakumin.htm.

27. George A. de Vos and William O. Wetherall, *Japan's Minorities: Burakumin, Koreans, Ainu and Okinawans*, updated by Kay Stearman (London: Minority Rights Group, 1983), p. 5.

28. University of Adelaide, "Academic Book Prompts Japanese War Apology," Press Release (April 23, 2002).

29. Bodiford, "Zen."

30. Stephen Turnbull, *The Kakure Kirishitan of Japan: A Study of Their Development, Beliefs and Rituals to the Present Day* (Richmond, Surrey: Japan Library, 1998), p. 40.

31. Geoffrey Samuel, *Civilized Shamans: Buddhism in Tibetan Societies* (Washington: Smithsonian Institution Press, 1993), pp. 119–121, 129, 137 and 145.

32. Franz Michael, *Rule by Incarnation: Tibetan Buddhism and Its Role in Society and the State* (Boulder, CO: Westview Press, 1982), pp. 46 and 116.

33. Passin, "Untouchability," p. 38.

34. Melvyn C. Goldstein, *A History of Modern Tibet, 1913–1951: The Demise of the Lamaist State* (Berkeley: University of California Press, 1989), pp. 208–209.

35. Rebecca Redwood French, *The Golden Yoke: The Legal Cosmology of Buddhist Tibet* (Ithaca, NY: Cornell University Press, 1995), pp. 110–115. The tripartite division of the outcastes is according to the Dalai Lama Code (p. 114.)

36. Samuel, *Civilized Shamans*, p. 121.

37. Israel Epstein, *Tibet Transformed* (Beijing: New World Press, 1983), pp. 52–53.

38. See chapter 13, document 24.

39. Alan Sponberg, "TBMSG: A Dhamma Revolution in Contemporary India," in Christopher S. Queen and Sallie B. King, *Engaged Buddhism: Buddhist Liberation Movements in Asia* (Albany: State University of New York Press, 1996).

40. Eleanor Zelliot, *From Untouchable to Dalit: Essays on the Ambedkar Movement*, 2nd ed. (Delhi: Manohar, 1996), pp. 187 and 263.

41. Zelliot, *From Untouchable to Dalit*, p. 192; Christopher S. Queen, "Dr. Ambedkar and the Hermeneutics of Buddhist Liberation" in Queen and King, *Engaged Buddhism*, p. 51.

42. B. R. Ambedkar, *The Buddha and His Dhamma*, 2nd ed. (Bombay: Siddarth Publication, 1974), p. 23.

43. Ambedkar, *Buddha*, p. xlii.

44. Queen, "Ambedkar," p. 55.

45. Ambedkar, *Buddha*, p. 83.

46. Ibid., p. 89.

47. Zelliot, *From Untouchable to Dalit*, pp. 79–85; Queen, "Ambedkar," pp. 64–65.

48. Queen, "Ambedkar," pp. 59–60.

49. Zelliot, *From Untouchable to Dalit*, pp. 226–227.

50. Ibid., p. 224; paraphrased.

Chapter 9. The Status of Women in Buddhism

1. T. W. Rhys Davids and Hermann Oldenberg, trans., *Vinaya Texts*, in *Sacred Books of the East*, vols. 13, 17, and 20 (Oxford: Clarendon Press, 1881–1885; reprint, Delhi: Motilal Banarsidass, 1966), vol. 20, pp. 320–328.

2. Jonathan S. Walters, "Gotami's Story," in Donald S. Lopez Jr., ed., *Buddhism in Practice* (Princeton, NJ: Princeton University Press, 1995), line 79.

3. Ibid., line 173.

4. Ibid., lines 179–189.

5. Ibid., line 185.

6. Ibid., line 152.

7. Davids and Oldenberg, *Vinaya Texts*, SBE, vol. 20, p. 323.

8. Ibid., p. 328.

9. Ibid., pp. 330ff.

10. Rita Gross, *Buddhism after Patriarchy: A Feminist History, Analysis, and Reconstruction of Buddhism* (Albany: State University of New York Press, 1993), p. 34. She credits I. B. Horner for this observation.

11. Gross, *Buddhism after Patriarchy*, p. 39.

12. Nancy Auer Falk, "The Case of the Vanishing Nun: The Fruits of Ambivalence in Ancient Indian Buddhism," in Nancy Auer Falk and Rita M. Gross, *Unspoken Worlds: Women's Religious Lives* (Belmont, CA: Wadsworth Publishing Company, 1989), pp. 156–157.

13. Gross, *Buddhism after Patriarchy*, p. 51.

14. E. B. Cowell, ed., *The Jataka or Stories of the Buddha's Former Births* (Cambridge: Cambridge University Press, 1895; reprint, London: Pali Text Society, 1957), vol. IV, pp. 219–246.

15. Ibid., vol. IV, p. 223.

16. Ibid., vol. IV, p. 236.

17. John Garrett Jones, *Tales and Teachings of the Buddha: The Jataka Stories in Relation to the Pali Canon* (London: Allen and Unwin, 1979), p. 100.

18. Cowell, *Jataka*, Jataka 31, vol. I, p. 79.

19. Ibid., Jataka 519, vol. V, p. 53.

20. Ibid., Jataka 320, vol. IV, p. 46.

21. Ibid., Jataka 544, vol. VI, pp. 114–126.

22. Gross, *Buddhism after Patriarchy*, pp. 49–51.

23. Sigalaka Sutta, see chapter 13, document 7.

24. Susan Murcott, *The First Buddhist Women: Translations and Commentary on the Therigatha* (Berkeley, CA: Parallax Press, 1991), p. 106.

25. Alexandra R. Kapur-Fic, *Thailand, Buddhism, Society, and Women* (New Delhi: Abinav Publications, 1998), pp. 359–360. She references I. B. Horner, *Women under Primitive Buddhism* (London: Routledge, 1930; reprint, Delhi: Motial Banarsidass, 1975), p. 121, first published.

26. Murcott, *First Buddhist Women*, pp. 21–26.

27. Ibid., pp. 97–99.

28. Liz Wilson, *Charming Cadavers: Horrific Figurations of the Feminine in Indian Buddhist Hagiographic Literature* (Chicago: University of Chicago Press, 1996), chs. 2 and 3.

29. Diana Y. Paul, *Women in Buddhism: Images of the Feminine in Mahayana Tradition* (Berkeley, CA: Asian Humanities Press, 1979), pp. 27–29.

30. Paul, *Women in Buddhism*, p. 29.

31. Ibid., p. 31.

32. Ibid., p. 37.

33. Ibid., pp. 26–27.

34. Ibid., p. 50.

35. Murcott, *First Buddhist Women*, p. 122. See also Peter Harvey, *An Introduction to Buddhist Ethics: Foundations, Values and Issues* (Cambridge: Cambridge University Press, 2000), pp. 359–360.

36. Gross, *Buddhism after Patriarchy*, p. 46.

37. Murcott, *First Buddhist Women*, p. 64.

38. Ibid., pp. 65–66.

39. Gross, *Buddhism after Patriarchy*, pp. 67–75; Nancy Shuster, "Changing the Female Body: Wise Women and the Bodhisattva Career in Some *Maharatnakutasutras*," *The Journal of the International Association of Buddhist Studies* 4:1 (1981).

40. Gross, *Buddhism after Patriarchy*, pp. 70–71.

41. Paul, *Women in Buddhism*, p. 230.

42. Bhiksuni Karma Lekshe Tsomo, "Nuns of Japan: Part II," in Bhiksuni Karma Lekshe Tsomo, ed., *Sakyadhita: Daughters of the Buddha* (Ithaca, NY: Snow Lion Publications, 1988), p. 129.

43. Reverend Tessho Kondo, "Nuns of Japan: Part I," in Karma Lekshe Tsomo, ed., *Sakyadhita*.

44. Nancy J. Barnes, "Buddhist Women and the Nuns' Order in Asia," in Christopher S. Queen and Sallie B. King, *Engaged Buddhism: Buddhist Liberation Movements in Asia* (Albany: State University of New York Press, 1996), pp. 277–285.

45. Ven Ani Jutima, "Full Ordination for Nuns Restored in Sri Lanka," *Insight* (Spring 2002).

46. Sanitsuda Ekachai, "The Dhammananda Controversy," *Bangkok Post* (September 22, 2001).

47. Barnes, "Buddhist Women," p. 283.

48. See Rita Gross, *Buddhism after Patriarchy*, ch. 4, for an excellent discussion of the relevant issues. Generally speaking, I am convinced by Gross's arguments throughout her book.

49. Ibid., p. 30.

50. Ibid., p. 33.

51. Cowell, *Jataka*, Jataka 536, vol. V, pp. 219–245.

52. Ibid., Jataka 62, vol. I, pp. 151–155.

53. T. W. Rhys Davids, *The Questions of King Milinda* (Oxford: Oxford University Press, 1890, 1894; reprint, New York: Dover, 1963), vol. I, p. 294.

54. Gross, *Buddhism after Patriarchy*, p. 36.

55. Ibid., p. 35.

56. Ibid., pp. 30 and 51.

Chapter 10. Japanese Buddhism, Militarism, and Human Rights

1. Ryusaku Tsunoda, William Theodore de Bary, and Donald Keene, eds., *Sources of Japanese Tradition*, vol. 1 (New York: Columbia University Press, 1958), p. 48.

2. James C. Dobbins, *Jodo Shinshu: Shin Buddhism in Medieval Japan* (Bloomington: Indiana University Press, 1989), pp. 138ff; Sir Charles Eliot, *Japanese Buddhism* (London: Routledge and Kegan Paul, 1964), p. 198.

3. Minor Rogers and Ann Rogers, *Rennyo: The Second Founder of Shin Buddhism, with a Collection of his Letters* (Berkeley, CA: Asian Humanities Press, 1991).

4. Brian Daizen Victoria, *Zen at War* (New York: Weatherhill, 1997), p. 6.

5. Ibid., pp. 23–25.

6. Christopher Ives, "Ethical Pitfalls in Imperial Zen and Nishida Philosophy: Ichikawa Hakugen's Critique," in James W. Heisig and John C. Maraldo, eds., *Rude Awakenings: Zen, the Kyoto School and the Question of Nationalism* (Honolulu: University of Hawaii Press, 1995), p. 17.

7. Victoria, *Zen at War*, p. 29.

8. Ibid.

9. Ibid., p. 25.

10. Ibid., p. 30.

11. Ibid., chs. 6 and 7.

12. Ibid., pp. 137–138.

13. D. T. Suzuki, *Zen and Its Influence on Japanese Culture* (Kyoto: Eastern Buddhist Society, 1938), which was revised and reissued as *Zen and Japanese Culture* (Princeton, NJ: Princeton University Press, 1959), p. 145. All quotations are from the 1959 edition.

14. Ibid., p. 89.

15. Ibid., p. 63.

16. Arthur Koestler, *The Lotus and the Robot* (London: Hutchinson and Co., 1960; and New York: Macmillan, 1961), p. 274.

17. Brian Daizen Victoria, *Zen War Stories* (Richmond, Surrey: Curzon Press, 2003), p. 106.

18. Victoria, *Zen at War*, p. 111.

19. Victoria, *War Stories*, p. 120.

20. Kiyohide Kirita, "D. T. Suzuki on Society and the State," in Heisig and Maraldo, *Rude Awakenings*, pp. 60–61.

21. Victoria, *Zen War Stories*, pp. 144–145.

22. Victoria, *Zen at War*, pp. 63ff; Victoria, *War Stories*, chs. 6, 9, and 10; Charles Brewer Jones, *Buddhism in Taiwan: Religion and the State, 1660–1990* (Honolulu: University of Hawaii Press, 1999).

23. See chapter 6.

24. Saburo Ienaga, *The Pacific War: World War II and the Japanese, 1931–1945* (1968; trans., New York: Pantheon, 1978), p. 181.

25. Victoria, *Zen War Stories*, pp. 164–166, translates the wartime memoir, quotation from p. 166.

26. Kurebayashi Kodo, cited in Victoria, *Zen at War*, p. 133.

27. Ibid., p. 143.

28. Shinsho Hanayama, *The Way of Deliverance: Three Years with the Condemned Japanese War Criminals* (London: Victor Gollancz, 1955), p. 256.

29. Iris Chang, *The Rape of Nanking: The Forgotten Holocaust of World War Two* (New York: Basic Books, 1997), pp. 50–52.

30. Hanayama, *Way of Deliverance*, p. 186.

31. Ibid., p. 256.

32. Hanayama, *Way of Deliverance*, passim. Some of the war criminals were Japanese Christians, who also had embraced the Imperial ideology during the war, and came to regret it for religious reasons before their execution (pp. 106–113). See also, Victoria, *War Stories*, ch. 10, "Buddhism—the Last Refuge of War Criminals."

33. Victoria, *Zen War Stories*, p. 7; for Genjo's wartime memoir, published in 1999, pp. 4–11.

34. Ibid., pp. 164–170.

35. Ibid., p. 169.

36. Victoria, *Zen at War*, p. 139ff.

37. Ives, "Ethical Pitfalls," pp. 18–19.

38. Victoria, *Zen at War*, p. 138.

39. Ibid.

40. Ibid., p. 139.

41. Brian Daizen Victoria, "Yasutani Roshi: The Hardest Koan," *Tricycle: The Buddhist Review* 9:1 (Fall 1999), p. 65.

42. Abhi Subedi, *Ekai Kawaguchi: The Trespassing Insider* (Kathmandu: Mandala Book Point, 1999), ch. 6.

43. Ibid., p. 129.

44. Ives, "Ethical Pitfalls," pp. 16–17.

45. Ibid., p. 22.

46. Ibid., p. 17.

47. Victoria, *Zen at War*, pp. 171–174.

48. Ives, "Ethical Pitfalls," pp. 25ff.

49. James W. Heisig, "Tanabe's Logic of the Specific and Nationalism," in Heisig and Maraldo, *Rude Awakenings*, p. 257.

50. Rogers and Rogers, *Rennyo*, p. 326.

51. Ibid., ch. 7.

52. Ibid., pp. 329–331.

53. Ibid., p. 332.

54. For example, Makiguchi Tsunesaburo (1871–1944), the founder of Soka Gakkai, was imprisoned during the war for refusing to toe the ideological line. He died from malnutrition. Robert Kisala, *Prophets for Peace: Pacificism and Cultural Identity in Japan's New Religions* (Honolulu: University of Hawaii Press, 1999), pp. 74–78.

55. Jacqueline I. Stone, "When Disobedience is Filial and Resistance is Loyal: The Lotus Sutra and Social Obligations in the Medieval Nichiren Tradition," in Gene Reeves, ed., *A Buddhist Kaleidoscope: Essays on the Lotus Sutra* (Tokyo: Kosei Publishing Co., 2002), p. 279.

56. Jiun Kubota, The 3rd Patriarch of the Religious Foundation Sanbo-kyodan, "Apology for What the Founder of the Sanbo-Kyodan, Haku'un Yasutani Roshi, Said and Did during World War II," *Tricycle: The Buddhist Review*, 10:1 (Fall 2000), pp. 18–19.

57. Bodhin Kjolhede, in Victoria, "Yasutani," p. 69.

58. Brian Daizen Victoria, "Engaged Buddhism: A Skeleton in the Closet," *Journal of Global Buddhism* 2 (2001).

59. Victoria, *Zen at War*, p. 154.

60. Victoria, *Zen War Stories*, pp. 232–233.

61. Ibid., pp. 232–233.

Chapter 11. Tibetan Buddhism, Social Structure, and Violence

1. David Snellgrove, *Indo-Tibetan Buddhism: Indian Buddhists and Their Tibetan Successors* (Boston: Shambhala, 1987), p. 386.

2. Donald S. Lopez Jr., ed., *Religions of Tibet in Practice* (Princeton, NJ: Princeton University Press, 1997), "Introduction," p. 19.

3. Turrell V. Wylie, "Monastic Patronage in 15th Century Tibet," *Acta Orientalia Academiae Scientiarum Hungarica* 34 (1980), pp. 319–328.

4. Lopez, *Religions of Tibet*, p. 23.

5. This discussion of class is based primarily on Geoffrey Samuel, *Civilized Shamans: Buddhism in Tibetan Societies* (Washington, DC: Smithsonian Institution Press, 1993), pp. 116–125; and Melvyn C. Goldstein, *A History of Modern Tibet, 1913–1950: The Demise of the Lamaist State* (Berkeley: University of California Press, 1989), pp. 3–8; Goldstein's various articles; and Franz Michael, *Rule by Incarnation: Tibetan Buddhism and Its Role in Society and the State* (Boulder, CO: Westview Press, 1982), pp. 46–49 and 115–124.

6. Israel Epstein, *Tibet Transformed* (Beijing: New World Press, 1983), p. 406; Melvyn C. Goldstein, "Reexamining Choice, Dependency and Command in the Tibetan Social System: 'Tax Appendages' and other Landless Serfs," *Tibet Journal* 11:4 (1986), p. 86 and p. 110 n5; Goldstein thinks that these Chinese estimates are in the right order of magnitude.

7. Samuel, *Civilized Shamans*, pp. 119–121.

8. Ibid., p. 145.

9. Franz Michael, "Traditional Tibetan Polity and Its Potential for Modernization," *Tibet Journal* 11:4 (1986), pp. 70–78.

10. Goldstein, "Reexamining Choice."

11. Melvyn C. Goldstein, "On the Nature of the Tibetan Peasantry: A Rejoinder," *Tibet Journal* 13:4 (1988), pp. 61–65.

12. Beatrice Miller, "A Response to Goldstein's 'Reexamining Choice, Dependency and Command in the Tibetan Social System,'" *Tibet Journal* 12:2 (1987), pp. 65–67.

13. Samuel, *Civilized Shamans*, p. 117.

14. Melvyn C. Goldstein, "Serfdom and Mobility: An Examination of the Institution of 'Human Lease' in Traditional Tibetan Society," *Journal of Asian Studies* 30:3 (1970), p. 521.

15. Hsi Chang-hao and Kao Yuan-mei, *Tibet Leaps Forward* (Peking: Foreign Languages Press, 1977), p. 26.

16. Jin Zhou, ed., *Tibet: No Longer Mediaeval* (Beijing: Foreign Languages Press, 1981), pp. 50–60.

17. Epstein, *Tibet Transformed*, chs. 2, 3, and 9.

18. Melvyn C. Goldstein, "Introduction," in Melvyn C. Goldstein and Matthew T. Kapstein, *Buddhism in Contemporary Tibet: Religious Revival and Cultural Indentity* (Berkeley: University of California Press, 1998) reviews the Chinese record in regard to freedom of religion in Tibet. For a chronology of events in Tibet from 1949 to the present, as compiled by the Tibetan Government in Exile, see http://www.tibet.net/eng/tgie/chrono/ (October 22, 2002).

19. Goldstein, "Reexamining Choice," p. 109, n2.

20. Nancy E. Levine, *The Dynamics of Polyandry: Kinship, Domesticity, and Population on the Tibetan Border* (Chicago: University of Chicago Press, 1988); and Nancy E. Levine, "Opposition and Interdependence: Demographic and Economic Perspectives on Nyinba Slavery," in James L. Watson, ed. *Asian and African Systems of Slavery* (Oxford: Basil Blackwell, 1980), p. 199.

21. Lopez, *Religions of Tibet*, p. 31.

22. Goldstein, *History of Modern Tibet*, pp. 41–42.

23. Goldstein, *History of Modern Tibet*, p. 21; and Melvyn C. Goldstein, "The Revival of Monastic Life in Drepung Monastery," in Goldstein and Kapstein, *Buddhism in Contemporary Tibet*, p. 15–22.

24. Goldstein, *History of Modern Tibet*, p. 25.

25. Figures from the Mey College of the Sera Monastery, Goldstein, *History of Modern Tibet*, p. 24.

26. For the *dobdo*, or *dobdob* (*ldab ldob*, in standard transliteration from Tibetan) see, Melvyn C. Goldstein, "A Study of the Ldab Ldob," *Central Asiatic Journal* 9:2 (1964), pp. 125–141; Goldstein, "Revival," p. 19; David Snellgrove and Hugh Richardson, *A Cultural History of Tibet* (Boulder, CO: Prajna Press, 1980), pp. 240–241; R. A. Stein, *Tibetan Civilization* (London: Faber and Faber, 1972), pp. 140–141.

27. Abhi Subedi, *Ekai Kawaguchi: The Trespassing Insider* (Kathmandu: Mandala Book Point, 1999).

28. Ekai Kawaguchi, *Three Years in Tibet* (Madras: Theosophical Publishing Society, 1909), pp. 326–328.

29. Ibid., p. 292.

30. Goldstein, "Ldab Ldob," p. 134.

31. Kawaguchi, *Three Years*, pp. 291–294, and 301.

32. Goldstein, *History of Modern Tibet*, p. 37.

33. Ibid.

34. Tsering Shakya, *The Dragon in the Land of Snows* (New York: Columbia University Press, 1999), p. 5.

35. Goldstein, *History of Modern Tibet*, p. 106.

36. The failure of the reformers was sealed in the struggle at the beginning of the regency after the death of the thirteenth Dalai Lama, when Lungshar, the leader of the progressive forces, was condemned and sentenced to being blinded by mutilation. See Goldstein, *History of Modern Tibet*, ch. 6, for details.

37. Charles Bell, *Portrait of the Dalai Lama* (London: Collins, 1946), pp. 252–253.

38. Goldstein, *History of Modern Tibet*, pp. 427–445, reviews the disputed events of this complex incident. The present study presents a bare outline of what happened. An important underlying factor was the rivalry between the regent (Taktra), who was currently governing on behalf of the young Dalai Lama, and the former regent (Reting), who was eager to regain the position. Most of the monks and the abbot of Sera Che college strongly supported Reting.

39. Ibid., p. 429.

40. Again, events were very complicated and centered in large point on the struggle between the two main contenders for the regency. See Goldstein, *History of Modern Tibet*, ch. 14.

41. Ibid., p. 521.

42. Ibid., p. 521n.

43. Dalai Lama, [His Holiness the Dalai Lama of Tibet], *My Land and My People* (New York: Potala Corporation, 1962), pp. 60–61.

44. Ibid., pp. 64–67.

45. Ibid., p. 231.

46. Sections of the Draft Constitution are included in chapter 13, document 24.

47. John F. Avendon, *Exile from the Land of Snows* (New York: Alfred A. Knopf, 1984), pp. 107–109.

48. See chapter 13, document 24.

49. Dalai Lama, *Freedom in Exile: The Autobiography of His Holiness The Dalai Lama of Tibet* (London: Hodder and Stoughton, 1990), pp. 186–187.

50. Stephen Batchelor, et al., "Deity or Demon, The Controversy over Tibet's Dorje Shugden," *Tricycle*, 7:3 (Spring 1998), pp. 58–84.

51. See chapter 13, documents 1 and 24.

52. For details see, Avendon, *Exile*, and Kevin Boyle and Juliet Sheen, eds., *Freedom of Religion and Belief: A World Report* (London: Routledge, 1997), pp. 186–187.

53. José Ignacio Cabezón, "Buddhist Principles in the Tibetan Liberation Movement," in Christopher S. Queen and Sallie B. King, *Engaged Buddhism: Buddhist Liberation Movements in Asia* (Albany: State University of New York Press, 1996), pp. 295–299.

54. Ibid., pp. 301–302.

55. Dalai Lama, *Kindness, Clarity, and Insight*, J. Hopkins and E. Napper, eds. (Ithaca, NY: Snow Lion, 1984; reprint, Delhi: Motilal Banarsidass, 1997), p. 11.

56. Dalai Lama, *Kindness, Clarity, and Insight*, p. 65. This theme, in very similar words, recurs very often in his speeches and writings. See Cabezón, "Buddhist Principles," pp. 302–304.

57. Dalai Lama, "Universal Rights and Human Responsibility," statement made at The United Nations World Conference on Human Rights, Vienna, June 15, 1993, see chapter 13, document 23.

58. Georges Dreyfus, "Law, State, and Political Ideology in Tibet," *Journal of the International Association of Buddhist Studies* 18:1 (1995), pp. 122–123.

59. Shakya, *Dragon*, p. 5.

60. Kawaguchi, *Three Years*, p. 430.

61. Goldstein, "Revival."

Chapter 12. Concluding Reflections

1. Minor Rogers and Ann Rogers, *Rennyo: The Second Founder of Shin Buddhism, with a Collection of His Letters* (Berkeley, CA: Asian Humanities Press, 1991), p. 362.

2. No doubt the reader is thinking, how can it be explained that one R. E. Florida dares query the Dalai Lama and Aung San Suu Kyi?

3. Dalai Lama (His Holiness the XIVth Dalai Lama of Tibet), *Kindness, Clarity, and Insight*, ed. J. Hopkins and E. Napper (Ithaca, NY: Snow Lion, 1984; reprint, Delhi: Motilal Banarsidass, 1997), pp. 84–85.

4. *Dhammapada*, verse 183, in Walpola Rahula, *What the Buddha Taught*, 2nd ed. (New York: Grove Press, 1974), p. 131.

5. P. A. Payutto [Phra Prayudh Payutto], *A Constitution for Living: Buddhist Principles for a Fruitful and Harmonious Life*, trans. Bruce Evans (Bangkok: Buddhadhamma Foundation, 1996), p. viii.

6. Robert Aitken, *The Mind of Clover: Essays in Zen Buddhist Ethics* (San Francisco: North Point Press, 1984), p. 164.

7. Masaharu Anesaki, *History of Japanese Religion: With Special Reference to the Social and Moral Life of the Nation* (London: Kegan Paul, Trench, and Trubner, 1930), Book VI, see especially p. 373. See also Thomas Freeman Yarnall, "Engaged Buddhism: New and Improved? Made in the USA of Asian Material," in Christopher Queen, Charles Prebish, and Daniel Keown, eds., *Action Dharma: New Studies in Engaged Buddhism* (London: RoutledgeCurzon, 2003).

8. Darrel Wratten, "Engaged Buddhism in South Africa," in Christopher S. Queen, ed., *Engaged Buddhism in the West* (Boston: Wisdom Publications, 2000), p. 449. The italics in the first quotation are Wratten's.

9. Robert E. Goss, "Naropa Institute: The Engaged Academy," in Queen, *Engaged Buddhism in the West*, p. 338.

10. Damien Keown, Charles Prebish, and Wayne Husted, eds., *Buddhism and Human Rights* (Richmond, Surrey: Curzon Press, 1998), pp. 221–222.

ANNOTATED BIBLIOGRAPHY

Buddhist Studies, General Works

Asvaghosa. *Buddhacarita: or Acts of the Buddha*. Translated by E. H. Johnston. 1936. Reprint, Delhi: Motilal Banarsidass, 1972. A lovely, richly detailed life of the Buddha written in Sanskrit verse in India, perhaps dating from around the turn of the common era.

Basham, A. L. *The Wonder That Was India*. New York: Grove Press, 1959.

Burlingame, Eugene Watson, trans. *Buddhist Legends Translated from the Original Pali Text of the Dhammapada Commentary*. 1921. Reprint, London: Pali Text Society, 1969.

Carrithers, M. *The Buddha*. Oxford: Oxford University Press, 1983. Very good short introduction to the historical Buddha.

Conze, Edward, ed. and trans. *Buddhist Scriptures*. Harmondsworth: Penguin, 1959. Useful selection, especially of the Indian Buddhist texts.

Cowell, E. B., ed. *The Jataka or Stories of the Buddha's Former Births*. 6 vols. Cambridge: Columbia University Press, 1895. Reprint, London: Pali Text Society, 1957. Important and rich source of information about early Buddhism. The Jataka tales are widely used in Buddhist lands to teach the basics of the faith.

Davids, T. W. Rhys. *The Questions of King Milinda.* Oxford: Oxford University Press, 1890, 1894. Reprint, New York: Dover, 1963.

Davids, T. W. Rhys, and Hermann Oldenberg, trans. *Vinaya Texts.* In *Sacred Books of the East,* vols. 13, 17, and 20. Oxford: Clarendon, 1881–1885. Reprint, Delhi: Motilal Banarsidass, 1966. The *vinaya* is the prime source for our knowledge about the early life of the monks and nuns and how the early religious community related with the secular world.

Dharmasiri, Gunapala. *A Buddhist Critique of the Christian Conception of God.* Antioch, CA: Golden Leaves, 1988.

Gombrich, Richard. "Buddhist Karma and Social Control." *Comparative Studies in Society and History* 17:1 (1975).

———. *Theravada Buddhism: A Social History from Ancient Benares to Modern Colombo.* London: Routledge and Kegan Paul, 1988. An excellent social history of Theravada Buddhism, with much valuable material on human rights and related issues.

Gross, Rita. "Karma and Social Justice." *World Faiths Encounter* 29 (2001). A very fine discussion on whether or not the doctrine of karma forecloses any possibility of justice.

Hisao Inagaki, in collaboration with Harold Stewart. *The Three Pure Land Sutras: A Study* and *Translation from Chinese.* Kyoto: Nagata Bunshodo, 1995. The fundamental scriptures of Pure Land Buddhism.

Hurvitz, Leon. *Scripture of the Lotus Blossom of the Fine Dharma.* New York: Columbia University Press, 1976.

Jones, John Garrett. *Tales and Teachings of the Buddha: The Jataka Stories in Relation to the Pali Canon.* London: George Allen and Unwin, 1979. Indispensable guide to these important scriptures.

Kitagawa, Joseph M., and Mark D. Cummings. *Buddhism and Asian History: Readings from the Encyclopedia of Religion.* New York: Macmillan, 1989.

Ling, Trevor. *The Buddha: Buddhist Civilization in India and Ceylon.* 1973. Reprint, Harmondsworth: Penguin, 1976. This useful book traces the history of Buddhism in India and Sri Lanka, taking into account social and political factors.

————. *The Buddha's Philosophy of Man: Early Indian Buddhist Dialogues.* London: Dent, 1981. This useful annotated selection and translation from the *Digha Nikaya* focuses on Buddha's social and political teachings.

————. *Buddhism, Imperialism and War.* London: George Allen and Unwin, 1979. Valuable on Southeast Asia.

————, ed. *Buddhist Trends in Southeast Asia.* Singapore: Institute of Southeast Asian Studies, 1993.

Lopez, Donald S., Jr., ed. *Buddhism in Practice.* Princeton, NJ: Princeton University Press, 1995. Excellent selections, which are drawn from writers at the cutting edge of scholarship.

————. *Curators of the Buddha: The Study of Buddhism under Colonialism.* Chicago: University of Chicago Press, 1995.

Misra, G.S.P. *The Age of Vinaya.* Delhi: Munshiram Manoharlal, 1972. Rich in social and historical detail about India in the time of Buddha.

Mookerji, Radhakumud. *Asoka.* 3rd ed. Delhi: Motilal Banarsidass, 1962. Contains translations of all of Asoka's inscriptions as well as exhaustive historical notes.

Nanamoli, Bhikku, and Bhikku Bodhi. *The Middle Length Discourses of the Buddha: A Translation of the Majjhima Nikaya.* 2nd ed. Boston: Wisdom Publications, 2001. A very fine translation of a critically important primary text.

Neumaier, Eva. "The Dilemma of Authoritative Utterance in Buddhism." In Harold Coward, ed., *Experiencing Scripture in World Religions.* Maryknoll, NY: Orbis Books, 2000. Excellent concise introduction to the complexities of Buddhist scriptures.

Nikam, N. A., and Richard McKeon, eds. and trans. *The Edicts of Asoka.* Chicago: University of Chicago Press, Phoenix Books, 1966. A scholarly and readable translation of these key texts.

Prebish, Charles S. *Buddhist Monastic Discipline: The Sanskrit Pratimoksa Sutras of the Mahasamghikas and Mulasarvastivadins.* University Park: Pennsylvania University Press, 1975. Very useful on the early *vinaya* and monastic sangha.

Pye, Michael. *Skilful Means: A Concept in Mahayana Buddhism*. London: Duckworth, 1978. Good treatment of an important topic.

Rahula, Walpola. *What the Buddha Taught*. 2nd ed. New York: Grove Press, 1974. Still one of the best introductions to the basic teachings of the Theravada school, with little sociological or historical application.

Santideva. *The Bodhicaryavatara*. Translated by Kate Crosby and Andrew Skilton. Oxford: Oxford University Press, 1995. Primary text from the Mahayana path.

Sopa, Geshe Lhundub. "The Special Theory of Pratityasamutpada: The Cycle of Dependent Origination." *Journal of the International Association of Buddhist Studies* 9:1 (1986).

Suzuki, D. T. *Outlines of Mahayana Buddhism*. 1907. Reprint, New York: Schocken, 1963.

Swearer, Donald K. *The Buddhist World of Southeast Asia*. Albany: State University of New York Press, 1995.

Walshe, Maurice trans. *Thus Have I Heard: The Long Discourses of the Buddha, The Digha Nikaya*. London: Wisdom Publications, 1987. A very fine translation of a critically important primary text.

Warren, Henry Clarke. *Buddhism in Translations*. Cambridge, MA: Harvard University Press, 1900. A useful selection of texts, well translated.

Watson, Burton, trans. *The Lotus Sutra*. New York: Columbia University Press, 1993.

Buddhist Ethics, General Works

De Silva, Lily. "The Scope and the Contemporary Significance of the Five Precepts." In Charles Wei-hsun Fu and Sandra A. Wawrytko, eds., *Buddhist Ethics: An International Symposium*. Westport, CT: Greenwood Press, 1991.

Florida, R. E. "Buddhism and Abortion." In Damien Keown, ed., *Contemporary Buddhist Ethics*. Richmond, Surrey: Curzon Press, 2000.

———. "Buddhism and the Four Principles." In Raanan Gillon, ed., *Principles of Health Care Ethics*. Chichester: John Wiley and Sons, 1994.

Florida, Robert E. "Buddhism and Violence in Modernity." In David J. Hawkin, ed., *The Twenty-First Century Confronts Its Gods: Globalization, Technology, and War.* Albany: State University of New York Press, 2004. Some of the material in this essay is found in the present volume.

Fu, Charles Wei-hsun, and Sandra A. Wawrytko, eds. *Buddhist Ethics and Modern Society: An International Symposium.* Westport, CT: Greenwood Press, 1991. Noteworthy for how little is said about human rights in this collection of essays.

Granoff, Phyllis. "The Violence of Non-Violence: A Study of Some Jain Responses to Non-Jain Religious Practices." *The Journal of the International Association for Buddhist Studies* 15:1 (1992). Casts light on the Mahayana willingness to break the precepts, including taking human life.

Harvey, Peter. *An Introduction to Buddhist Ethics: Foundations, Values and Issues.* Cambridge: Cambridge University Press, 2000. The first survey of Buddhist ethics to take into account historical and sociological data from a wide array of Buddhist cultures. Human rights issues are only occasionally in the foreground.

Kalupahana, David J. *Ethics in Early Buddhism.* Honolulu: University of Hawaii Press, 1995.

Keown, Damien. *Buddhism and Bioethics.* London: Macmillan, 1995.

———. *The Nature of Buddhist Ethics.* New York: St. Martin's Press, 1992.

———, ed. *Contemporary Buddhist Ethics.* Richmond, Surrey: Curzon Press, 2000.

King, Sally B. "It's a Long Way to a Global Ethic: A Response to Leonard Swidler." *Buddhist-Christian Studies* (1995). Prof. King sees the attempt to forge a global ethic as barely concealed Christian imperialism, and the evidence seems to be on her side.

Knitter, Paul F. "Pitfalls and Promises for a Global Ethics." *Buddhist-Christian Studies* (1995). A Roman Catholic supporter of the Global Ethic movement fears that it is an expression of the developed world's dominance.

Lee, Chung Ok. "Unity beyond Religious and Ethnic Conflict Based on a Universal Declaration of a Global Ethic: A Buddhist Perspective." *Buddhist-Christian Studies* (1995).

McCarthy, Stephen. "Why the Dalai Lama Should Read Aristotle." *Journal of Buddhist Ethics* 8 (2001). Perhaps could be retitled "Why Stephen McCarthy Should Read the *Heart Sutra*"—a very interesting, but not convincing argument that the similarities in Buddhist and Aristotelian ethics could provide a framework for absolute, universal human rights that Eastern Buddhists and politicians could embrace.

Norman, K. R. "Asoka and Capital Punishment: Notes on a Portion of Asoka's Fourth Pillar Edict, with an Appendix on the Accusative Absolute Construction." *Journal of the Royal Asiatic Society* (1975).

Reynolds, Frank. "Buddhism and Law—Preface." *The Journal of the International Association of Buddhist Studies* 18:1 (1995).

Schopen, Gregory. "The Monastic Ownership of Servants or Slaves: Local and Legal Factors in the Redactional History of Two *Vinayas*." *The Journal of the International Association of Buddhist Studies* 17:2 (1994). Illuminating on Buddhist monastic slavery.

Sizemore, Russell F., and Donald K. Swearer. *Ethics, Wealth, and Salvation: A Study in Buddhist Social Ethics*. Columbia: University of South Carolina Press, 1990. First rate collection, much valuable material on Theravada ethical life.

Strauss, Virginia. "Peace, Culture, and Education Activities: A Buddhist Response to the Global Ethic." *Buddhist-Christian Studies* (1995). A Soka Gakkai response.

Thurman, Robert A. F. "Buddhist Ethics: The Emptiness That Is Compassion." *Religious Traditions* (November 1981).

Von Hinuber, Oskar. "Buddhist Law According to the Theravada-Vinaya: A Survey of Theory and Practice." *The Journal of the International Association of Buddhist Studies* 18:1 (1995).

———. "Buddhist Law According to the Theravada-Vinaya II: Some Additions and Corrections." *The Journal of the International Association of Buddhist Studies* 20:2 (1997).

Human Rights, General Works

Boyle, Kevin, and Juliet Sheen, eds. *Freedom of Religion and Belief: A World Report*. London: Routledge, 1997. A survey of the actual state of religious freedom in a large number of selected countries. Good sections on China (Tibet), Japan, Sri Lanka, and Vietnam, but nothing on Burma.

Brownlie, Ian, ed. *Basic Documents on Human Rights*. Oxford: Clarendon Press, 1992.

Feinberg, Joel. "The Nature and Value of Rights." In Morton E. Winston, ed., *The Philosophy of Human Rights*. Belmont, CA: Wadsworth, 1989. A fine philosophical discussion.

Finnis, J. M. *Natural Law and Natural Rights*. Oxford: Oxford University Press, 1980. One of the major theoretical sources for the present study.

Harris J. W. *Legal Philosophies*, Clarendon Law Series, H.L.A. Hart, ed. London: Butterworth, 1980. Good for the relation of rights and duties.

Sucharitkul, Sompong. "A Multi-Dimensional Concept of Human Rights in International Law." *Notre Dame Law Review* 62 (1987). Thai legal scholar argues that although everyone is a "duty-bearer" of human rights, human rights are not the same from culture to culture.

Winston, Morton E. *The Philosophy of Human Rights*. Belmont, CA: Wadsworth Publishing Company, 1989.

———. "Understanding Human Rights." In Morton E. Winston, ed. *The Philosophy of Human Rights*. Belmont, CA: Wadsworth Publishing Company, 1989.

Human Rights in Asia

Bloom, Irene, J. Paul Martin, and Wayne L. Proudfoot, eds. *Religious Diversity and Human Rights*. New York: Columbia University Press, 1996. Contains very strong essays about human rights in the major religious traditions of Asia.

Chanana, Dev Raj. *Slavery in Ancient India as Depicted in Pali and Sanskrit Texts*. New Delhi: People's Publishing House, 1960. Detailed, useful book.

Chung, Young-Sun. "Asian Values and Challenges to Universal Human Rights." *Peace Forum* 15:27 (1999).

Ghee, Lim Teck, ed. *Reflections on Development in Southeast Asia*. Singapore: Institute of Southeast Asian Studies, 1988.

Kung, Hans, and Karl-Josef Kuschel, eds. *A Global Ethic: The Declaration of the Parliament of the World's Religions*. London: SCM Press, 1993.

Panikkar, R. "Is the Notion of Human Rights a Western Concept?" *Diogenes* 20 (1982). This important essay raises some fundamental questions.

Queen, Christopher S., and Sallie B. King, eds. *Engaged Buddhism: Buddhist Liberation Movements in Asia*. Albany: State University of New York Press, 1996. This storehouse of treasures contains very fine essays with excellent bibliographies and other resources on contemporary engaged Buddhist movements in Asia.

Queen, Christopher, Charles Prebish, and Damien Keown, eds. *Action Dharma: New Studies in Engaged Buddhism*. London: RoutledgeCurzon, 2003. Excellent group of essays on Buddhist ethical theory and practice, including considerable material on human rights. This volume was received too late to be integrated into the present study.

Reid, Anthony. *Slavery, Bondage, and Dependency in Southeast Asia*. St. Lucia: University of Queensland Press, 1983.

Watson, James L., ed. *Asian and African Systems of Slavery*. Oxford: Basil Blackwell, 1980.

Welch, C. E., and V. Leary. *Asian Perspectives on Human Rights*. Boulder, CO: Westview Press, 1990. Useful bibliography.

Human Rights and Religion, General

Lasker, Bruno. *Human Bondage in Southeast Asia*. Chapel Hill: University of North Carolina Press, 1950. Reprint, Westport, CT: Greenwood Press, 1972. Important study on the most critical issue in human rights.

Rouner, Leroy S. *Human Rights and the World's Religions*. South Bend, IN: University of Notre Dame Press, 1988. Contains useful essays by Thurman and Unno.

Swidler, Arlene, ed. *Human Rights in Religious Traditions.* New York: Pilgrim Press, 1982. Good essay by Kenneth Inada.

Swidler, Leonard, ed. *Religious Liberty and Human Rights in Nations and in Religions.* Philadelphia: Ecumenical Press, 1986.

Traer, Robert. *Faith in Human Rights: Support in Religious Traditions for a Global Struggle.* Washington, DC: Georgetown University Press, 1991. Argues that all religious traditions "affirm human rights as part of their faith." The section on Buddhism does not prove its case.

Human Rights and Buddhism, General Works

Abe, Maseo. "Religious Tolerance and Human Rights: A Buddhist Perspective." In Leonard Swidler, ed., *Religious Liberty and Human Rights.* Philadelphia: Ecumenical Press, 1986.

Barnhart, Michael. "Buddhist Ethics and Social Justice." In Ron Bontekoe and Marietta Stepaniants, eds., *Justice and Democracy: Cross-Cultural Perspectives.* Honolulu: University of Hawaii Press, 1997.

Deitrick, James E. "Engaged Buddhist Ethics: Mistaking the Boat for the Shore." In Christopher Queen, Charles Prebish, and Damien Keown, eds., *Action Dharma: New Studies in Engaged Buddhism.* London: RoutledgeCurzon, 2003. Suggests that engaged Buddhist ethical theory is not "basically Buddhist." This volume was received too late to be integrated into the present study.

Holt, John C. "The Radical Egalitarianism of Mahayana Buddhism." In R. Siriwardena, ed., *Equality and the Religious Traditions of Asia.* London: Frances Pinter, 1987.

Ihara, Craig K. "Why There Are No Rights in Buddhism: A Reply to Damien Keown." In Damien Keown, Charles Prebish, and Wayne Husted, eds., *Buddhism and Human Rights.* Richmond, Surrey: Curzon Press, 1998.

Inada, Kenneth. "A Buddhist Response to the Nature of Human Rights." In Damien Keown, Charles Prebish, and Wayne Husted, eds., *Buddhism and Human Rights.* Richmond, Surrey: Curzon Press, 1998. First published in Claude E. Welch Jr. and Virginia A. Leary, eds., *Asian Perspectives on Human Rights.* Boulder, CO: Westview Press, 1990.

Jeffreys, Derek S. "Does Buddhism Need Human Rights." In Christopher Queen, Charles Prebish, and Damien Keown, eds., *Action Dharma: New Studies in Engaged Buddhism*. London: RoutledgeCurzon, 2003. An excellent essay which generally supports the positions taken in chapters 2 and 12 of the present study. It was received too late to be treated at length.

Junger, Peter D. "Why the Buddha Has No Rights." In Damien Keown, Charles Prebish, and Wayne Husted, eds., *Buddhism and Human Rights*. Richmond, Surrey: Curzon Press, 1998.

Keown, Damien, Charles Prebish, and Wayne Husted, eds. *Buddhism and Human Rights*. Richmond, Surrey: Curzon Press, 1998. This essential text is a collection of the major papers presented in the *Journal of Buddhist Ethics* 1995 online conference on Buddhism and human rights.

Krishan, Y. "Buddhism and the Caste System." *The Journal for the International Association of Buddhist Studies* 9:1 (1996). Argues that Buddhism actually strengthened the caste system.

McConnell, John A. "The Rohini Conflict and the Buddha's Intervention." In Sulak Sivaraksha et al., eds., *Radical Conservatism: Buddhism in the Contemporary World*. Bangkok: Thai Inter-Religious Commission for Development, 1990.

Morgante, Amy, ed. *Buddhist Perspectives on the Earth Charter*. Boston: Boston Research Center for the 21st Century, 1997.

Perera, L.P.N. *Buddhism and Human Rights: A Buddhist Commentary on the Universal Declaration of Human Rights*. Colombo, Sri Lanka: Karunaratne and Sons, 1991. The first monograph on Buddhism and human rights. It carefully reviews each article of the Universal Declaration of Human Rights in light of the Pali scriptures of Theravada Buddhism, little historical application.

————, ed. *Human Rights and Religions in Sri Lanka: A Commentary on the Universal Declaration of Human Rights*. Colombo: Sri Lanka Foundation, 1988.

Saddhatissa, Hamalawa. *Buddhist Ethics*, rev. ed. Boston: Wisdom Publications, 1997.

Silk, Jonathan. "The Problem of Slavery or Unfree Labor in Indian Buddhism." Paper delivered at the American Academy of Religion, 1997.

Swearer, Donald K. " 'Rights' Because of Intrinsic Nature or 'Responsibilities' Because of Mutual Interdependence?" In Amy Morgante, ed., *Buddhist Perspectives on the Earth Charter*. Boston: Boston Research Center for the 21st Century, 1997.

Tanaguchi, Shoyo. "Human Rights and the Buddha's Teachings: A Soteriological Perspective." *The Pacific World Journal of the Institute of Buddhist Studies*, NS, 6 (1990). An early attempt to show that Pali texts support human rights, but not convincing in detail.

Thurman, Robert A. F. "Human Rights and Human Responsibilities: Buddhist Views on Individualism and Altruism." In Irene Bloom, J. Paul Martin, and Wayne L. Proudfoot, eds., *Religious Diversity and Human Rights*. New York: Columbia University Press, 1996. A provocative interpretation of the relationship through history of the varieties of Buddhism to human rights and responsibilities.

Tilaratne, Asanga. "Buddhism on Slavery." *Dialogue* (Colombo, Sri Lanka), NS, 23 (1996). A review of the Pali Texts and early Sri Lankan literature on slavery.

Traer, Robert. "Buddhist Affirmations of Human Rights." *Buddhist Christian Studies* 8 (1988), pp. 13–19.

Yarnall, Thomas Freeman. "Engaged Buddhism: New and Improved? Made in the USA of Asian Materials." In Christopher Queen, Charles Prebish, and Damien Keown, eds., *Action Dharma: New Studies in Engaged Buddhism*. London: RoutledgeCurzon, 2003. A detailed and valuable 48-paged consideration of the key writers and issues concerning Buddhism, human rights, and social action. This volume was received too late to be integrated into the present study.

Women and Human Rights in Buddhism

Aung San Suu Kyi, for the works of this female Burmese Buddhist Nobel Laureate, please see the Burmese section of the bibliography.

Ekachai, Sanitsuda. "The Dhammananda Controversy." *Bangkok Post* (22 September 2001). Reactions to the ordination of the first Thai nuns ever.

Falk, Nancy Auer. "The Case of the Vanishing Nun: The Fruits of Ambivalence in Ancient Indian Buddhism." In Nancy Auer Falk and Rita

M. Gross, *Unspoken Worlds: Women's Religious Lives*. Belmont, CA: Wadsworth Publishing Company, 1989.

Falk, Nancy Auer, and Rita M. Gross. *Unspoken Worlds: Women's Religious Lives*. Belmont, CA: Wadsworth Publishing Company, 1989. Collection of essays with some useful Buddhist sections.

Findly, Ellison Banks, ed. *Women's Buddhism Buddhism's Women*. Boston: Wisdom Publications, 2000. Selection of good essays, on both historical and contemporary issues.

Goonatilake, Hema. "Women and Family in Buddhism." In Sulak Sivaraksa, ed., *Buddhist Perception for Desirable Societies in the Future*. Bangkok: The Inter-Religious Commission for Development, 1992.

Gross, Rita. *Buddhism after Patriarchy: A Feminist History, Analysis, and Reconstruction of Buddhism*. Albany: State University of New York Press, 1993. Indispensable, very influential book, and very well done.

———. *Soaring and Settling: Buddhist Perspectives on Contemporary Social and Religious Issues*. New York: Continuum, 1998.

Havnevik, Hanna. *Tibetan Buddhist Nuns: History, Cultural Norms and Social Reality*. Oslo: Norwegian University Press, 1989. Fieldwork based study with nuns in the exile community in India, with good historical material as well.

Horner, I. B. *Women Under Primitive Buddhism*. London: Routledge, 1930. Reprint, Delhi: Motilal Banarsidass, 1975. One of the earliest and one of the best works on Buddhism and women.

Kabilsingh, Chatsumarn. *Thai Women in Buddhism*. Berkeley, CA: Parallax Press, 1991. Central work on the topic.

Kapur-Fic, Alexandra R. *Thailand, Buddhism, Society, and Women*. New Delhi: Abinav Publications, 1998. Good title, disappointing book.

Murcott, Susan. *The First Buddhist Women: Translations and Commentary on the Therigatha*. Berkeley, CA: Parallax Press, 1991. Useful, but does not replace Horner's book.

"No Female Monks for Thailand." *Bangkok Post* (17 May 2001).

Paul, Diana Y. *Women in Buddhism: Images of the Feminine in Mahayana Tradition*. Berkeley, CA: Asian Humanities Press, 1979. Key work in the area.

Peach, Linda Joy. "Buddhism and Human Rights in the Thai Sex Trade." In Courtney W. Howland, ed., *Religious Fundamentalisms and the Human Rights of Women*. New York: St. Martin's Press, 1999. Well-done study, which opens up some lines for further investigation.

Shuster, Nancy. "Changing the Female Body: Wise Women and the Bodhisattva Career in Some *Maharatnakutasutras*." *The Journal of the International Association of Buddhist Studies* 4:1 (1981). Very useful paper.

Tsomo, Bhiksuni Karma Lekshe. "Nuns of Japan: Part II." In Karma Lekshe Tsomo, ed., *Sakyadhita: Daughters of the Buddha*. Ithaca, NY: Snow Lion Publications, 1988.

———, ed. *Innovative Buddhist Women: Swimming against the Stream*. Richmond, Surrey: Curzon Press, 2000. Very useful collection of papers.

———, ed. *Sakyadhita: Daughters of the Buddha*. Ithaca, NY: Snow Lion Publications, 1988. Good on contemporary Buddhist nuns.

Walters, Jonathan S. "Gotami's Story." In Donald S. Lopez, Jr., ed., *Buddhism in Practice*. Princeton, NJ: Princeton University Press, 1995.

Wilson, Liz. *Charming Cadavers: Horrific Figurations of the Feminine in Indian Buddhist Hagiographic Literature*. Chicago: University of Chicago Press, 1996.

Engaged Buddhism

Chappell, David, ed. *Buddhist Peacework: Creating Cultures of Peace*. Boston: Wisdom Publications, 1999. A collection of essays, most of which have some direct relevance to human rights issues.

Hanh, Thich Nhat. *For a Future to Be Possible: Commentaries on the Five Wonderful Precepts*. Berkeley, CA: Parallax Press, 1993.

Kraft, Kenneth, ed. *Inner Peace, World Peace: Essays on Buddhism and Nonviolence*. Albany: State University of New York Press, 1992. Includes essays by Thurman, Swearer, Sulak, and others.

Queen, Christopher S., ed. *Engaged Buddhism in the West*. Boston: Wisdom Publications, 2000. An excellent resource for Buddhist approaches to a number of social issues, including human rights. Europe, South Africa, Australia, and North America are all covered.

Buddhism and Human Rights: Individual Countries

Burma

Aung, Maung Htin. *A History of Burma*. New York: Columbia University Press, 1967. Very interesting on the British colonial period from a Burmese viewpoint.

Aung San Suu Kyi. *Aung San of Burma: A Biographical Portrait by his Daughter*. London: Kiscadale Publications, 1991. Also collected as "My Father" in Aung San Suu Kyi, *Freedom from Fear and Other Writings*, 2nd ed. London: Penguin, 1995. Useful to understand her political and religious convictions.

———. *Freedom from Fear and Other Writings*, 2nd ed. London: Penguin, 1995. Inspiring writings by and about the Nobel Peace Laureate from Burma.

Aung San Suu Kyi and Alan Clements. *The Voice of Hope: Conversations: Aung San Suu Kyi with Alan Clements*. New York: Seven Stories Press, 1997. These conversations contain much of relevance to the issues in Buddhism and human rights.

Badgley, John. "Burmese Ideology: A Comment." In Josef Silverstein, ed., *Independent Burma at Forty Years: Six Assessments*. Ithaca, NY: Southeast Asia Program, Cornell University, 1989.

Ba Maw. *Breakthrough in Burma: Memoirs of a Revolution, 1939–1946*. New Haven: Yale University Press, 1968. Very interesting, self-justifying autobiography by the Premier of the Burmese puppet government under the Japanese occupation.

Bunge, Frederica M. *Burma: A Country Study*. Washington, DC: American University, 1983. Quite a good handbook, much of value on religion and politics.

Burma Socialist Programme Party. *The System of Correlation of Man and His Environment: The Philosophy of the Burma Socialist Programme Party*.

Rangoon: Sarpay Beikman Press, 1973. The military government's philosophical blueprint.

Cady, John F. A *History of Modern Burma*. Ithaca, NY: Cornell University Press, 1959. The best, most detailed historical study for Burma before the military takeover in 1962.

Chakravarti, Nalini Ranjan. *The Indian Minority in Burma: The Rise and Decline of an Immigrant Community*. London: Institute of Race Relations, 1971.

Clements, Alan, and Leslie Kean. *Burma's Revolution of the Spirit: the Struggle for Democratic Freedom and Dignity*. Foreword by His Holiness the Dalai Lama; preface by Sein Win. New York: Aperture, 1994. Important documentation of human rights abuses under the military government in Burma.

Crosthwaite, Sir Charles. *The Pacification of Burma*. London: Frank Cass, 1968. Written by the British official in charge of the pacification of Burma in the 1880s.

Ferguson, John P. "The Quest for Legitimation by Burmese Monks and Kings: The Case of the Shwegyin Sect (19th–20th Centuries)." In Bardwell L. Smith, ed., *Religion and Legitimation of Power in Thailand, Laos, and Burma*. Chambersburg, PA: Anima Books, 1978.

Fernando, Laskiri. "The Burmese Road to Development and Human Rights." In Alice Tay, ed., *East Asia: Human Rights, Nation-Building, Trade*. Baden-Baden: Nomos Verlagsgesellschaft, 1999. A strong paper that provides evidence for the lack of human rights concern throughout Burmese history.

Human Rights Watch. "Burma: Rape, Forced Labor and Religious Persecution in Northern Arakan." *Human Rights Watch/Asia* 4:13 (May 7, 1992).

———. "Crackdown on Burmese Muslims." July 2002. Available online at: http://www.hrw.org.

———. *World Report 1998*, "Burma." http//www.hrw.org/worldreport/Asia-01.htm#P127_40364.

Huxley, Andrew. "Buddhism and the Law—The View from Mandalay." *Journal of the International Association of Buddhist Studies* 18:1 (1995).

Detailed introduction to an important aspect of Buddhist civilization in Burma.

Kreager, Philip. "Aung San Suu Kyi and the Peaceful Struggle for Human Rights in Burma." In Aung San Suu Kyi, *Freedom from Fear and Other Writings*, 2nd ed. London: Penguin, 1995.

Matthews, Bruce. "Buddhism under a Military Regime: The Iron Heel in Burma." *Asian Survey* 33:4 (April 1993). A solid, detailed study of this issue, and one of the very few that look extensively into religious factors.

Maung Maung, U. *Burma and General Ne Win*. London: Asia Publishing House, 1969.

Mendelson, E. Michael. *Sangha and State in Burma: A Study of Monastic Sectarianism and Leadership*. Ithaca, NY: Cornell University Press, 1975. Excellent detailed study.

Naw, Angelene. *Aung San and the Struggle for Burmese Independence*. Chiang Mai: Silkworm Books, 2001.

Nu, Thakin. See U Nu.

Nu, U. See U Nu.

Sarkisyanz, E. "Buddhist Backgrounds of Burmese Socialism." In Bardwell L. Smith, ed., *Religion and Legitimation of Power in Thailand, Laos, and Burma*. Chambersburg, PA: Anima Books, 1978.

———. *Buddhist Backgrounds of the Burmese Revolution*. The Hague: Martinus Nijhoff, 1965. Solid, detailed European scholarship.

Silverstein, Josef, ed. *Independent Burma at Forty Years: Six Assessments*. Ithaca, NY: Southeast Asia Program, Cornell University, 1989. Essays on religion, economics, politics, and history detail the horrendous problems Burma has faced since independence.

Smeaton, Donald Mackenzie. *The Loyal Karens of Burma*. London: Kegan Paul, Trench, 1887. Fascinating glimpse from a contemporary observer into the problems in upper Burma after the British takeover.

Smith, Bardwell L., ed. *Religion and Legitimation of Power in Thailand, Laos, and Burma*. Chambersburg, PA: Anima Books, 1978.

Smith, Donald Eugene. *Religion and Politics in Burma*. Princeton, NJ: Princeton University Press, 1965.

Smith, Martin. *Burma: Insurgency, and the Politics of Ethnicity*. London: Zed Books, 1991.

Spiro, Melford E. *Buddhism and Society: A Great Tradition and Its Burmese Vicissitudes*. New York: Harper and Row, 1970.

Steinberg, David I. "Neither Silver nor Gold: The 40th Anniversary of the Burmese Economy." In Josef Silverstein, ed., *Independent Burma at Forty Years: Six Assessments*. Ithaca, NY: Southeast Asia Program, Cornell University, 1989.

Thakin Nu [U Nu]. *Burma Under the Japanese: Pictures and Portraits*. London: Macmillan, 1954. Fresh first-hand recollections of a very difficult time.

U Nu. *U Nu Saturday's Child*. Translated by U Law Yone. New Haven: Yale University Press, 1975. A fascinating account of his political career, not at all glossing over his errors.

Victor, Barbara. *Lady: Burma's Daw Aung San Suu Kyi*. London: Faber and Faber, 1998.

Win, Kanbawza. *Daw Aung San Suu Kyi, the Nobel Laureate: a Burmese Perspective*. Bangkok: CPDSK Publications, 1992. A useful study.

Zan, Myint. "Law and Legal Culture, and Constitutions and Constitutionalisms in Burma." In Alice Tay, ed., *East Asia: Human Rights, Nation-Building, Trade*. Baden-Baden: Nomos Verlagsgesellschaft, 1999. A long, detailed and fascinating account of the consistent lack of human rights in Burmese history.

Cambodia

Fernando, Laskiri. "Khmer Socialism, Human Rights, and the UN Intervention." In Alice Tay, ed., *East Asia: Human Rights, Nation-Building, Trade*. Baden-Baden: Nomos Verlagsgesellschaft, 1999. Gives a historical overview of traditional Cambodian social structure, slavery, and kingship, and discusses what has happened in Cambodia in modernity—first rate and very useful.

Suksamran, Somboon. "Buddhism, Political Authority, and Legitimacy in Thailand and Cambodia." In Trevor Ling, ed., *Buddhist Trends in Southeast Asia*. Singapore: Institute of Southeast Asian Studies, 1993. An excellent review of the travails of Buddhism in Cambodia.

China

Ch'en, Kenneth. *Buddhism in China: A Historical Survey*. Princeton, NJ: Princeton University Press, 1964. Somewhat dated in approach, but still very useful.

————. *The Chinese Transformation of Buddhism*. Princeton, NJ: Princeton University Press, 1973. Very good on the ethical, political, and economic aspects.

de Bary, Wm. Theodore, Wing-tsit Chan, and Burton Watson, eds. *Sources of Chinese Tradition*. New York: Columbia University Press, 1960.

Gernet, Jacques. *les Aspects économiques du bouddhisme dans la société chinoise du V au X siècle*. Paris: École Française d'Extreme-orient, 1956. A classic study.

Hevia, James. "Lamas, Emperors, and Rituals: Political Implications in Qing Imperial Ceremonies." *The Journal of the International Association of Buddhist Studies* 16:2 (1993).

Jones, Charles Brewer. *Buddhism in Taiwan: Religion and the State, 1660–1990*. Honolulu: University of Hawaii Press, 1999.

Lopez, Donald S., Jr., ed. *Religions of China in Practice*. Princeton, NJ: Princeton University Press, 1996. Indispensable selection of primary texts and contemporary scholarship.

Orzech, Charles. *Politics and Transcendent Wisdom: The Scripture for Humane Kings in the Creation of Chinese Buddhism*. University Park: The Pennsylvania State University Press, 1998. Important for understanding the role of "state-protection" Buddhism.

Welch, Holmes. *The Buddhist Revival in China*. Cambridge, MA: Harvard University Press, 1968. Excellent source on the practice of Buddhism in twentieth-century China before 1949.

Wright, Arthur F. *Buddhism in Chinese History*. Stanford, CA: Stanford University Press, 1959. Well-written and thoughtful short introduction.

Wu-tsung, Emperor. "Edict on the Suppression of Buddhism." In Wm. Theodore de Bary, Wing-tsit Chan, and Burton Watson, eds., *Sources of Chinese Tradition*. New York: Columbia University Press, 1960.

India

Ambedkar, B. R. *The Buddha and His Dhamma*, 2nd ed. Bombay: Siddharth Publication, 1974. This controversial work lays out the reasons that Dr. Ambedkar had for converting from Hinduism to Buddhism to free himself and his followers from the disadvantages of being "untouchables" in the Hindu caste system.

————. *Buddha and the Future of His Religion*, 3rd ed. Jullundur: Bheem Patrika Publications, 1950.

Blackburn, Anne M. "Religion, Kinship and Buddhism: Ambedkar's Vision of a Moral Community." *The Journal of the International Association of Buddhist Studies* 16:1 (1993).

Keer, Dhananjay. *Dr. Ambedkar: Life and Mission*, 3rd ed. Delhi: D. K., 1987. The leading biography of this important Buddhist reformer.

Queen, Christopher S. "Dr. Ambedkar and the Hermeneutics of Buddhist Liberation." In Christopher S. Queen and Sallie B. King, eds., *Engaged Buddhism: Buddhist Liberation Movement in Asia*. Albany: State University of New York Press, 1996.

Sangharakshita. *Ambedkar and Buddhism*. Glasgow, Scotland: Windhorse Publications, 1986. Important account by the Western Buddhist who helped Dr. Ambedkar on his journey to Buddhism.

Sponberg, Alan. "TBMSG: A Dhamma Revolution in Contemporary India." In Christopher S. Queen and Sallie B. King, eds., *Engaged Buddhism: Buddhist Liberation Movement in Asia*. Albany: State University of New York Press, 1996.

Zelliot, Eleanor. *From Untouchable to Dalit: Essays on the Ambedkar Movement*, 2nd ed. (New Delhi: Manohar, 1996.) Excellent collection of studies on the Dalit movement.

Japan

Aitken, Robert. *The Mind of Clover: Essays in Zen Buddhist Ethics*. San Francisco: North Point Press, 1984.

Alldritt, Leslie D. "The *Burakumin*: The Complicity of Japanese Buddhism in Oppression and an Opportunity for Liberation." *Journal of Buddhist Ethics* 7 (2000). Thoughtful survey of the problem of the "outcastes" of Japan and how Buddhist organizations aided and abetted their oppression.

Amstutz, Galen. *Interpreting Amida: History and Orientalism in the Study of Pure Land Buddhism*. Albany: State University of New York Press, 1997. This important study on Japan's largest Buddhist group has some insights to Buddhism and human rights.

Anesaki, Masaharu. *History of Japanese Religion: With Special Reference to the Social and Moral Life of the Nation*. London: Kegan Paul, Trench, and Trubner, 1930. Good on the modernization of Japan and the transfer of human rights concepts from the West.

Bodiford, William. "Zen and the Art of Religious Prejudice: Efforts to Reform a Tradition of Social Discrimination." *Japanese Journal of Religious Studies* 23:1–2, 1996, pp. 1–27. Documentation of Zen Buddhist complicity in the oppression and humiliation of Japan's "outcastes" and the attempts to make amends.

Buraku Liberation Research Institute. *Long-Suffering Brothers and Sisters, Unite! The Buraku Problem, Universal Human Rights and Minority Problems in Various Countries*. Osaka: Buraku Liberation Research Institute, 1981. Papers from an international symposium on human rights.

———. *The Reality of Buraku Discrimination in Japan*. Osaka: Buraku Liberation Research Institute Publications, 1994. Insiders' insights into Japan's "outcaste" community.

———. *The Road to a Discrimination-Free Future*. Osaka: Buraku Liberation Research Institute, 1983. A useful collection of papers from an international conference.

Chang, Iris. *The Rape of Nanking: The Forgotten Holocaust of World War Two*. New York: Basic Books, 1997. A readable account of one of the worst Japanese atrocities of World War II.

Deal, William E. "Buddhism and the State in Early Japan." In Donald S. Lopez, Jr., ed., *Buddhism in Practice*. Princeton, NJ: Princeton University Press, 1995.

Demiéville, Paul. Review of Suzuki's *Zen and Japanese Culture. Orientalische Literaturzeitung* 61:1.2 (1966). Reprinted in Paul Demiéville, *Choix d'études bouddhiques (1929–1970)*. Leiden: Brill, 1973.

De Vos, George, and Hiroshi Wagatsuma. *Japan's Invisible Race: Caste in Culture and Personality*. Berkeley: University of California Press, 1966. Major study on the burakumin "outcastes" of Japan.

De Vos, George A., and William O. Weatheral. *Japan's Minorities: Burakumin, Koreans, Ainu and Okinawans*. Updated by Kay Stearman. London: Minority Rights Group, 1983. Has an excellent succinct summary of the burakumin issue.

Dobbins, James C. *Jodo Shinshu: Shin Buddhism in Medieval Japan*. Bloomington: Indiana University Press, 1989. Background material on Japan's largest Buddhist movement, some details useful for human rights issues.

Eliot, Sir Charles. *Japanese Buddhism*. London: Routledge and Kegan Paul, 1964. Basic reference on Japanese Buddhism.

Futaba, Kenko. "Shinran and Human Dignity: Opening an Historic Horizon." *The Pacific World* 4 (1988). Useful on Japan's largest Buddhist movement and human rights.

Hanayama, Shinsho. *The Way of Deliverance: Three Years with the Condemned Japanese War Criminals*. London: Victor Gollancz, 1955. Reflections by the Buddhist chaplain who took care of those Japanese sentenced to die for war crimes.

Heisig, James W. "Tanabe's Logic of the Specific and Nationalism." In James W. Heisig and John C. Maraldo, eds., *Rude Awakenings: Zen, the Kyoto School and the Question of Nationalism*. Honolulu: University of Hawaii Press, 1995.

Heisig, James W., and John C. Maraldo, eds. *Rude Awakenings: Zen, the Kyoto School and the Question of Nationalism*. Honolulu: University of Hawaii Press, 1995. A collection of excellent essays on the philosophy of Nishida, Japan's leading thinker of mid–twentieth-century, Zen, and their relationship to the Imperial Buddhist ideology that fueled Japan's war machine.

Herrigel, Eugen. *Zen in the Art of Archery*. New York: Pantheon, 1953. Austrian who studied Zen and became a Nazi supporter.

Hirakawa, Akira. "The History of Buddhist Nuns in Japan." *Buddhist-Christian Studies* 1992. There was never full ordination of nuns in Japan, but there continues to be an active tradition of women taking the bodhisattva precepts.

Hubbard, Jamie, and Paul. L. Swanson, eds. *Pruning the Bodhi Tree: The Storm over Critical Buddhism*. Honolulu: The University of Hawaii Press, 1997. A collection of essays with many useful points on social issues and Buddhism in Japan, including, for example discrimination against the outcastes.

Humphries, Christmas. "No Stink of Zen: A Reply to Koestler." *Encounter* 15:6 (1960). Part of the Koestler-Suzuki controversy.

Ienaga, Saburo. *The Pacific War: World War II and the Japanese, 1931–1945.* Translated by Frank Baldwin. New York: Pantheon, 1978. Antimilitarist account.

Ives, Christopher. "Ethical Pitfalls in Imperial Zen and Nishida Philosophy: Ichikawa Hakugen's Critique." In James W. Heisig and John C. Maraldo, eds., *Rude Awakenings: Zen, the Kyoto School and the Question of Nationalism*. Honolulu: University of Hawaii Press, 1995.

———. *Zen Awakenings and Society*. Honolulu: University of Hawaii Press, 1992. Rare to find a study focused on the ethics of Zen, useful book.

Jalon, Allan M. "Meditating on War and Guilt, Zen Says It is Sorry." *New York Times* (January 11, 2003). Brian Daizen Victoria and Zen war guilt.

Jung, C. G. "A Letter from C. G. Jung: Yoga, Zen, and Koestler." *Encounter* 16:2 (1961). Part of the Koestler-Suzuki controversy.

Kasahara, Toshinori. "Shin Buddhism and the Buraku-min," Shin Dharma Net. Available online at http//shindharmanet.com/writings/burakumin.htm. Stresses that discrimination against "outcastes" continues although formally abolished more than one hundred years ago.

Kisala, Robert. *Prophets for Peace: Pacifism and Cultural Identity in Japan's New Religions*. Honolulu: University of Hawaii Press, 1999. Indirectly useful for human rights.

Kitaguchi, Suehiro. *An Introduction to the Buraku Issue: Questions and Answers*. Richmond, Surrey: Curzon, 1999. About Japan's "outcastes."

Koestler, Arthur. *The Lotus and the Robot*. London: Hutchinson and Co., 1960 and New York: Macmillan, 1961. Contains Koestler's spirited attack on D. T. Suzuki's teaching.

———. "Neither Lotus nor Robot." *Encounter* 16:2 (1961), p. 58.

———. "A Stink of Zen: The Lotus and the Robot." *Encounter* 15:4 (1960). Reprinted in Arthur Koestler, *The Lotus and the Robot*. London: Hutchinson and Co., 1960 and New York: Macmillan, 1961.

Kubota, Jiun, The 3rd Patriarch of the Religious Foundation Sanbo-kyodan. "Apology for What the Founder of the Sanbo-Kyodan, Haku'un Yasutani Roshi, Said and Did during World War II." *Tricycle: The Buddhist Review* 10:1 (Fall 2000), pp. 18–19. Important apology for Japanese Buddhist activities in World War II.

Miayata, Koichi. "Critical Comments on Brian Victoria's 'Engaged Buddhism: A Skeleton in the Closet.'" *Journal of Global Buddhism* 3 (2002). A rejoinder to Victoria's tying Japanese Buddhist leaders to the fascist ideology and war effort, particularly in regard to Soka Gakkai.

Michio, Arakai. "The Schools of Japanese Buddhism." In Joseph M. Kitagawa and Mark D. Cummings, eds., *Buddhism and Asian History: Readings from the Encyclopedia of Religion*. New York: Macmillan, 1989. Basic historical background material.

Neary, Ian. *Political Protest and Social Control in Pre-War Japan: The Origins of Buraku Liberation*. Manchester: Manchester University Press, 1989. Interesting on Japan's "outcastes" and on Japanese totalitarian state. Good on religious factors.

Ninomiya, Shigeaki. "An Inquiry Concerning the Origin, Development, and Present Situation of the Eta in Relation to the History of Social Classes in Japan." *Transactions of the Asiatic Society of Japan* 10 (1968), pp. 47–154. Very detailed consideration of the history of the "outcastes" of Japan.

Noriyoshi, Tamaru. "Buddhism in Japan." In Joseph M. Kitagawa and Mark D. Cummings, eds., *Buddhism and Asian History: Readings from the Encyclopedia of Religion.* New York: Macmillan, 1989.

Passin, Herbert. "Untouchability in the Far East." *Monumentica Nipponica* 11:3 (October 1955). An interesting study of untouchability in India, Japan, Korea, and Tibet.

Rogers, Minor, and Ann, Rogers. *Rennyo: The Second Founder of Shin Buddhism; With a Collection of his Letters.* Berkeley, CA: Asian Humanities Press, 1991. Some very useful material on Japan's largest Buddhist movement and human rights.

Scholem, Gershom. "Zen Nazism?" *Encounter* 16:2 (1961). Part of the Koestler-Suzuki controversy.

Sharf, Robert H. "The Zen of Japanese Nationalism." *History of Religions* 33:1 (1993). This essay presents a very intelligent assessment of the role of Buddhism in creating Japanese nationalist ideology.

Stephen, Christopher. "Zen's Holy War." *Kansai Times* (April 2003). Short article based on an interview with Brian Victoria.

Stone, Jacqueline I. "When Disobedience is Filial and Resistance is Loyal: The Lotus Sutra and Social Obligations in the Medieval Nichiren Tradition." In Gene Reeves, ed., *A Buddhist Kaleidoscope: Essays on the Lotus Sutra.* Tokyo: Kosei Publishing Co., 2002.

Storry, Richard. *The Double Patriots: A Study of Japanese Nationalism.* 1957. Reprint, Westport, CT: Greenwood Press, 1973.

Suzuki, D. T. "A Reply from D. T. Suzuki." *Encounter* 17:4 (1961). Part of the Koestler-Suzuki controversy.

———. *Zen and Its Influence on Japanese Culture.* Kyoto: Eastern Buddhist Society, 1938; revised and reissued as *Zen and Japanese Culture.* Princeton, NJ: Princeton University Press, 1959.

Tanaka, Kenneth K., and Eicho Nasu. *Engaged Pure Land Buddhism: Challenges Facing Jodo Shinshu in the Contemporary World.* Berkeley: Wisdom Ocean Publications, 1998. Contains some useful material on Shin Buddhism and human rights.

Tsunoda, Ryusaku, Wm. Theodore de Bary, and Donald Keene, eds. *Sources of Japanese Tradition*. New York: Columbia University Press, 1958. Very valuable collection of primary sources.

Turnbull, Stephen. *The Kakure Kirishitan of Japan: A Study of Their Development, Beliefs and Rituals to the Present Day*. Richmond, Surrey: Japan Library, 1998. Clear on the Buddhist involvement in the persecution of Christians in Japan from 1614–1873.

Ueda, Takumi. "A Discriminated-Against Minority in Japan—The Present Situation of the Burakumin and the Buraku liberation Movement." In Buraku Liberation Research Institute, *The Road to a Discrimination-Free Future*. Osaka: Buraku Liberation Research Institute, 1983.

University of Adelaide. "Academic Book Prompts Japanese War Apology." Press Release (April 23, 2002).

Victoria, Brian Daizen. "Engaged Buddhism: A Skeleton in the Closet." *Journal of Global Buddhism* 2 (2001). Documents Japanese Zen masters' and other Buddhists' fervent support for Japanese militarism and their Western students' attempts to justify it. See Koichi Miyata article for a reply.

———. "Yasutani Roshi: The Hardest Koan." *Tricycle: The Buddhist Review* 9:1 (Fall 1999), pp. 60–75. Victoria's important article on Japanese Buddhist complicity in human rights violations in World War II.

———. *Zen at War*. New York: Weatherhill, 1997. This well-written monograph details the involvement of Buddhism in the formulation and popularization of the militaristic ideology that led Japan into World War II and to war crimes.

———. *Zen War Stories*. Richmond, Surrey: Curzon Press, 2003. Digs deeper to reveal links between Zen and Japanese fascism.

Wagatsuma, Heroshi. See de Vos and Wagatsuma.

Weiner, Michael, ed. *Japan's Minorities: The Illusion of Homogeneity*. London: Routledge, 1997. Includes a useful chapter on the *burakumin*, Japanese outcastes, by Ian Neary.

Yukihiro, Ohashi. "New Perspectives on the Early Tokugawa Persecution." In John Breen and Mark Williams, eds. *Japan and Christianity: Impacts and Responses.* New York: St. Martin's Press, 1996. How persecution against the Christians in Japan developed.

Zerblowsky, R. J. Zwi. "Some Observations on Recent Studies of Zen." In E. E. Urbach, R. J. Zwi Werblowsky, and Ch. Wirszubski, eds., *Studies in Mysticism and Religion Presented to Gershom G. Scholem.* Jerusalem: The Hebrew University, 1967. A very lively discussion of important issues concerning Zen, history, and ethics.

Korea

Buswell, Robert Evans Jr. "Buddhism in Korea." In Joseph M. Kitagawa, and Mark D. Cummings, eds., *Buddhism and Asian History: Readings from the Encyclopedia of Religion.* New York: Macmillan, 1989. Basic historical data, shows how Buddhists in Korea were repressed for centuries, both by their own government and by their Japanese occupiers.

Lancaster, Lewis R., and Chai-shin Yu. *Introduction of Buddhism to Korea.* Berkeley: Asian Humanities Press, 1989.

Tedesco, Frank. "Questions for Buddhist and Christian Cooperation in Korea." *Buddhist-Christian Studies* 17 (1997). Contemporary persecution of Korean Buddhists by Korean Christians.

Laos

Stuart-Fox, Martin. *Buddhist Kingdom, Marxist State: The Making of Modern Laos.* Bangkok: White Lotus, 1996.

Mongolia

Brown, William A., and Urgurge Onon, trans. *History of Mongolian People's Republic.* Cambridge, MA: Harvard University Press, 1976. Translated from the Mongolian, a communist account of their government tells how the high lamas "were defeated and liquidated by revolutionary violence."

Hyer, Paul, and Sechin Jagchild. *A Mongolian Living Buddha: Biography of the Kanjurwa Khutughtu.* Albany: State University Press of New York,

1983. This biography covers the period of 1914–1978 and has insights on the Japanese occupation of Mongolia (1931–1945) and the Soviet oppression of Buddhism.

Moses, Larry W. *The Political Role of Mongol Buddhism*, Indiana University Uralic Altaic Series, 133. Bloomington: Asian Studies Research Institute, Indiana University, 1977. Detailed chapter on the extermination of Mongolia's Buddhist leaders and extirpation of their religious way of life.

Russia

Batchelor, Stephen. "The Trials of Dandaron." *Tricycle* 1:3 (Spring 1992). Fascinating story of Stalin's liquidation of Russian Buddhists in the great purges.

Sri Lanka

General

Ani Jutima, Ven. "Full Ordination for Nuns Restored in Sri Lanka." *Insight* (Spring 2002). An account of the reestablishment of full ordination for women in Sri Lanka by one of the ordinands.

Carrithers, Michael. *The Forest Monks of Sri Lanka: An Anthropological and Historical Study*. Delhi: Oxford University Press, 1983. Good on an important movement in Sri Lanka, also some valuable insights into the civil war.

Gombrich, Richard. *Buddhist Precept and Practice: Traditional Buddhism in the Rural Highlands of Ceylon*. Oxford University Press, 1971. Reprint, Delhi: Motilal Banarsidass, 1991. Masterful blending of social science theory, fieldwork, and Buddhist scholarship.

Gombrich, Richard, and Gananath Obeyesekere. *Buddhism Transformed: Religious Change in Sri Lanka*. Princeton, NJ: Princeton University Press, 1988. Two masters have produced a masterful study of the fluid nature of contemporary religion in Sri Lanka.

Gunawardana, R.A.L.H. *Robe and Plow: Monasticism and Economic Interest in Early Medieval Sri Lanka*. Tucson: University of Arizona Press, 1979. Useful on slavery and many other details.

Guruge, Ananda, ed. *Return to Righteousness: A Collection of Speeches, Essays, and Letters of Anagarika Dharmapala.* Colombo, Sri Lanka: The Government Press, 1965. Primary texts from the major progenitor of "Protestant Buddhism."

Harris, Elizabeth J. "Slavery in Sri Lanka: Reflections on Nineteenth Century Evidence about the Kandyan Kingdom and Maritime Provinces." *Dialogue* (Colombo, Sri Lanka), NS, vol. 23 (1996). The British Colonists' negative reaction to Sri Lankan Slavery, which was a relatively humane form of bondage.

Malalgoda, Kitsiri. *Buddhism in Sinhalese Society 1750–1900: A Study of Religious Revival and Change.* Berkeley: University of California Press, 1976.

Olcott, Henry. *Buddhist Catechism.* Colombo, Ceylon: Theosophical Society, Buddhist Section, 1881.

―――. *Old Diary Leaves.* 6 vols. 1895–1935. Reprint, Adyar, India: Theosophical Publishing House, 1972–1975.

Prothero, Stephen. *The White Buddhist: The Asian Odyssey of Henry Steel Olcott.* Bloomington: Indiana University Press, 1996.

Rahula, Walpola. *History of Buddhism in Ceylon: The Anuradhapura Period, 3rd Century B.C.-10th Century A.C.*, 2nd ed. Colombo, Ceylon: M.D. Gunasena, 1966. Detailed monograph by a leading scholar.

Buddhism, Human Rights, and Ethnic Violence

Although the current civil war between the Sinhalese Buddhist majority and the Tamil Hindu minority in Sri Lanka raises many important human rights issues, it is not covered directly in the text of the present study. Burma, another Theravada country with a similar pattern of history, served as the test case. This section of the bibliography is meant to lead the interested reader to the Sri Lankan situation. A very good place to start is Tessa Bartholomeuz's "In Defense of Dharma," a short, very intelligent theoretical introduction to the issues involved, cited below.

Almond, Gabriel A., Emmanuel Sivan, and R. Scott Appleby. "Examining the Cases." In Martin E. Marty and R. Scott Appleby, eds., *Fundamentalisms Comprehended.* Chicago: The University of Chicago Press,

1995. Contains an excellent succinct background section to the Buddhist-Tamil civil war in Sri Lanka.

Bandaranaike, S.W.R.D. *The Government and the People: A Collection of the Speeches of S.W.R.D. Bandaranaike*. Colombo: Government Press, 1959. A collection of speeches by the prime minister of Sri Lanka, who was elected with the help of Buddhist nationalists, under whom the current civil war began.

———. *Towards a New Era: Selected Speeches of S.W.R.D. Bandaranaike*. Colombo, Government Press, 1961. More speeches.

Bartholomeusz, Tessa, J. "In Defense of Dharma: Just-War Ideology in Buddhist Sri Lanka." *Journal of Buddhist Ethics* 6 (1999). An excellent introduction to a horrendous and horrendously complex conflict. This article includes a thoughtful discussion of the passage in the *Mahavamsa*, a noncanonical but extremely important history of the establishment of Buddhism in Sri Lanka, which notoriously states that killing a non-Buddhist is not killing a human being. She makes excellent use of contemporary popular sources in newspapers and journals.

Bartholomeusz, Tessa, J., and Chandra R. de Silva, eds. *Buddhist Fundamentalism and Moral Identities in Sri Lanka*. Albany: State University of New York Press, 1998. This good collection of essays makes it very clear that there is no one Buddhist voice in Sri Lanka, and that the roots of the violence are very complex.

Bechert, Heinz. "S.W.R.D. Bandaranaike and the Legitimation of Power through Buddhist Ideals." In Bardwell L. Smith, ed., *Religion and Legitimation of Power in Thailand, Laos, and Burma*. Chambersburg, PA: Anima Books, 1978. Excellent on the Buddhist background to the civil war in Sri Lanka.

Bond, George D. "A. T. Ariyaratne and Sarvodaya Shramadana Movement in Sri Lanka." In Christopher S. Queen and Sallie B. King, eds., *Engaged Buddhism: Buddhist Liberation Movement in Asia*. Albany: State University of New York Press, 1996.

Canagaretna, Sujit M. "Nation Building in a Multi-Ethnic Setting: the Sri Lankan Case." *Asian Affairs* 14 (1987) pp. 1–19.

Guardian. "Obituary of Sirimavo Bandaranaike." October 11, 2000.

Kemper, Steven. *The Presence of the Past: Chronicles, Politics, and Culture in Sinhala Life*. Ithaca, NY: Cornell University Press, 1991. Good for the background to the conflict.

Macy, Joanna. *Dharma and Development*. West Hartford, CT: Kumarian Press, 1983.

Obeyesekere, Gananath. "Buddhism, Nationhood, and Cultural Identity." In Martin E. Marty and R. Scott Appleby, eds., *Fundamentalisms Comprehended*. Chicago: University of Chicago Press, 1995. Traces the roots of the current crisis to the Sri Lankan historical tradition and to the British Colonial period.

Seneviratne, H. L. *The Work of Kings: The New Buddhism in Sri Lanka*. Chicago: the University of Chicago Press, 1999. A sombre assessment of contemporary Sri Lankan Buddhism.

Tambiah, S. J. *Buddhism Betrayed? Religion, Politics and Violence in Sri Lanka*. Chicago: University of Chicago, 1992. Another first-rate, detailed study by this major author.

————. *Sri Lanka: Ethnic Fratricide and the Dismantling of Democracy*. Chicago: University of Chicago Press, 1986. Passionate work by one of the great sociologists of Buddhism.

Wickremeratne, Ananda. *Buddhism and Ethnicity in Sri Lanka: A Historical Analysis*. Delhi: International Centre for Ethnic Studies (Kandy, Sri Lanka) in association with Vikas Publishing House, 1995. Very good study on many levels—Buddhist social and doctrinal background, Sri Lankan history, and the current troubles. He notes, "The belief that violence is incompatible with Buddhism in Sri Lanka, or any Buddhist country, somewhat gratuitously flatters Buddhism" (p. 283).

Thailand

Note that Thais nearly always refer to themselves by their first names, but in Western sources, the last name is often used. In the present Bibliography, the Western style is used, and the two names are cross-referenced.

Akin. See Rabibhadana.

Barnes, Nancy J. "Buddhist Women and the Nun's Order in Asia." In Christopher S. Queen and Sallie B. King, eds., *Engaged Buddhism: Buddhist Liberation Movement in Asia*. Albany: State University of New York Press, 1996.

Batson, Benjamin A. *The End of the Absolute Monarchy in Siam*. Singapore: Oxford University Press, 1984. A sympathetic account of King Prajadhipok (Rama VII) of Siam, who lost absolute powers in the 1932 democracy revolution.

Bowering, Sir John. *The Kingdom and People of Siam*, 2 vols. Hong Kong: Government House, 1856. Reprint, Oxford: Oxford University Press, 1969.

Brailey, Nigel J. *Thailand and the Fall of Singapore: A Frustrated Asian Revolution*. Boulder, CO: Westview Press, 1986. A detailed and balanced study of Thailand since 1932.

Bunnang, Tej. *The Provincial Administration of Siam (1892–1915)*. Kuala Lumpur: Oxford University Press, 1977.

Chatsumarn. See Kabilsingh.

Chattip and Suthy. See Nartsupha.

Chit or Jit. See Poumisak.

Chomchai, Prachoom. *Chulalongkorn the Great*. Tokyo: The Centre for East Asian Cultural Studies, 1965. A solid biography of Thailand's most beloved king.

Cruikshank, R. B. "Slavery in Nineteenth Century Siam." *Journal of the Siam Society* 63:2 (1975). Some useful material, but not a strong study.

Fickle, Dorothy H. *Images of the Buddha in Thailand*. Singapore: Oxford University Press, 1989. A good study, which puts the art in context.

Hongladarom, Soraj. "Buddhism and Human Rights in the Thoughts of Sulak Sivaraksa and Phra Dammapidok (Prayudh Prayutto)." Damien Keown, Charles Prebish, and Wayne Husted, eds., *Buddhism and Human Rights*. Richmond, Surrey: Curzon Press, 1998.

Ingram, James C. *Economic Change in Thailand 1850–1970*. Stanford: Stanford University Press, 1971.

Ishii, Yoneo. *Sangha, State, and Society: Thai Buddhism in History.* Translated by Peter Hawkes. Honolulu: University of Hawaii Press, 1986.

Jackson, Peter. *Buddhadasa: A Buddhist Thinker for the Modern World.* Bangkok: The Siam Society, 1988. The most detailed study of this important thinker.

Jit or Chit. See Poumisak.

Jumsai, Manich. *Popular History of Thailand,* 3rd ed. Bangkok: Chalermnit, 1993. Very useful handbook.

Keyes, Charles F. "Political Crisis and Militant Buddhism in Contemporary Thailand." In Bardwell L. Smith, ed., *Religion and Legitimation of Power in Thailand, Laos, and Burma.* Chambersburg, PA: Anima Books, 1978.

Lingat, R. *L'esclavage privé dans le vieux droit siamois (avec une traduction des anciennes lois siamoises sur l'esclavage).* Paris: Les editions Domat-Montchrestien, 1931. Very important study of slavery in Thailand with primary documents in translation.

Manich. See Jumsai.

Moffat, Abbot Low. *Mongkut: The King of Siam.* Ithaca, NY: Cornell University Press, 1960.

Mongkut, King of Siam. *A King of Siam Speaks.* Edited by M. R. Seni Pramoj and M. R. Kukrit Pramoj. Bangkok: The Siam Society, 1987. Selected writings of one of Thailand's most important kings.

Nartsupha, Chattip, and Suthy Prasartset. *The Political Economy of Siam, 1851–1910.* Bangkok: The Social Science Association of Thailand, 1981. Contains much useful primary material.

————. *Socio-economic Institutions and Cultural Change in Siam, 1851–1910: A Documentary Survey.* Southeast Asian Perspectives No. 4. Singapore: Institute of Southeast Asian Studies, 1977. Much of the same material as is found in the preceding source.

Nyanavarotama, Phra. *The Plan of Life.* Bangkok: Mahamakuta Rajavidyalaya Foundation, 2535/1992. Insight into how mainstream Thai Buddhists understand their faith.

Pallegoix, J. B. *Description du royaume Thai ou Siam*, 2 Vols. Paris: Se vend au profit de la mission de Siam, 1854. Reprint Westmead, England: Gregg International, 1969.

Panyarachun, Anand, ed. *Thailand: King Bumibol Adulyadej: The Golden Jubilee, 1946–1996*. Bangkok: Asia Books, 1996. A coffee-table book with some excellent critical essays amongst the beautiful photographs.

Payutto, Phra Prayudh. *Buddhadhamma: Natural Law and Values for Life*. Translated by Grant A. Olson. Albany: State University of New York Press, 1995. The most important of Payutto's works that has been translated.

———. *Buddhist Economics: A Middle Way for the Market Place*. Translated by Dhammavijaya and Bruce Evans. Bangkok: Buddhadhamma Foundation, 1994.

——— [P. A. Payutto]. *A Constitution for Living: Buddhist Principles for a Fruitful and Harmonious Life*. Translated by Bruce Evans. Bangkok: Buddhadhamma Foundation, 1996.

——— [Phra Rajavaramuni]. "Foundations of Buddhist Social Ethics." In Russell F. Sizemore and Donald K. Swearer, *Ethics, Wealth, and Salvation: A Study in Buddhist Social Ethics*. Columbia: University of South Carolina Press, 1990. Lengthy, detailed work.

——— [Phra Debvedi]. *Freedom: Individual and Social*. Bangkok: Buddhadhamma Foundation, 1987. Somewhat more positive on human rights than his other works.

——— [Bhikku P. A. Payutto]. *Good, Evil and Beyond: Kamma in the Buddha's Teaching*. Bangkok: Buddhadhamma Foundation, 1993.

——— [P. A. Payutto]. *Phuttavithii Kae Panha Phua Satawad Thii 21 (A Buddhist Solution for the Twenty-first Century)*. Bangkok: Sahathammik, 1994. Translated into in English and cited in Soraj Hongladarom, "Buddhism and Human Rights in the Thoughts of Sulak Sivaraksa and Phra Dhammapidok (Prayudh Payutto)." In Keown, Prebish, and Husted, *Buddhism and Human Rights*.

Poumisak, Jit [or Chit]. "The Real Face of Thai Saktina Today." In Craig J. Reynolds, ed., *Thai Radical Discourse: The Real Face of Thai Feudalism*

Today. Ithaca: Studies on Southeast Asia, Cornell University, 1987. Interesting book by a radical Thai thinker, a man who died in the jungle insurrections against military dictatorship.

Prachoom. See Chomchai.

Rabibhadana, Akin. "The Organization of Thai Society in the Early Bangkok Period, 1782–1874." Data Paper No. 74. Ithaca, NY: Southeast Asia Program, Cornell University, 1969. Excellent detail on traditional Thai social structures.

Rama II, King of Siam. *Sang Thong: A Dance Drama from Thailand*. Translated and introduction by Fern S. Ingersoll. Rutland VT: C. E. Tuttle Company, 1973.

Reynolds, Craig J., ed. See Poumisak.

Roberts, Edmund. *Embassy to the Eastern Courts of Cochin-China, Siam, and Muscat; in the U.S. Sloop-of-war Peacock, David Geisinger, Commander, During the Years 1832-3-4.* 1837. Reprint, Wilmington, Delaware: Scholarly Resources, 1972.

Sivaraksa, Sulak. "Being in the World: A Buddhist Ethical and Social Concern." Paper presented at the conference, "Buddhism and Christianity: Toward the Human Future," at Berkeley, CA in August 1987, cited in Robert Traer, "Buddhist Affirmations of Human Rights," *Buddhist Christian Studies* 8 (1988), p. 17.

———. "Buddhism and Human Freedom." *Buddhist-Christian Studies* 18 (1998). Short paper outlining Sulak's basic Buddhist approach.

———. "Buddhism and Human Rights in Siam." In Sulak Sivaraksa, ed. *Socially Engaged Buddhism for the New Millennium*. Berkeley, CA: Parallax Press, 1999. A personal account of Buddhism and human rights issues by a major figure in contemporary Thai Buddhism.

———. "Buddhism and Thai Politics." In Sulak Sivaraksa, *A Socially Engaged Buddhism*. Bangkok: Thai Inter-Religious Commission for Development, 1988. Excerpted in chapter 13, document 19.

———. "Buddhist Ethics and Modern Politics: A Theravada Viewpoint." In Fu and Wawrytko, eds., *Buddhist Ethics*.

————. "In Exile from Siam, an Interview with Sulak Sivaraksa." *Tricycle* 1:4 (Summer 1992).

————. *A Socially Engaged Buddhism*. Bangkok: Thai Inter-Religious Commission for Development, 1988. Vintage Sulak.

————, ed. *Buddhist Perception for Desirable Societies in the Future*. Bangkok: Thai Inter-Religious Commission for Development, 1992.

————, ed. *Socially Engaged Buddhism for the New Millennium: Essays in Honour of Ven. Phra Dammapitaka (Bhikku P.A. Payutto [Phra Prayudh Payutto] on his 60th Birthday Anniversary*. Bangkok: Sathirakoses-Nagapradipa Foundation, 1999. Another very useful collection.

Sivaraksa, Sulak et al., eds. *Radical Conservatism: Buddhism in the Contemporary World*. Bangkok: Thai Inter-Religious Commission for Development, 1990. Useful on engaged Buddhism in Asia.

Smyth, H. Warrington. *Five Years in Siam: From 1891–96*. New York: Scribner's, 1898. Reprint with an introduction by Tamaro Loos, Bangkok: White Lotus, 1994.

Somboon. See Suksamran.

Soraj. See Hongladarom.

Sulak. See Sivaraksa.

Suksamram, Somboon. *Buddhism and Politics in Thailand: A Study of Socio-Political Change and Political Activism of the Thai Sangha*. Singapore: Institute of Southeast Asian Studies, 1982. Perhaps the most useful of his many writings on the topic.

————. "A Buddhist Approach to Development: The Case of 'Development Monks' in Thailand." In Lim Teck Ghee, ed., *Reflections on Development in Southeast Asia*. Singapore: Institute of Southeast Asian Studies, 1988.

————. *Political Buddhism in Southeast Asia: The Role of the Sangha in the Modernization of Thailand*. London: C. Hurst, 1977.

Swearer, Donald K. "Sulak Sivaraksa's Buddhist Vision for Renewing Society." In Christopher S. Queen and Sallie B. King, eds., *Engaged*

Buddhism: Buddhist Liberation Movement in Asia. Albany: State University of New York Press, 1996.

Tej. See Bunnang.

Terwiel, B. J. "Bondage and Slavery in Early Nineteenth Century Siam." In Anthony Reid, *Slavery, Bondage, and Dependency in Southeast Asia.* St. Lucia: University of Queensland Press, 1983. Very useful on slavery in traditional Siam.

————. *A History of Modern Thailand 1762–1942.* St. Lucia: University of Queensland Press, 1983. A good single volume history.

Tips, Walter E. J. *Gustave Rolin-Jaequemyns (Chao Phraya Aphai Raja) and The Belgian Advisers in Siam (1892–1902).* Bangkok: Published by the Author, 1992.

Turton, Andrew. "Thai Institutions of Slavery." In James L. Watson, ed., *Asian and African Systems of Slavery.* Oxford: Basil Blackwell, 1980.

van Vliet, Jeremias. *The Short History of the Kings of Siam.* Translated by Leonard Andaya from a 1640 MS. Bangkok: The Siam Society, 1975.

Vella, Walter Francis. *Chaiyo! King Vajiravudh and the Development of Thai Nationalism.* Honolulu: University Press of Hawaii, 1978. Rather too enthusiastic and rather too weak on telling detail.

Wales, H. G. Quaritch. *Ancient Siamese Government and Administration.* London: B. Quaritch, 1934. Reprint, New York: Paragon, 1965.

Wyatt, David K. *The Crystal Sands: The Chronicles of Nagara Sri Dharmaraja.* Data Paper Number 98. Ithaca, NY: Southeast Asia Program Cornell University, 1975. Throws considerable light on Buddhism in Siamese society in a region on the periphery of the culture.

————. *The Politics of Reform in Thailand: Education in the Reign of King Chulalongkorn.* New Haven: Yale University Press, 1969.

Tibet

Avendon, John F. *Exile from the Land of Snows.* New York: Alfred A. Knopf, 1984. A good study of the life of the Dalai Lama in exile.

Batchelor, Stephen et al. "Deity or Demon, The Controversy over Tibet's Dorje Shugden." *Tricycle* 7:3 (Spring 1998). Account of an incident where the Dalai Lama was accused of attempting to limit religious freedom to Tibetan Buddhists.

Bell, Charles. *Portrait of the Dalai Lama*. London: Collins, 1946. Account of Tibet's political life and of the thirteenth Dalai Lama by the British Political Representative in Tibet, Bhutan, and Sikkim. Full of first-hand detail.

Bishop, Peter. *Dreams of Power: Tibetan Buddhism and the Western Imagination*. London: The Athlone Press, 1993. Tends to bring out some of the darker side of Tibet.

Cabezón, José Ignacio. "Buddhist Principles in the Tibetan Liberation Movement." In Christopher S. Queen and Sallie B. King, eds., *Engaged Buddhism: Buddhist Liberation Movement in Asia*. Albany: State University of New York Press, 1996.

Chang-hao, Hsi, and Kao Yuan-mei. *Tibet Leaps Forward*. Peking: Foreign Languages Press, 1977. Party-line Chinese communist view of recent events in Tibet.

Dalai Lama. *Freedom in Exile: The Autobiography of His Holiness The Dalai Lama* of Tibet. London: Hodder and Stoughton. 1990. Autobiography.

———. "Human Rights and Universal Responsibility." Statement made at The United Nations World Conference on Human Rights, Vienna, June 15, 1993. An important primary text by the best-known Buddhist spokesman in the modern world.

———. *Kindness, Clarity, and Insight*. Edited by J. Hopkins and E. Napper. Ithaca, NY: Snowlion, 1984. Reprint, Delhi: Motilal Banarsidass, 1997. The collection of his Holiness's writings that is most on the topic of Buddhism and human rights.

——— [His Holiness the Dalai Lama of Tibet]. *My Land and My People*. New York: Potala Corporation, 1962. A memoir written shortly after the 1959 exile from Tibet—fresh and lively book.

———. *A Policy of Kindness: An Anthology of Writings by and about the Dalai Lama*. Ithaca NY: Snow Lion, 1990. Contains some material on the Dalai Lama's views on human rights.

Dargyay, Eva. *Tibetan Village Communities: Structure and Change*. Warminster, England: Aries and Phillips, 1982.

Dreyfus, Georges. "Law, State, and Political Ideology in Tibet." *Journal of the International Association of Buddhist Studies* 18:1 (1995). A well written contribution to a very important topic. He does not mention rights.

———. "The Shuk-den Affair: History and Nature of a Quarrel." *The Journal of the International Association of Buddhist Studies* 21:2 (1998). Detailed historical background and narration of the affair in which the current Dalai Lama has been accused of violating the religious freedom of some Tibetans who follow Shuk-den.

Epstein, Israel. *Tibet Transformed*. Beijing: New World Press, 1983. The best documented account of Tibet from a pro-communist Chinese view.

French, Rebecca Redwood. "The Cosmology of Law in Buddhist Tibet." *Journal of the International Association of Buddhist Studies* 18:1 (1995). Good introduction to the topic; no mention of rights.

———. *The Golden Yoke: The Legal Cosmology of Buddhist Tibet*. Ithaca, NY: Cornell University Press, 1995. A fascinating breakthrough study on the legal system of traditional Tibet, no mention of rights.

Goldstein, Melvyn C. *A History of Modern Tibet, 1913–1951: The Demise of the Lamaist State*. Berkeley: University of California Press, 1989. Huge, magisterial account of how the Tibetan elite spent their energies on court intrigues while their country was under mortal threat.

———. "On the Nature of the Tibetan Peasantry: A Rejoinder." *Tibet Journal* 13:4 (1988), pp. 61–65.

———. "Reexamining Choice, Dependency and Command in the Tibetan Social System: 'Tax Appendages' and other Landless Serfs." *Tibet Journal* 11:4 (1986), pp. 79–112.

———. "The Revival of Monastic Life in Drepung Monastery." In Melvyn C. Goldstein and Matthew T. Kapstein, eds., *Buddhism in Contemporary Tibet: Religious Revival and Cultural Identity*. Berkeley: University of California Press, 1998.

————. "Serfdom and Mobility: An Examination of the Institution of 'Human Lease' in Traditional Tibetan Society." *Journal of Asian Studies* 30:3 (1970).

————. "A Study of the Ldab Ldob." *Central Asiatic Journal* 9:2 (1964), pp. 125–141.

————. "Tibetan Refugees in South India: A New Face to the Indo-Tibetan Interface." *The Tibet Society Bulletin* 9 (1975).

Goldstein, Melvyn C., and Matthew T. Kapstein. *Buddhism in Contemporary Tibet: Religious Revival and Cultural Identity*. Berkeley: University of California Press, 1998. A fine, objective study of how Tibetan religion has fared under the Chinese.

Guenther, Herbert. "Buddhism in Tibet." In J. M. Kitagawa and M. D. Cummings, eds., *Buddhism and Asian History: Religion, History and Culture: Readings from the Encylopedia of Religion*. New York: Macmillan, 1989.

Hicks, Roger, and Ngakpa Chogyam. *Great Ocean: An Authorised Biography of the Dalai Lama*. Longmead, Dorset: Element Books, 1984.

Kawaguchi, Ekai. *Three Years in Tibet*. Madras: Theosophical Publishing Society, 1909. A unique account by a Japanese Buddhist priest who observed Tibetan monastic life from a century ago.

Levine, Nancy E. *The Dynamics of Polyandry: Kinship, Domesticity, and Population on the Tibetan Border*. Chicago: University of Chicago Press, 1988.

————. "Opposition and Interdependence: Demographic and Economic Perspectives on Nyinba Slavery." In Watson, James L., ed. *Asian and African Systems of Slavery*. Oxford: Basil Blackwell, 1980.

Lopez, Donald S., Jr., ed. *Religions of Tibet in Practice*. Princeton, NJ: Princeton University Press, 1997. Fine examples of current scholarship on the religions of Tibet.

Michael, Franz. *Rule by Incarnation: Tibetan Buddhism and Its Role in Society and the State*. Boulder, CO: Westview Press, 1982. Useful study.

————. "Traditional Tibetan Polity and Its Potential for Modernization." In the *Tibet Journal* 11:4 (1986), pp. 70–78.

Miller, Beatrice. "A Response to Goldstein's 'Reexamining Choice, Dependency and Command in the Tibetan Social System," in the *Tibet Journal*: vol. 12, no. 2, 1987, pp. 65–67.

Mullin, Chris, and Phuntsog Wangyal. *The Tibetans: Two Perspectives on Tibetan-Chinese Relations*. London: Minority Rights Group, 1983. Useful booklet, anti-Chinese viewpoints.

Samuel, Geoffrey. *Civilized Shamans: Buddhism in Tibetan Societies*. Washington, DC: Smithsonian Institution Press, 1993. Important study by an anthropologist that emphasizes the complexity and diversity of Tibetan peoples.

Shakya, Tsering. *The Dragon in the Land of Snows*. New York: Columbia University Press, 1999. Account of Tibet under Chinese occupation.

Snellgrove, David. *Indo-Tibetan Buddhism: Indian Buddhists and Their Tibetan Successors*. Boston: Shambhala, 1987.

Snellgrove, David, and Hugh Richardson. *A Cultural History of Tibet*. Boulder, CO: Prajna Press, 1980.

Stein, R. A. *Tibetan Civilization*. Translated from the French. 1962. London: Faber and Faber, 1972. Still a useful work.

Subedi, Abhi. *Ekai Kawaguchi: The Trespassing Insider*. Kathmandu: Mandala Book Point, 1999. A thorough biography of a very interesting Japanese Zen monk and scholar, who lived as a Tibetan monk one hundred years ago, when the country was closed to foreign travelers.

Thargyal, Rinzin. "The Applicability of the Concept of Feudalism to Traditional Tibetan Society." In Helga Uebach and Jampa L. Panglung, eds., *Tibetan Studies: Proceedings of the 4th Seminar of the International Association for Tibetan Studies*. Munich: Kommission für Zentralalsiatische Studien Bayerische Akademie Der Wissenschaften, 1988. Useful discussion on a topic important for Buddhism and human rights.

Wylie, Turrell V. "Monastic Patronage in 15th Century Tibet." *Acta Orientalia Academiae Scientiarum Hungarica* 34 (1980), pp. 319–328.

Zhou, Jin, ed. *Tibet: No Longer Mediaeval*. Beijing: Foreign Languages Press, 1981.

Vietnam

Matthews, Bruce. "The Place of Religion in Vietnam Today." *Buddhist-Christian Studies* (1992). A brief account of how Buddhism has adapted to the communist regime.

Nguyen Tai Thu, ed. *History of Buddhism in Vietnam.* Hanoi: Social Sciences Publishing House, 1992. Interesting on how the Buddhists adapted to French colonial rule.

Nhat Hanh, *Interbeing: Commentaries on the Tiep Hien Precepts.* Edited by Fred Eppsteiner. Berkeley, CA: Parallax Press, 1987.

———. *The Miracle of Mindfulness: A Manual on Meditation.* Revised edition. Boston: Beacon Press, 1981.

———. *Vietnam: Lotus in a Sea of Fire.* New York: Hill and Wang, 1967.

Western Buddhism

Field, Rick. *How the Swans Came to the Lake: A Narrative History of Buddhism in America.* Boulder, CO: Shambhala, 1981.

Goss, Robert E. "Naropa Institute: The Engaged Academy." In Christopher S. Queen, ed., *Engaged Buddhism in the West.* Boston: Wisdom Publications, 2000. Good account of America's only accredited Buddhist-inspired college, including a description of the master's program in engaged Buddhism.

Moon, Susan. "Activist Women in American Buddhism." In Christopher S. Queen, ed., *Engaged Buddhism in the West.* Boston: Wisdom Publications, 2000.

Sangharakshita. *The History of My Going for Refuge.* Glasgow: Windhorse, 1988. An autobiographical account by the founder of one of the strongest Western Buddhist groups.

Subhuti. *Bringing Buddhism to the West: A Life of Sangharakshita.* Birmingham: Windhorse, 1996. Sangharakshita's life as written by one of his major disciples.

Wratten, Darrell. "Engaged Buddhism in South Africa." In Christopher S. Queen, ed., *Engaged Buddhism in the West.* Boston: Wisdom Publications, 2000. This not only is very good on Buddhism in South Africa, it is generally interesting on Buddhism, rights, and social action.

INDEX

About the Author

ROBERT E. FLORIDA is Emeritus Fellow, Centre for Studies in Religion and Society, University of Victoria, British Columbia. He is former Professor of Religion and Dean of Arts at Brandon University in Manitoba. His works on the topic of Buddhism are widely published.